HISTORIC PHOTOS OF
BATON ROUG

TEXT AND CAPTIONS BY MARK E. MART

TURNER
PUBLISHING COMPANY

HISTORIC PHOTOS OF
BATON ROUGE

Turner Publishing Company
www.turnerpublishing.com

Historic Photos of Baton Rouge

Library of Congress Control Number: 2008901849

ISBN-13: 978-1-59652-441-5

Printed in the United States of America

ISBN 978-1-68442-017-9 (hc)

Contents

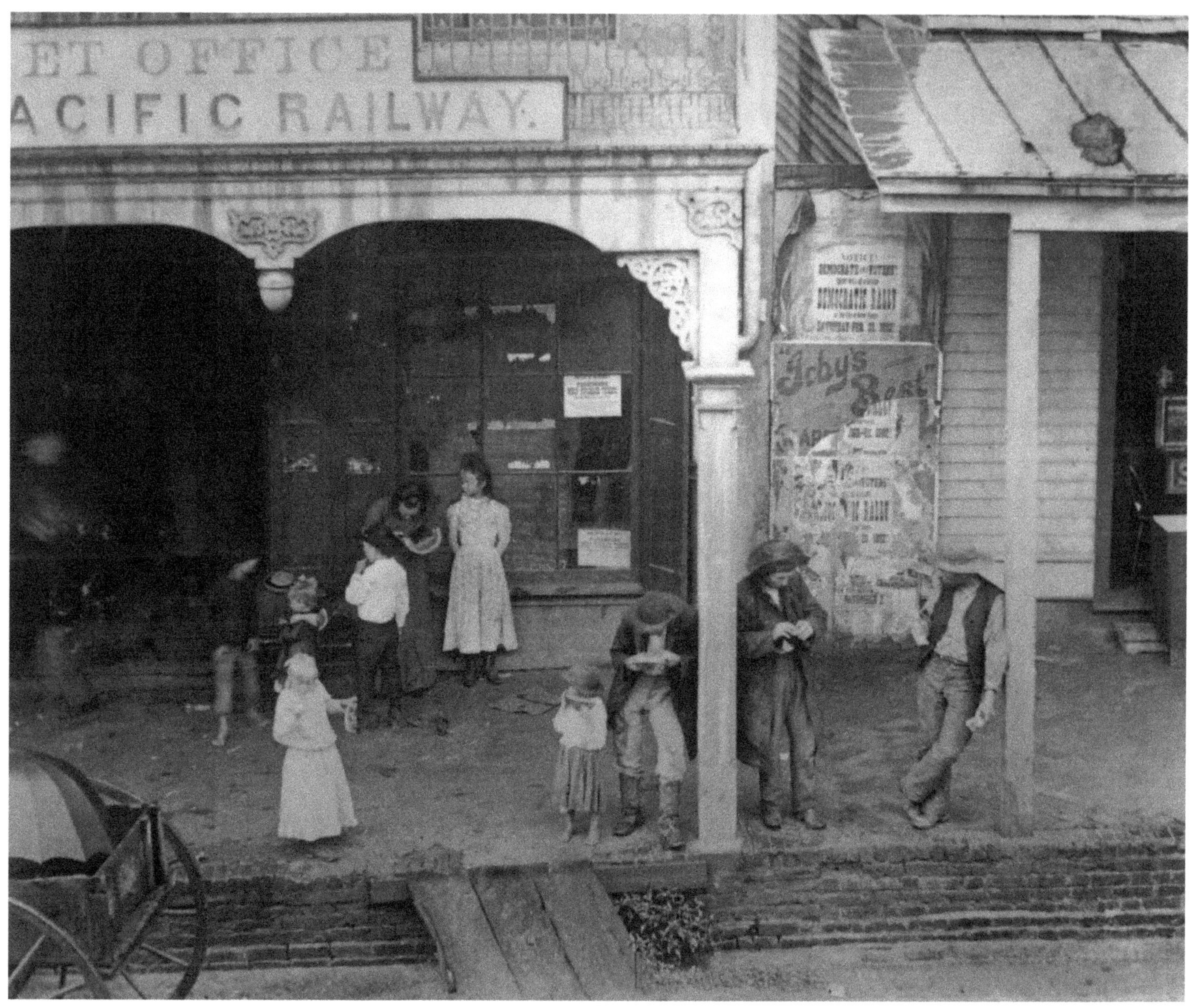

Citizens enjoy watermelon in the shade of the Texas & Pacific Railway office gallery on Main Street. Behind the three men, a poster announces a February 20, 1892, Democratic Party rally.

Acknowledgments

This volume, *Historic Photos of Baton Rouge,* is the result of the cooperation and efforts of many individuals, organizations, and corporations. It is with great thanks that we acknowledge the valuable contribution of the following for their generous support:

Library of Congress
Louisiana State University—Special Collections
State Library of Louisiana

My undying thanks to L. A. B. for her insightful comments and editorial advice.

—*Mark E. Martin*

PREFACE

Baton Rouge has thousands of historic photographs that reside in archives, both locally and nationally. This book began with the observation that, while those photographs are of great interest to many, they are not easily accessible. During a time when Baton Rouge is looking ahead and evaluating its future course, many people are asking, "How do we treat the past?" These decisions affect every aspect of the city—architecture, public spaces, commerce, infrastructure—and these, in turn, affect the way that people live their lives. This book seeks to provide easy access to a valuable, objective look into the history of Baton Rouge.

The power of photographs is that they are less subjective than words in their treatment of history. Although the photographer can make decisions regarding subject matter and how to capture and present it, photographs do not provide the breadth of interpretation that text does. For this reason, they offer an original, untainted perspective that allows the viewer to interpret and observe.

This project represents countless hours of review and research. The researchers and writer have reviewed thousands of photographs in numerous archives. We greatly appreciate the generous assistance of the individuals and organizations listed in the acknowledgments of this work, without whom this project could not have been completed.

The goal in publishing this work is to provide broader access to this set of extraordinary photographs that seek to inspire, provide perspective, and evoke insight that might assist people who are responsible for determining Baton Rouge's future. In addition, the book seeks to preserve the past with adequate respect and reverence.

With the exception of touching up imperfections caused by the damage of time and cropping where necessary, no other changes have been made to the photographs in this volume. The focus and clarity of many images is limited to the technology and the ability of the photographer at the time they were taken.

The work is divided into eras. Beginning with some of the earliest known photographs of Baton Rouge, the first section records photographs through the end of the nineteenth century. The second section spans the beginning of the twentieth century through World War I. Sections Three through Eight then move decade by decade from the 1920s through the 1970s.

In each of these sections we have made an effort to capture various aspects of life through our selection of photographs. People, commerce, transportation, infrastructure, religious institutions, and educational institutions have been included to provide a broad perspective.

We encourage readers to reflect as they go walking in Baton Rouge, strolling through the city, its parks, and its neighborhoods. It is the publisher's hope that in utilizing this work, longtime residents will learn something new and that new residents will gain a perspective on where Baton Rouge has been, so that each can contribute to its future.

—Todd Bottorff, Publisher

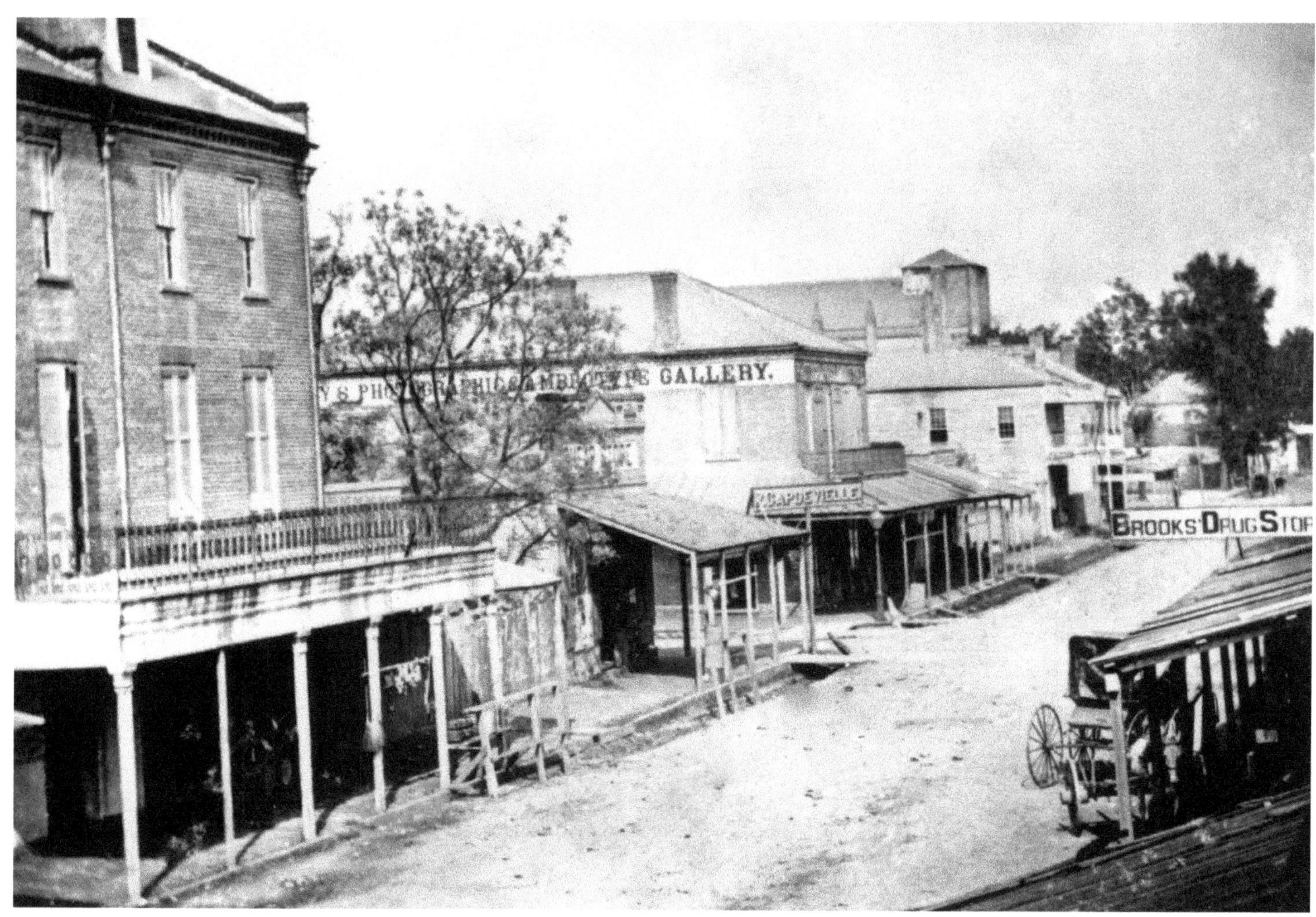

The photographer of numerous images in this collection, Andrew D. Lytle pointed his lens out his studio window sometime around 1866 and captured this view looking up Main Street away from the Mississippi River. Businesses visible include the Brooks Drug Store at 210 Main and Marion P. McCarthy's Photographic and Ambrotype Gallery at 314 Main. The blunt tower seen in the distance was part of Saint Joseph Catholic Church at 403 Main. Lytle's studio stood at 208 Main.

Nineteenth-Century Baton Rouge

(1850s–1899)

Having first arrived in the area in 1699, the French never really settled at Baton Rouge. It took the British, who acquired the Louisiana territory in 1763 following the French and Indian War, to found a true settlement, beginning with two fortifications: Fort Bute on Bayou Manchac and a much larger Fort New Richmond at Baton Rouge. In September 1779, Spanish forces under Governor Don Bernardo de Galvez captured both of the British forts and established Spanish rule. Baton Rouge became a true town under the Spanish; two areas, Beauregard Town and Spanish Town, were laid out and developed by 1805.

Changing international politics, however, removed from Spain the West Florida Territory of which Baton Rouge was a part. With the town completely surrounded by American territory by 1810, a small group of American rebels captured the Spanish Fort San Carlos (Fort New Richmond under the British) in Baton Rouge. On September 23, 1810, the new government declared all territory south of the 31st parallel, west of the Perdido River, east of the Mississippi River, and north of Lake Pontchartrain and along the coast of the Gulf of Mexico as the West Florida Republic. Ninety days later, the West Florida Republic became part of the American territory of Orleans. The small town growing up around the fort became Baton Rouge permanently.

By 1860 Baton Rouge had grown to include 4,181 whites and 1,247 slaves within its town limits. Much would change over the following decades: Louisiana would secede from the Union, fully one-third of Baton Rouge would be burnt by its occupying forces, the State Capitol would burn in a separate conflagration, African American legislators would serve in the Reconstruction government, the state would be readmitted to the Union, the Capitol would be rebuilt, and the Louisiana State University and Agricultural and Mechanical College (LSU A&M, or LSU) would settle in town and grow. Baton Rouge would very slowly recover from the Civil War until it stood on the edge of major changes at the end of the nineteenth century.

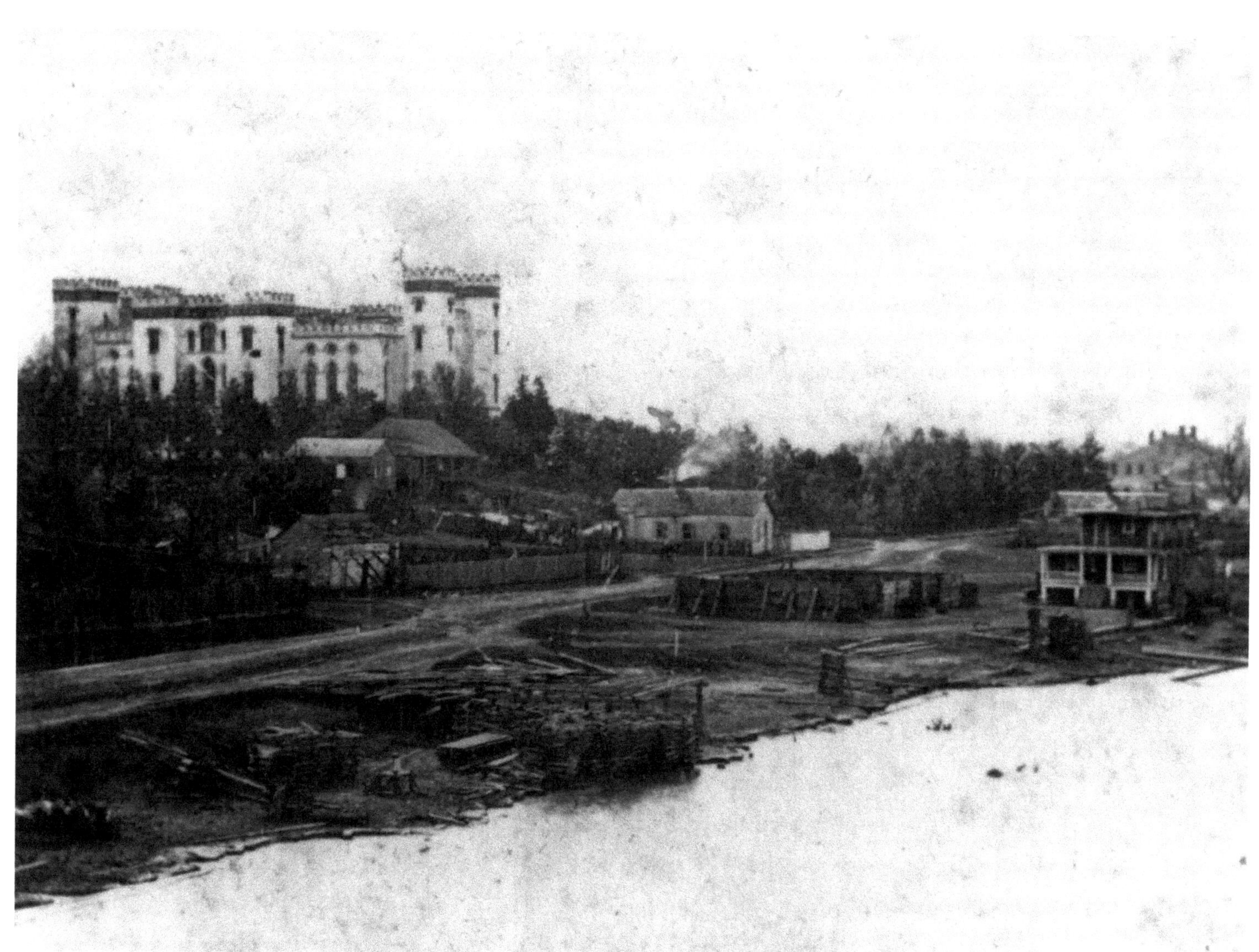

Architect James Harrison Dakin designed the Louisiana State Capitol in what he referred to as the "castellated Gothic" style. Construction took two years, 1847–1849, at a cost of nearly $400,000. This image from around 1860 also shows businesses that were built on the flood plane of the Mississippi River despite the lack of a riverfront levee.

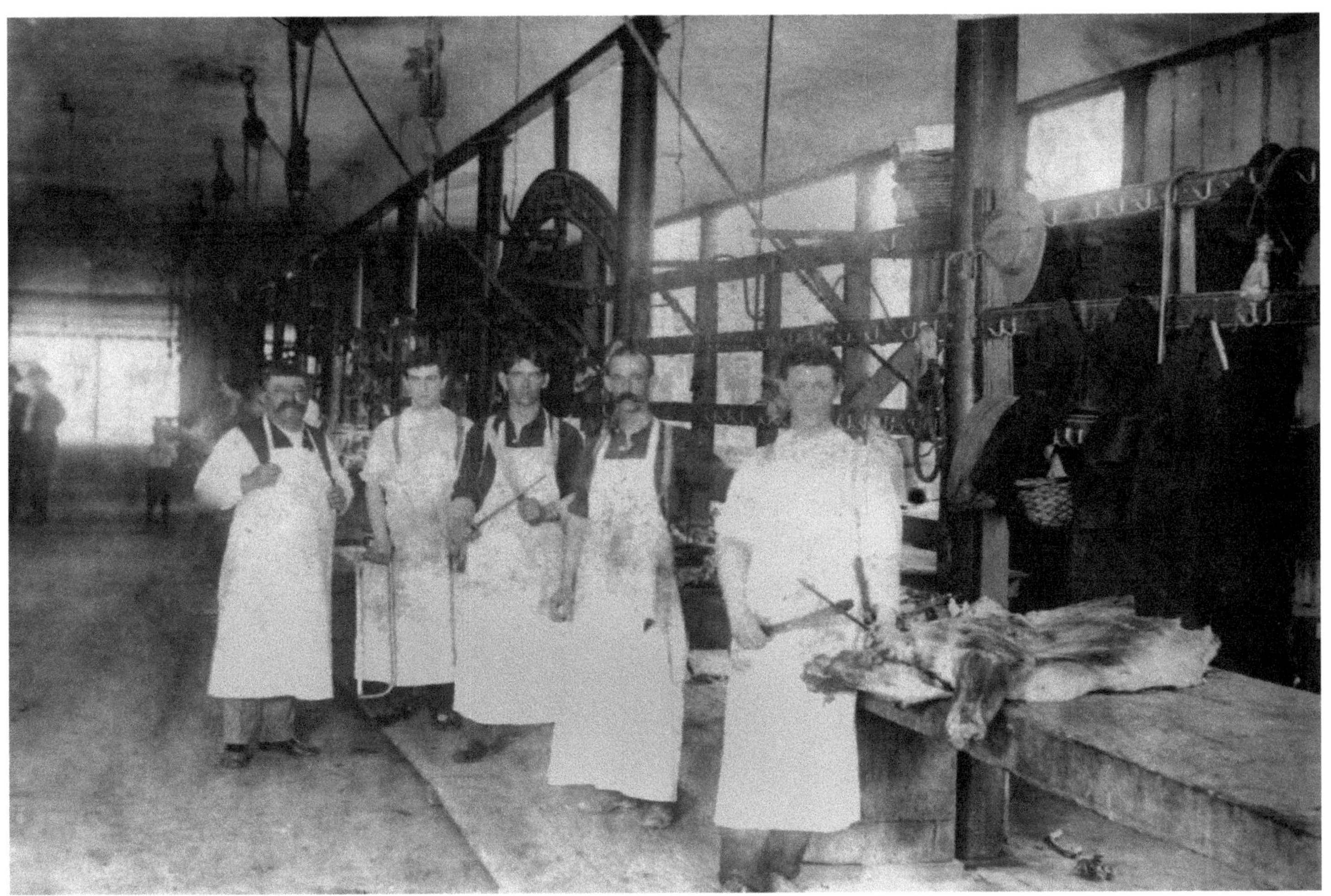

With a population of a little over 4,000 in 1860, Baton Rouge served as an important warehousing and transshipment port for plantations on both sides of the Mississippi. Local merchants catered not only to the permanent population but also to a large number of transients traveling the river. Photographed in 1859, these butchers worked in the central market a few blocks off the river.

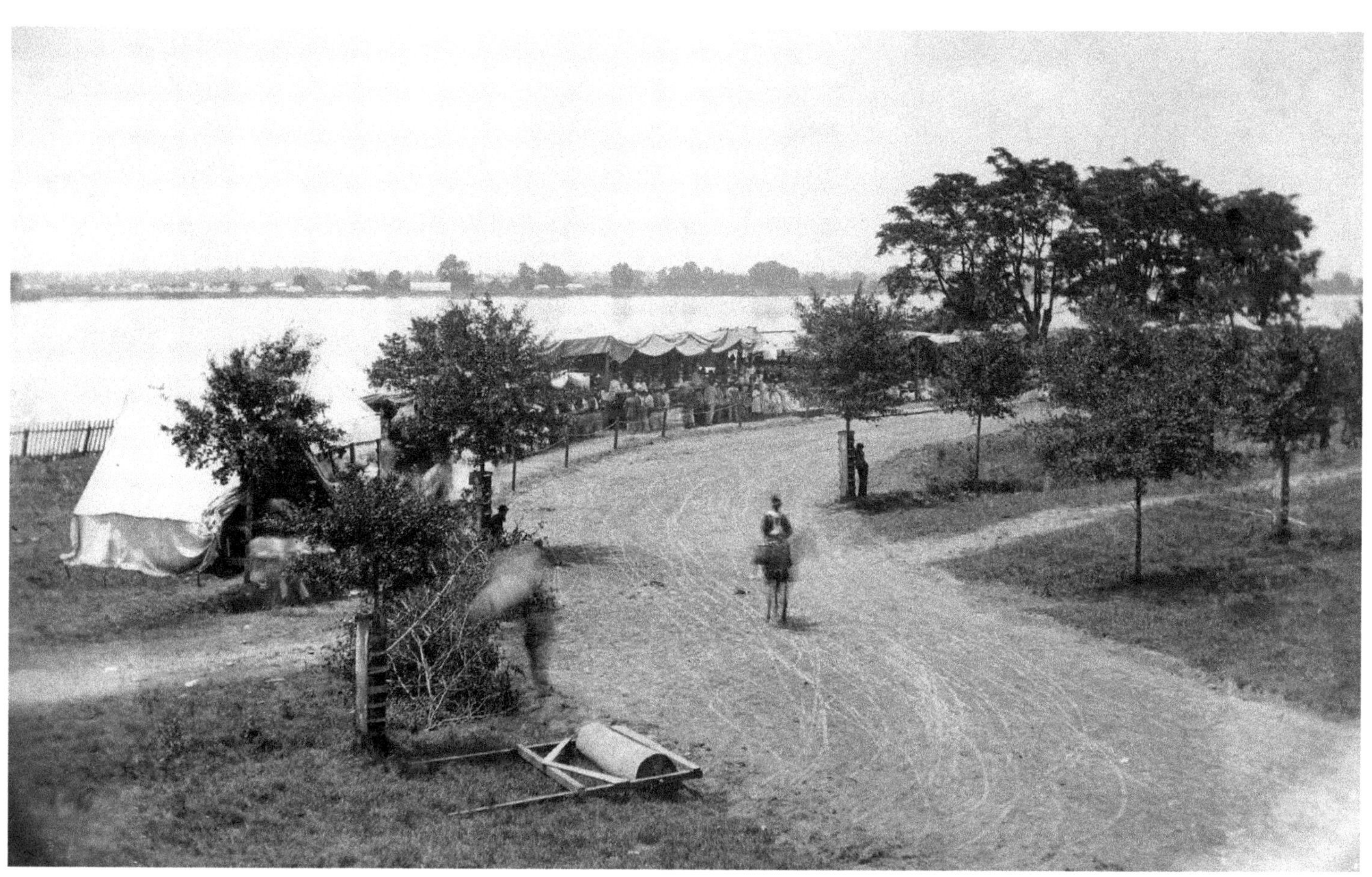

The western side of Baton Rouge ends at the Mississippi River. In the late 1850s, when Andrew D. Lytle took this photograph of a riverside social event, the townspeople attending would have ridden or walked dirt streets to the river's edge, in this case at the intersection of North and Lafayette streets.

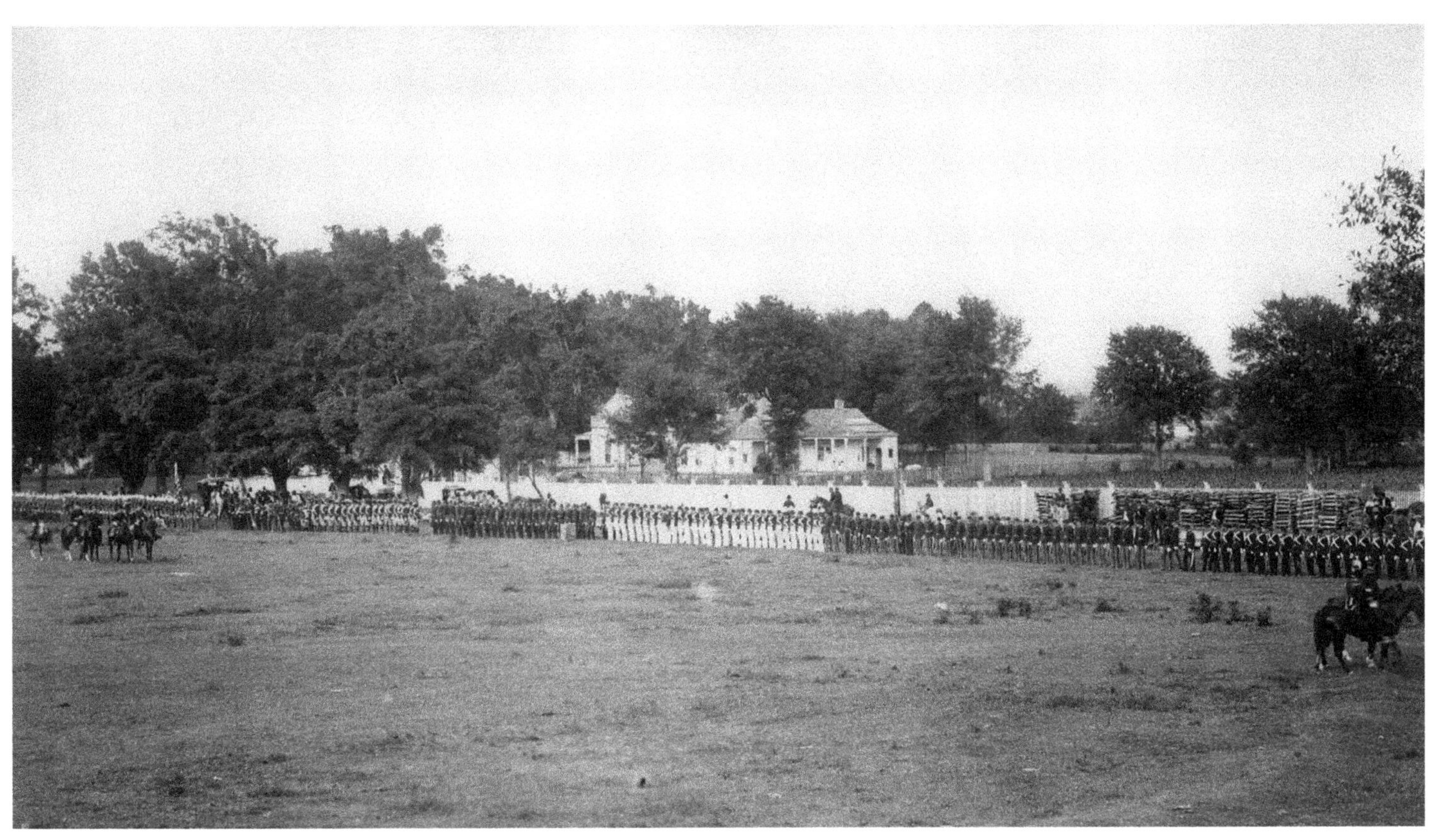

Around 1861, sometime before the capture of Baton Rouge, Lytle photographed these militia groups meeting in town. Artillery pieces taken from the Federal Arsenal provided them with weapons, powder, and ammunition. Among the groups here is the Washington Artillery of New Orleans, established in 1838 and still active as the 1st Battalion, 141st Field Artillery.

The traveling-photographer team of McPherson and Oliver is credited with this image of the camp of General Christopher Colon Augur's 19th Army Corps, 3rd Brigade, on the north edge of Baton Rouge around 1863. This area had been a United States Army arsenal and camp before the war. Tens of thousands of Federal troops and sailors lived in Baton Rouge before the fall of Port Hudson—the last Confederate stronghold on the Mississippi—less than 25 miles upriver.

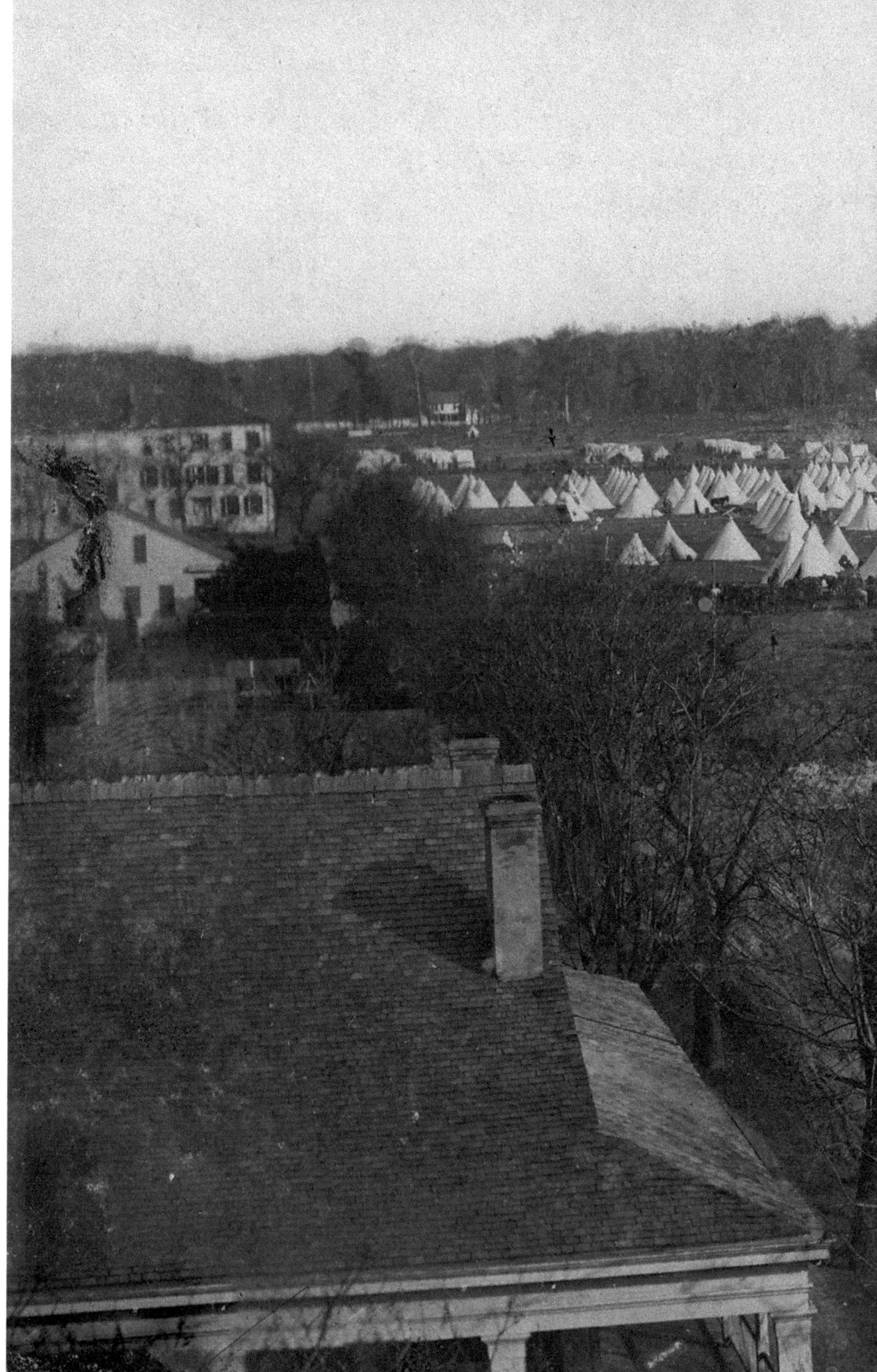

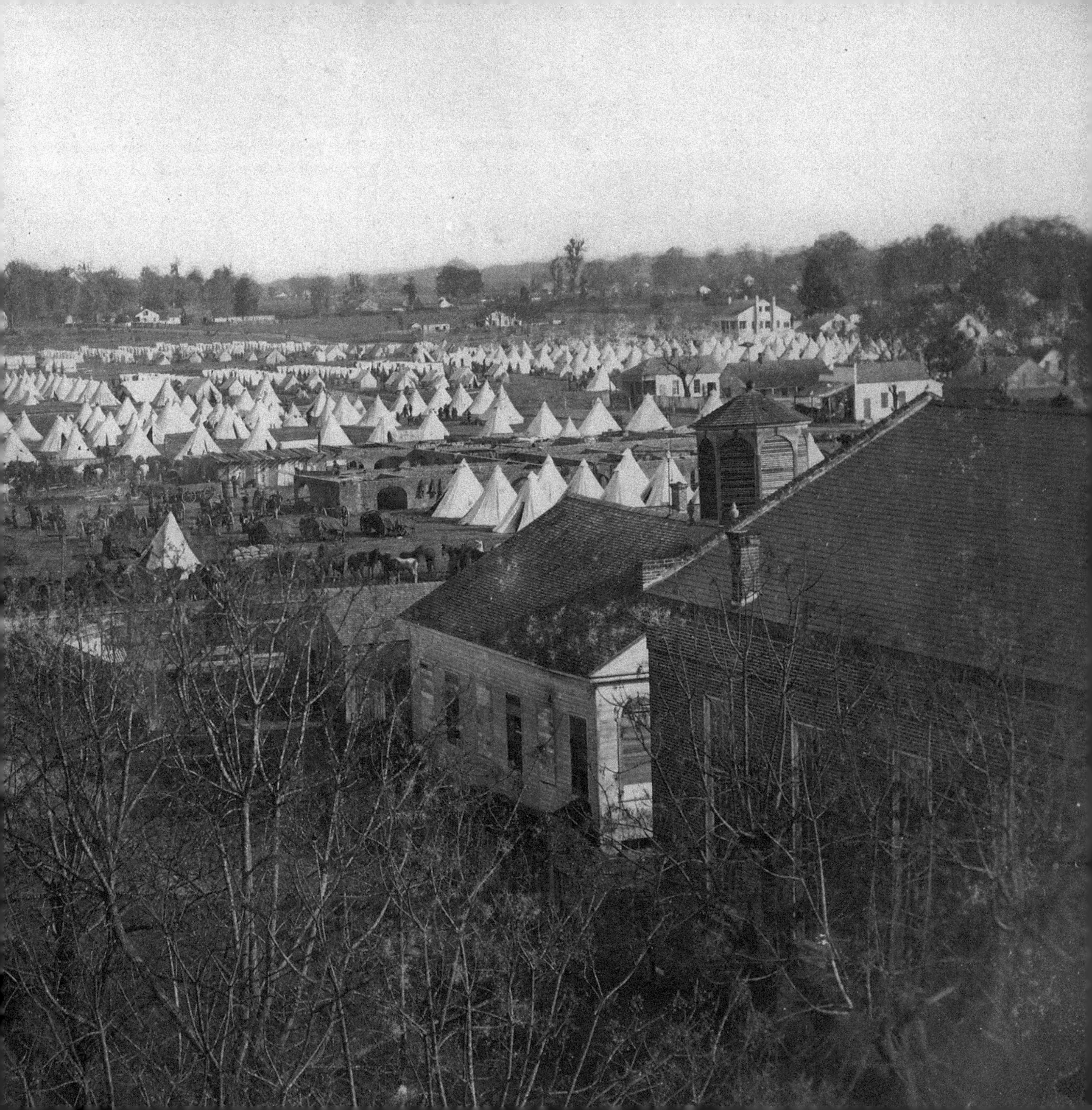

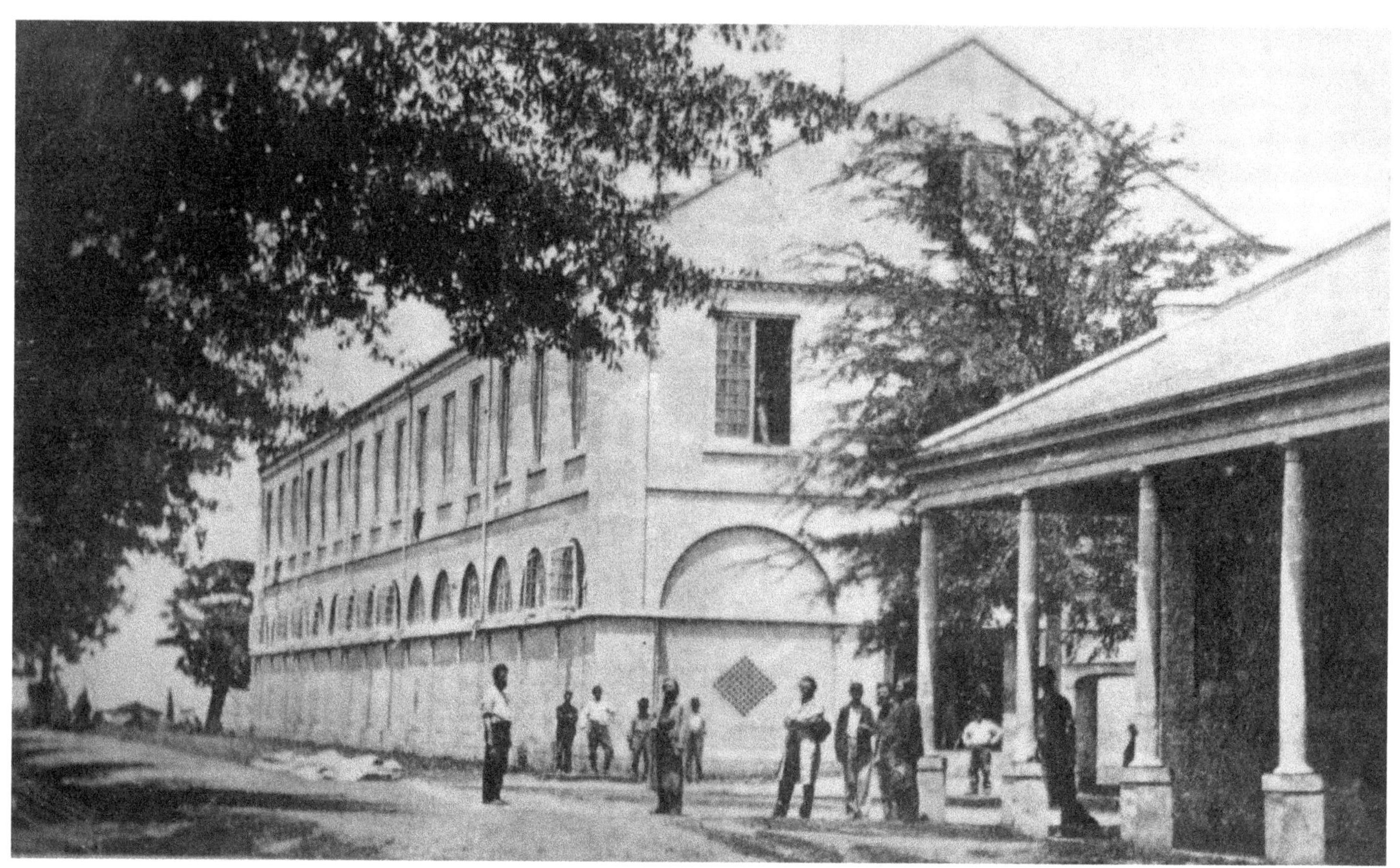

This building photographed about 1863 by L. I. Prince, a traveling photographer based out of New Orleans, was one of the many structures on the grounds of the Baton Rouge Arsenal. An important frontier military installation in the early nineteenth century and a major staging area for the Mexican War of 1848, the Arsenal hosted many illustrious military men including Zachary Taylor, Robert E. Lee, Jefferson Davis, William T. Sherman, George B. McClellan, P. G. T. Beauregard, and Ulysses S. Grant.

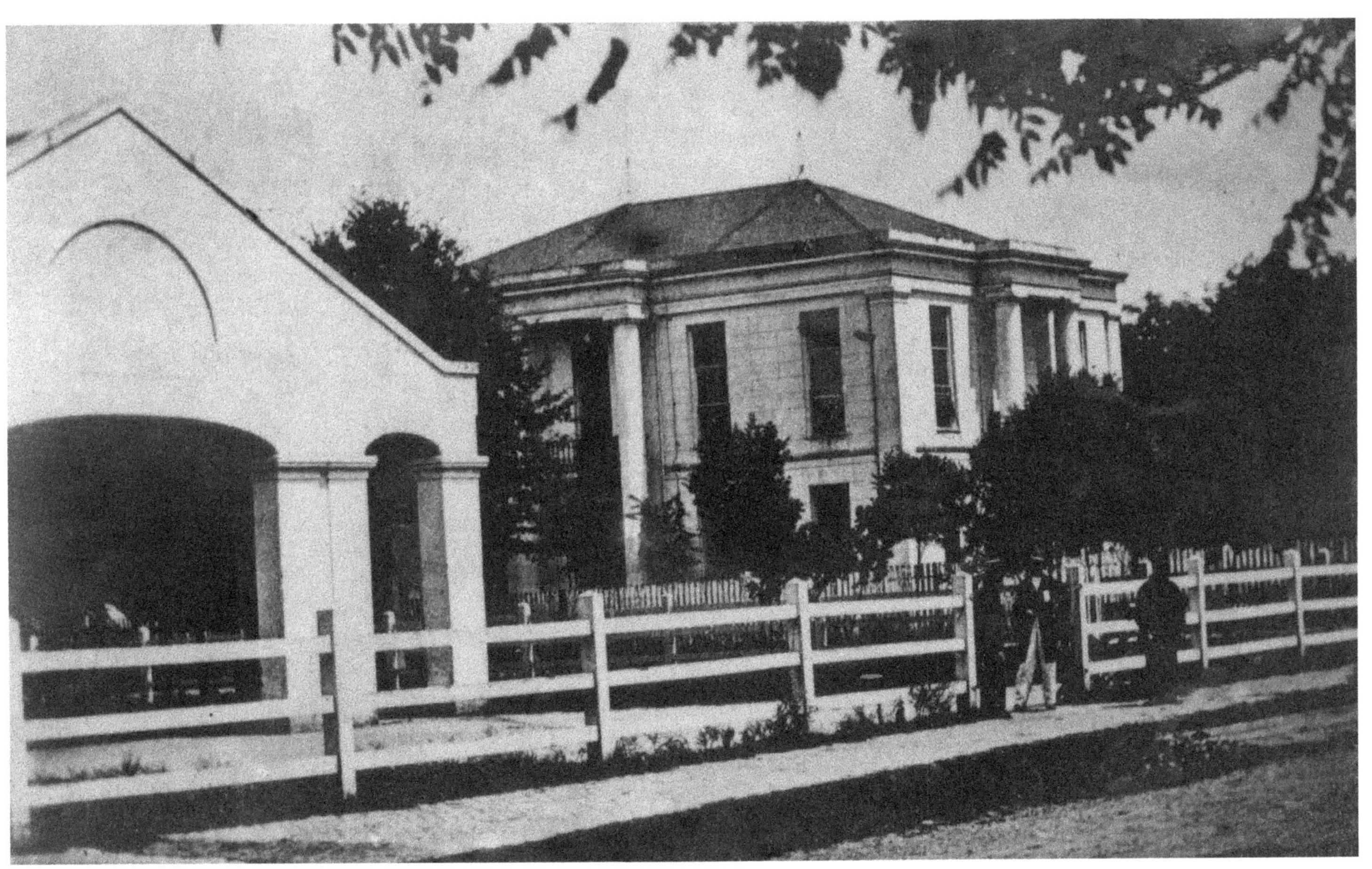

While L. I. Prince was in Baton Rouge, he photographed this view of the courthouse and market on Saint Louis Street. Baton Rouge was, and is, the parish governmental seat as well as the state capital. During the war, the Confederate Louisiana capital moved to other towns in unoccupied territory while the occupied capital moved to New Orleans. Only in 1882 did the capital return to Baton Rouge.

In this image of the Arsenal grounds around 1863, the main Arsenal building stands at right, while one of the Pentagon Barracks buildings can be seen at far left. At the time, Federal troops occupied Baton Rouge.

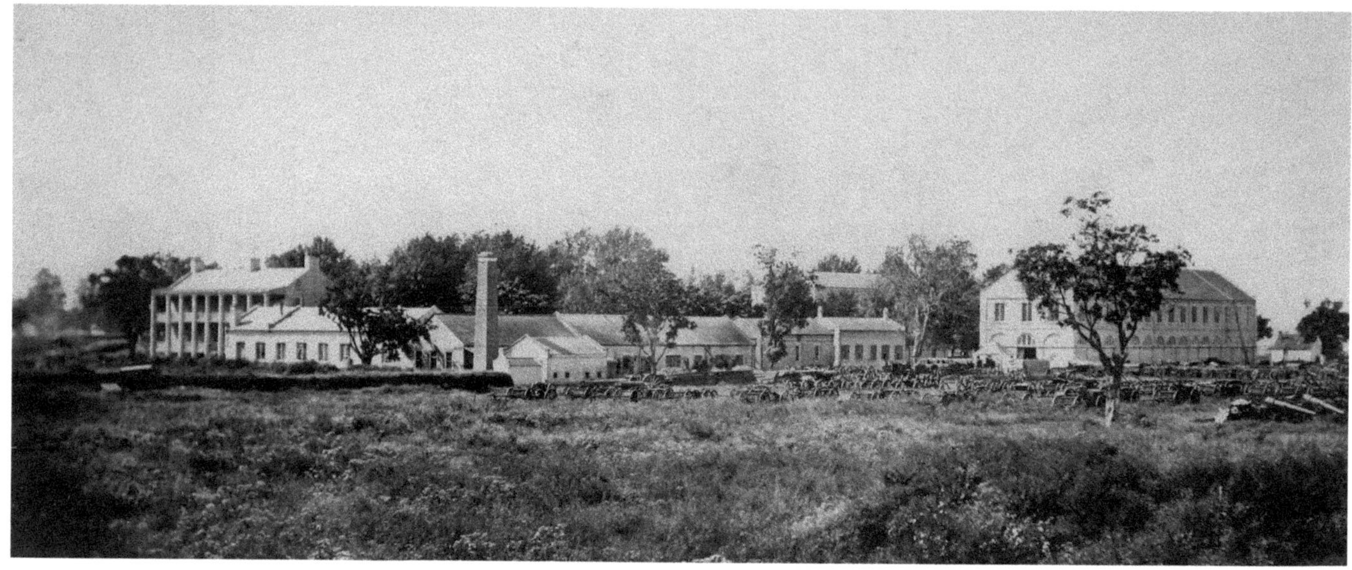

Federal forces were built up in Baton Rouge to maintain the siege of Port Hudson. McPherson and Oliver are credited with photographing this small segment of the 18th New York Artillery in Baton Rouge in 1863.

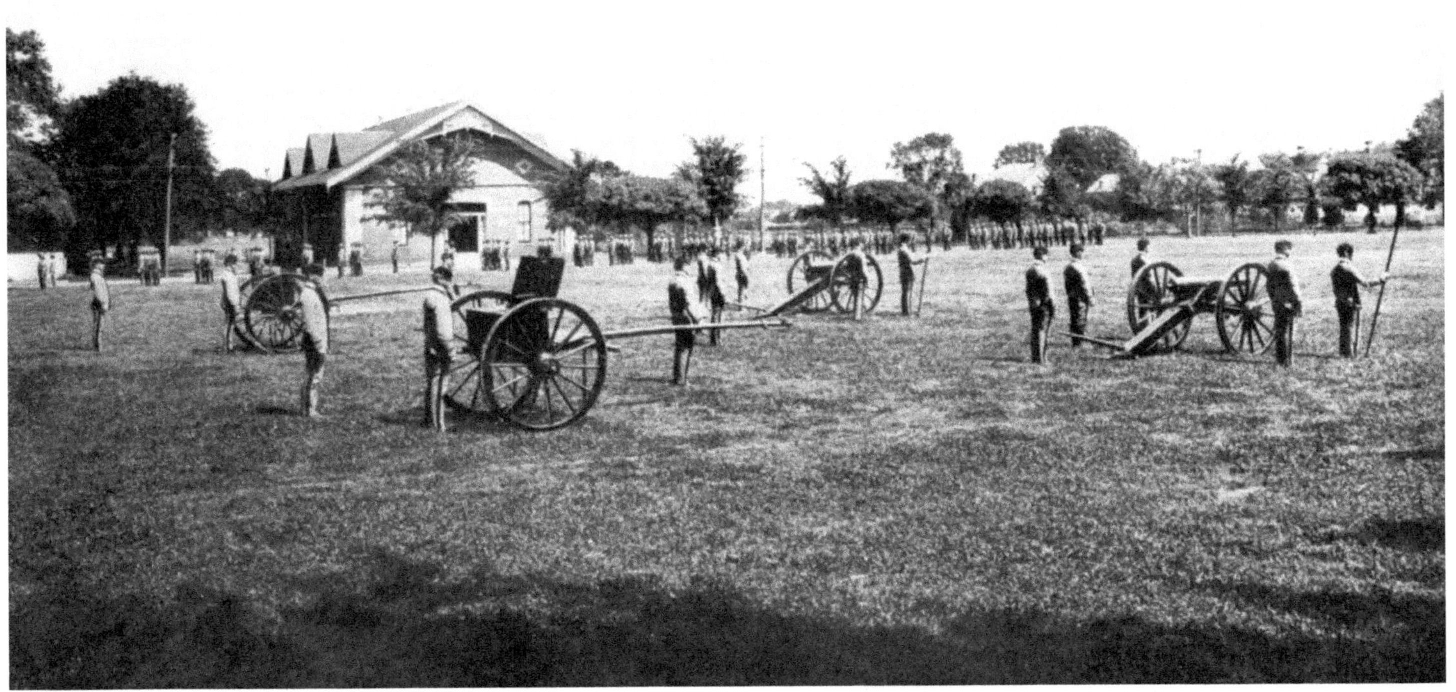

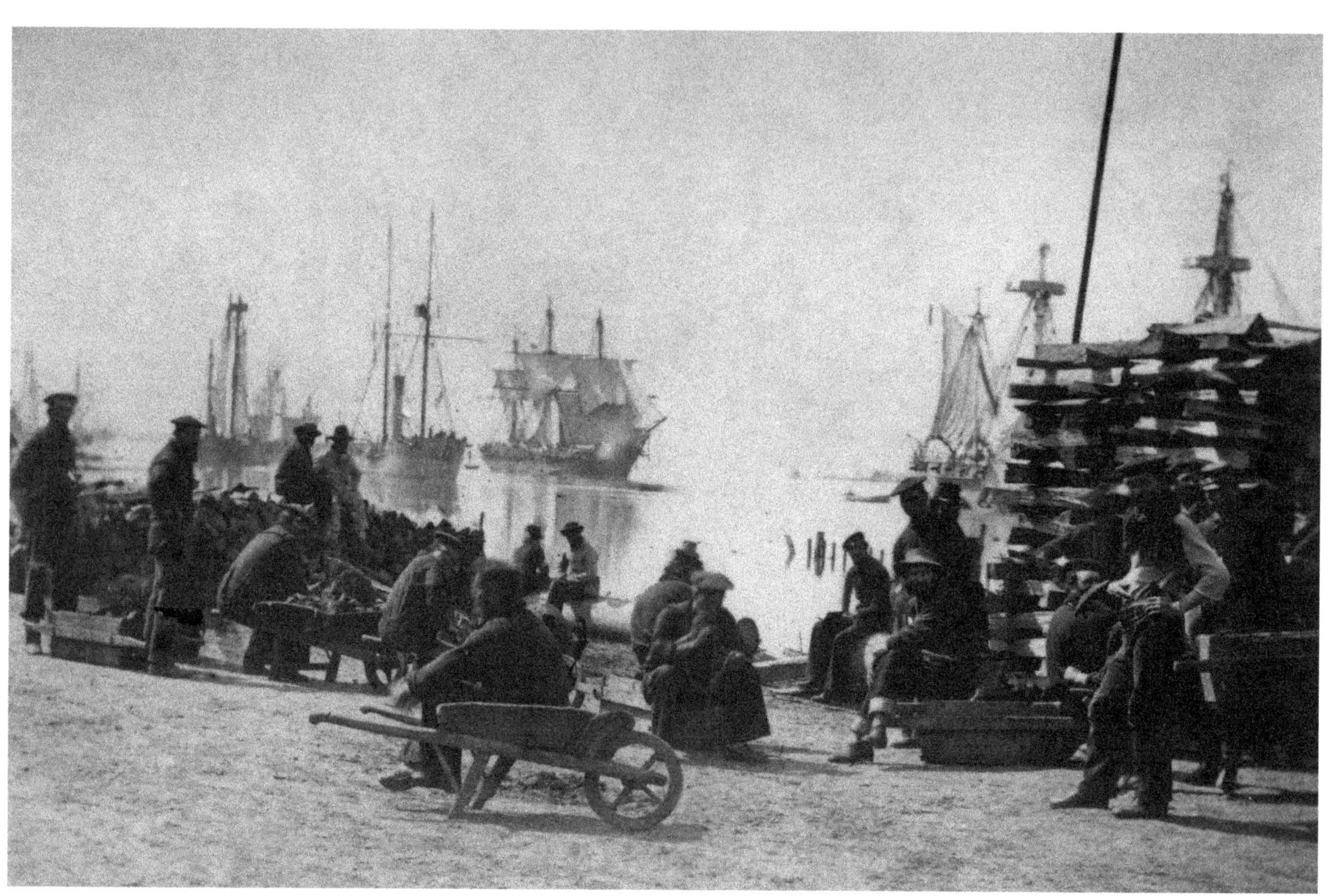

The Federal West Gulf Blockading Squadron under the command of Admiral David Farragut used Baton Rouge as a staging area for many operations on the Mississippi River, especially against Port Hudson. The fleet's coal-and-wood-burning steamers would take on fuel before conducting operations.

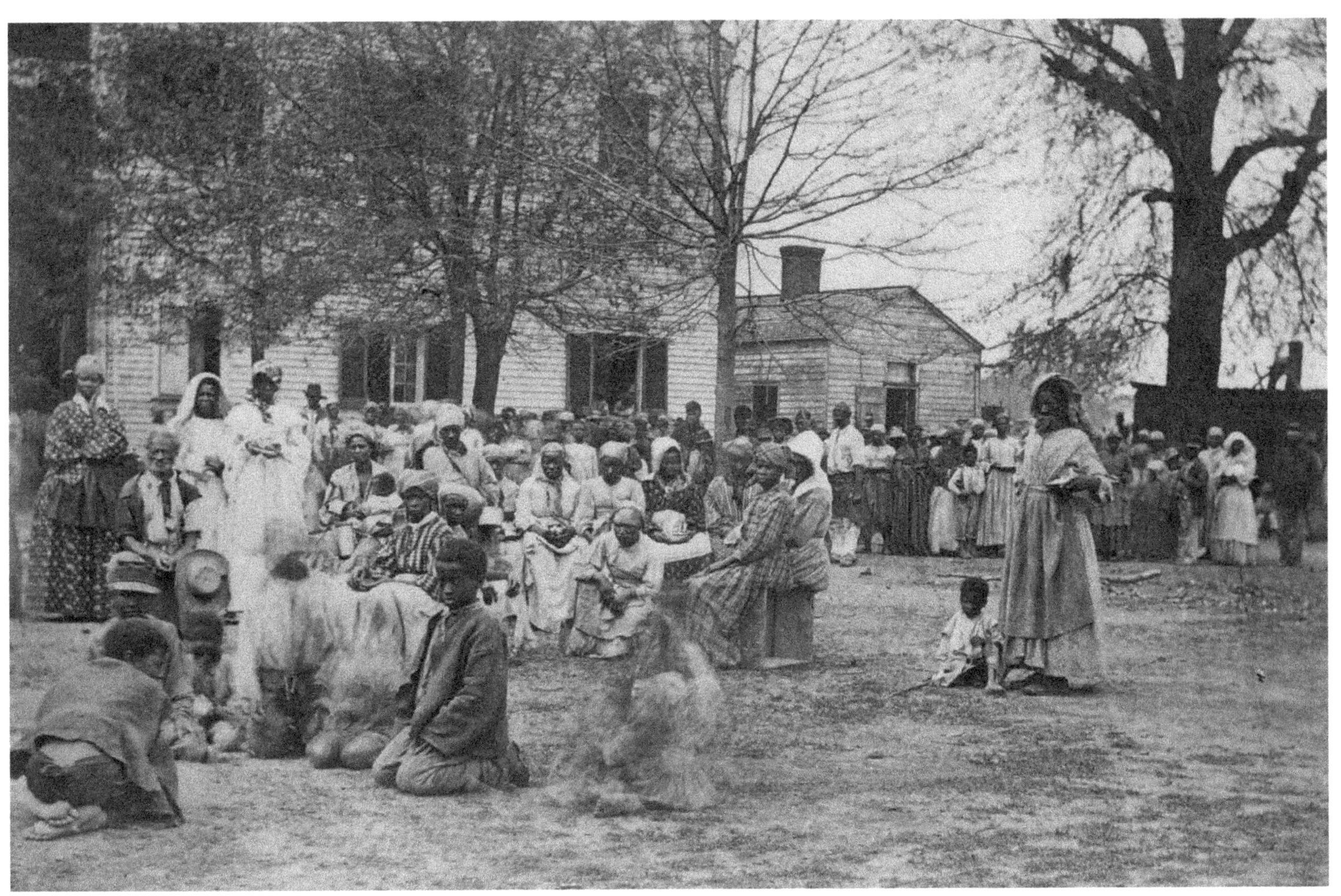

During the occupation of Louisiana, slaves fled captivity into territory controlled by Federal forces. Physically fit men and boys were often drafted into newly established blacks-only Federal military units. Women and children were interned in "contraband camps" like this one in Baton Rouge.

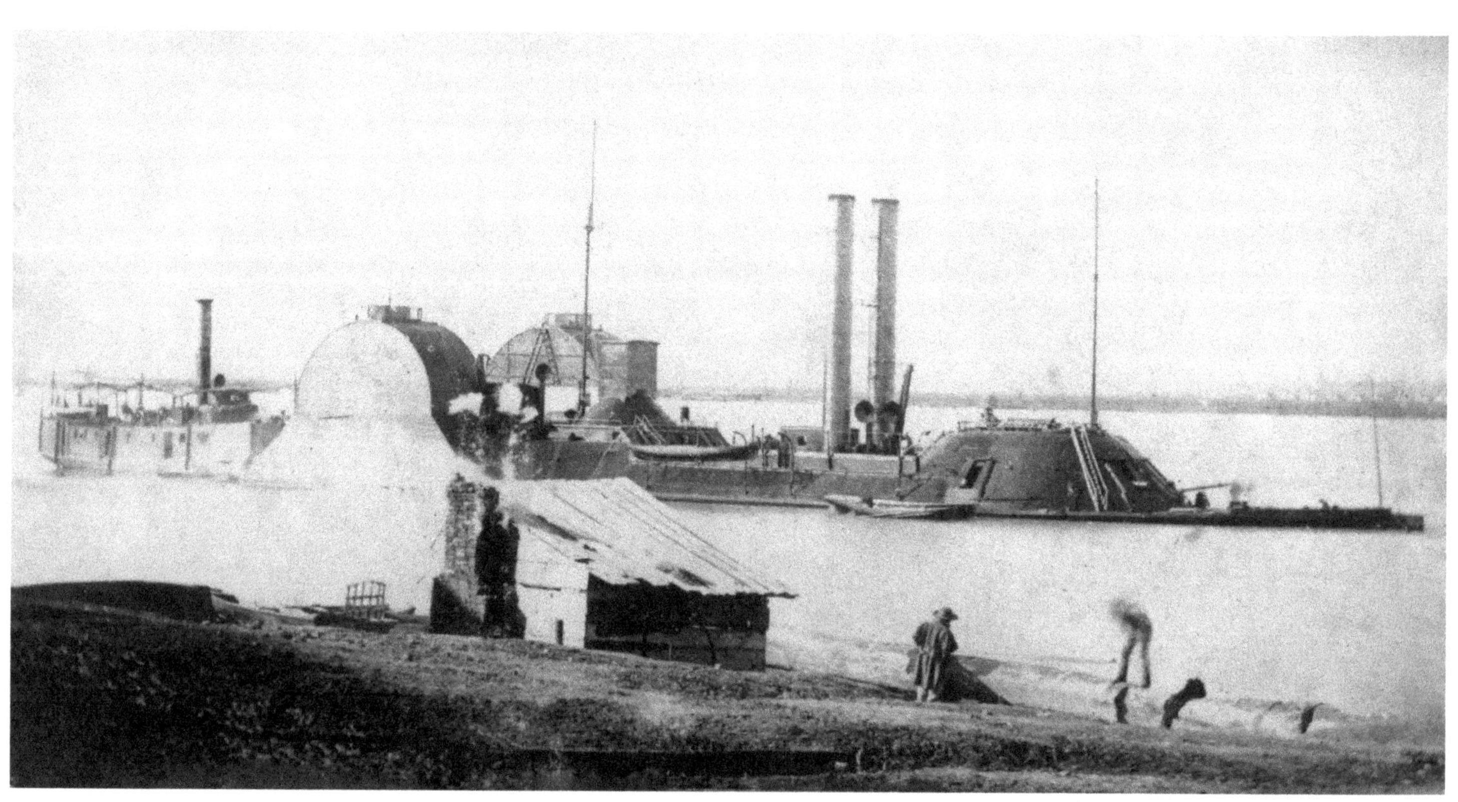

The USS *Choctaw,* part of the Federal West Gulf Blockading Squadron under Admiral David Farragut, often called on the port of Baton Rouge during the war.

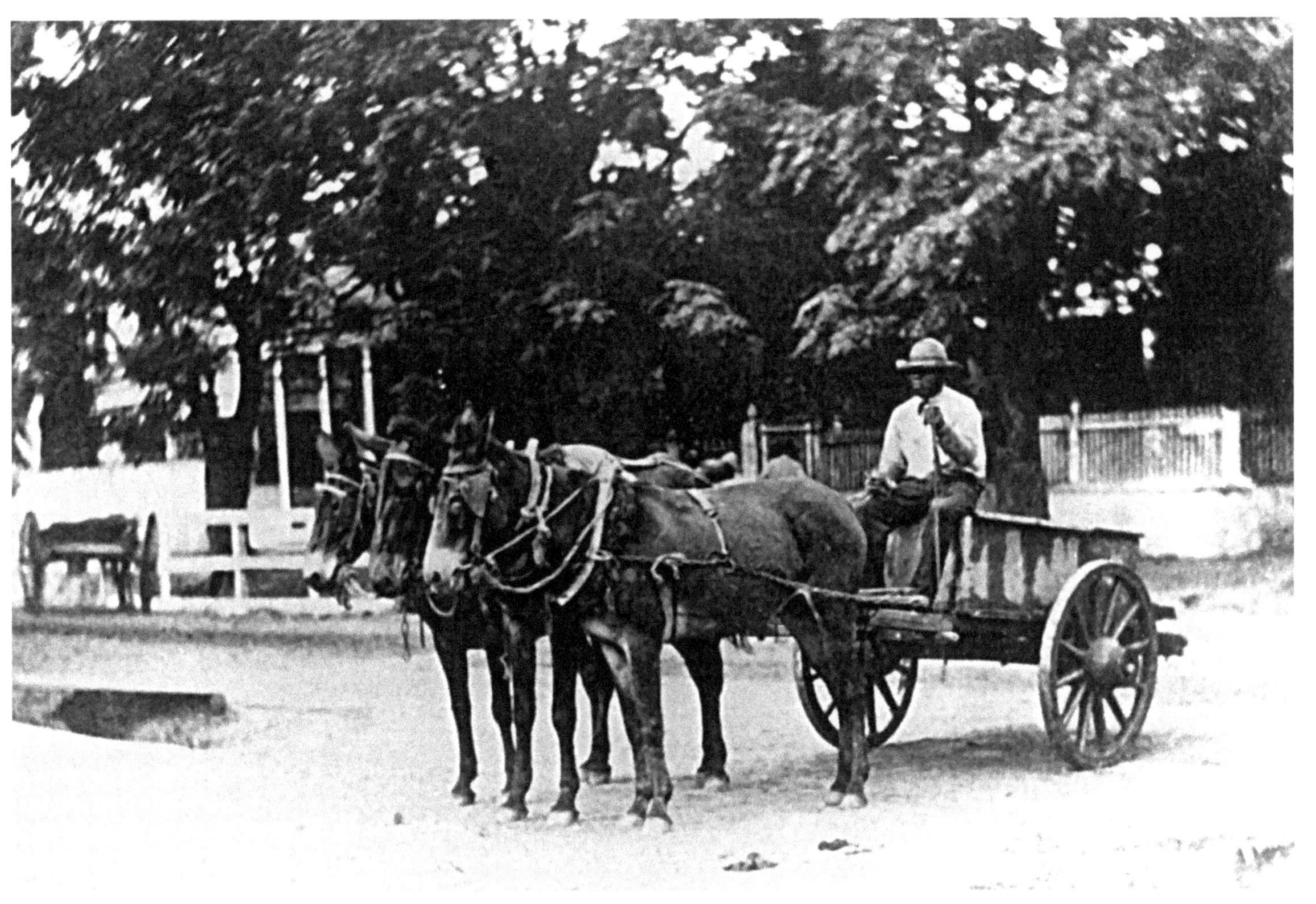

During the Federal occupation of Baton Rouge, beginning May 1862, traveling photographers visited to document the war. McPherson and Oliver may have captured this image at the intersection of Fourth and Church streets. The home that served as General Augur's headquarters until October 1863 is visible in the background.

This structure is the administration building of the Asylum for the Deaf and Dumb of Louisiana, completed in 1858 in Baton Rouge. Federal troops expelled what students remained in 1862 and used various buildings belonging to the institution as a hospital, barracks, and a prison, respectively, for the duration of the war.

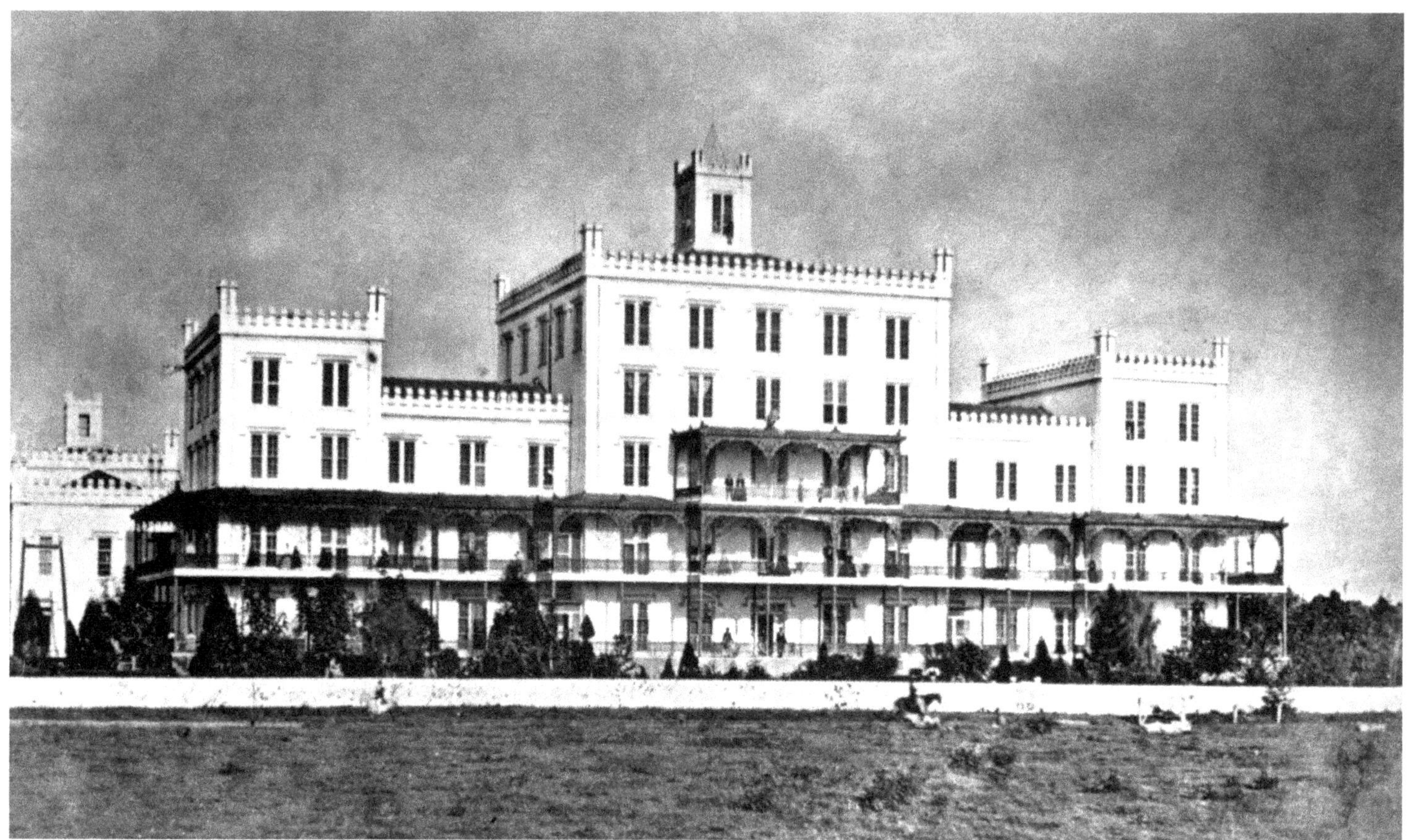

The Louisiana State Penitentiary, first built in Baton Rouge in 1835, occupied five blocks of the city beginning on Sixth Street and extending east to Eleventh Street. From 1844 until the Civil War, the penitentiary ran under a lease held by the private firm of McHatton Pratt and Company. During the war, Federal troops camped around the site and used the structure as a barracks facility.

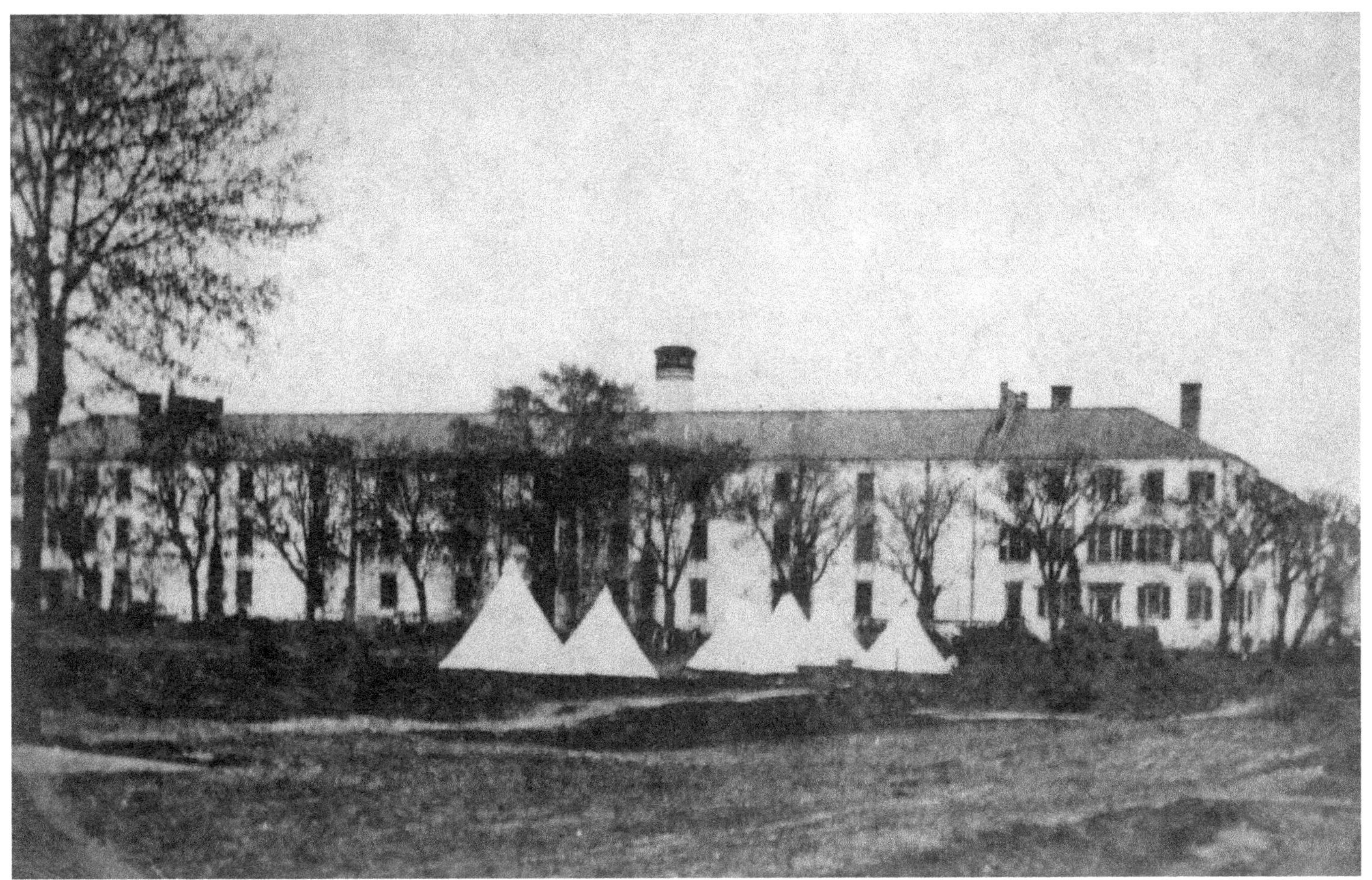

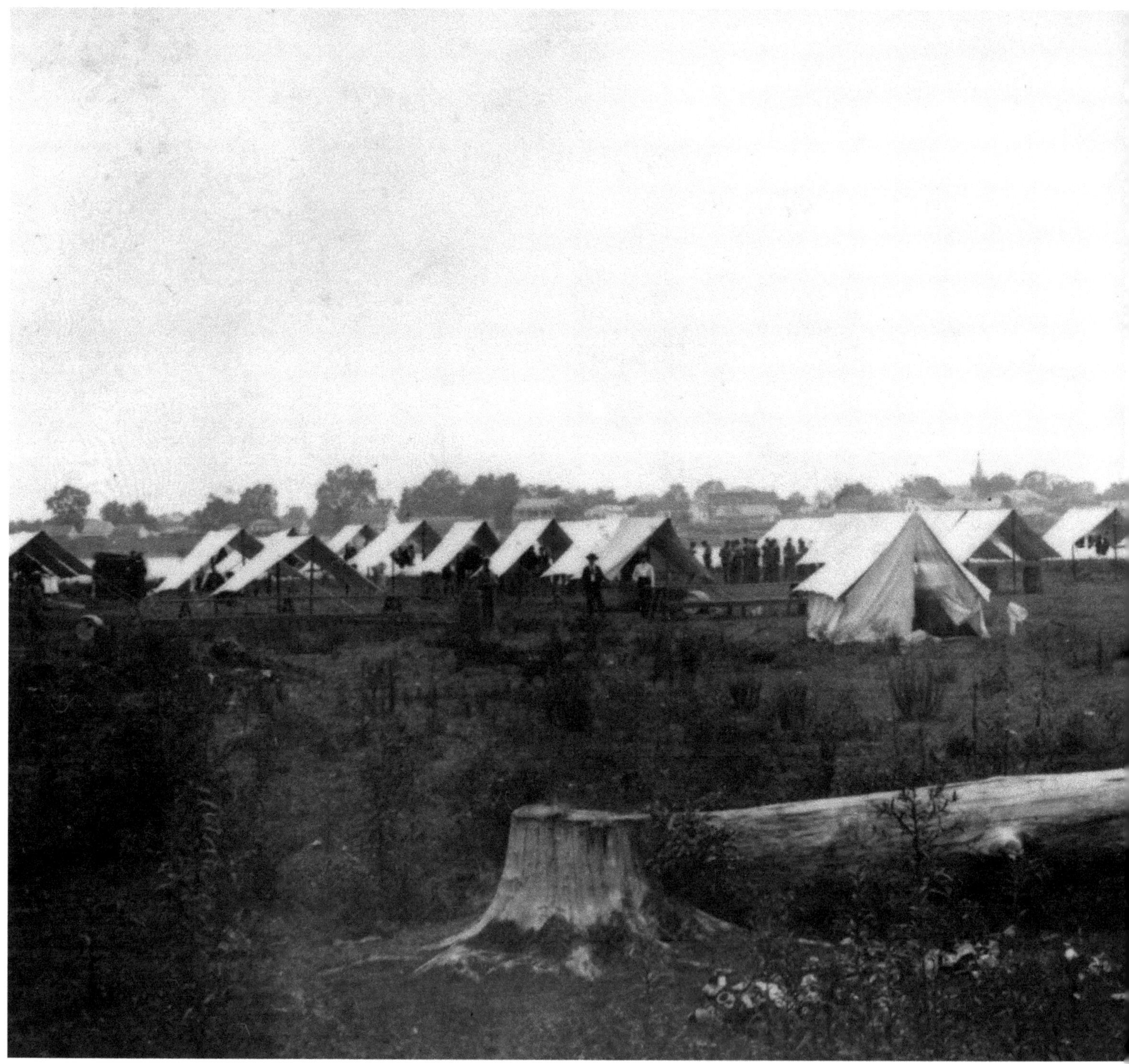

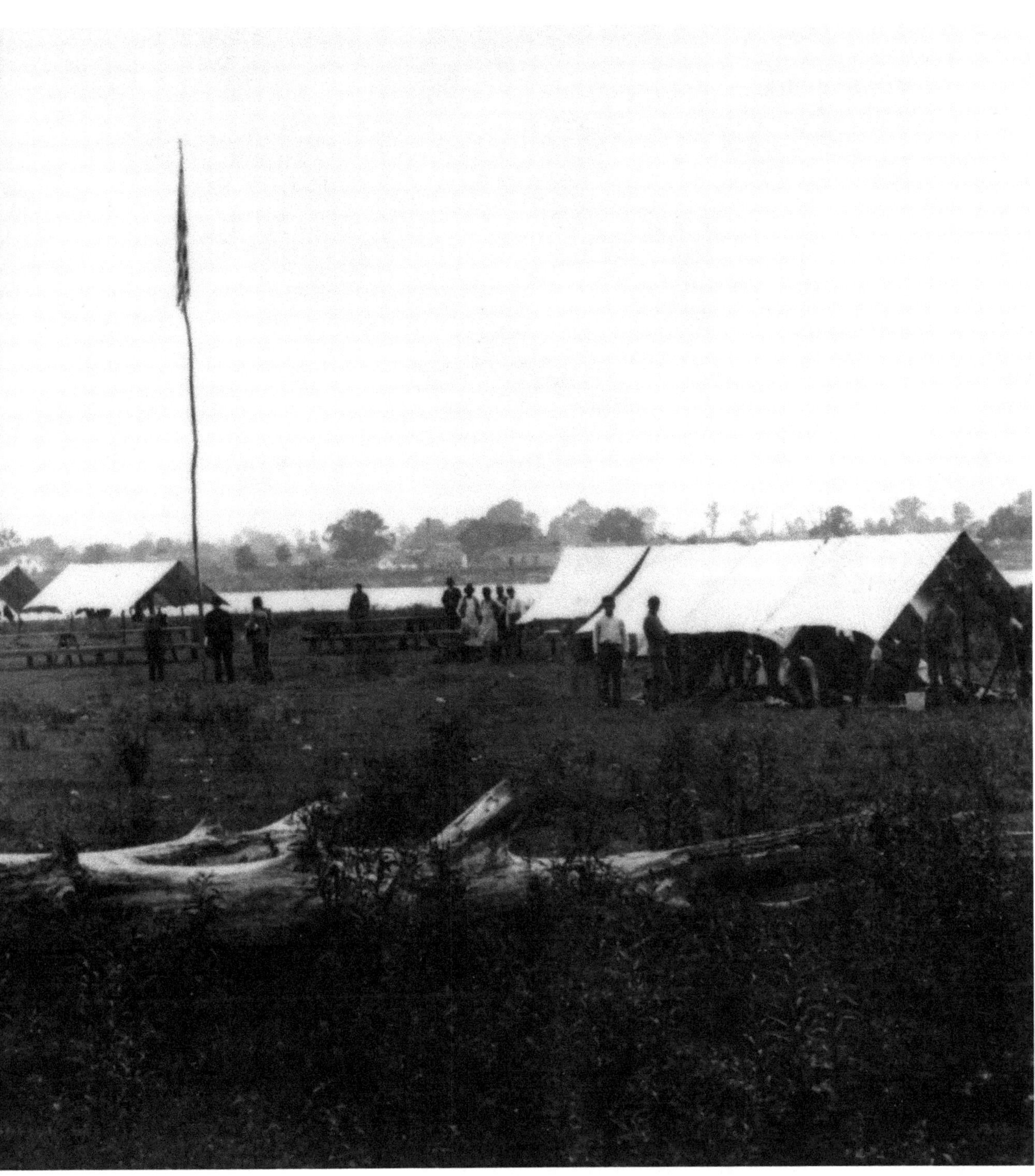

Andrew D. Lytle photographed this Federal Army encampment around 1863.

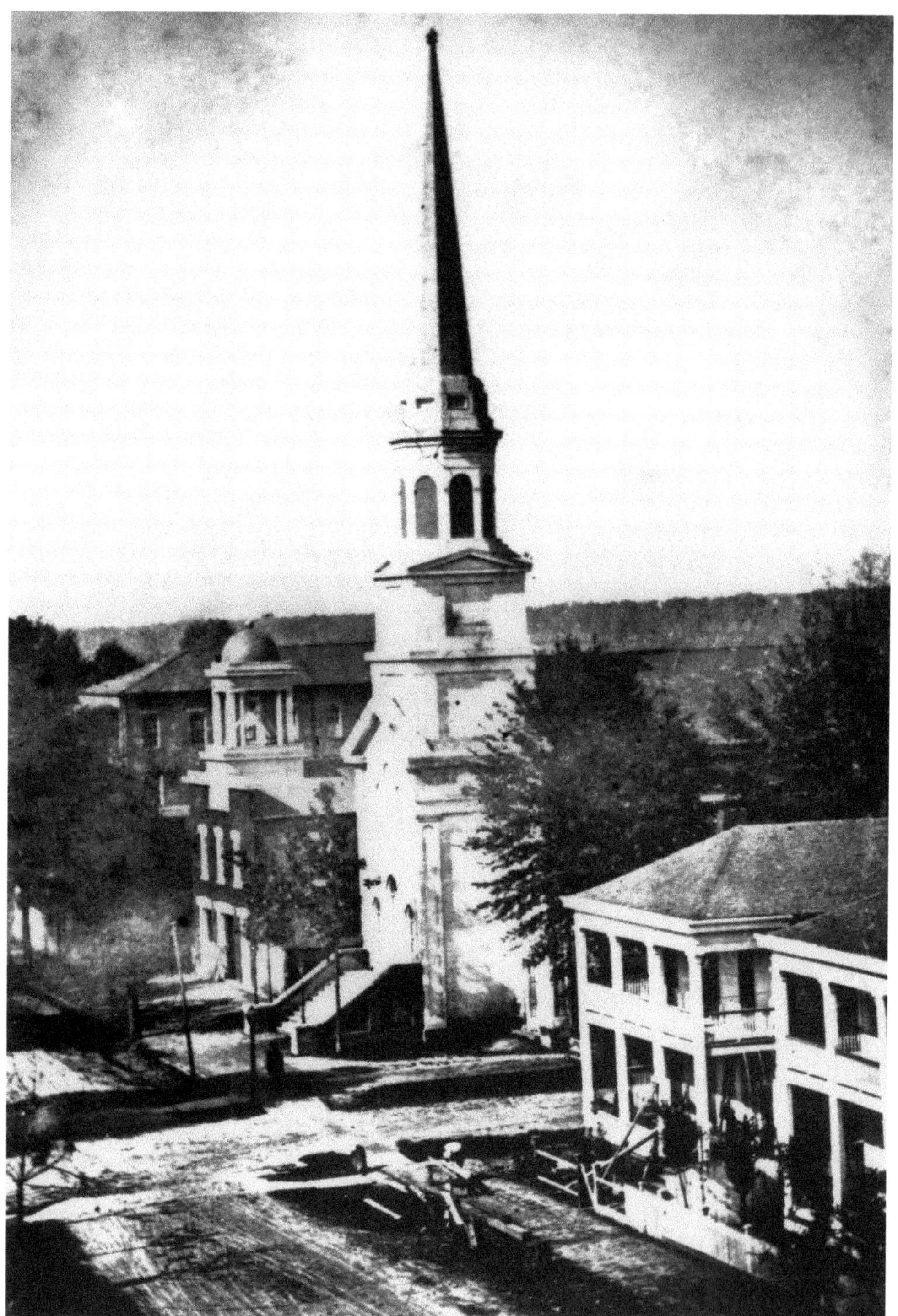

During the 1860s, the First Methodist Episcopal Church, South, on the corner of Church and Laurel streets was a frequent subject of photographers, including Andrew D. Lytle, who created this image around 1864.

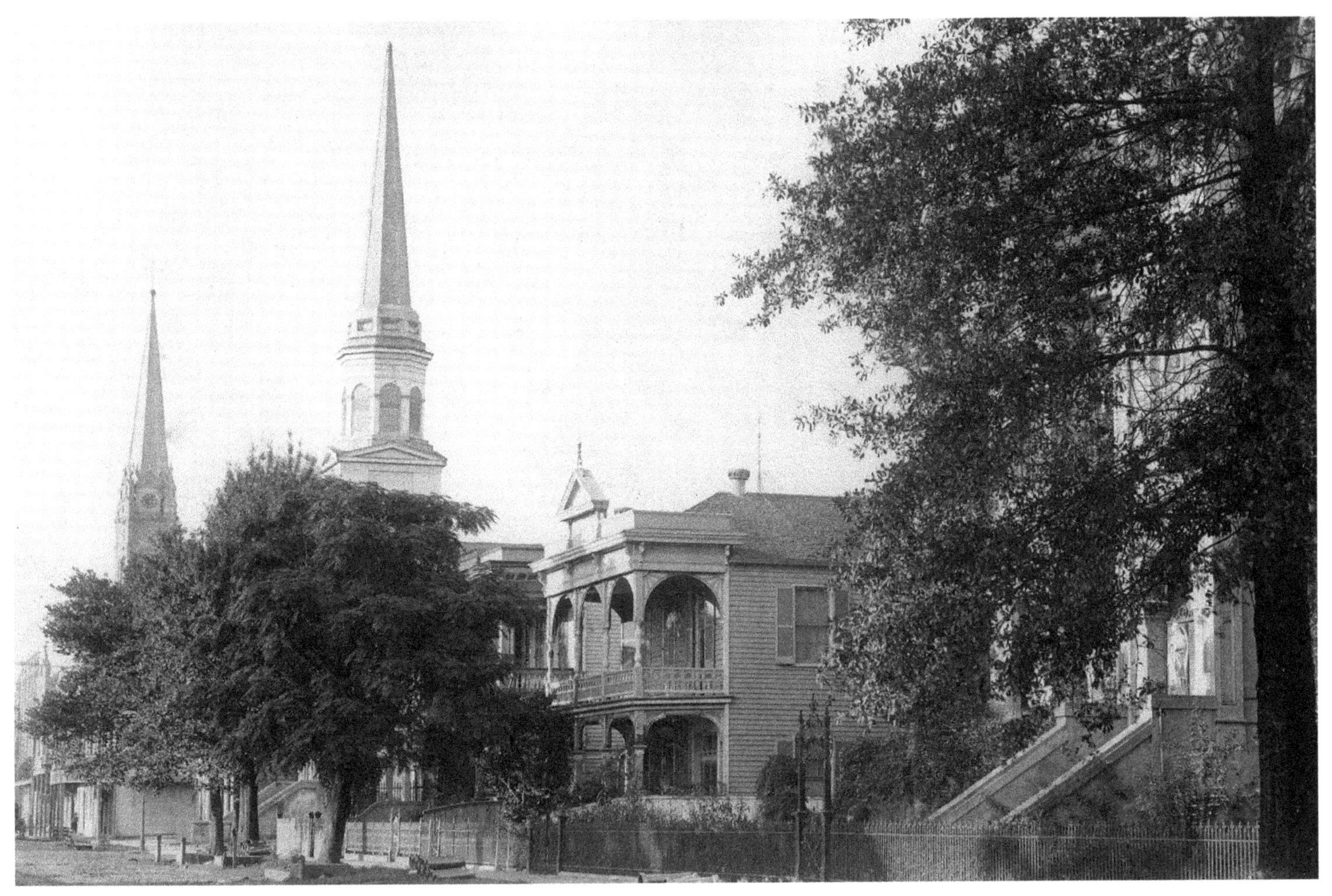

Church Street in Baton Rouge, seen here around 1880, was home to many of the town's houses of faith. In this view, the steeple in the distance belongs to Saint Joseph Catholic Church, now Saint Joseph Cathedral. The nearer steeple graces a church razed in the late 1800s.

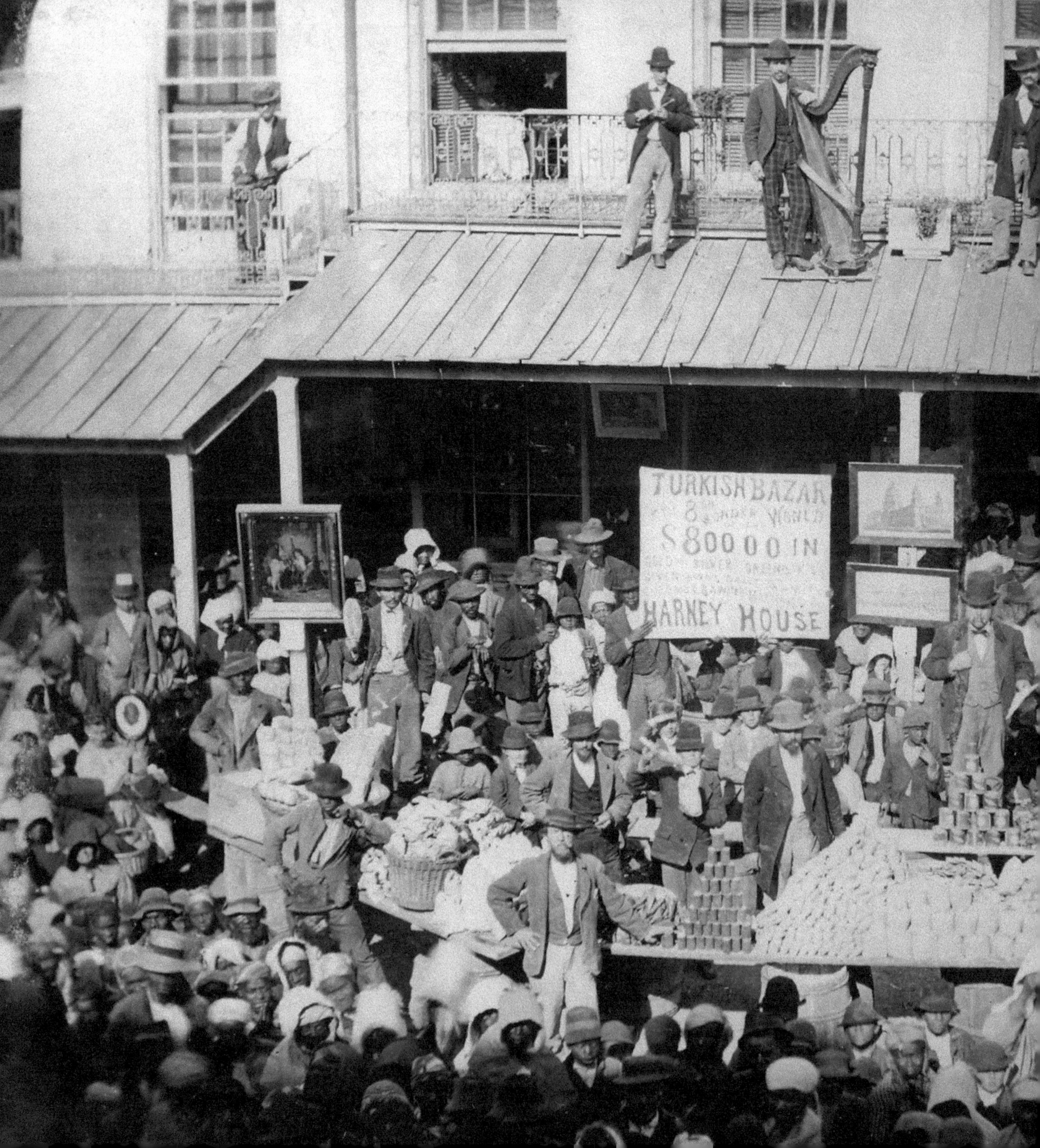
TURKISH BAZAR
$80000 IN
HARNEY HOUSE

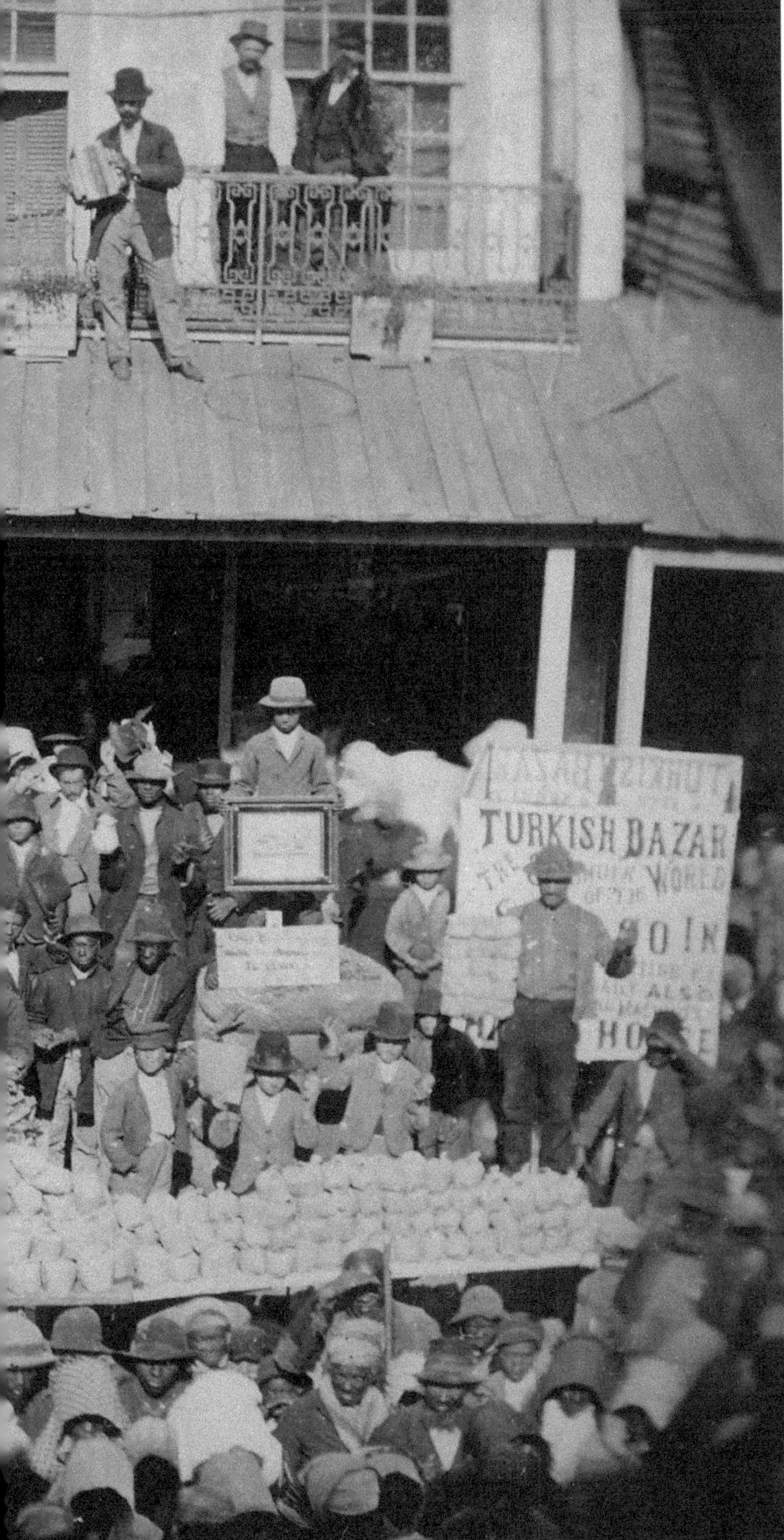

During the 1870s in Baton Rouge, the Harney House put on "Turkish Bazaar" events on Main Street. In 1875, a citizen's petition against the bazaars led the mayor to shut down the event permanently.

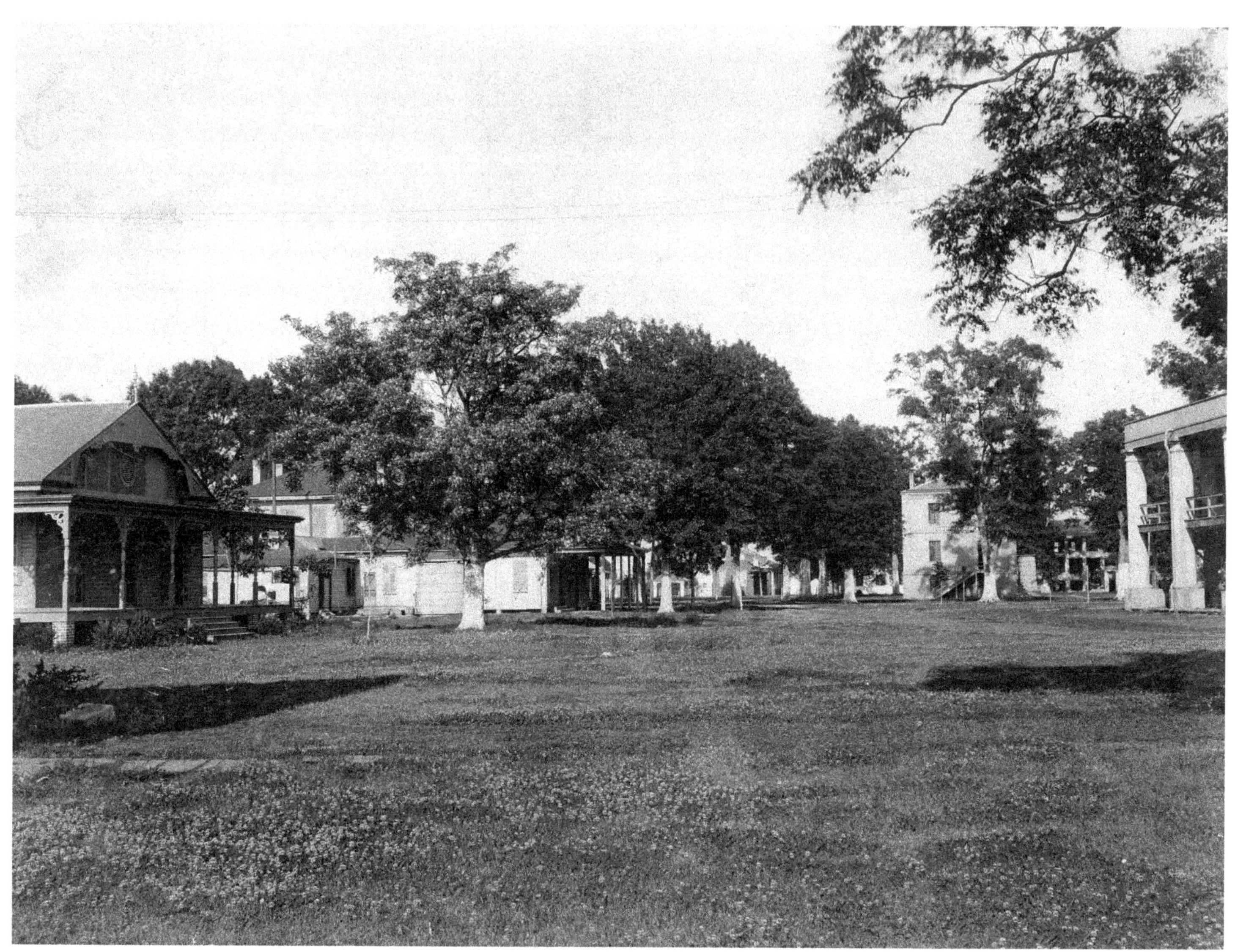

What became Louisiana State University began in 1860 as the Seminary of Learning of the State of Louisiana and was located near Pineville. Following the Civil War, the institution moved a number of times before settling on the old Arsenal grounds on the northern edge of Baton Rouge in 1886. This wide-angle view shows the LSU campus interior around 1890. From left to right are the hospital, mess hall, Treasurer's Office, Agricultural Hall, and barracks.

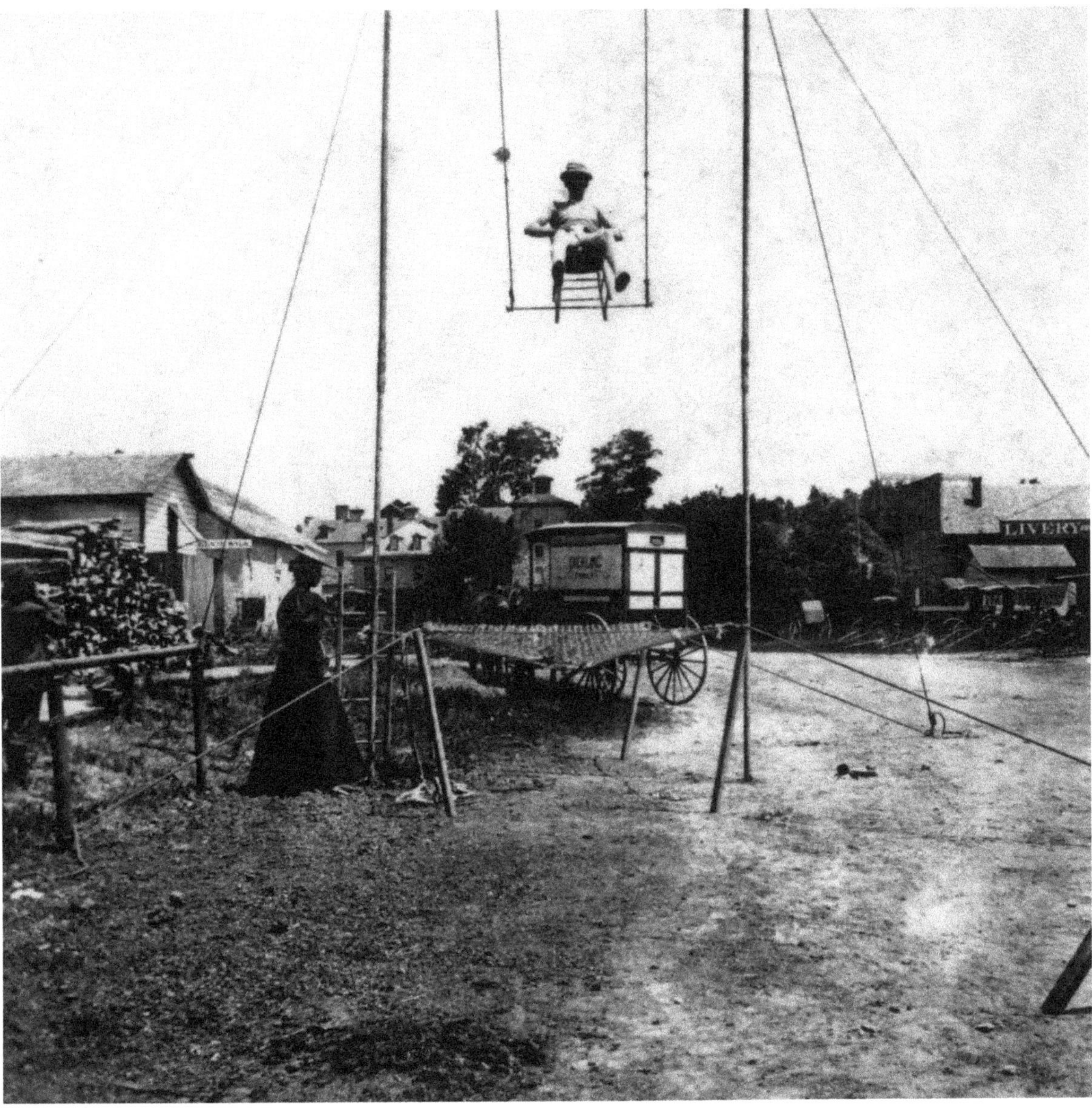

Traveling circuses crisscrossed the country in the late nineteenth and early twentieth centuries. Baton Rouge citizens enjoyed such traveling entertainments as this trapeze act seen about 1899.

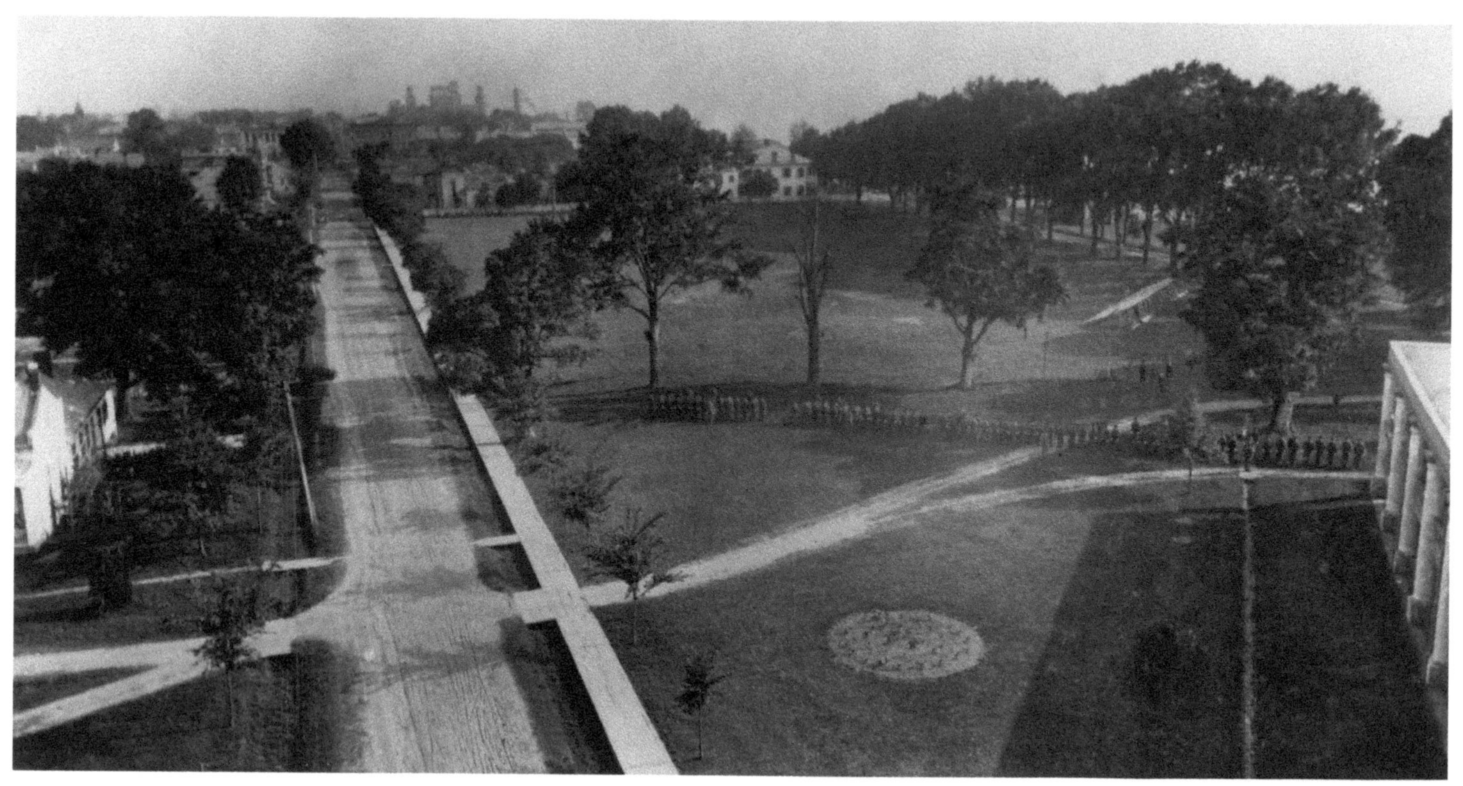

A photographer ran his camera up the flagpole at Third Street on the Louisiana State University campus on the old Arsenal grounds to take this picture of Baton Rouge around 1899. The State Capitol can be seen in the distance, and a part of one of the Pentagon Barracks buildings is visible to the right.

Trees and fencing surround this small church in Baton Rouge around 1890, with a streetlight also visible.

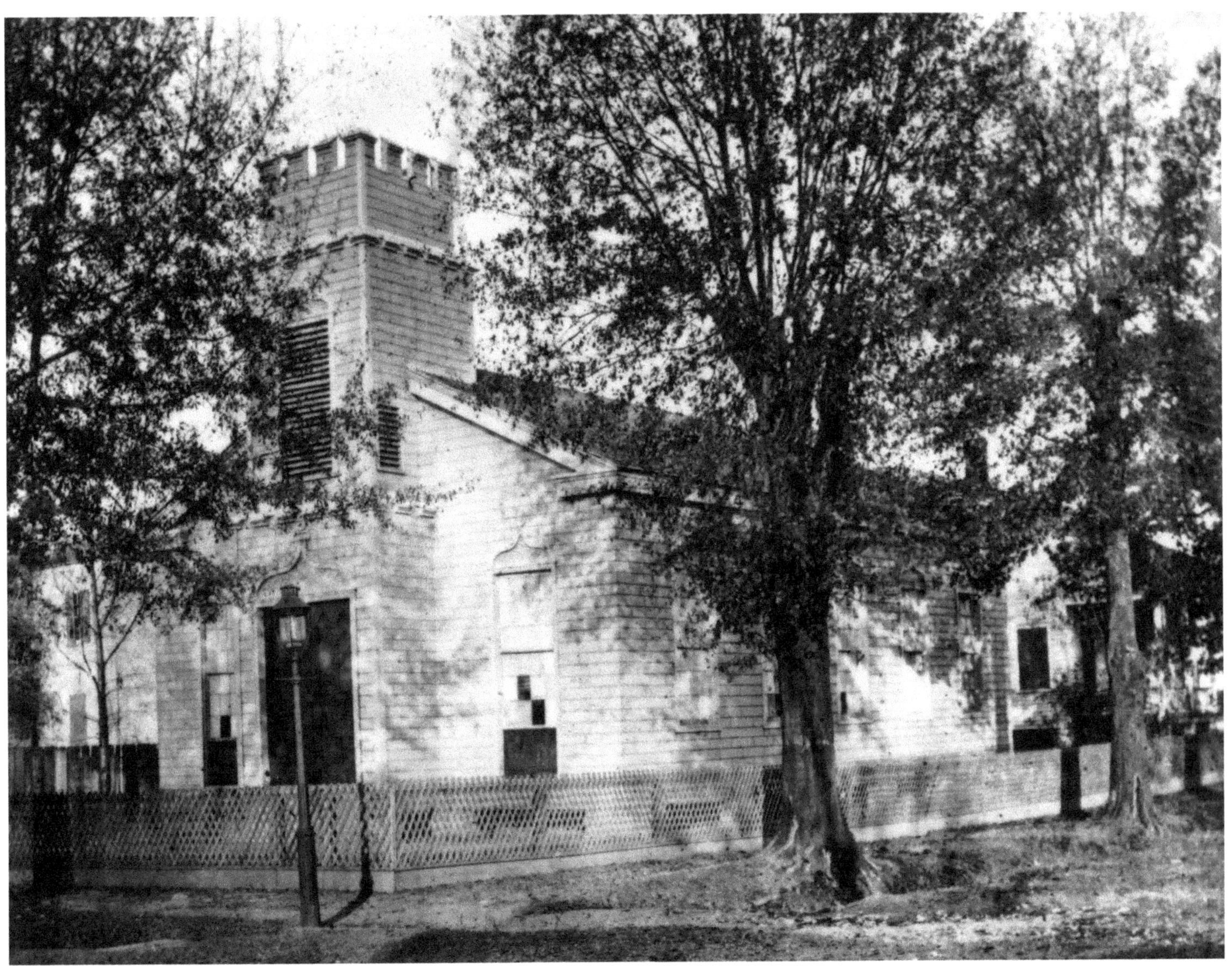

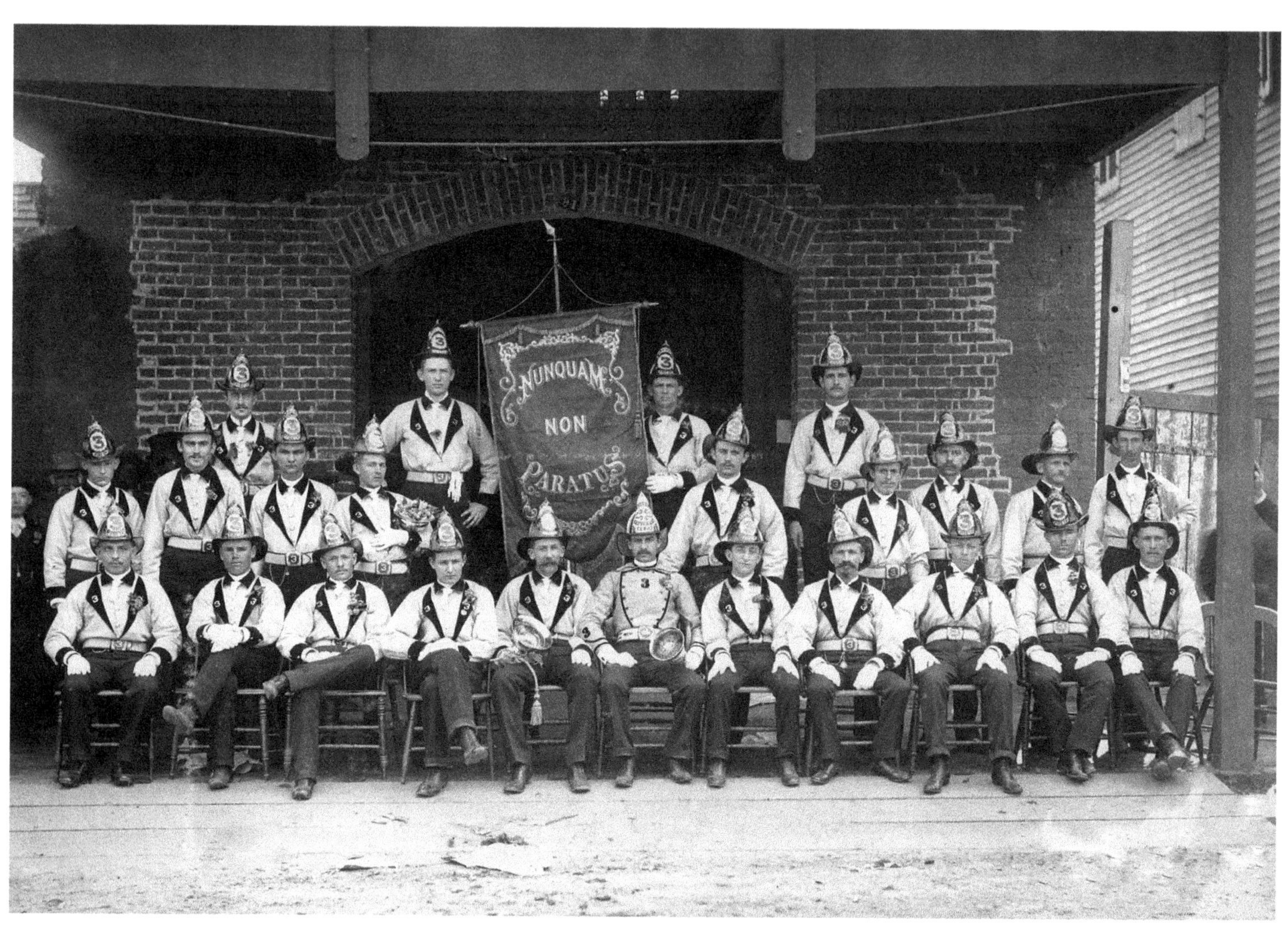

Volunteer fire fighters protected the city before the establishment of the city fire department. Here, in 1887, Washington Fire Company No. 3 sits for a group portrait. Their company motto, "Nunquam Non Paratus," translates as "Never Not Prepared." A better translation would be "Always Ready."

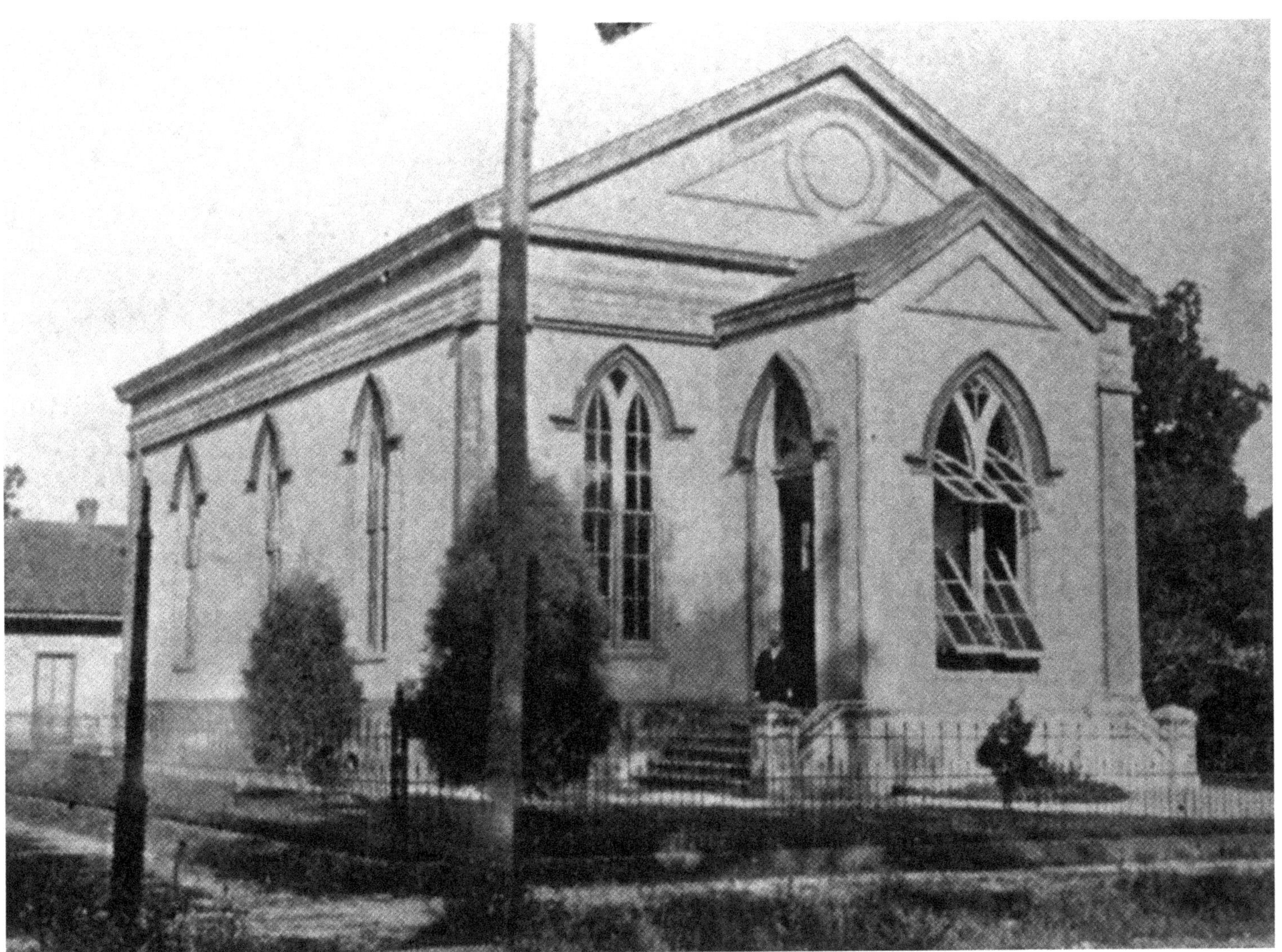

In 1858, Baton Rouge saw the establishment of its first organized Jewish congregation. This structure at 218 Fifth, one block east of Church Street, served as the synagogue of the Hebrew Congregation of Baton Rouge between 1877 and 1880.

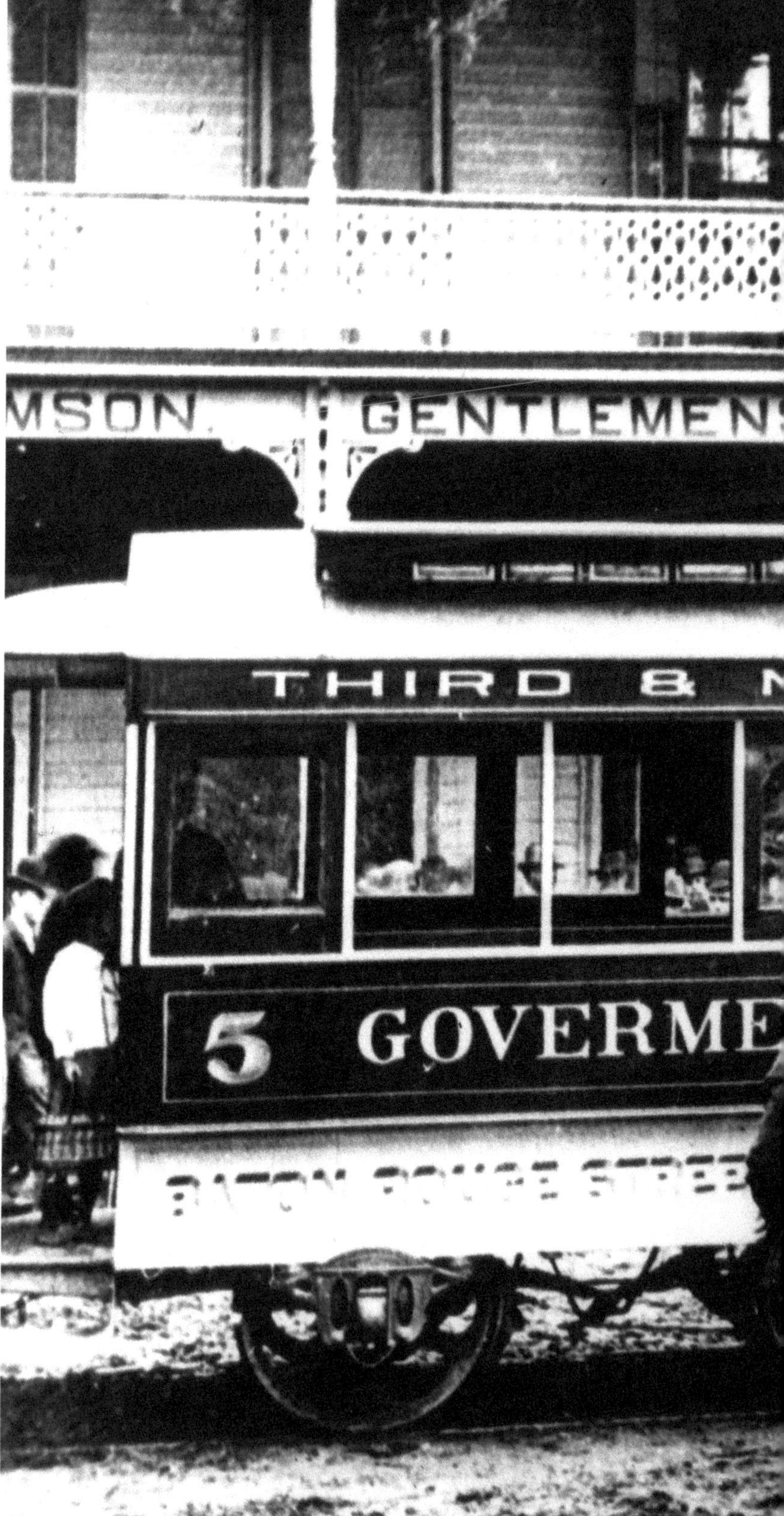

Trolleys decorated to celebrate the inaugural run of the Baton Rouge Street Railway system have stopped in front of Abe Abramson's dry goods store on the corner of Third Street and North Boulevard in October 1890. Within a few years, the system would upgrade from mule-drawn cars to electric-drive cars.

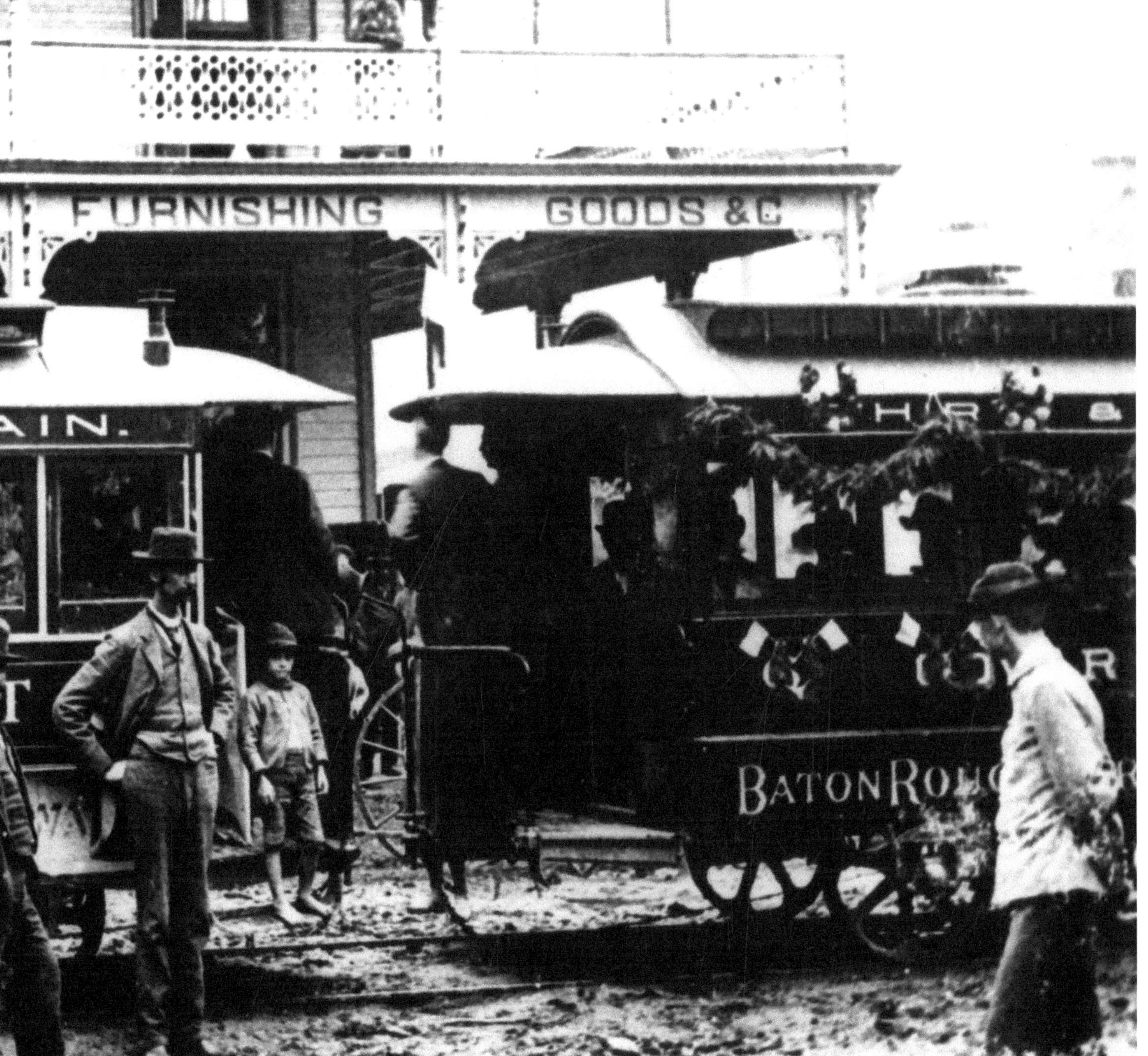
FURNISHING GOODS &C

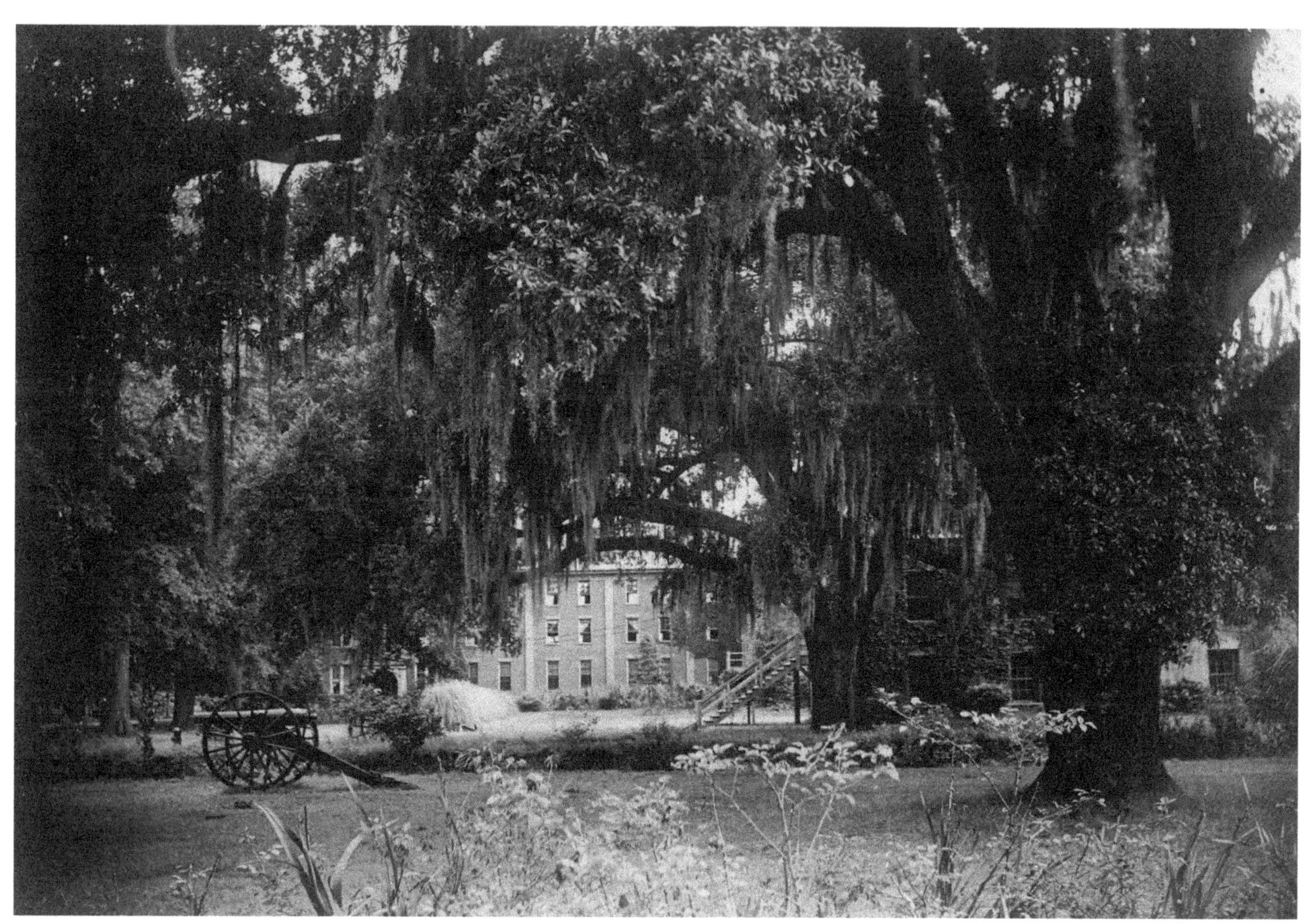

A cannon sits under a moss-draped oak on the campus of Louisiana State University, known as the "Old War Skule." Foster Hall is at center, while bits of Agricultural Hall can be seen on the right behind the trees.

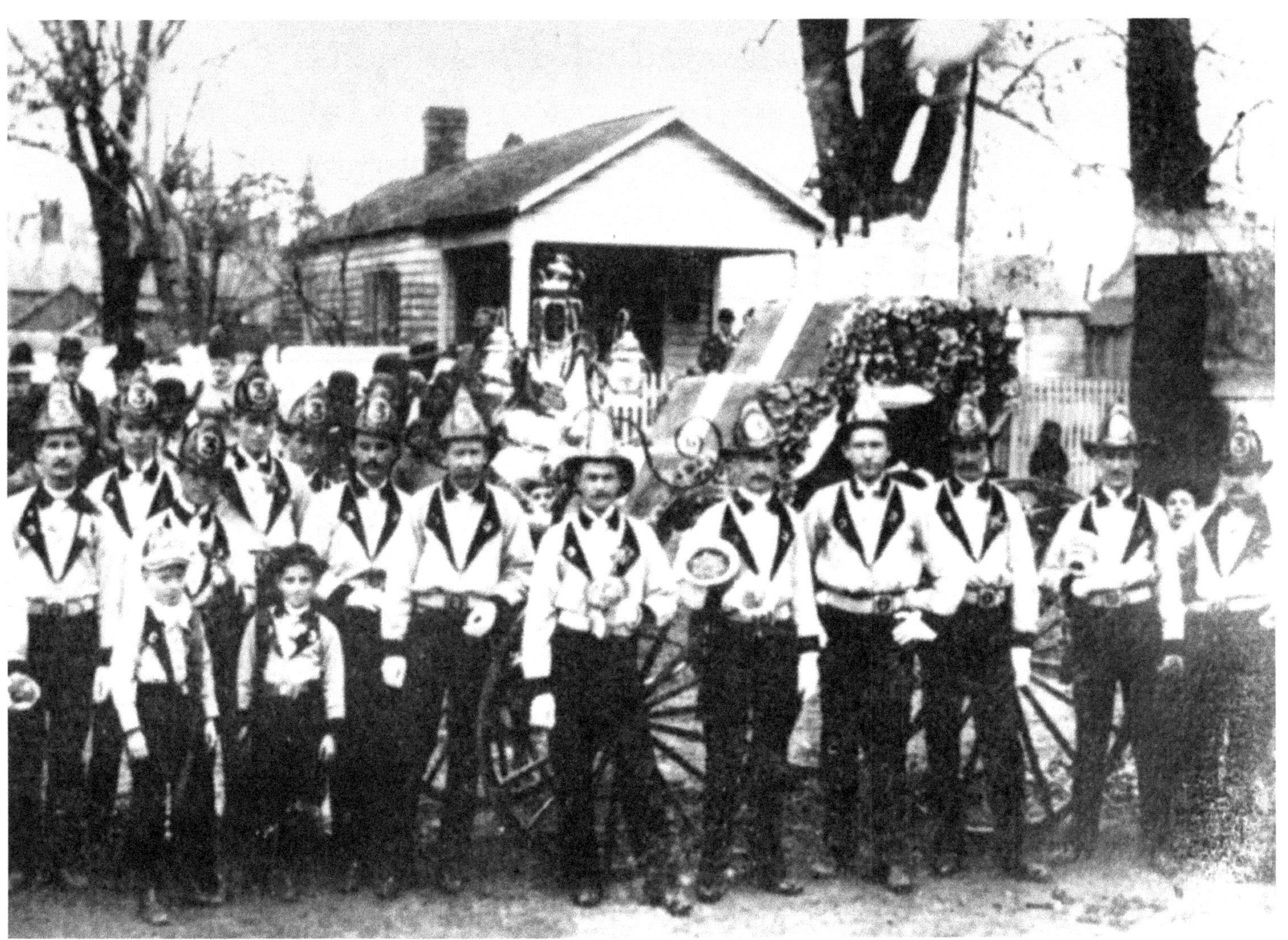

The Washington Fire Company No. 3 poses with its float created for the 1887 Washington's Birthday Firemen's Parade. Begun in the 1870s, this Baton Rouge annual event supplanted Mardi Gras as the winter social season's closing party.

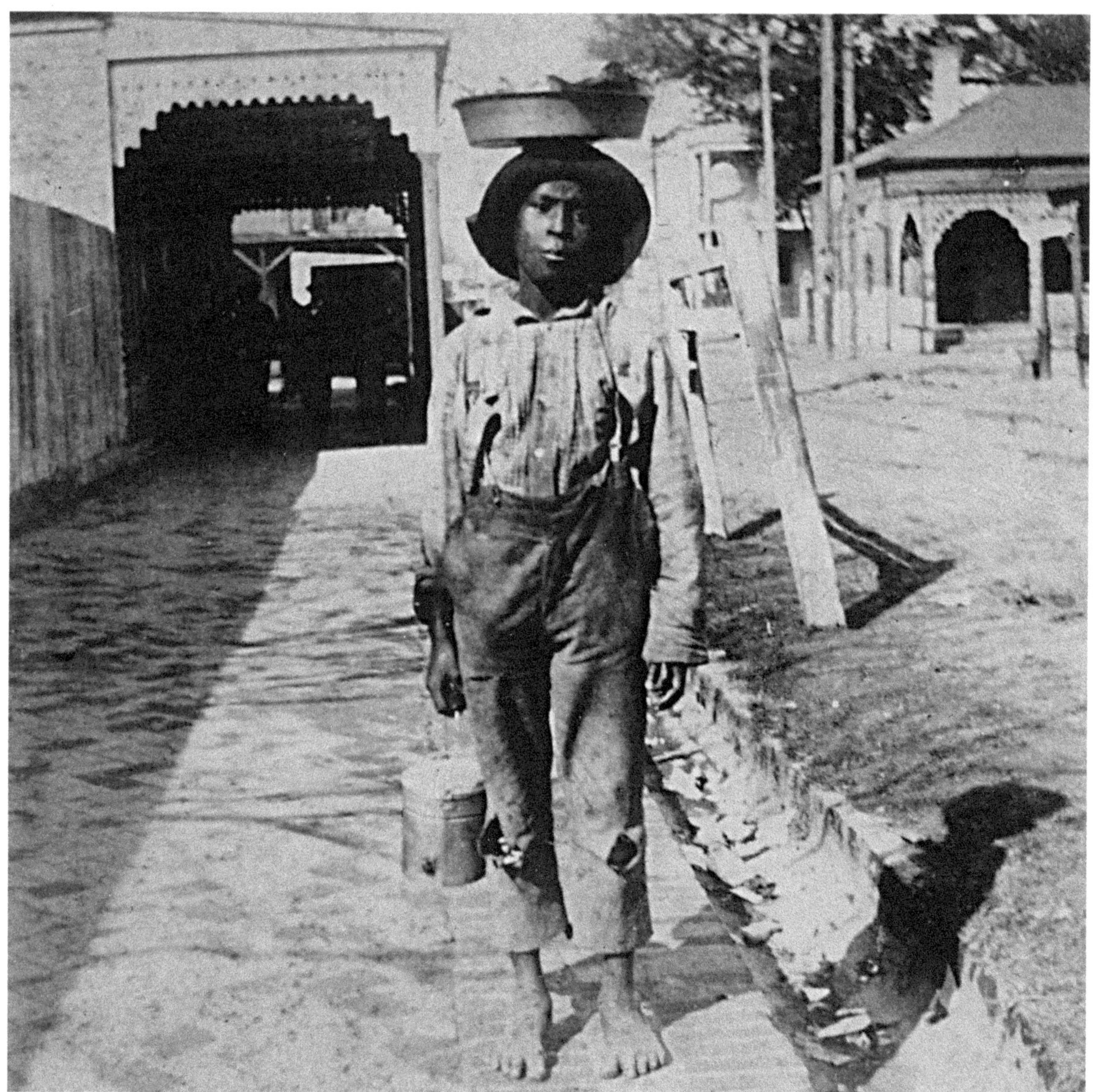

This young man may have been leaving the central market with his pan of fish and his bucket of oil. He stands on the sidewalk near the intersection of Third and Florida streets in downtown Baton Rouge around 1899.

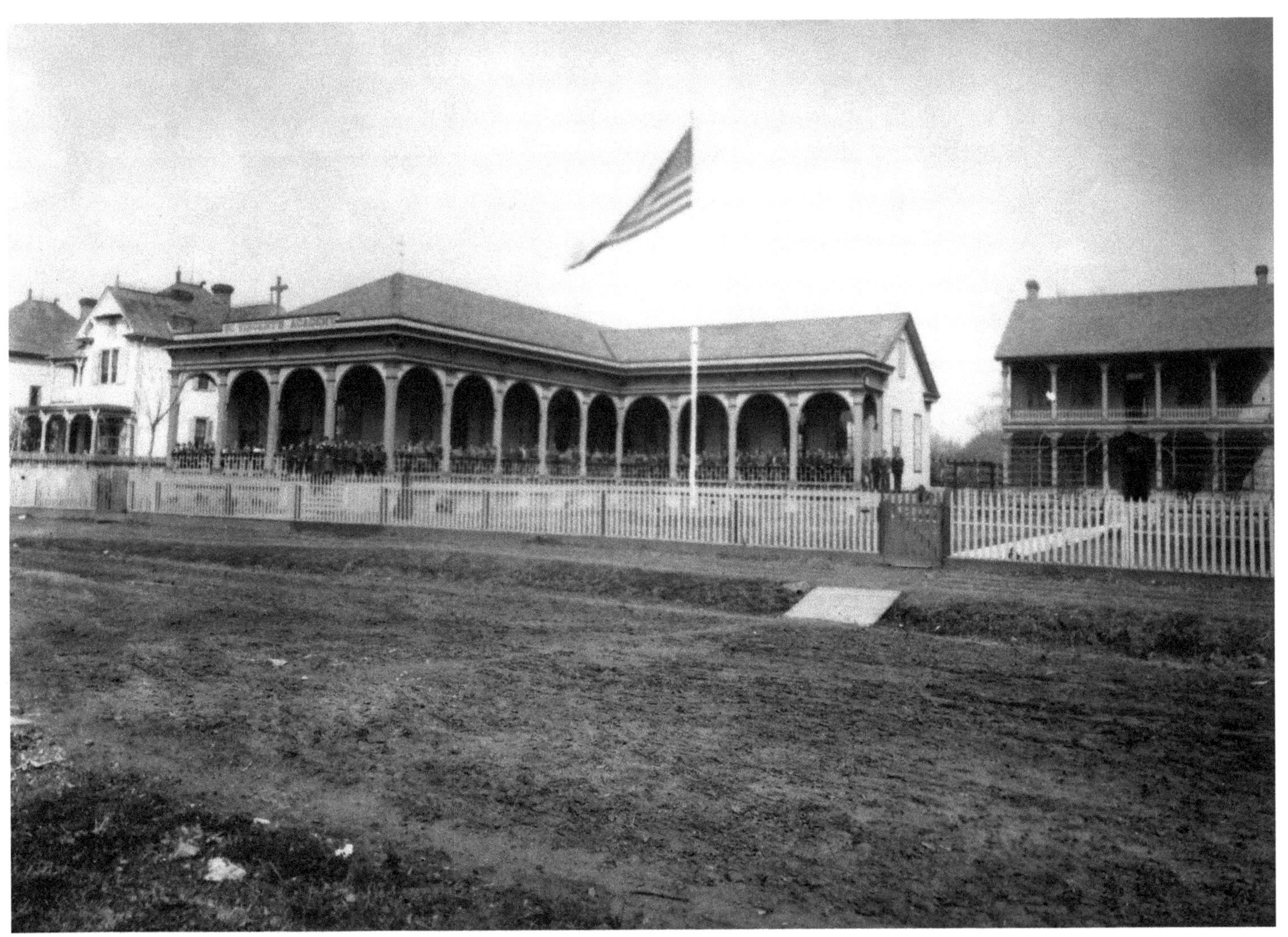

St. Vincent's Academy, built in 1894, was located at the intersection of North and Church streets. Thirty-five years later, a new structure would be built and the name would be changed to Catholic High School for Boys.

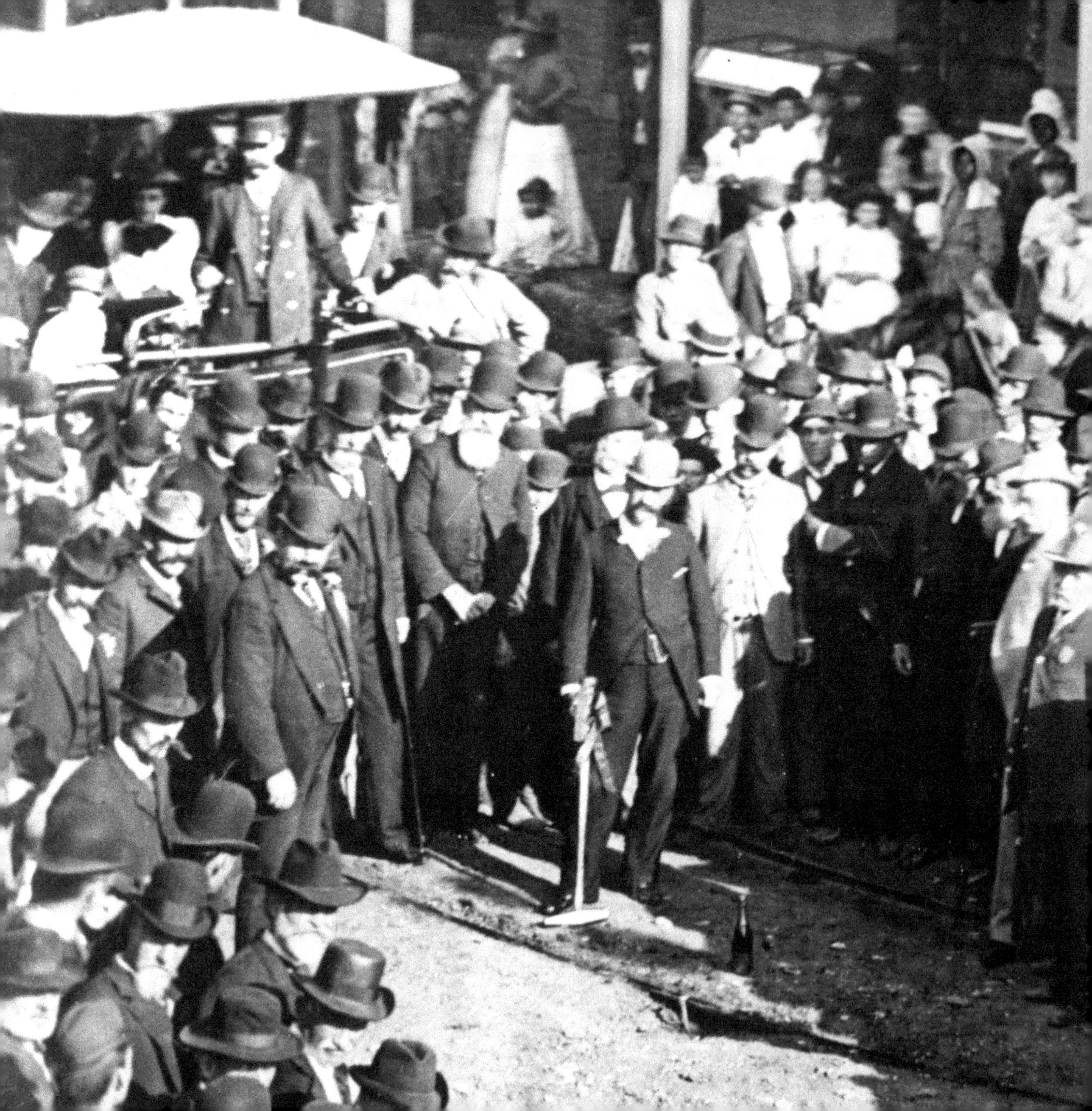

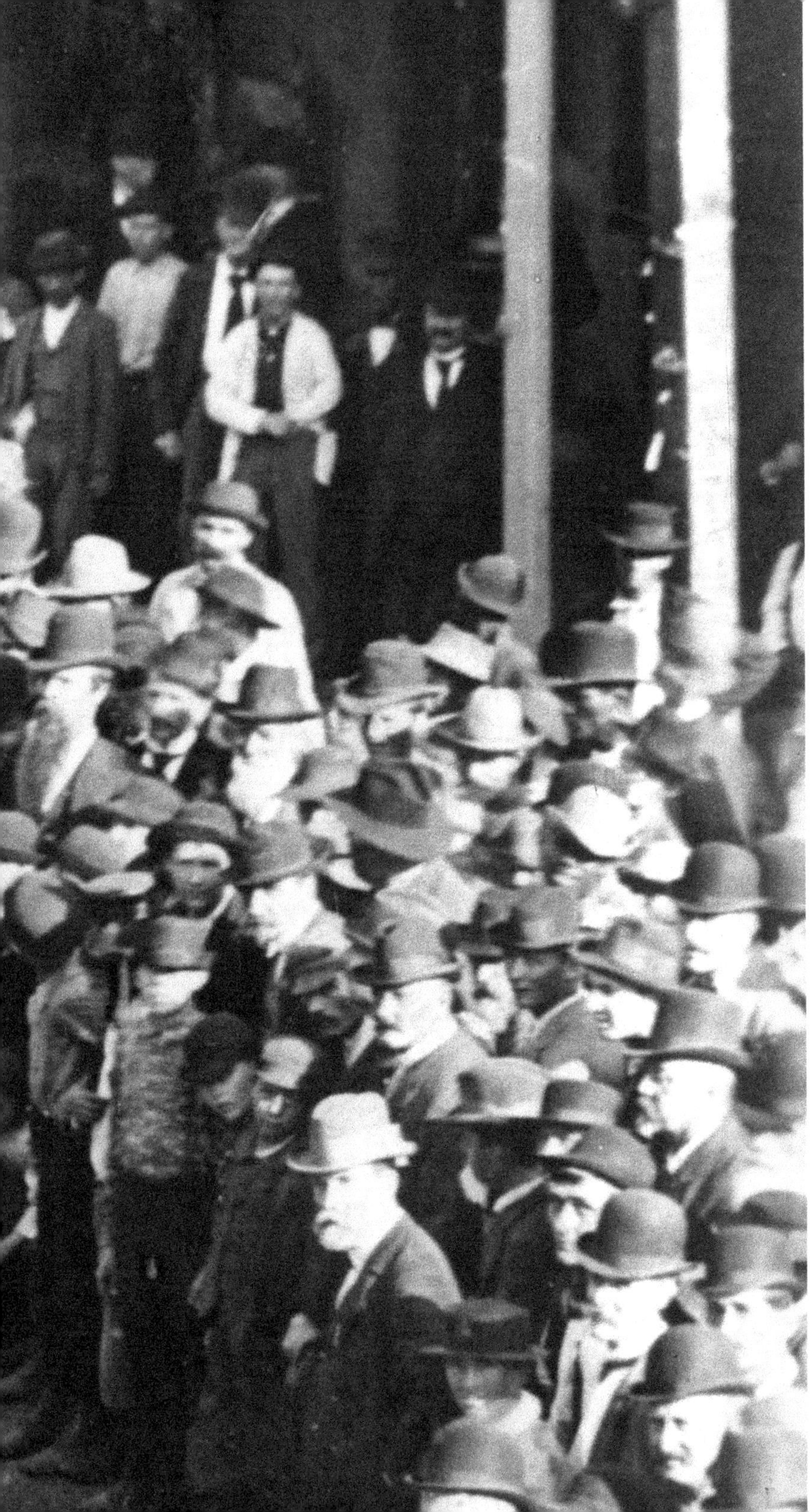

In April 1893, Baton Rouge celebrated the electrification of its street railway system, which would expand during the next few decades and serve as the city's mass transit system.

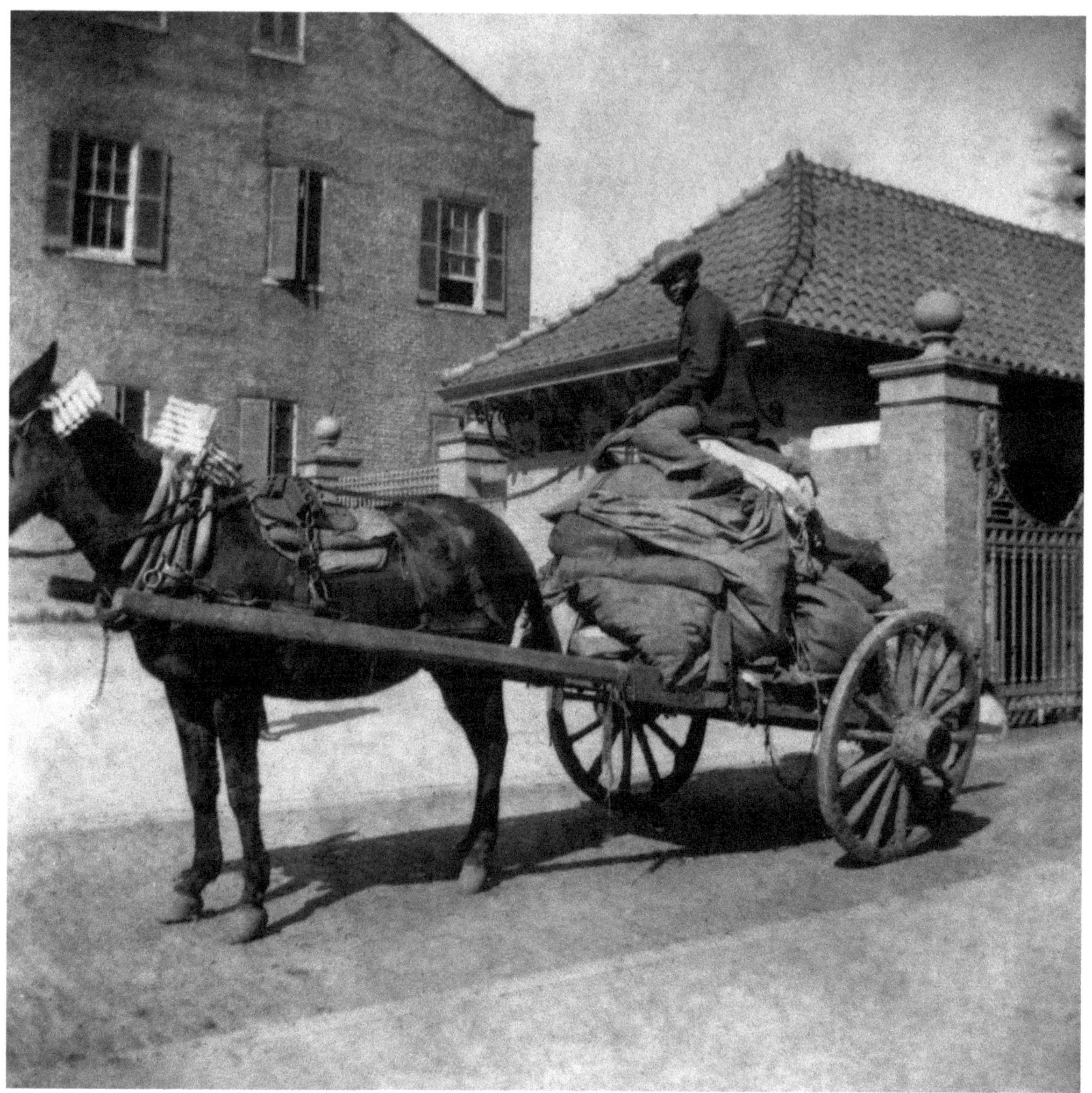

A United States Post Office dray loaded with mail sacks makes its way either to or from the post office on North Boulevard around 1899. The tile-roofed building seen behind the dray served as the post office stables.

Standing in front of the Washington Fire Company No. 1 firehouse, the float "Victory" prepares for the 1898 Washington's Birthday Firemen's Parade. The sign for Rabenhorst Undertakers, established in 1866, can be seen in the background.

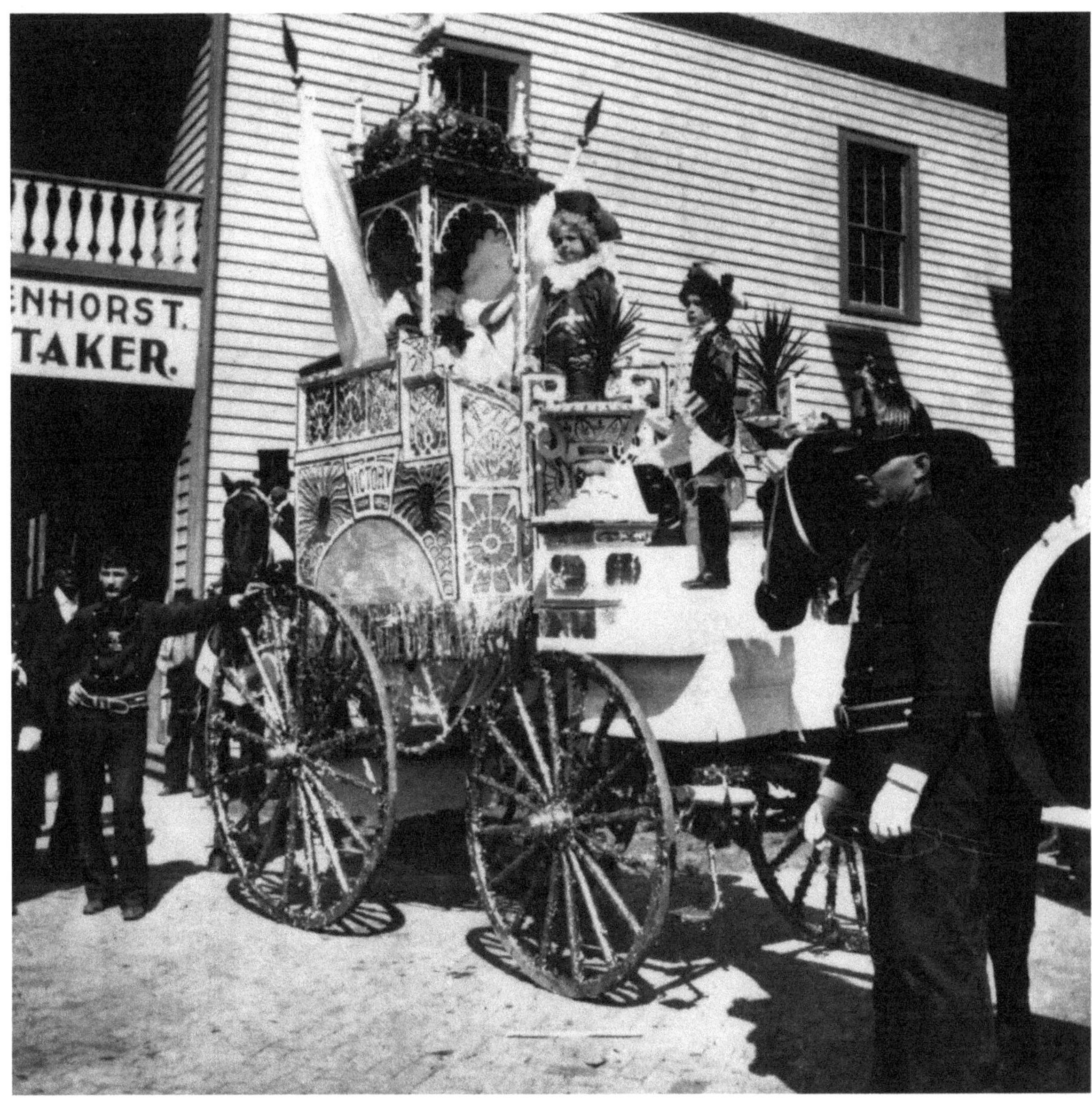

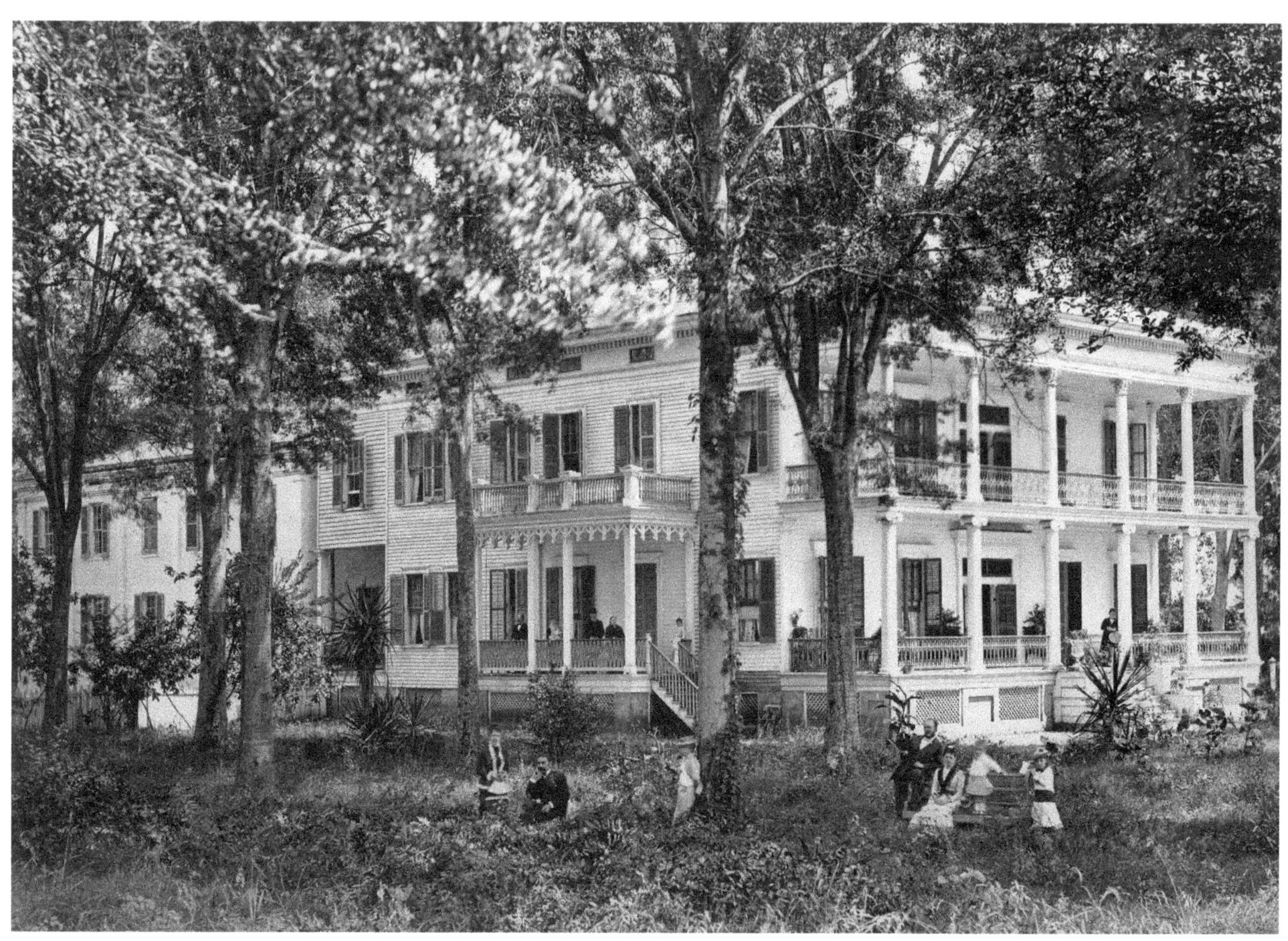

Woodstock Plantation, owned by the Walker family, sat near Bayou Manchac on the southeastern edge of East Baton Rouge Parish. It was one of nearly two dozen plantations in the parish. In this 1889 view, the Walker family poses before the main house.

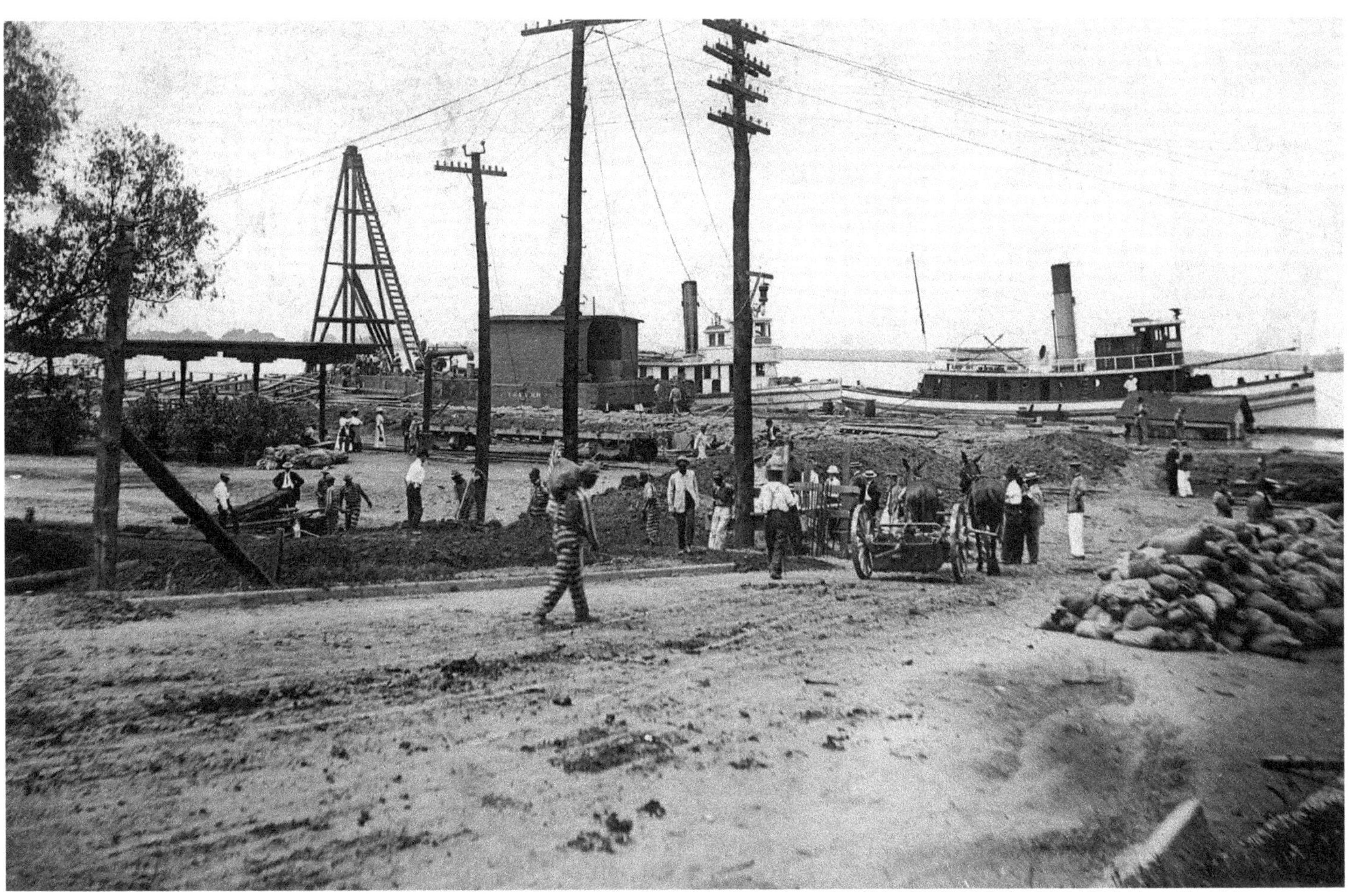

Without a levee until well into the twentieth century, Baton Rouge experienced periodic flooding by the Mississippi River. Sandbagging and temporary flood walls were the standard defense. Prisoners from the state penitentiary proved a ready source of conscripted labor during high-water emergencies, as this image from around 1897 demonstrates.

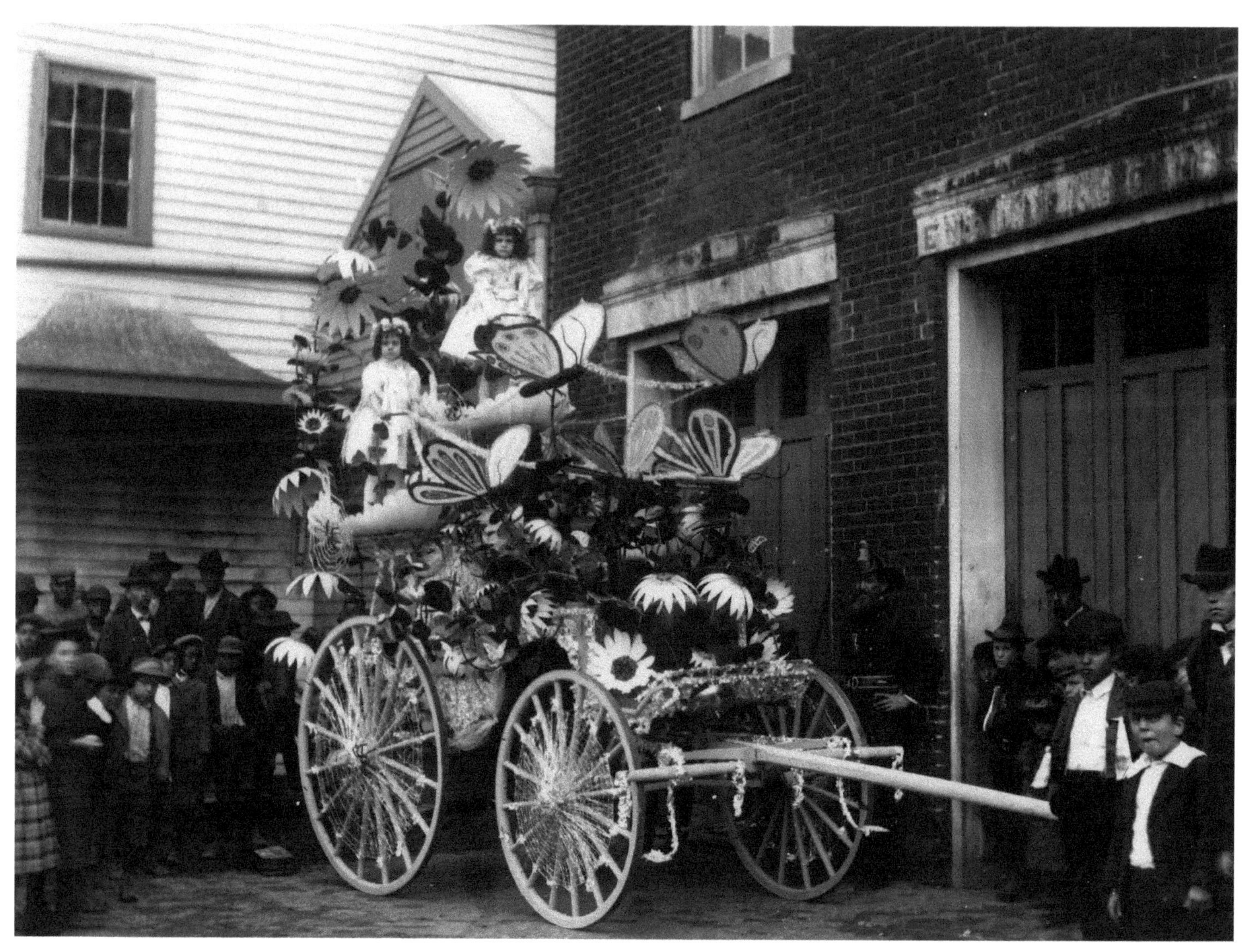

A highly decorated float for the annual Washington's Birthday Firemen's Parade stands in front of the firehouse of its sponsoring volunteer fire company.

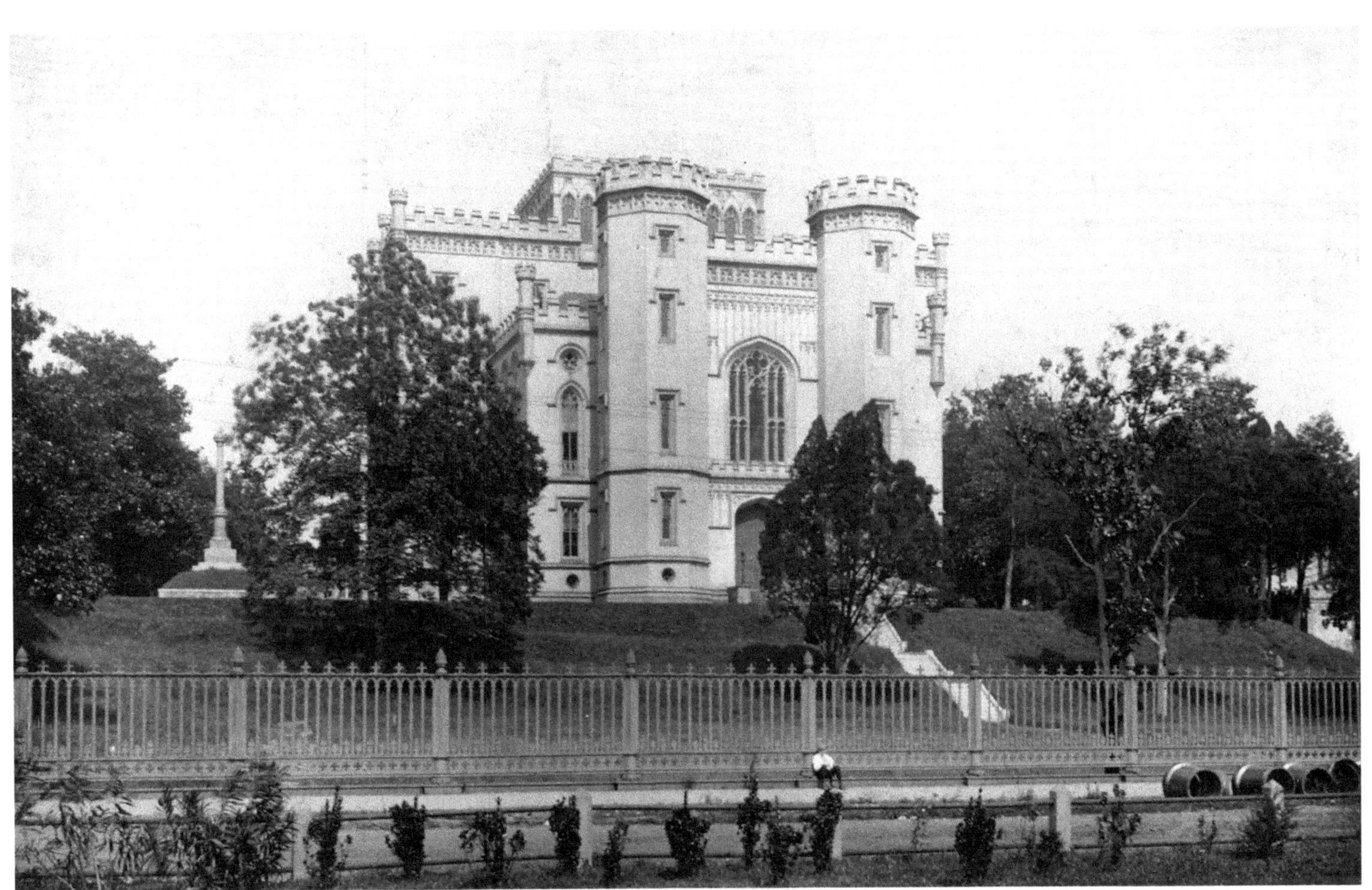

Gutted by a flue fire in December 1862 while occupied by Federal troops, the Capitol was later completely reconstructed under the direction of architect and engineer William A. Freret. The reconstruction was completed in 1882. This shot of the west side of the structure, taken from River Road about 1890, provides an excellent view of the cast-iron fence surrounding the grounds.

The Pelican Hook and Ladder Company No. 1 proudly displays its new ladder truck in this image from around 1895. Company members and other citizens stand outside the Pelican firehouse located at 78 Third Street in downtown Baton Rouge.

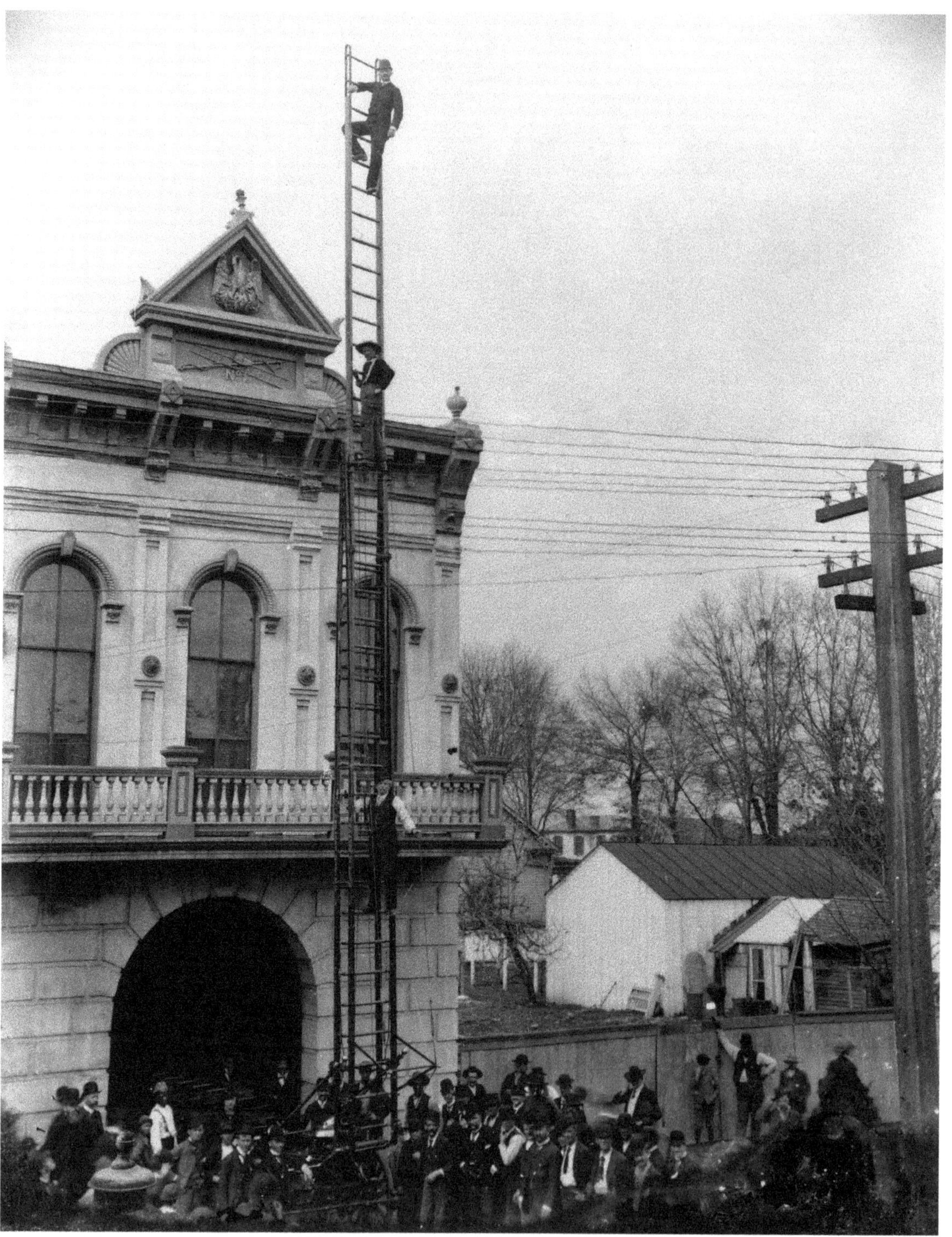

Football and a Strong Economy

(1900–1919)

As the century turned, so too did the fortunes of Baton Rouge. Robert A. Hart, elected mayor in 1898, applied a progressive agenda to city operations. Streets were paved, a mass transit system provided service in town, and a sanitary sewer system began to take shape, as did a clean, secure city water system. The city constructed new schools for white students and the first state-funded public school for African American students, bought property for a public hospital, and constructed a city abattoir, thereby reducing disease and contamination of foodstuffs.

The citizens of Baton Rouge, feeling the positive effects of a strong economy and increasing leisure time, turned to such pursuits as golf, tennis, theatergoing at the newly constructed Elks Theater and office building, and motion-picture viewing. Hunting and fishing, once necessary for many, became leisure pursuits.

For Baton Rouge, perhaps one of the most important changes was the introduction of college football at Louisiana State University. Although chronically underperforming in its early years, the Bayou Bengals, also known as the Fighting Tigers, set a school winning-streak record in 1907-09 that stood unbeaten until 1958. The university itself began a growth period that would leave it poised on the brink of a move to a new location south of town.

In 1914, Southern University and A&M College moved from New Orleans to the Scott's Bluff area of north Baton Rouge, offering classes from the sixth grade through a second year of college. Established by an act of the Louisiana legislature to provide for the education of persons of color, Southern University had opened its original New Orleans campus in 1881. Never well funded, Southern University and LSU did, however, together provide another stabilizing influence on the Baton Rouge economy.

The biggest, most far-reaching, and permanent change for Baton Rouge occurred in 1909. That year, Standard Oil of Louisiana incorporated in East Baton Rouge Parish. With that, the first of many petroleum refineries was built and the region experienced an unprecedented economic boom; construction wages alone equaled about two-thirds the value of the entire cotton crop. Baton Rouge irrevocably turned from agriculture to industry as the basis for its economy.

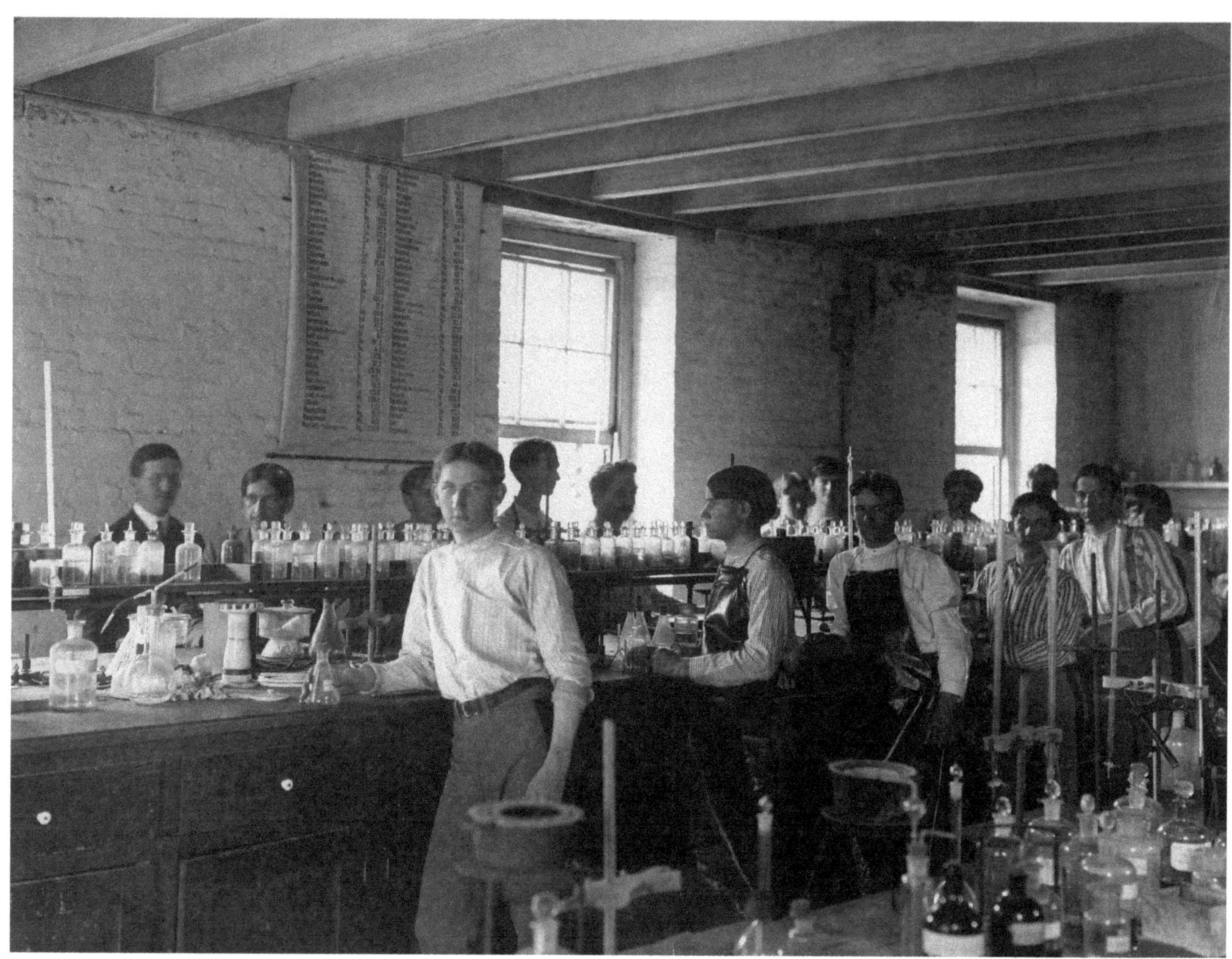

The Chemical Laboratory stood in the center of the LSU campus between Agricultural Hall and the President's Residence. This interior view of the laboratory, around 1900, shows cadets poised for experimentation.

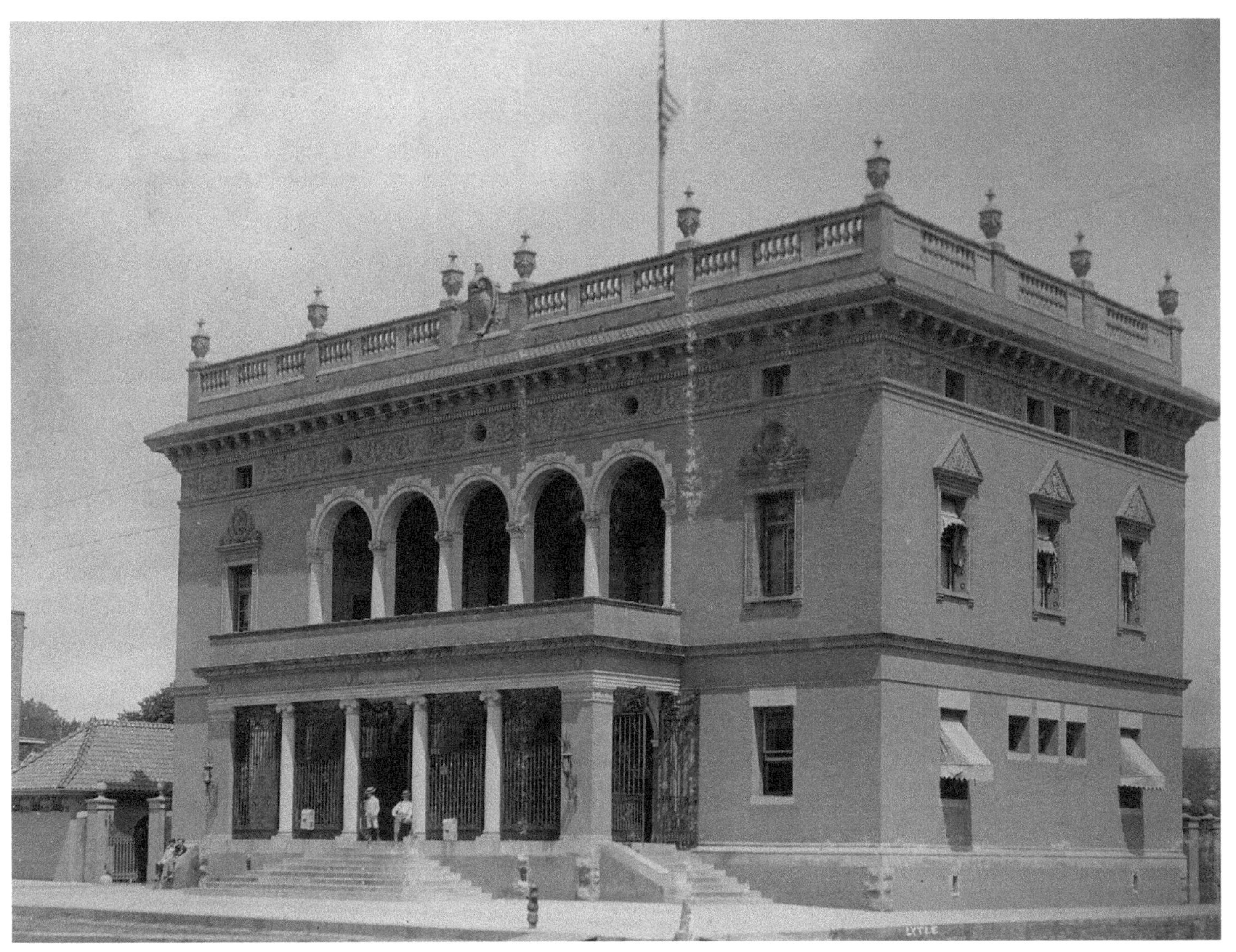

A new main post office and federal courthouse, completed in 1894 on North Boulevard between Third and Fourth streets in downtown Baton Rouge, served the growing community for decades. Seen here around 1900, its Italian Renaissance facade added interesting variety to the downtown architecture.

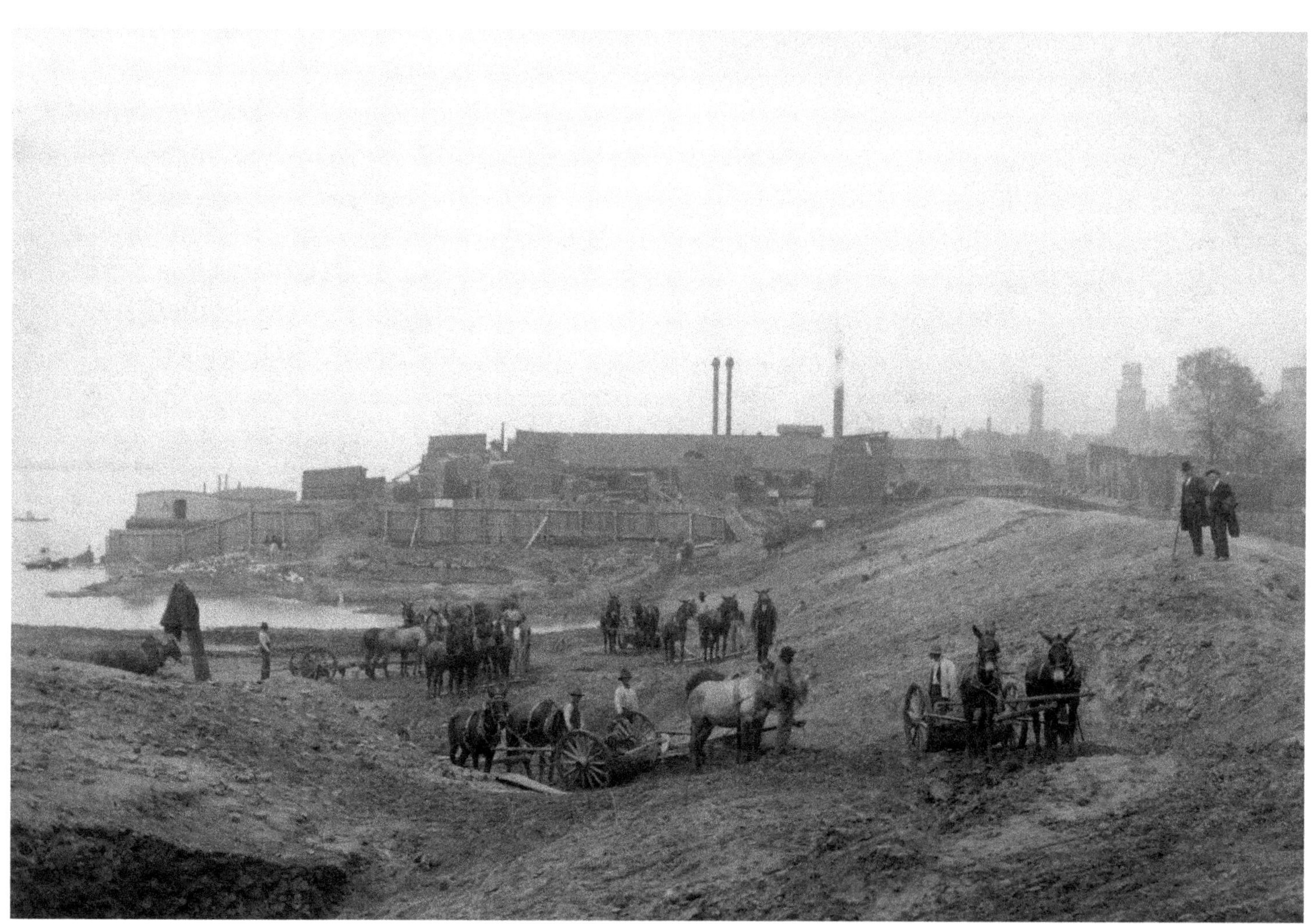

Levee construction began in earnest around the turn of the twentieth century. Until then, Baton Rouge had no levee and the town's business owners built as close to mean high water as they could. This meant periodic flooding for the businesses and the losses associated with it.

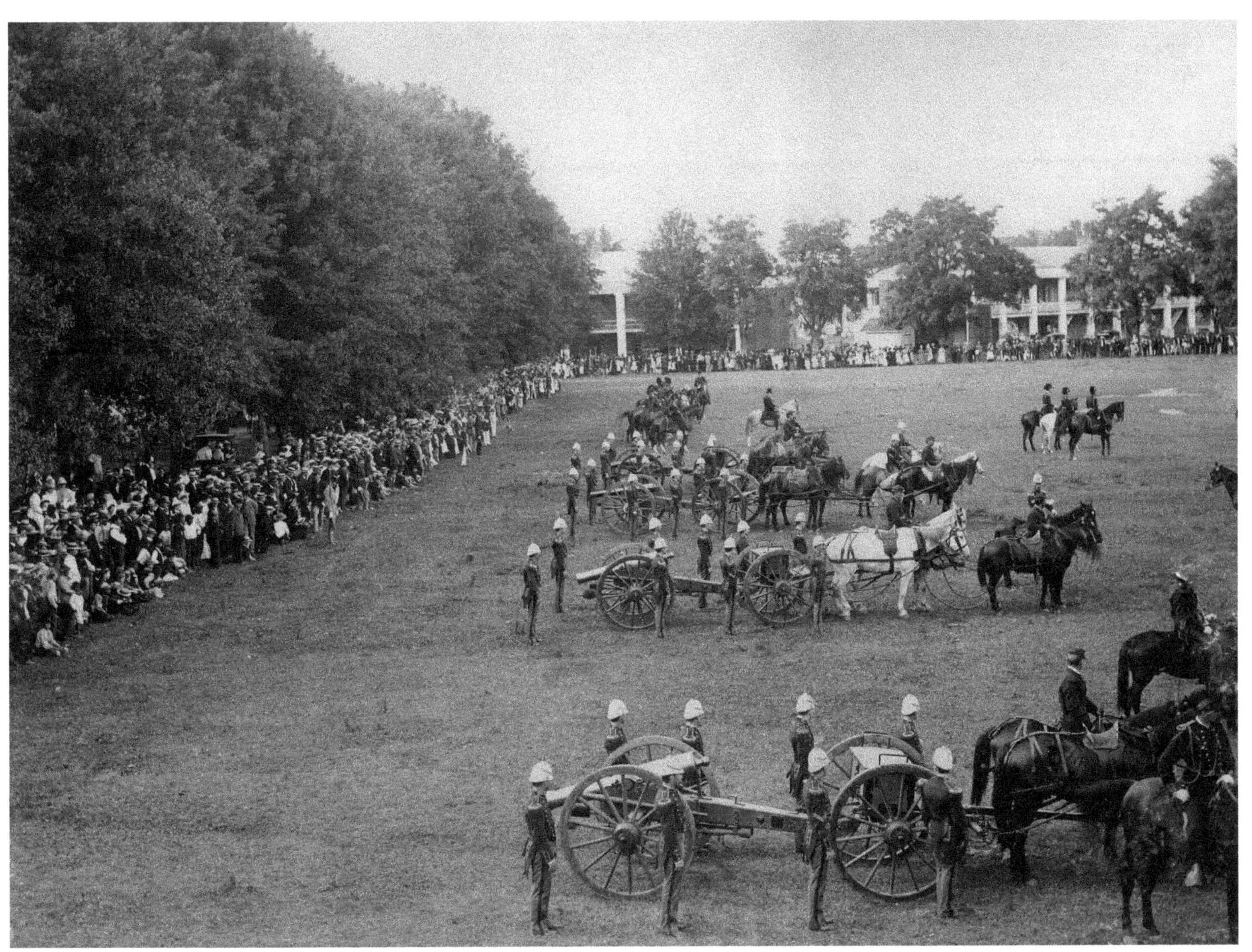

The cadets of Louisiana State University conduct a dress parade on the campus parade grounds around 1900 while the people of Baton Rouge look on.

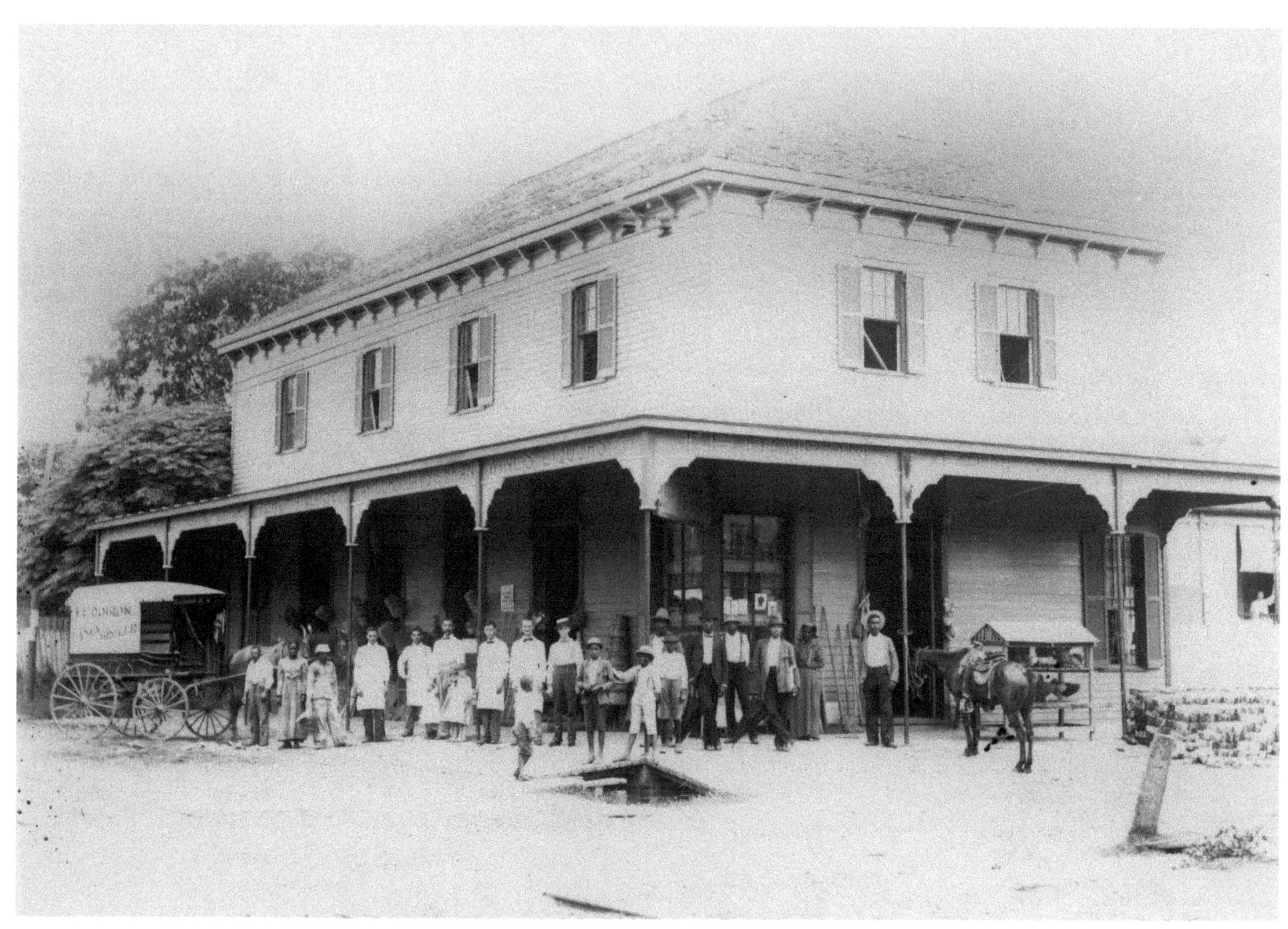

Tolbert Doiron owned and operated this grocery and liquor store at 617 Government Street. In 1906, within a few years of this image, there were 75 retail grocers in Baton Rouge.

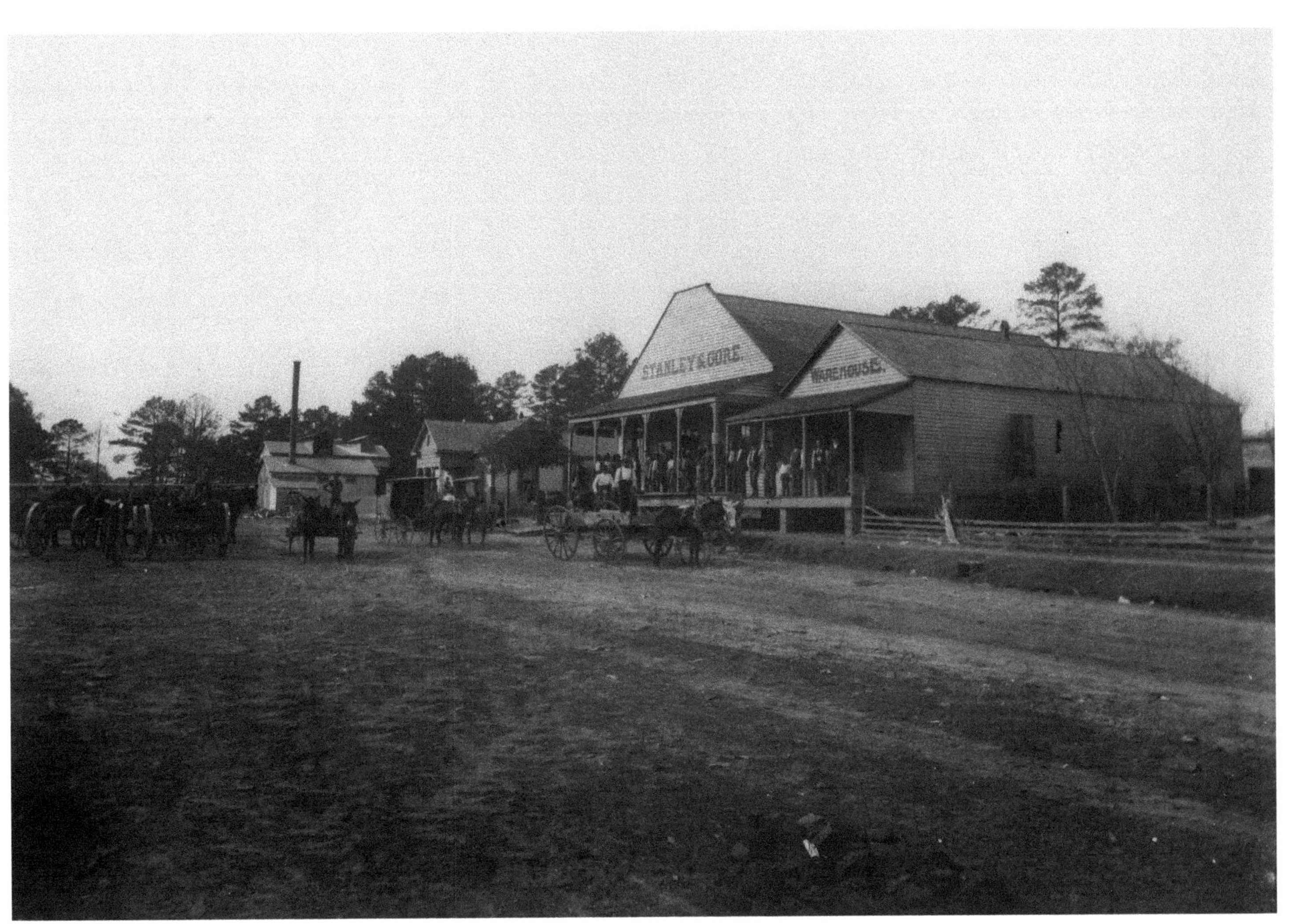

The Stanley & Gore store and warehouse served a plantation across the Mississippi River from Baton Rouge.

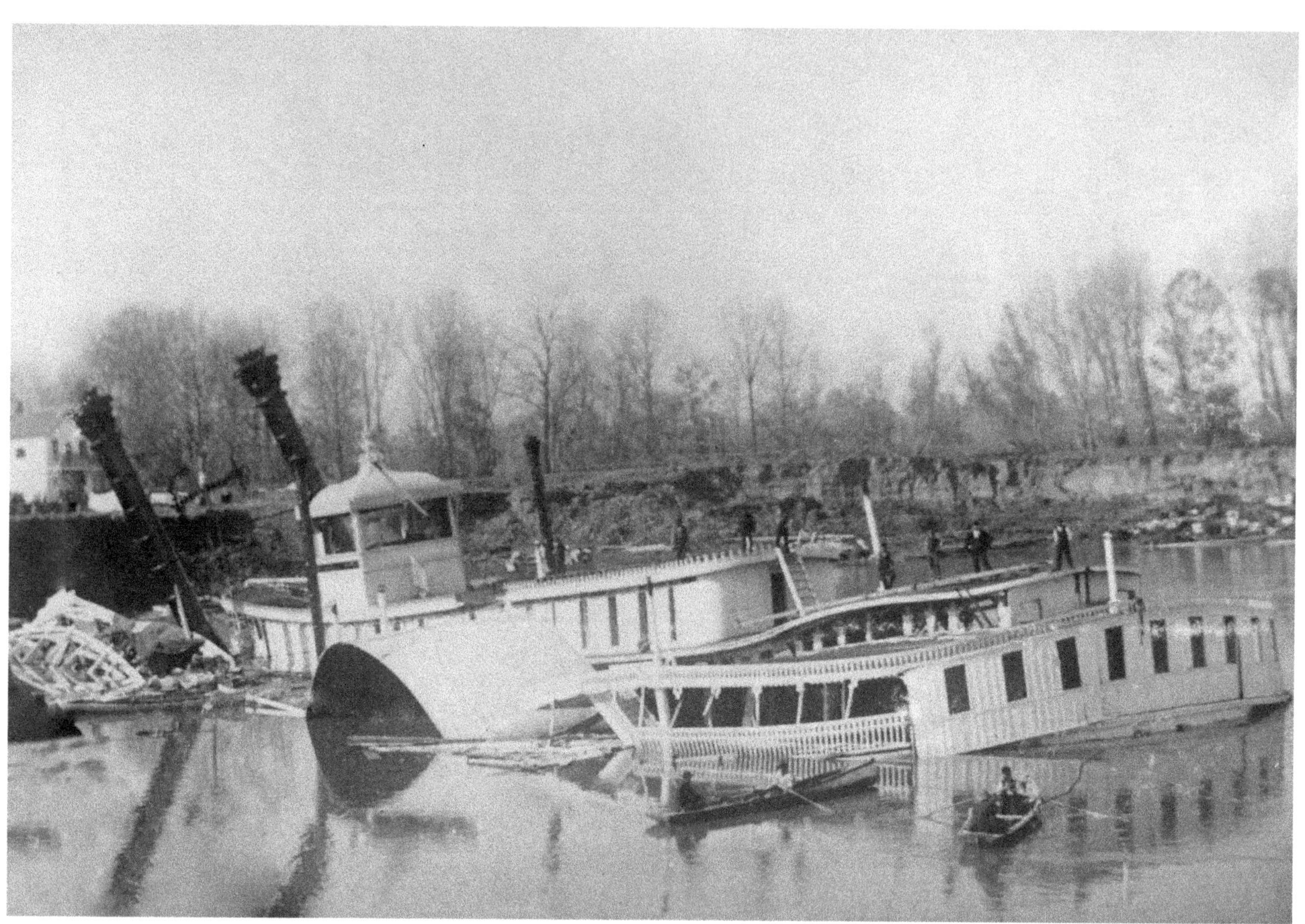

The Mississippi River served as the nation's highway well into the twentieth century. Hundreds of steamboats plied the river making hundreds of thousands of trips along the entire navigable reach of the river system, not all successfully. This scene from around 1900 demonstrates how many steamboats came to an end as wreckage partially sunken along the shore.

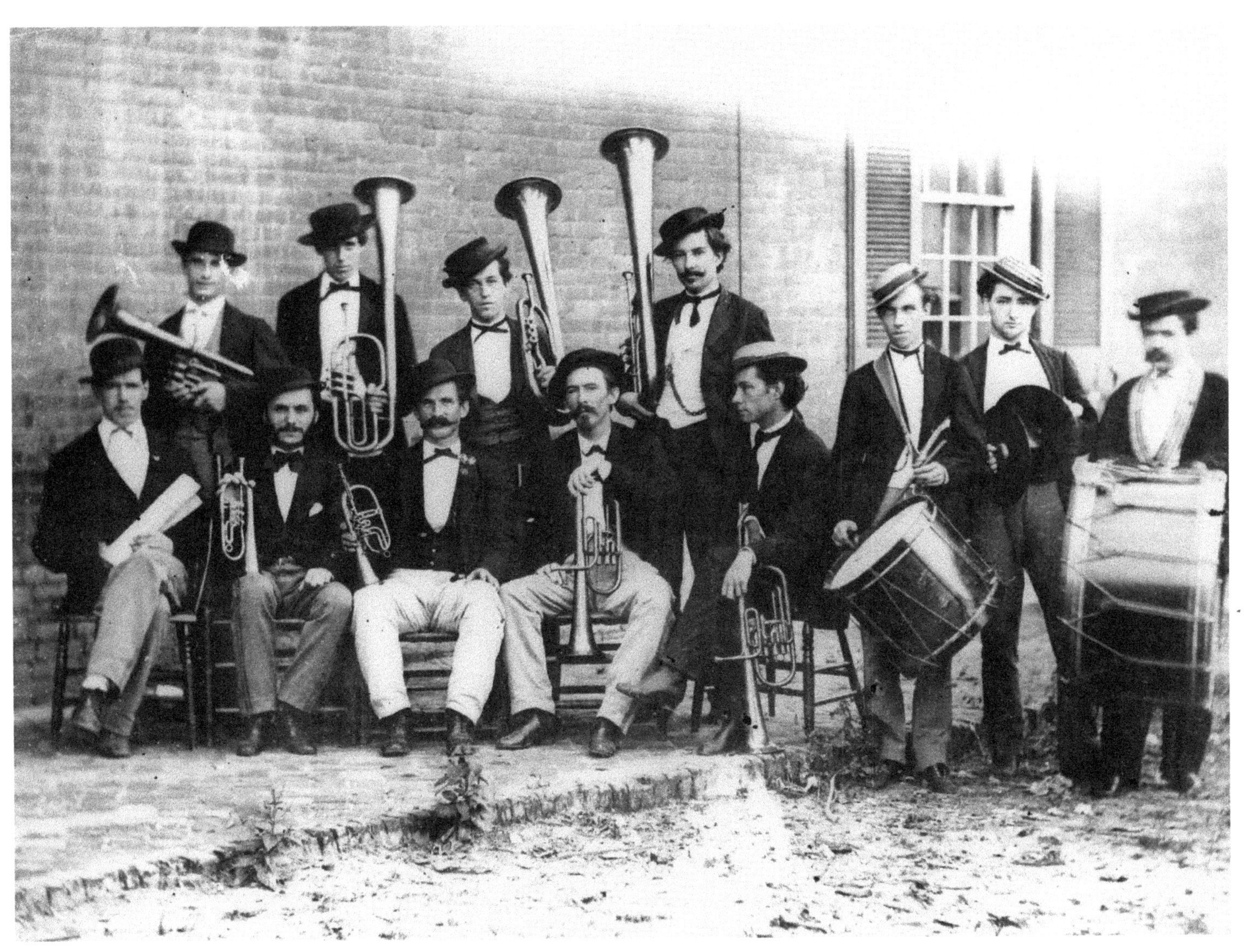

A glimpse at local entertainment—this brass band played in Baton Rouge around 1900.

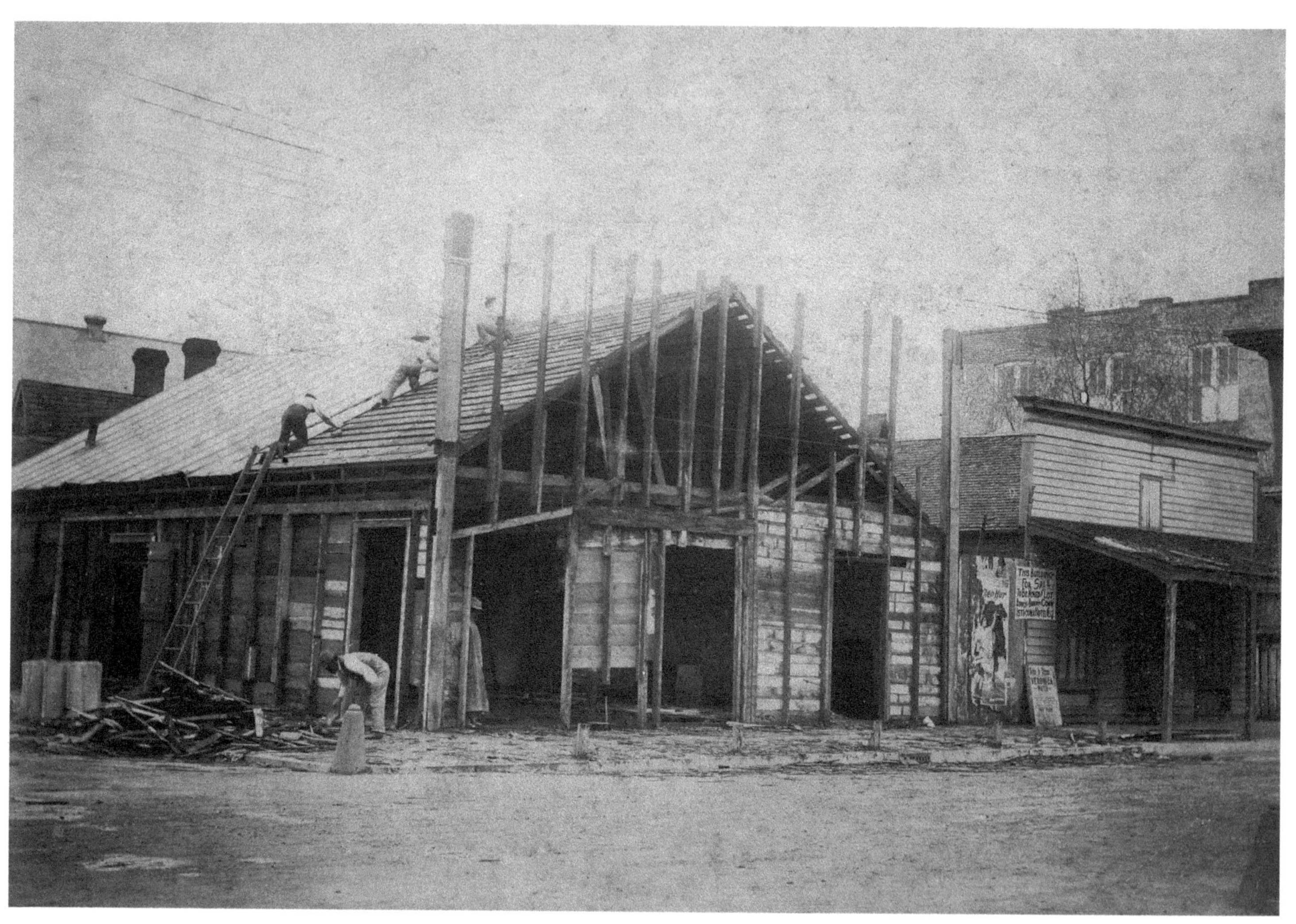

Workers demolish a building on the corner of Florida and Third streets around 1900. This site would later become the home of the Istrouma Hotel.

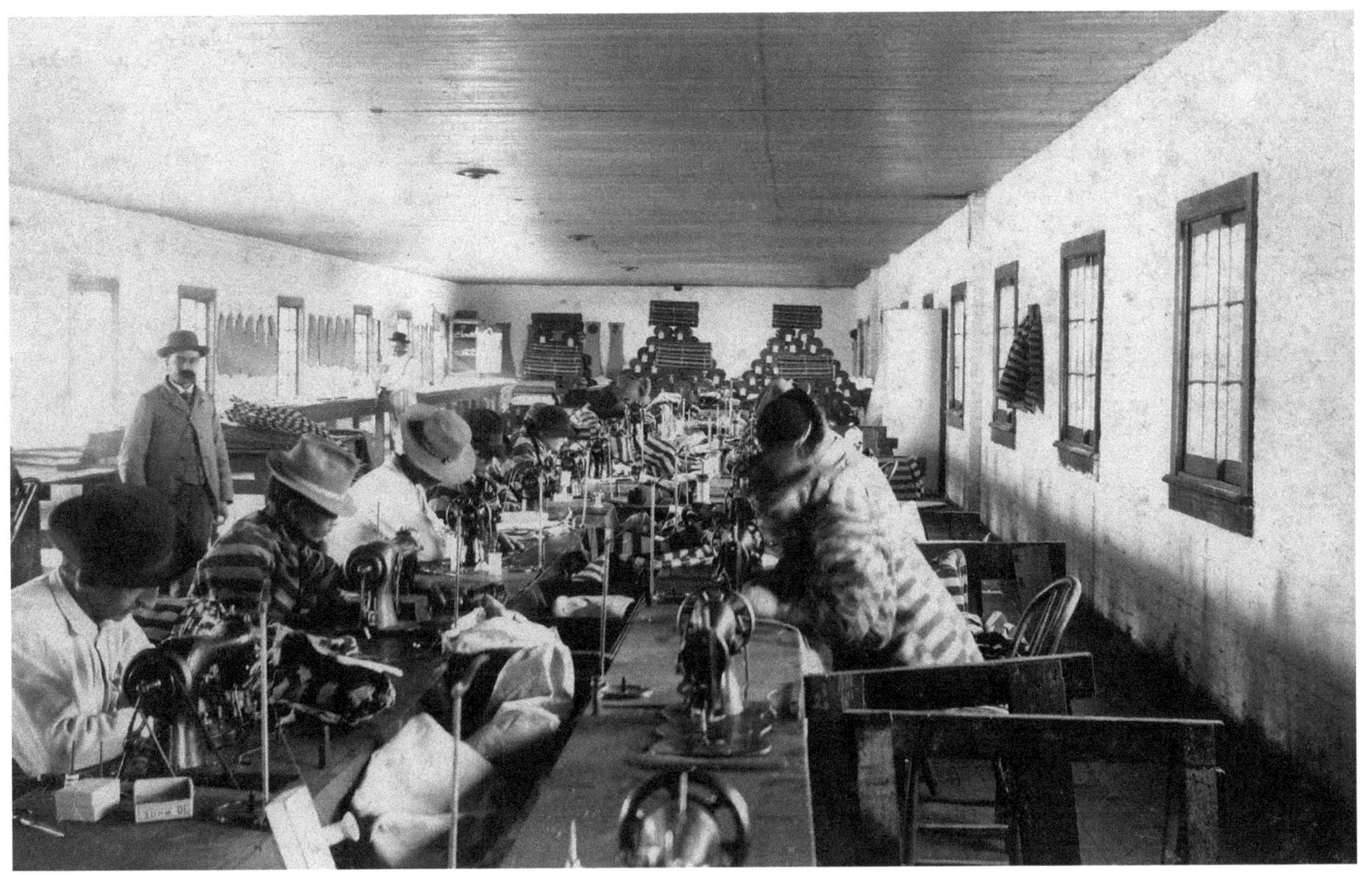

The state penitentiary sat squarely in the heart of Baton Rouge. From 1844 to 1861 the penitentiary ran under a lease held by a private firm. Beginning in 1869, the lease was awarded to Confederate Major Samuel James, who held the lease through 1900. On January 1, 1901, the State of Louisiana resumed control of all inmates. This image from around 1905 shows inmates working in the penitentiary's clothing factory.

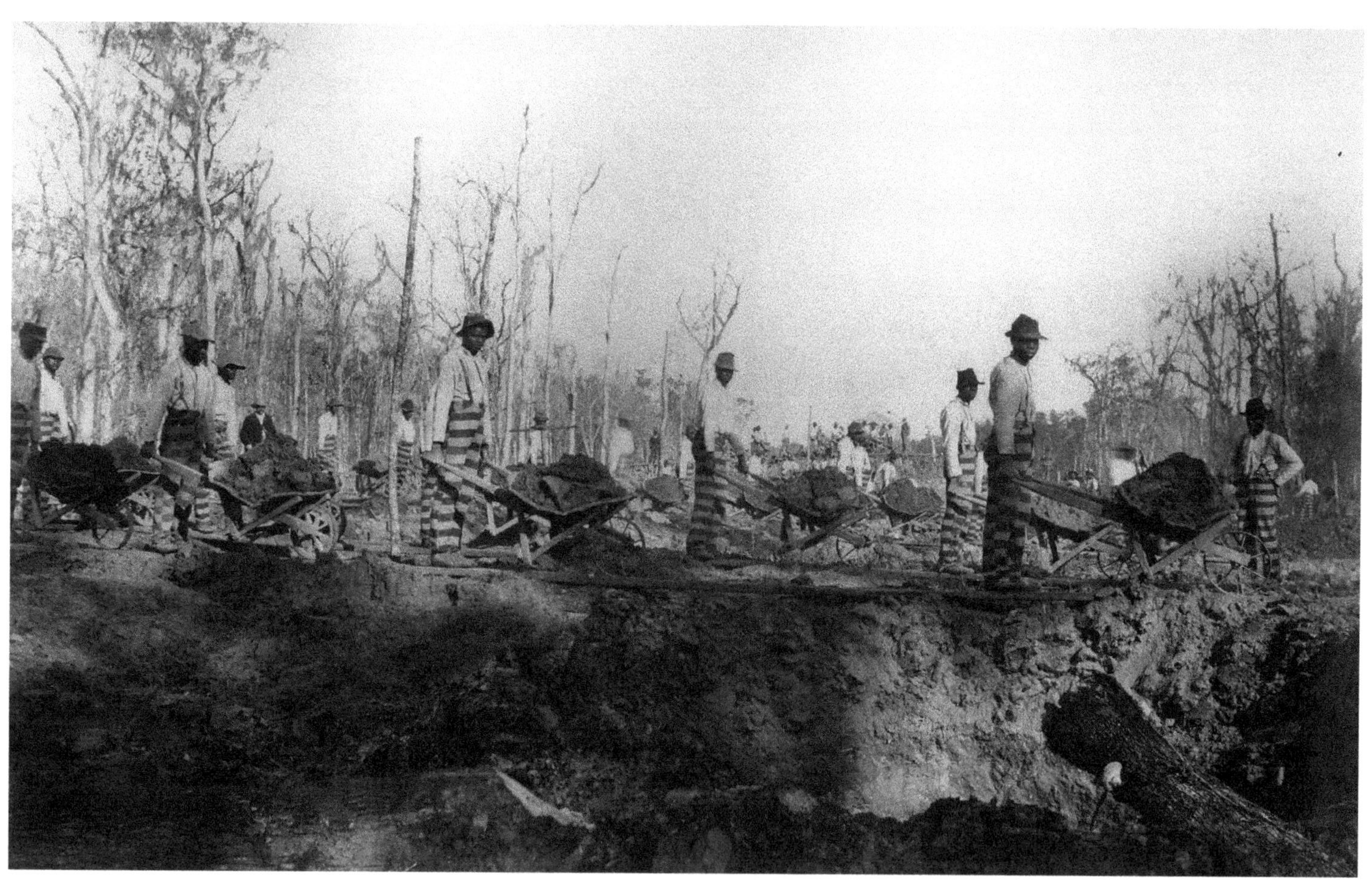

Levee construction became a major industry in Louisiana in the first decades of the twentieth century. State prisoners represented a cheap source of labor often leased to private contractors. Here, in about 1905, prison laborers push wheelbarrows full of dirt used to construct a levee somewhere near Baton Rouge.

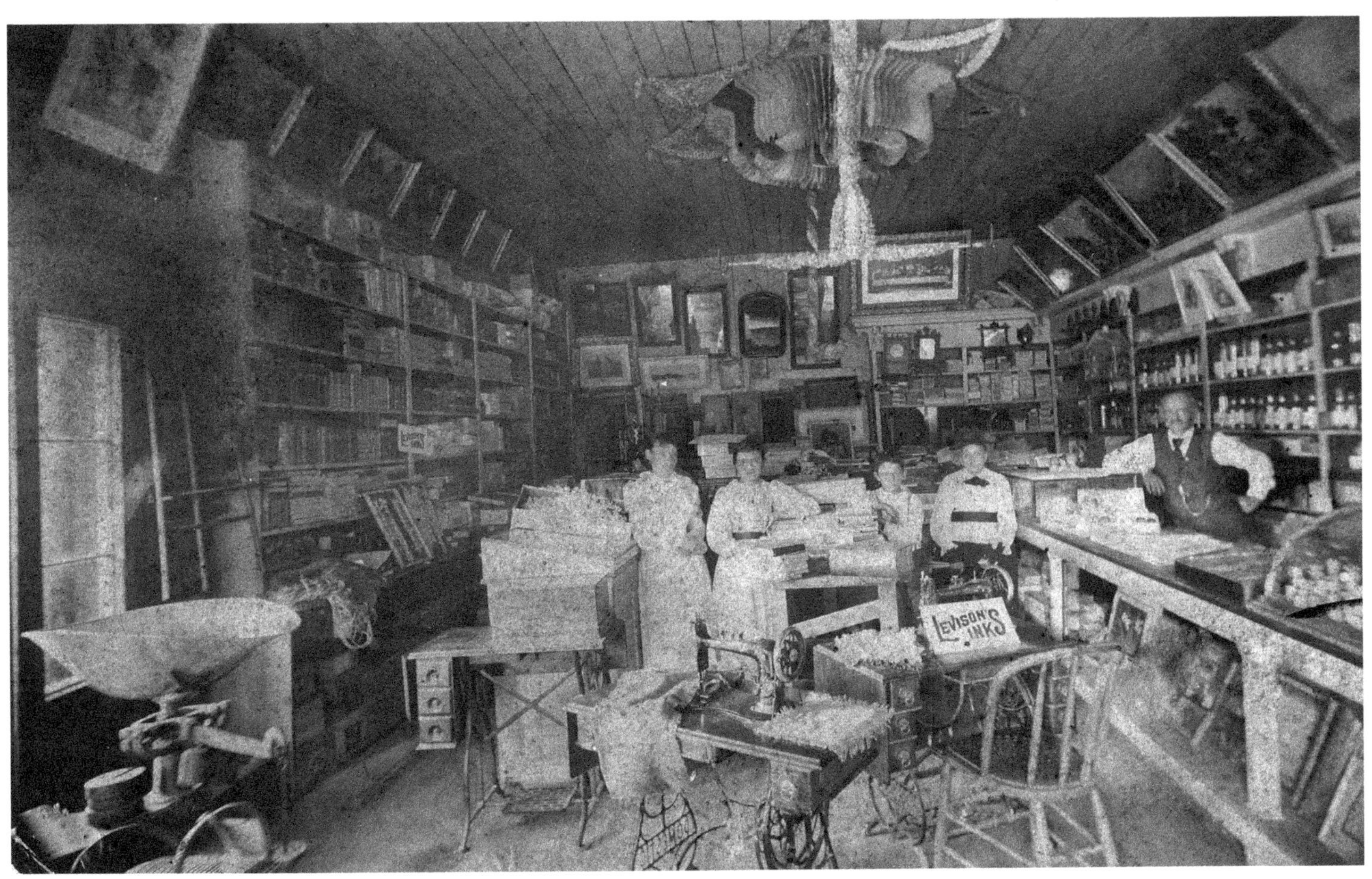

Many Baton Rouge businesses served both townsfolk and plantations in the vicinity. This may be the interior of the Garig Hardware Company, 401–403 Lafayette Street. Amateur photographer John B. Heroman, Sr., worked as a clerk at the hardware store between 1903 and 1908; he then moved on to become a bookkeeper at the First National Bank on the corner of Lafayette and Laurel streets.

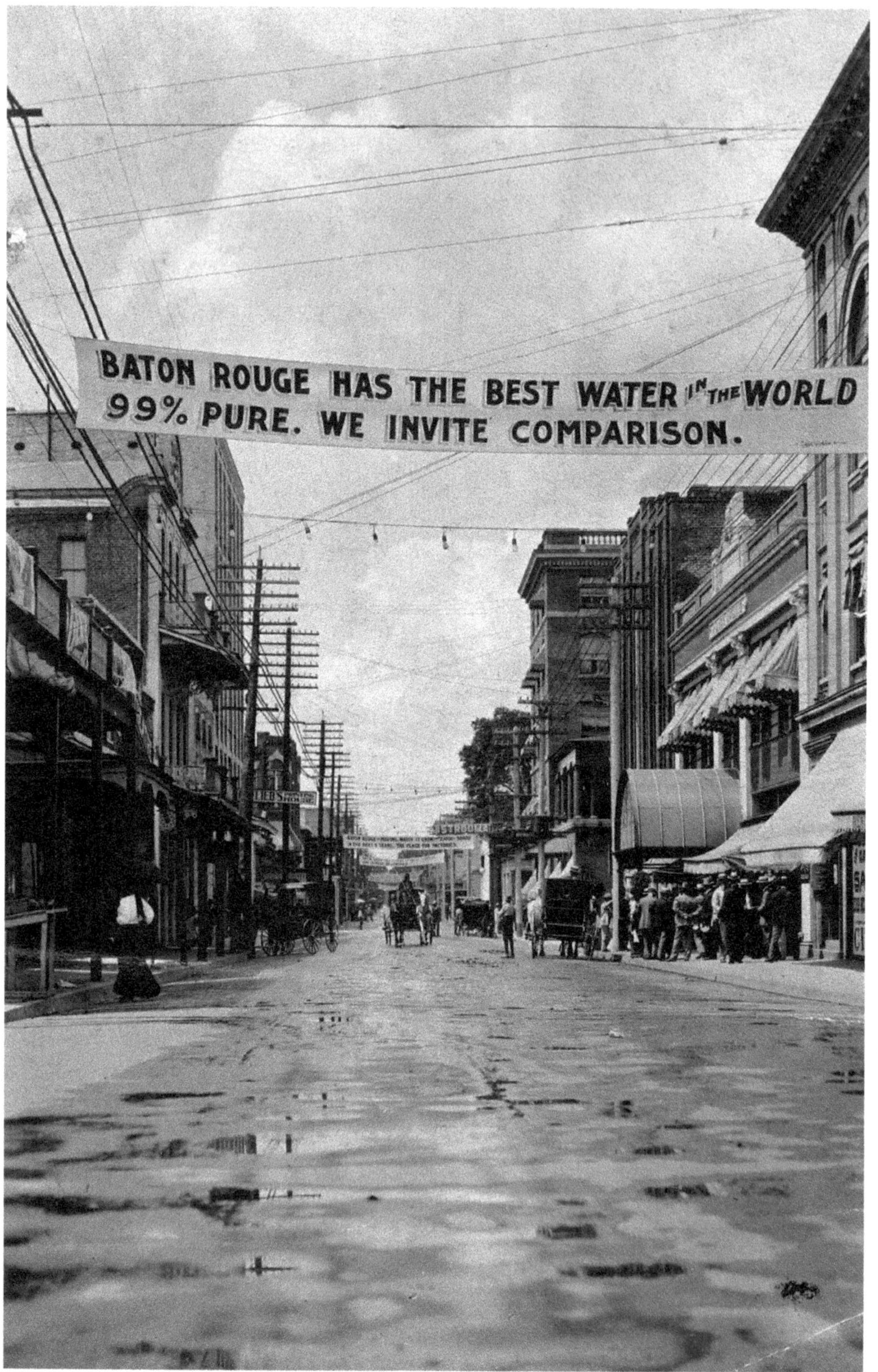

John B. Heroman lived his entire life in Baton Rouge. He entered many photography contests, and for one of them he provided this view of the town around 1910. While the front banner extols the quality of Baton Rouge water, the banner down the street reads: "Baton Rouge is moving, watch it grow from 25,000 to 50,000 in the next 5 years, the place for factories."

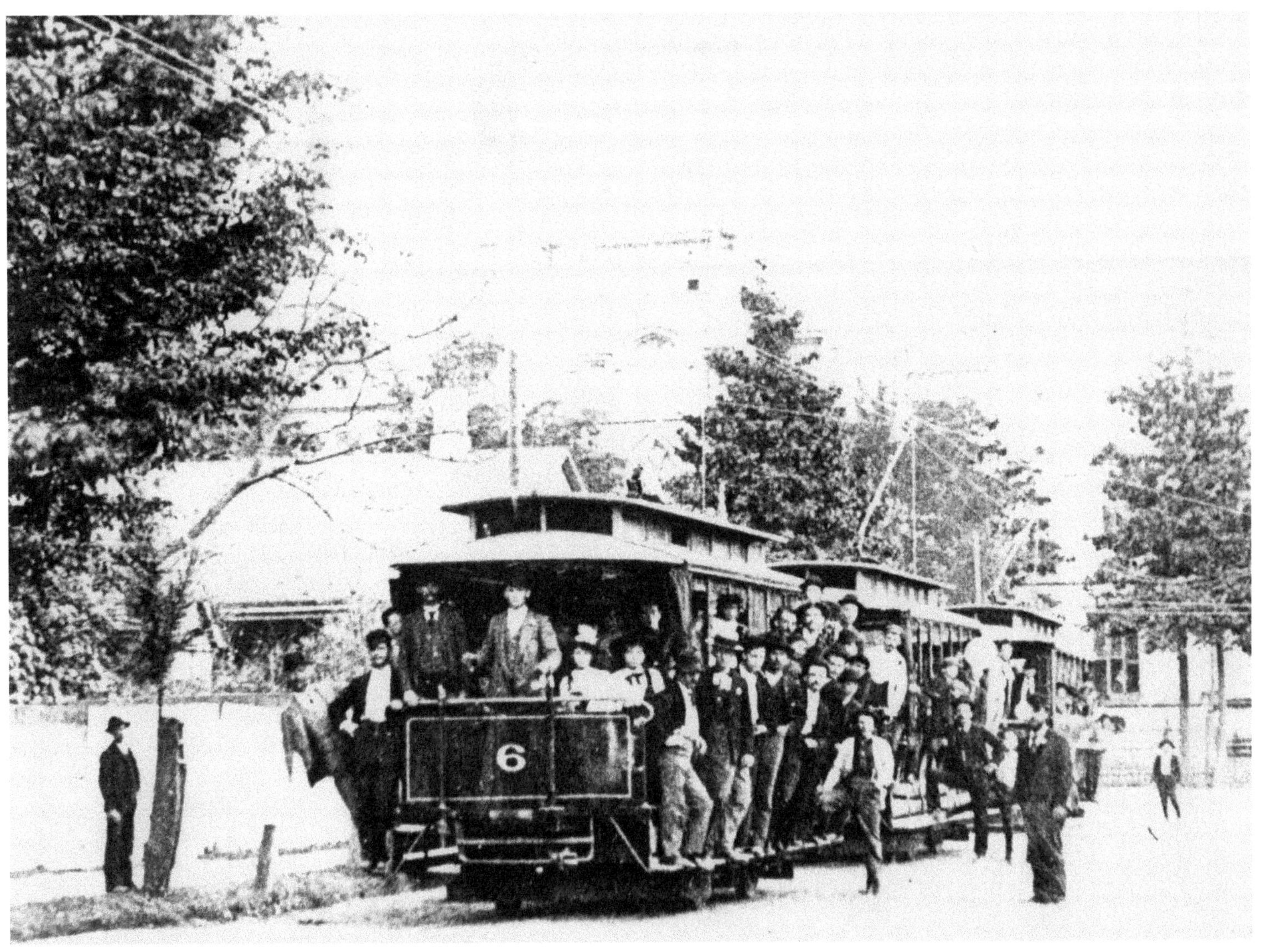

Filled to overflowing with riders, three of Baton Rouge's electric trolleys pause on Lafayette Street between North Boulevard and Convention Street, around 1900.

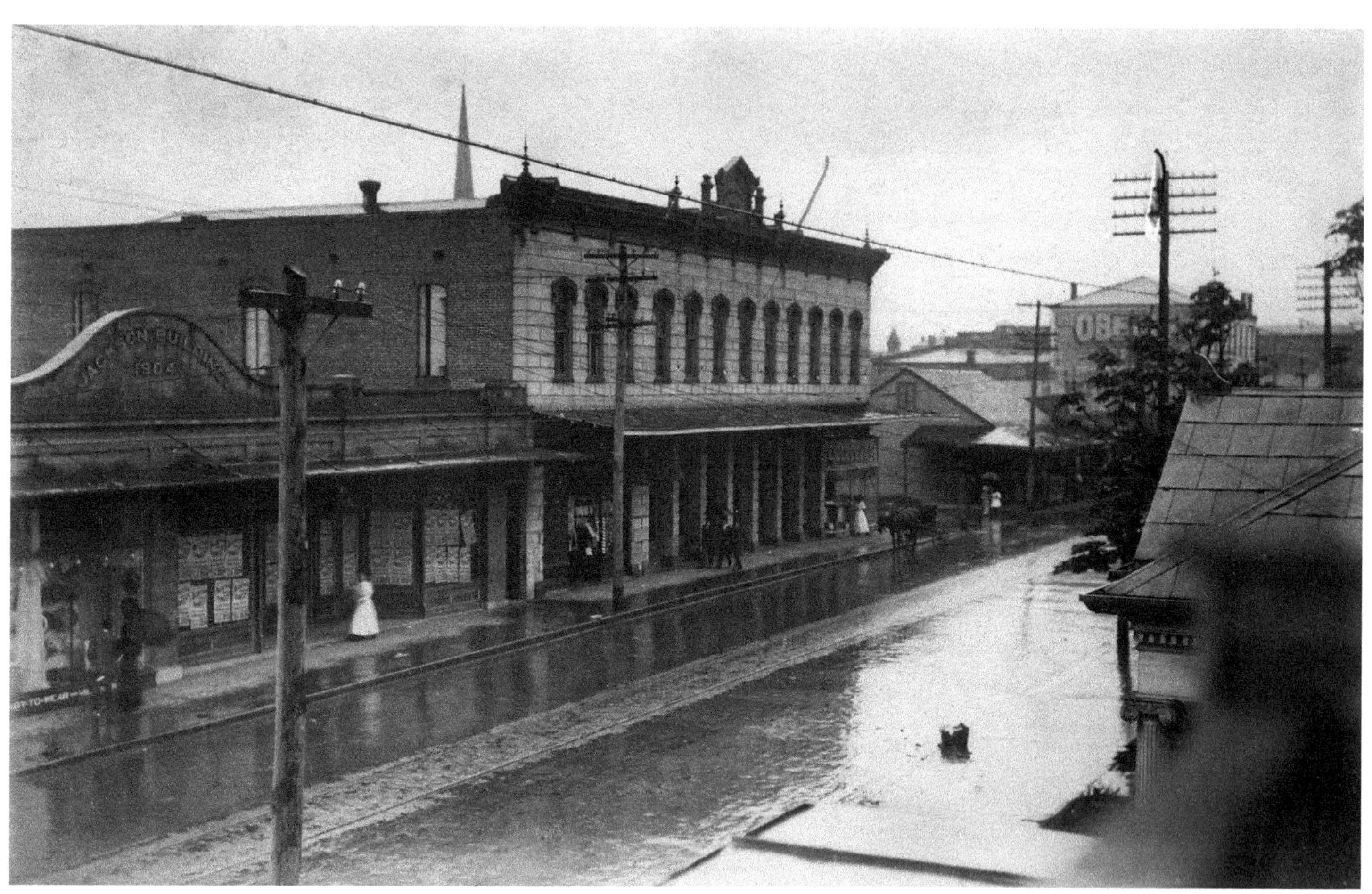

A rainy day in downtown Baton Rouge attracted the eye of photographer John B. Heroman sometime around 1910. As the power poles testify, the town had begun to be wired for electric service by then.

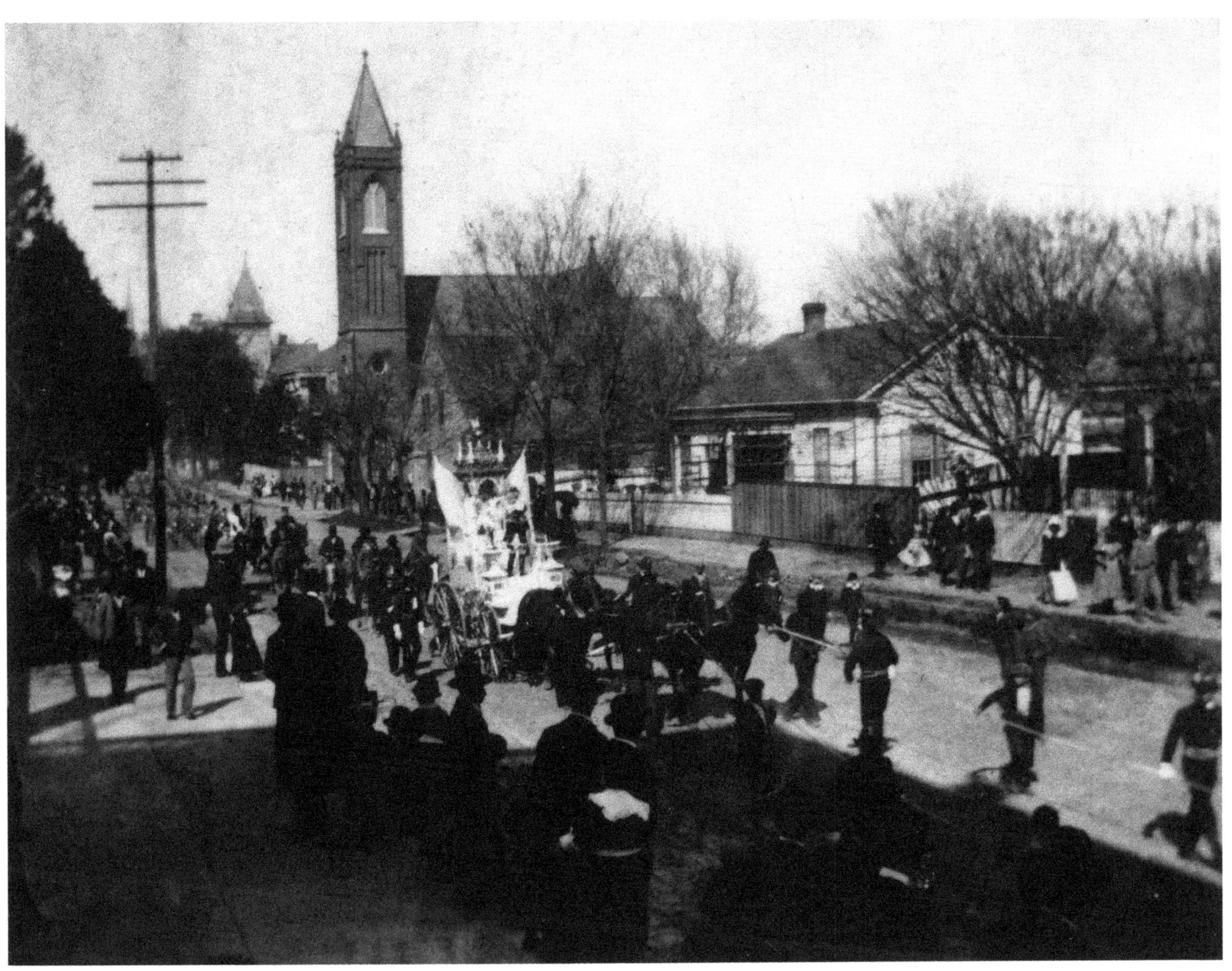

The Washington's Birthday Firemen's Parade moves down Church Street in downtown Baton Rouge around 1905. Each volunteer fire company would sponsor a float decorated around a common theme for that year's parade. The bell tower of Saint James Episcopal Church rises in the background.

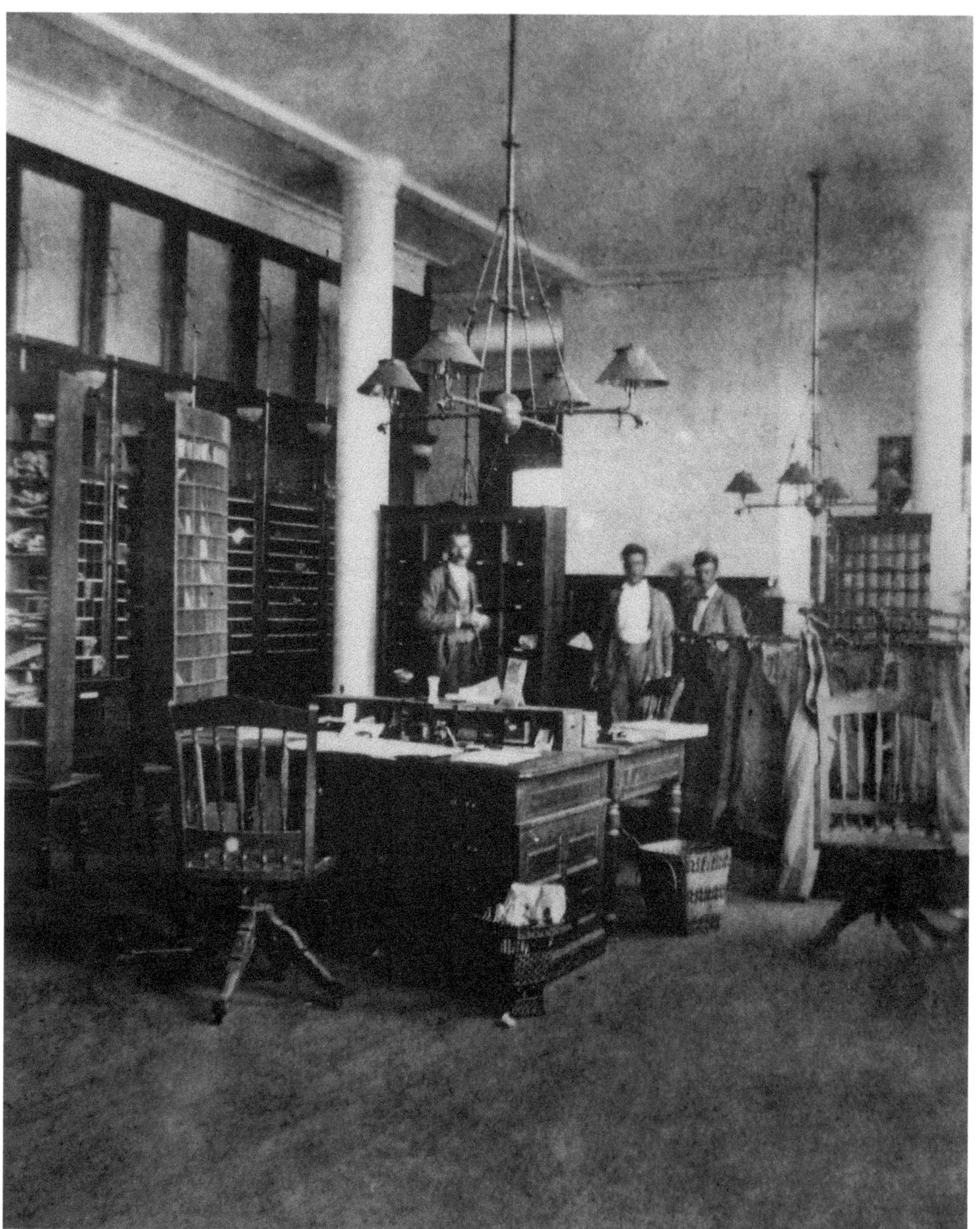

This interior view of the new post office from around 1905 documents what were then cutting-edge methods for delivering the mail.

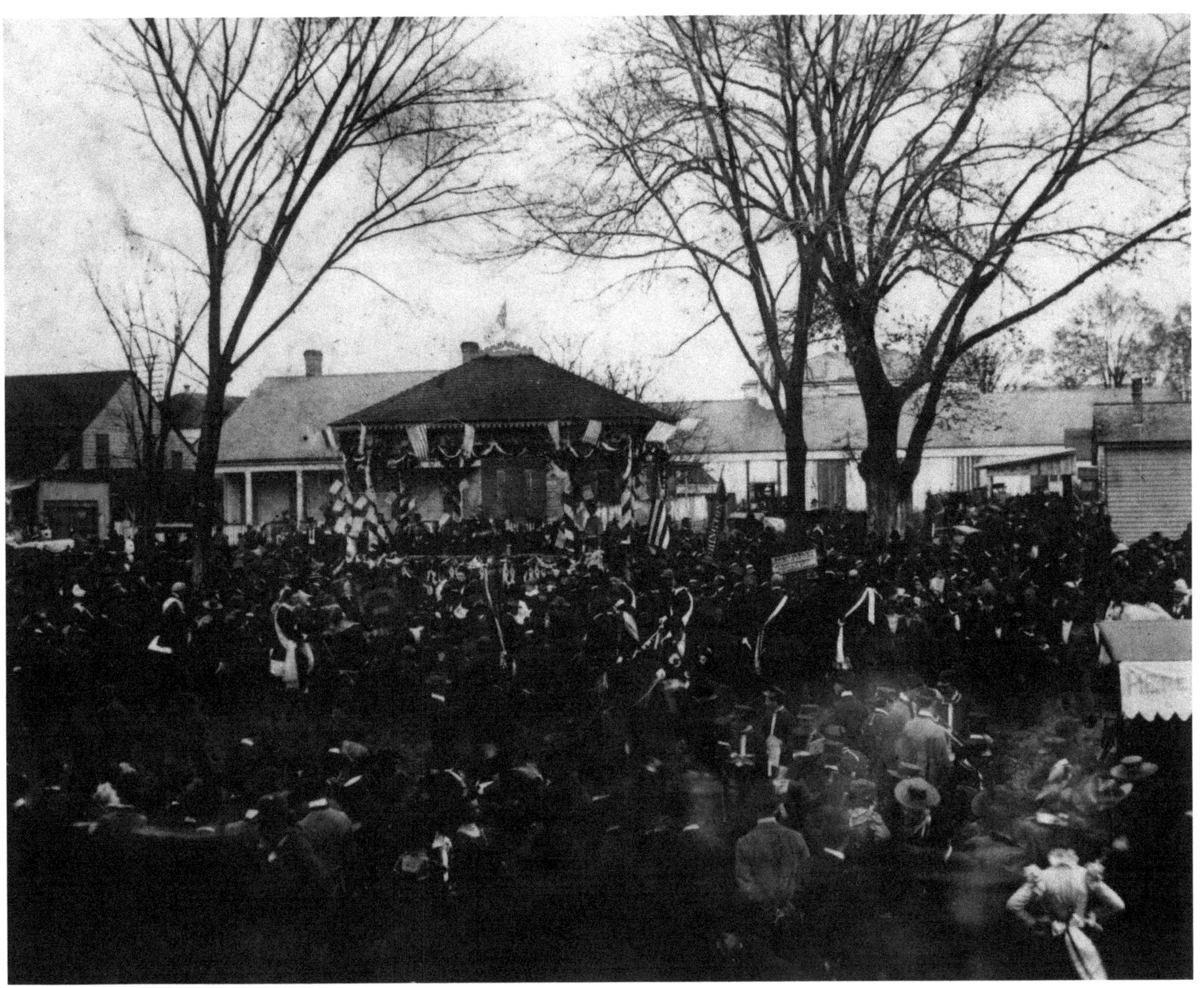

The annual Washington's Birthday Firemen's Parade began in the mid-1870s and continued into the mid-1910s. The crowd in this scene from around 1910 is gathered at the Public Market downtown near the Capitol.

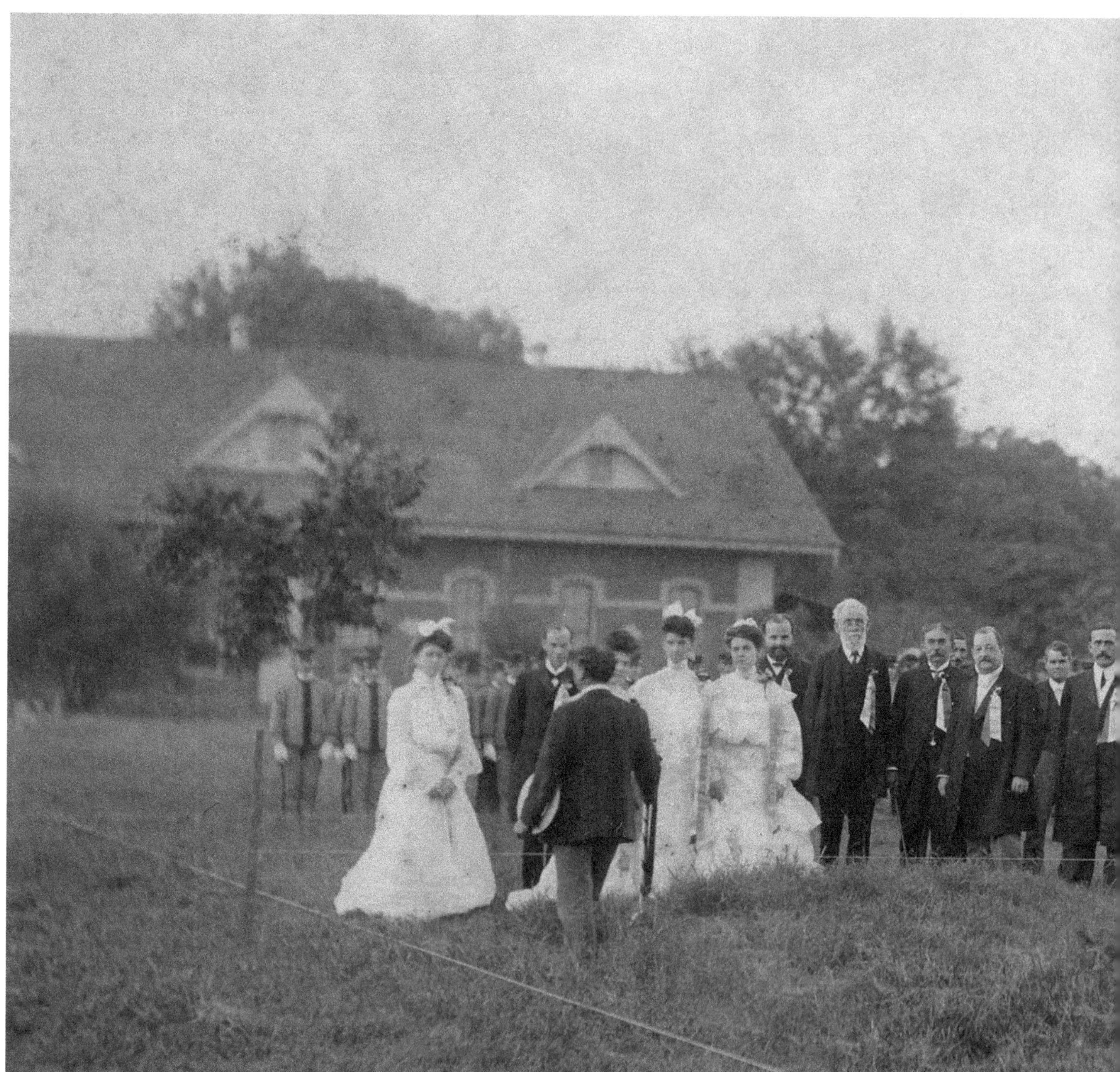

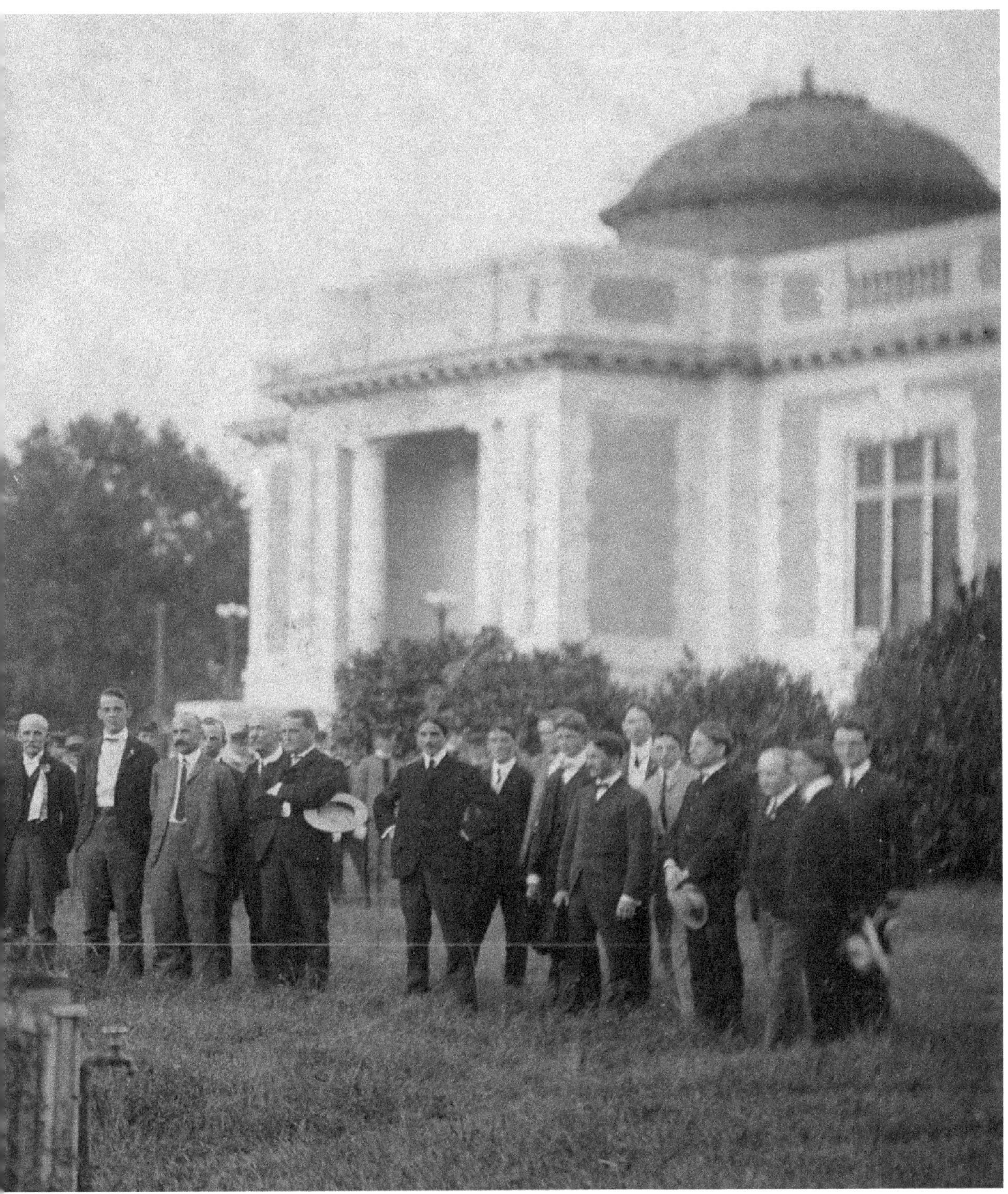

Here in September 1903, guests of honor, faculty, and cadets attend the groundbreaking for the Alumni Memorial Hall at Louisiana State University. At right stands Hill Memorial Library; behind the group is Garig Hall. When the university moved to its current site, the facade of the Alumni Hall was disassembled, moved to the new site, and reconstructed as the facade of the School of Journalism.

At the time of this image, around 1903, the Arsenal grounds had long since been transferred to the state and become the campus of Louisiana State University. "The Alley" ran from Lafayette Street to A Building, one of the Pentagon Barracks used for classrooms and a dormitory. The Professor's Residence can be seen at left.

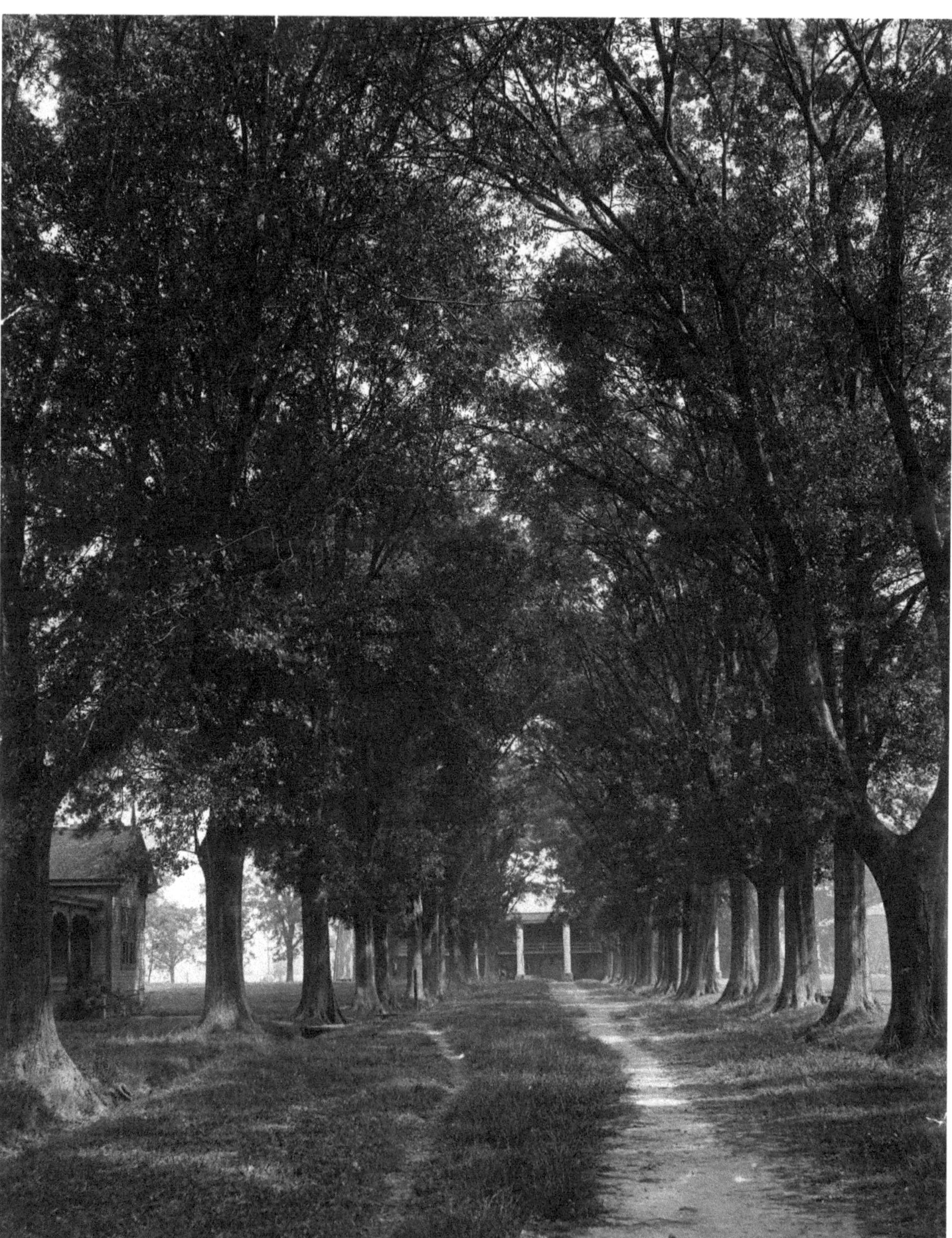

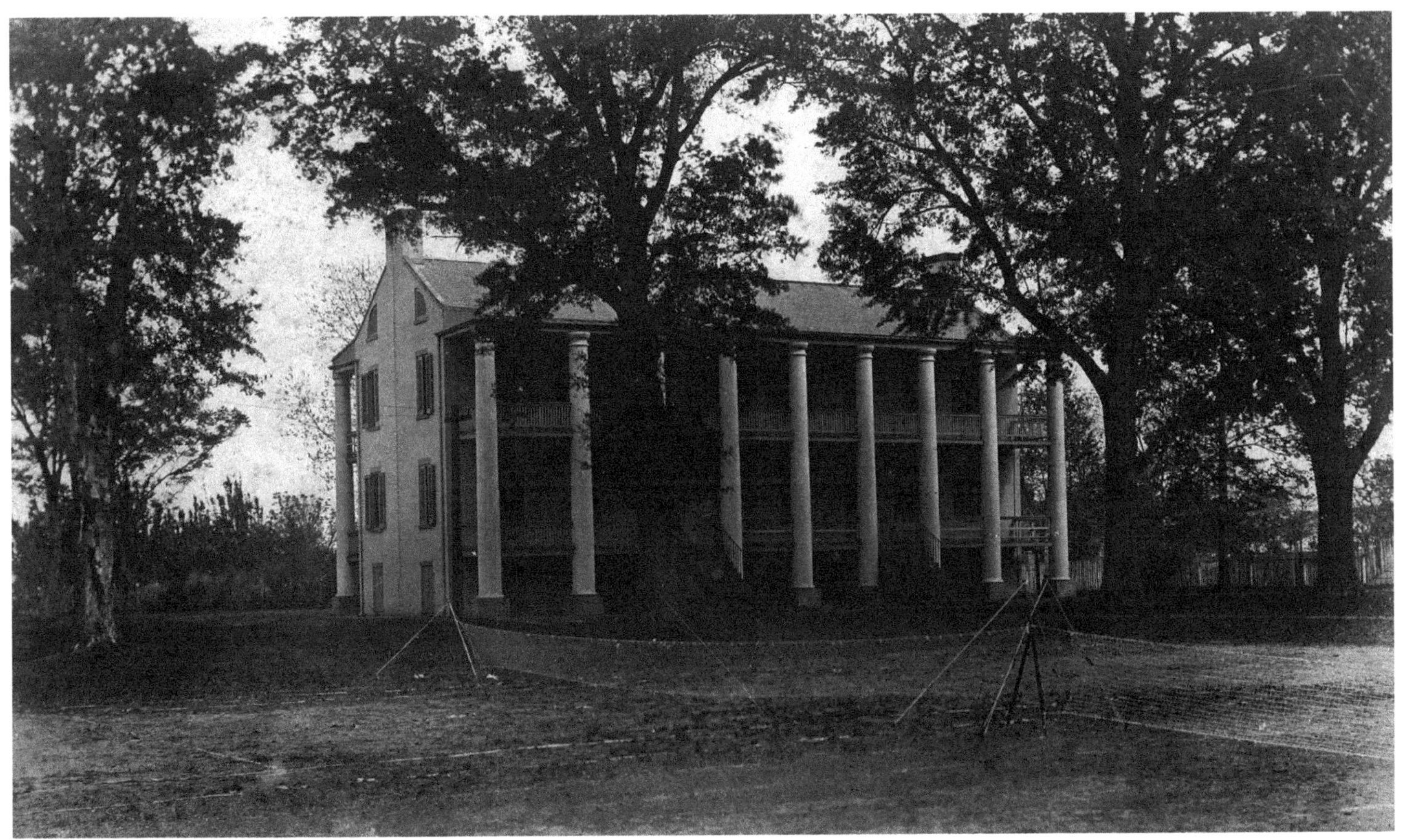

This building, the "Colony," served as an LSU dormitory. Evidently, the sport of lawn tennis had been introduced to the campus by 1903, with courts established near the dormitory.

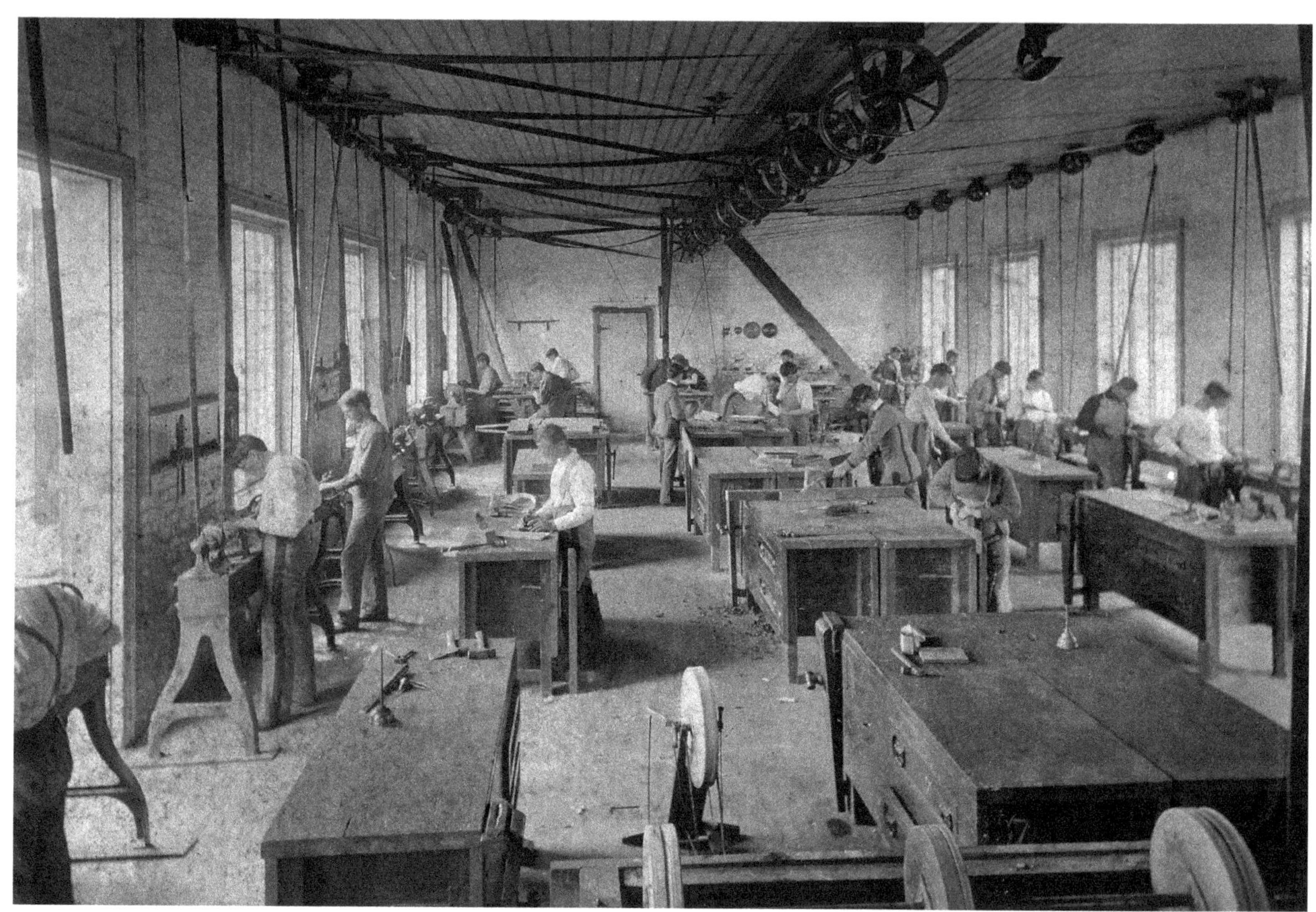

The LSU woodworking shop, occupying part of the ground floor of Robertson Hall, contained state-of-the-art equipment for 1903. A forge, foundry, and machine shop occupied the rest of the floor.

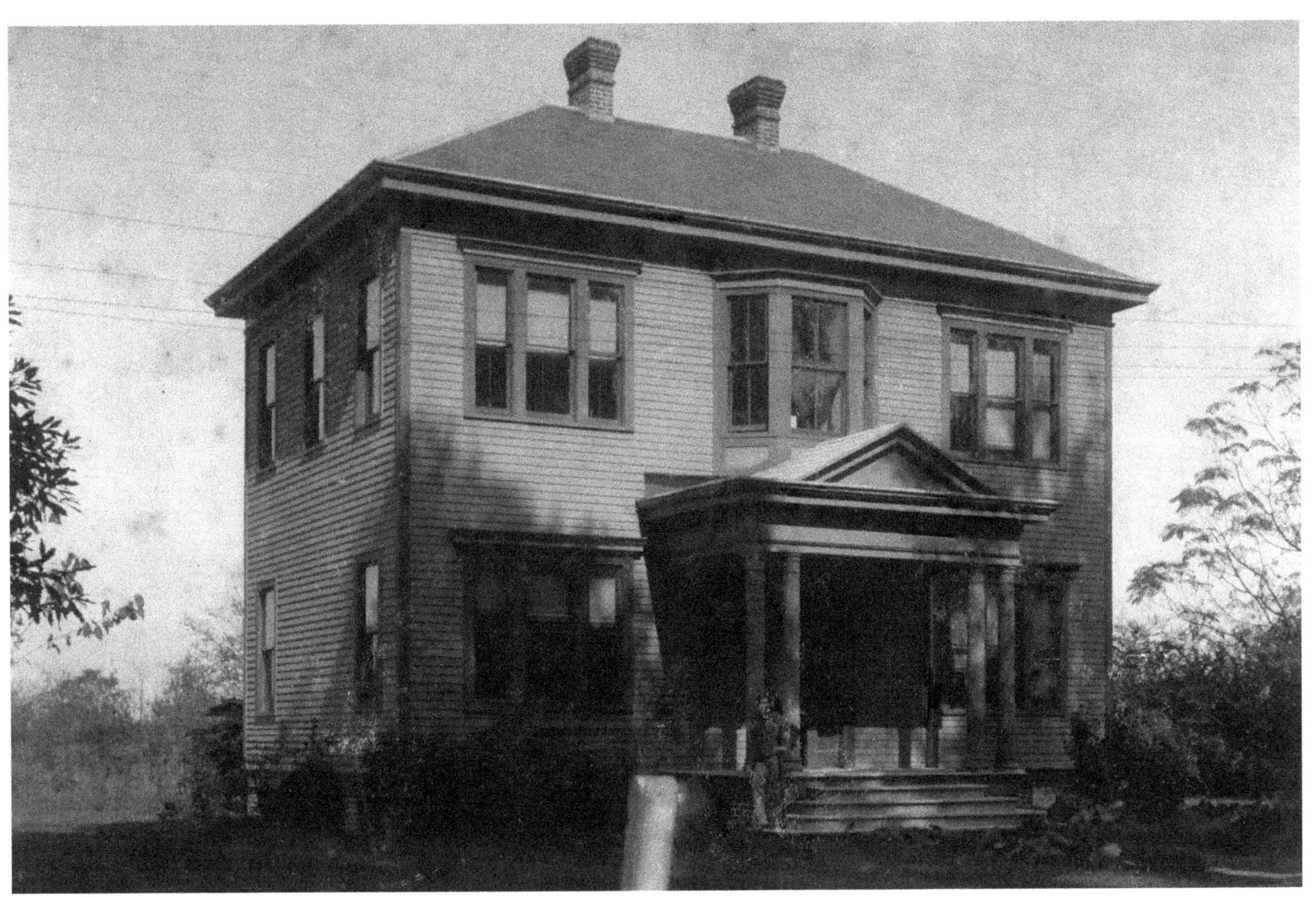

Louisiana State University and the Louisiana State Agricultural and Mechanical College merged under an act of the state legislature in 1877. The offices of the Agriculture Experiment Station moved into this LSU campus building, seen around 1905, from Audubon Park in New Orleans.

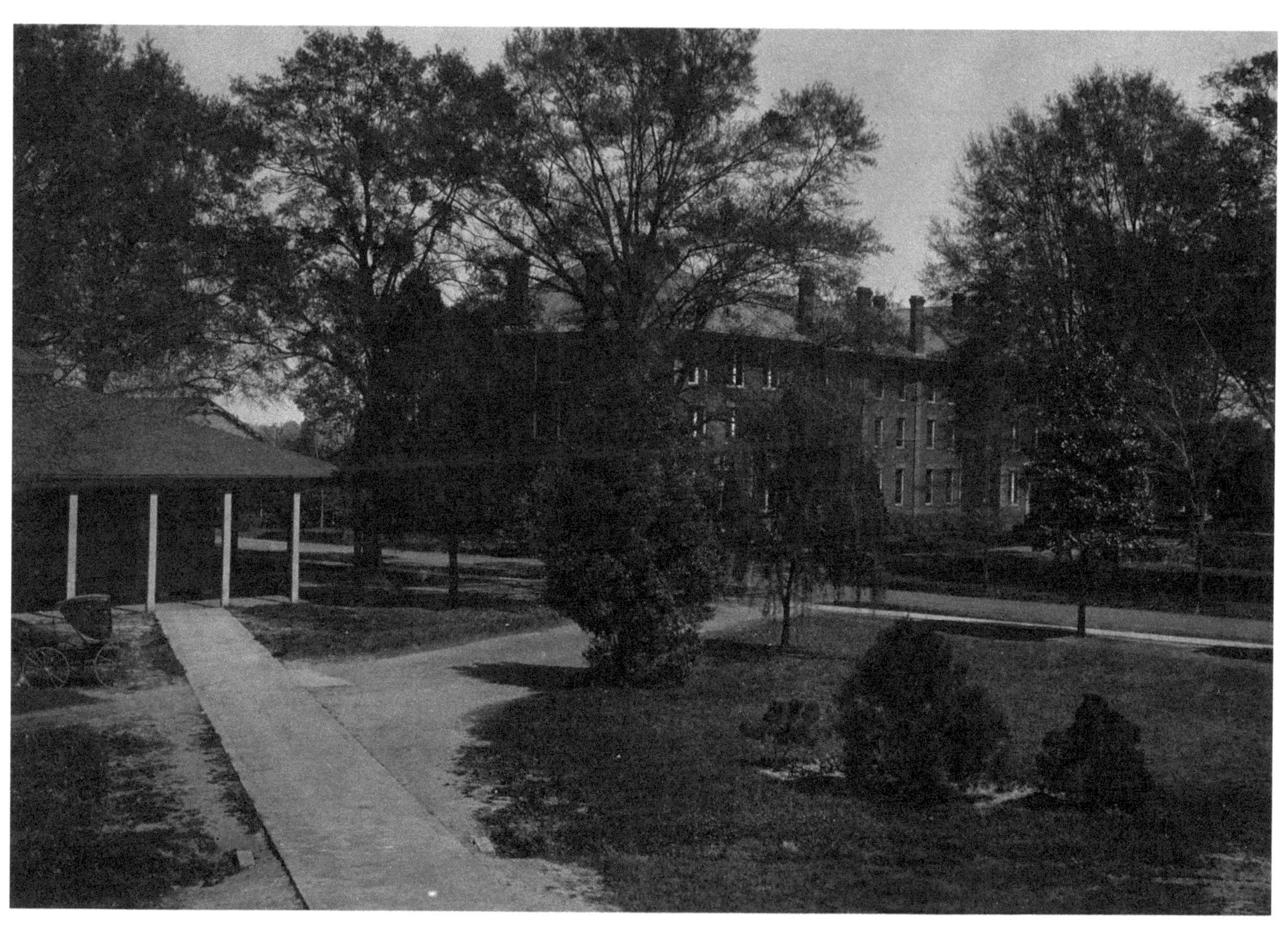

The university campus expanded greatly in the early 1900s. Foster Hall, at right, served as a dormitory and dining hall. The hospital, at left, looked after the cadets' health and well-being.

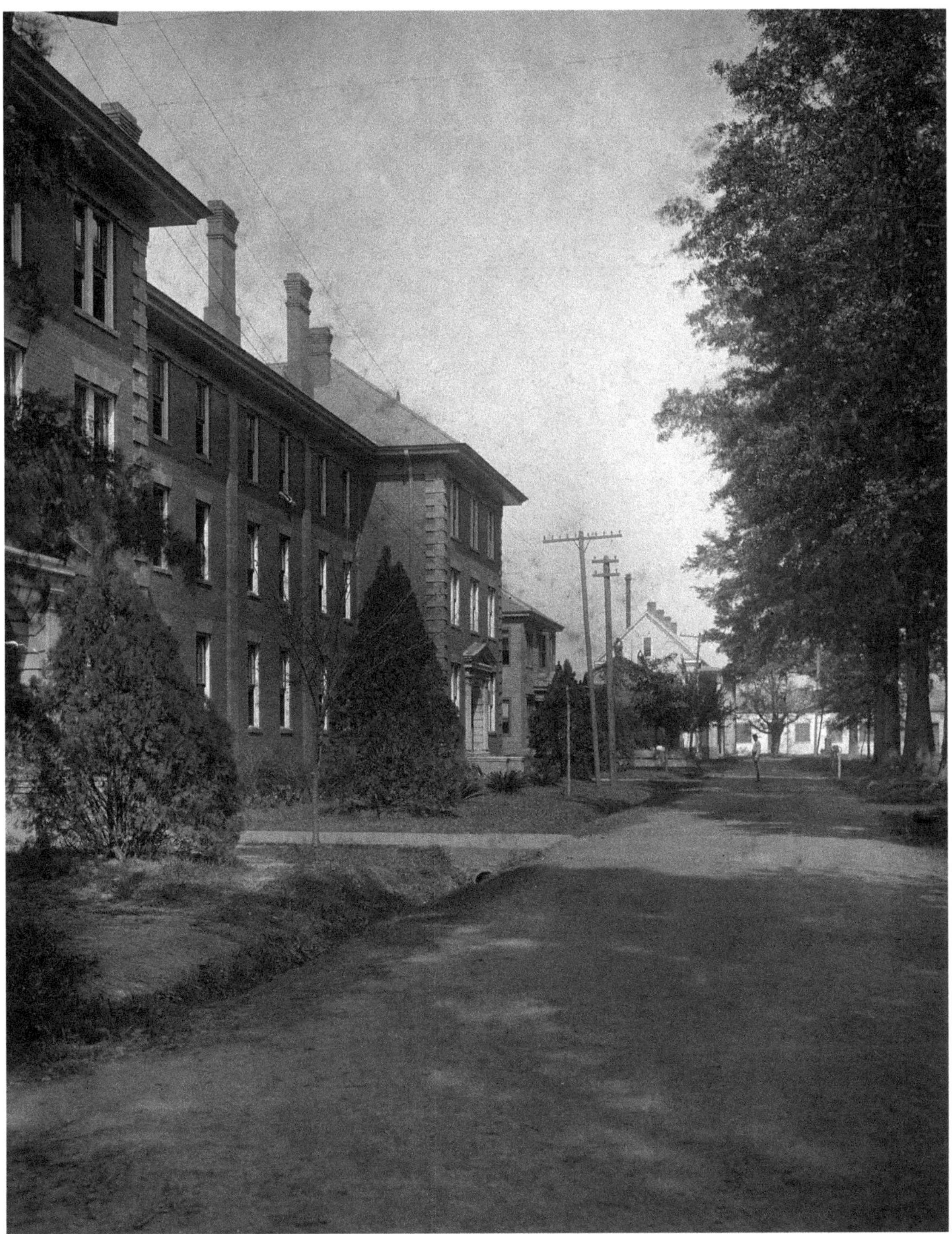

Over time, the old Arsenal grounds were transformed by the growth of the university. This view from around 1905 features Foster Hall, the Treasurer's Office, and, at the end of the street, a machine shop building.

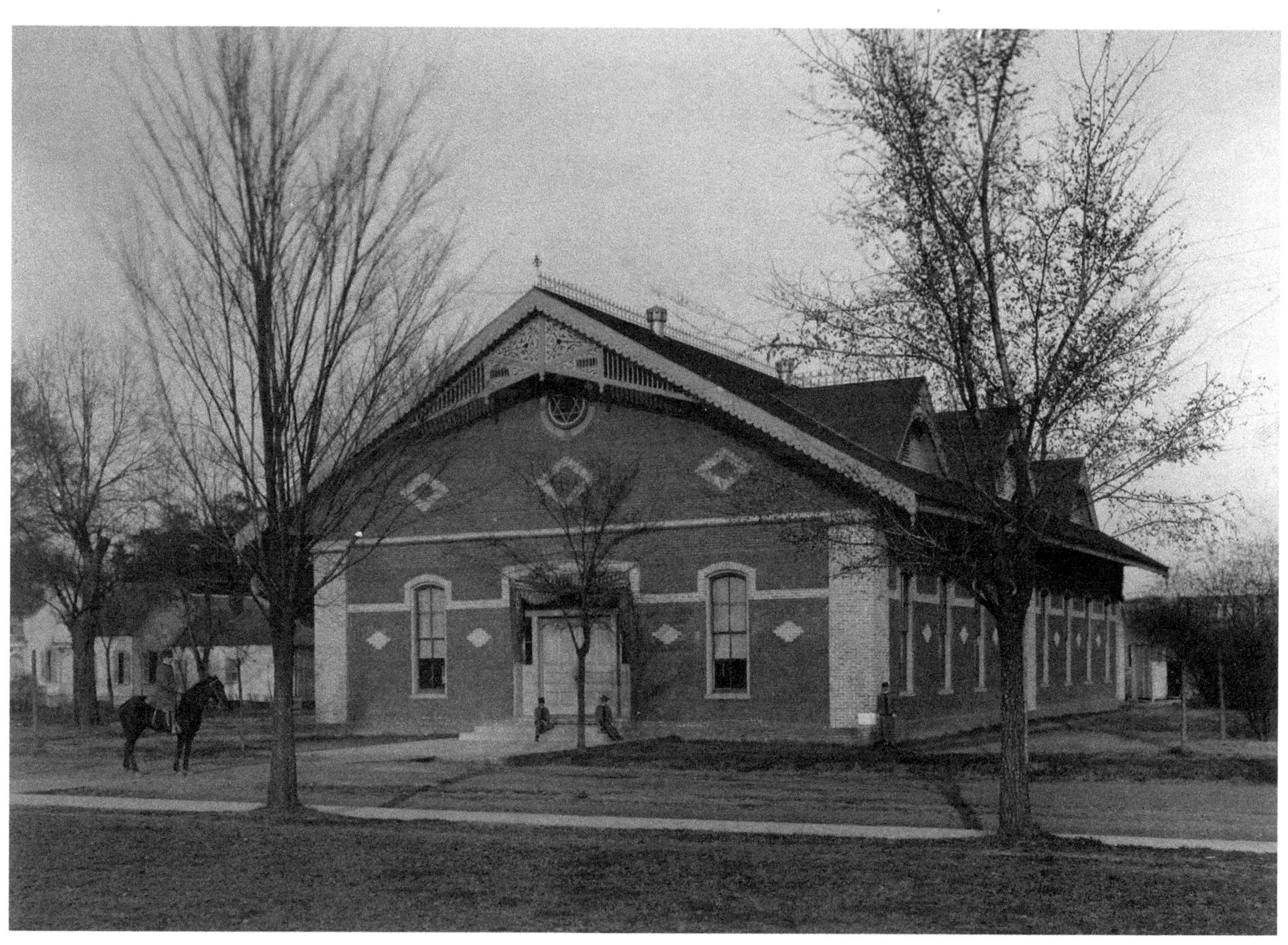

Able to hold 1,200 persons, LSU's Garig Hall, built 1899–1900, served as a meeting hall. The building was a gift of William Garig and is seen here around 1905.

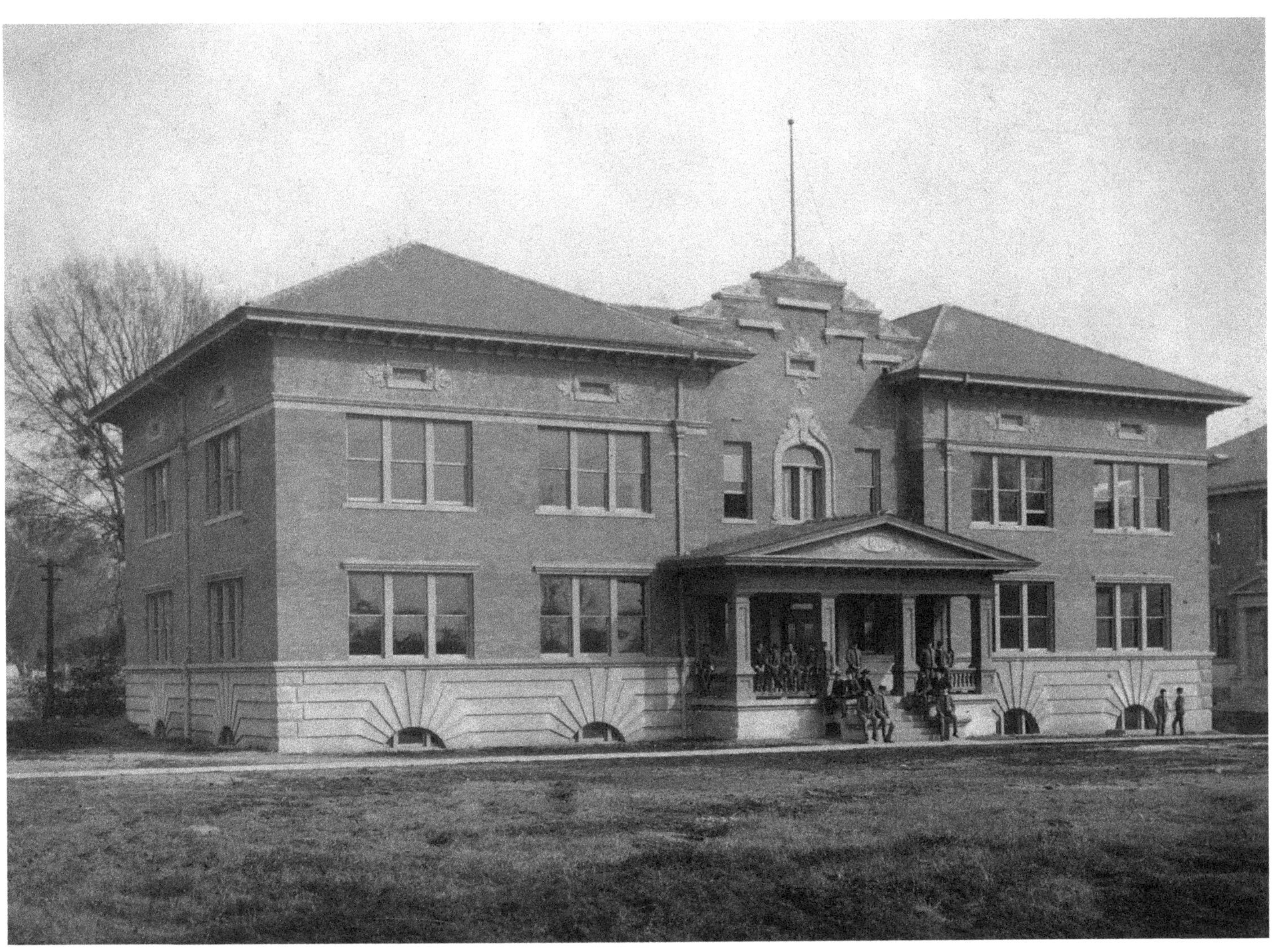

Heard Hall, built 1902–1903, housed the physics and civil engineering departments at the university. Occupying the first floor, the Department of Physics and Electricity maintained a laboratory specially designed for the study of magnetism. The Department of Civil Engineering occupied the second floor.

Hill Memorial Library, donated by John Hill of West Baton Rouge in memory of his son John Hill, Jr., occupied a prominent position on the LSU campus near the Third Street entrance. Its central rotunda was flanked by two reading rooms, one of which these studious cadets are utilizing around 1905.

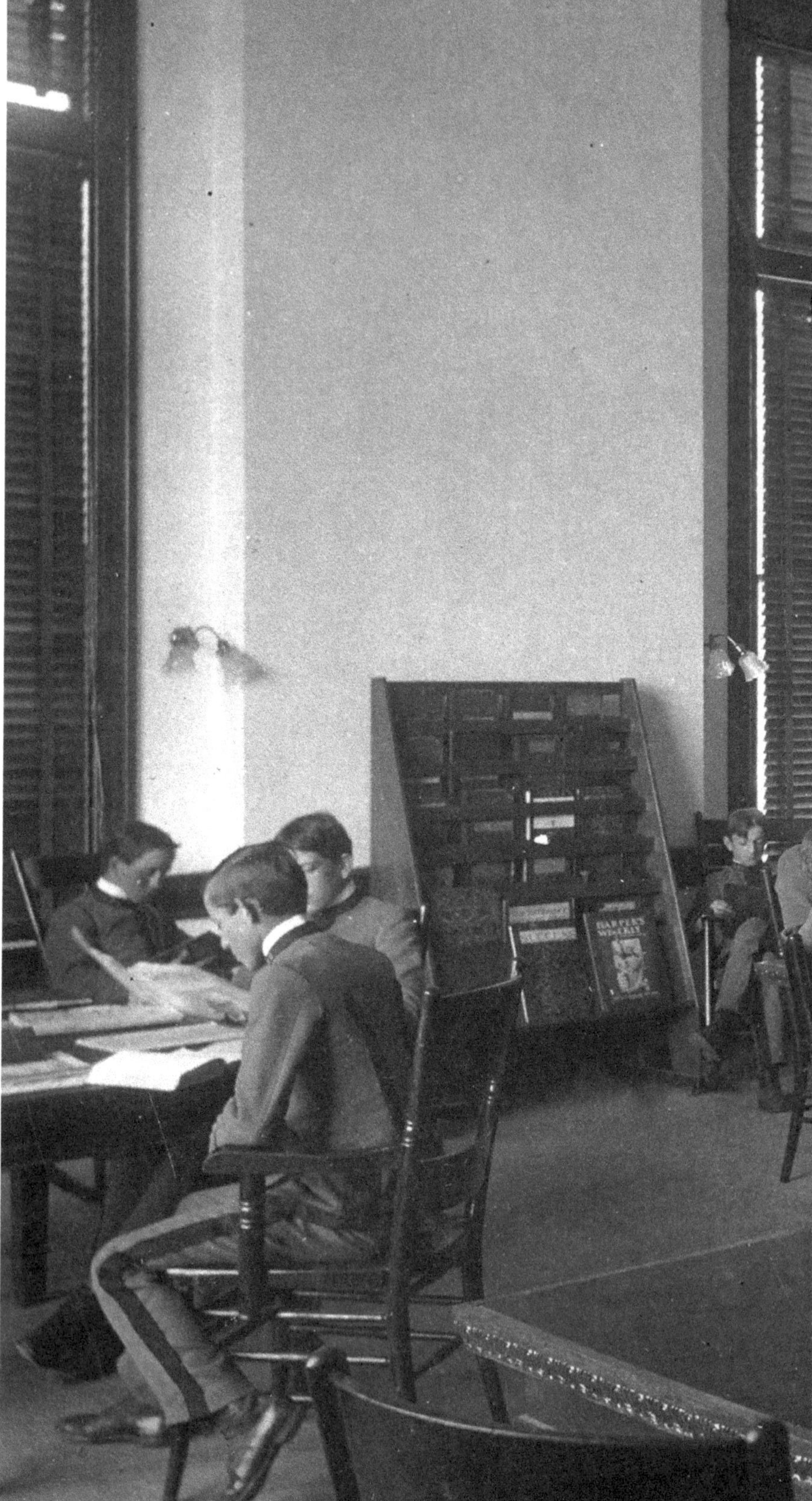

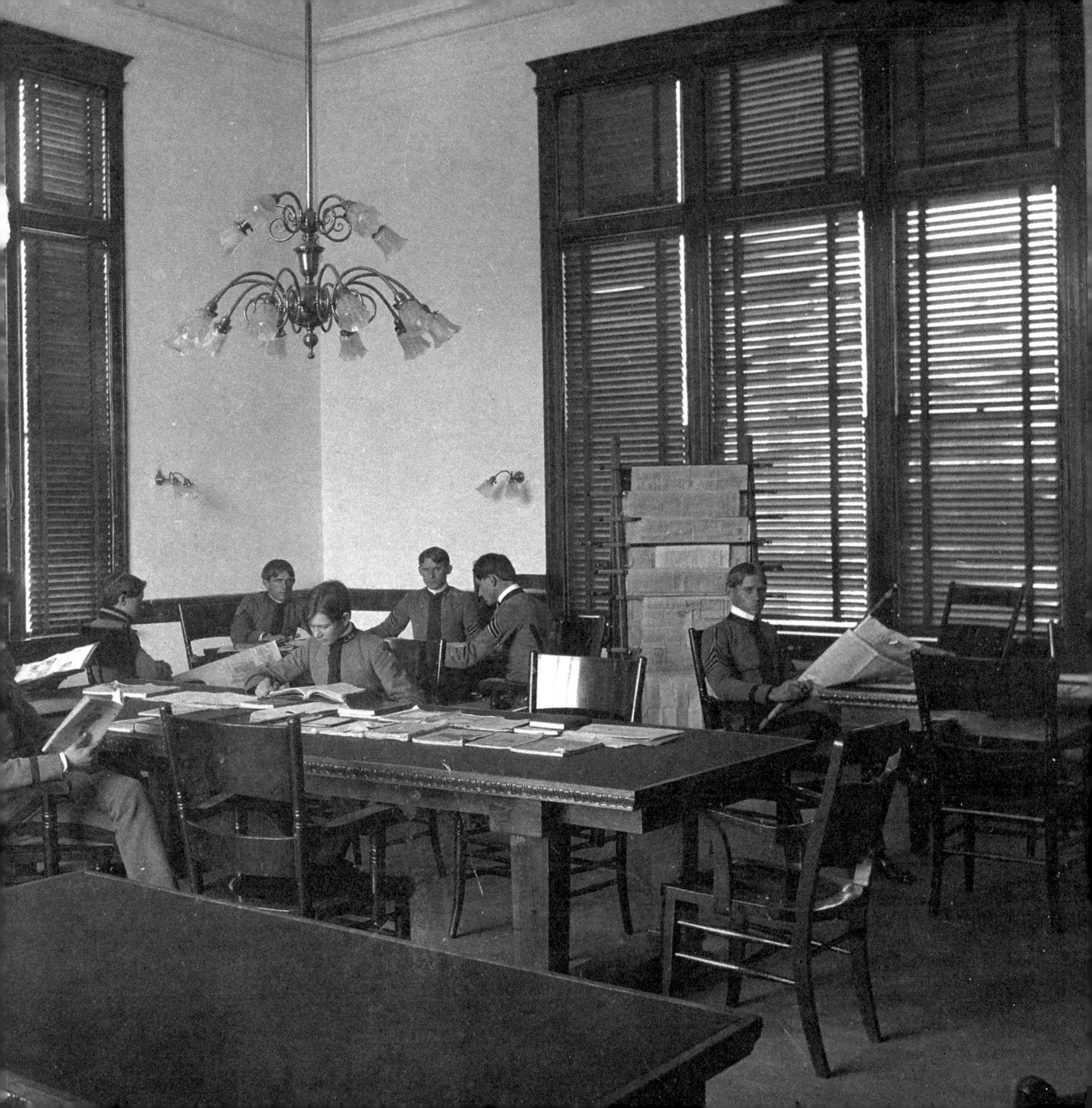

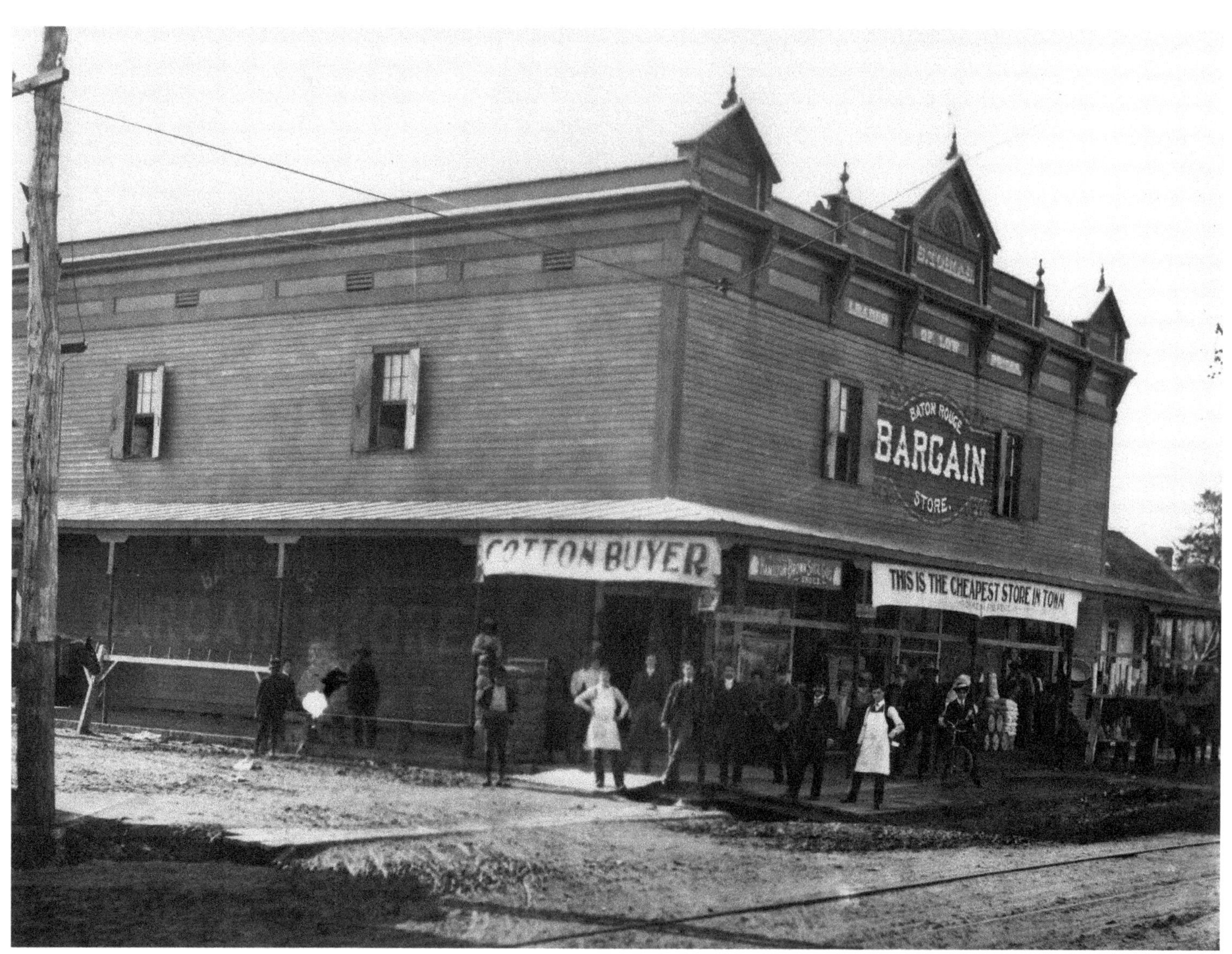

Advertising itself as the "cheapest store in town," the Baton Rouge Bargain Store, owned and operated by Sylvan Tobias, provided the citizens of Baton Rouge with a variety of goods. This image appears in the *Elks' souvenir of Baton Rouge; containing an historic, commercial and industrial review of prominent advantages of Parish of East Baton Rouge and the flower city of Louisiana,* published in 1901.

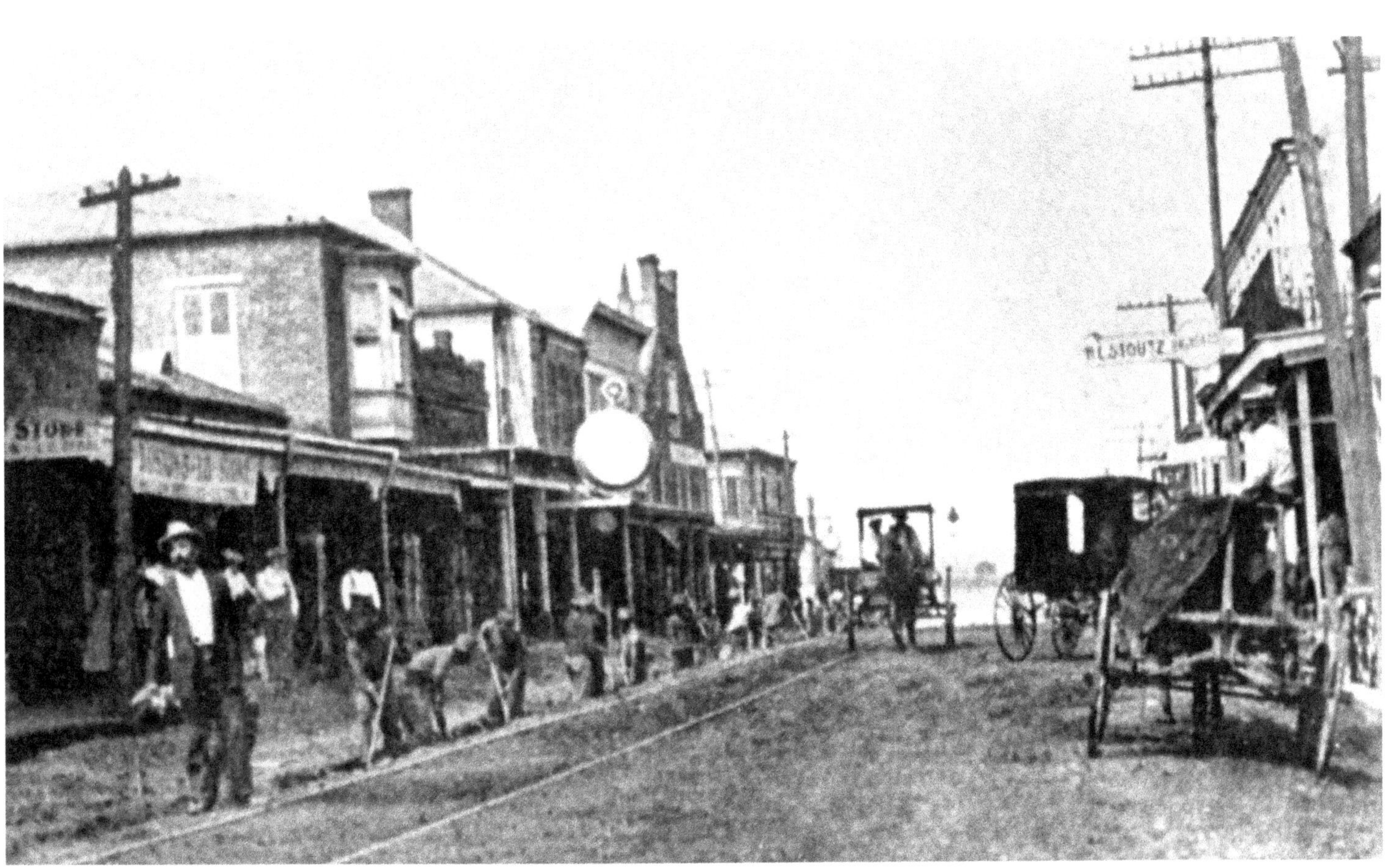

Baton Rouge began to grow and modernize at the beginning of the twentieth century. Here workers dig a trench for installation of a sanitary sewer system along Main Street near the river.

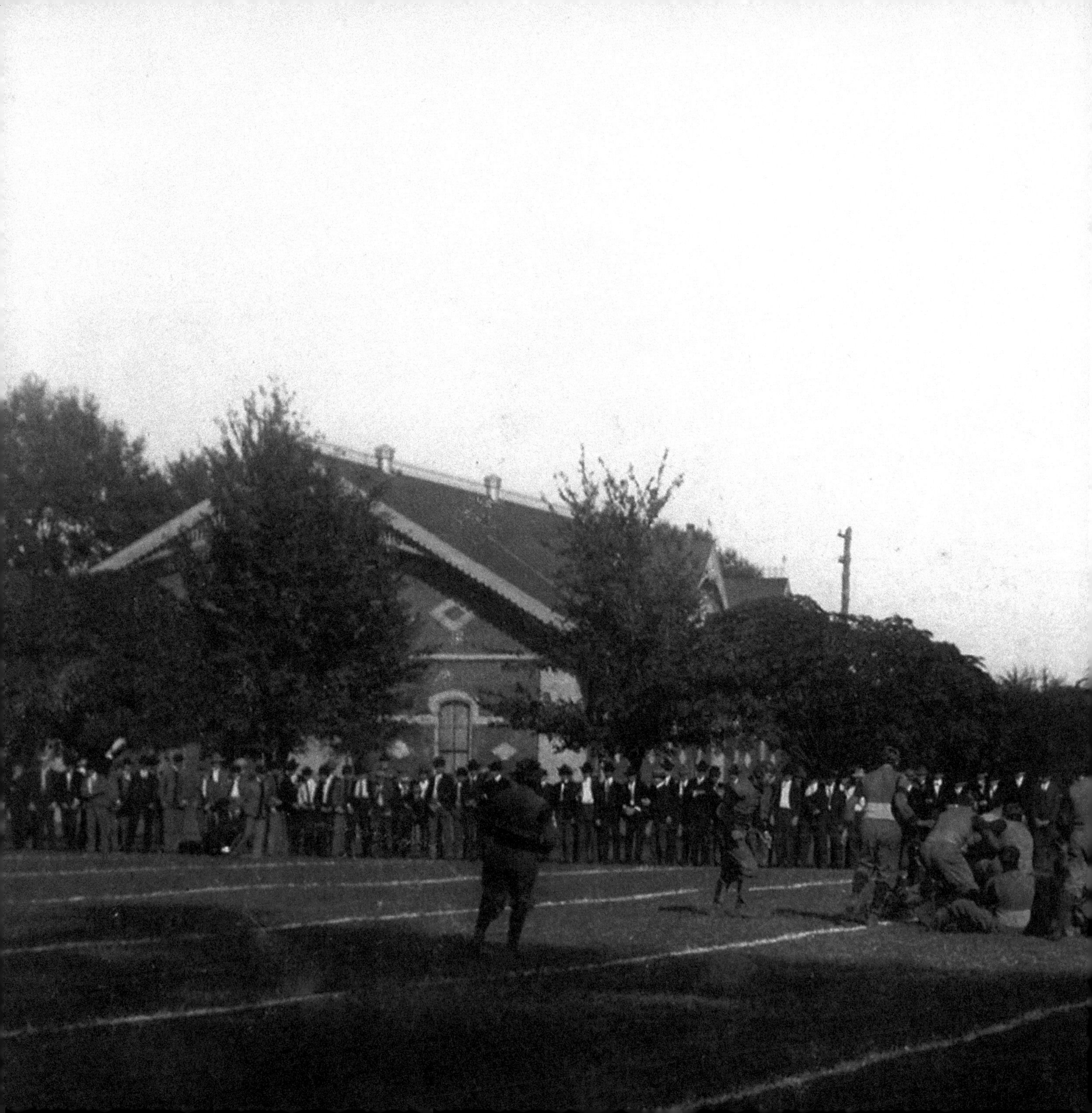

Introduced in an early modern form in the 1880s, football had become popular on university campuses by the early 1900s. But due to the relatively high number of injuries and to 18 deaths resulting from the sport, football was nearly banned on campuses by 1905. Here, around 1910, a game on the LSU campus draws a sizable crowd of onlookers.

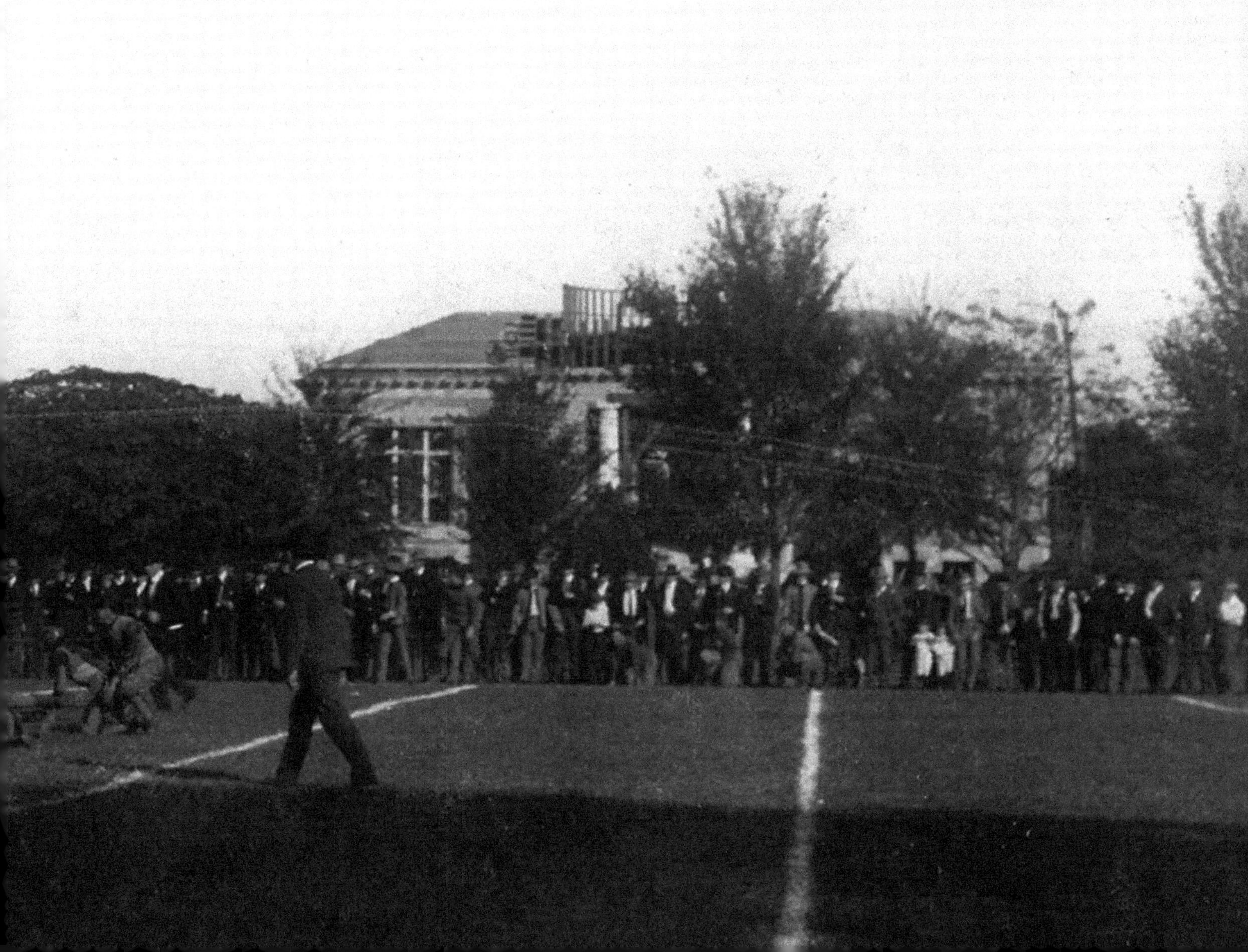

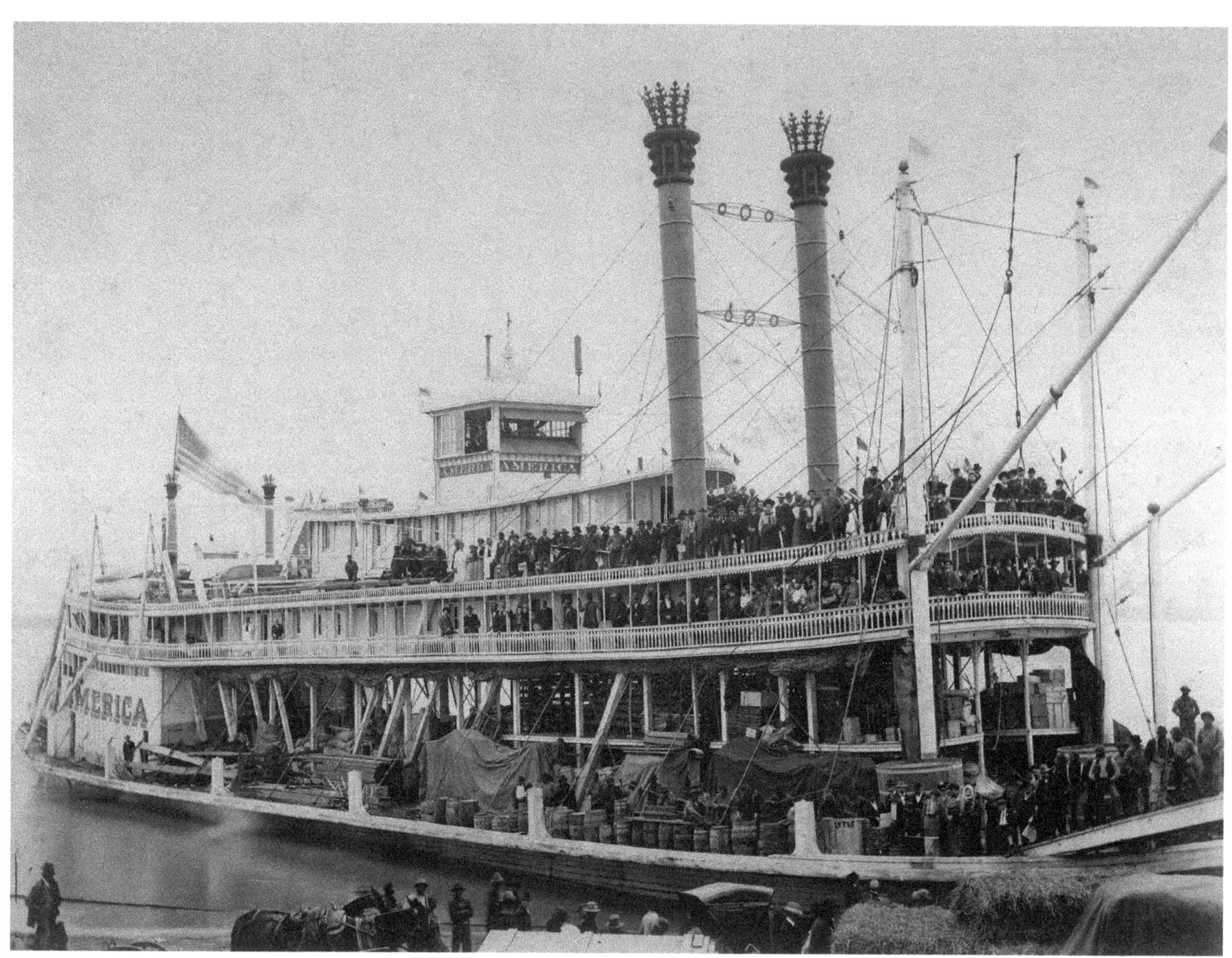

Baton Rouge grew through the years in large part due to its position on the Mississippi River. It was valued as a military post because of its command of the river and its natural harbor. These attributes grew in significance over time as the United States became established and trade developed. By the late 1800s, Baton Rouge had become an important entrepôt for steam-powered riverboats like the *America,* seen here around 1900.

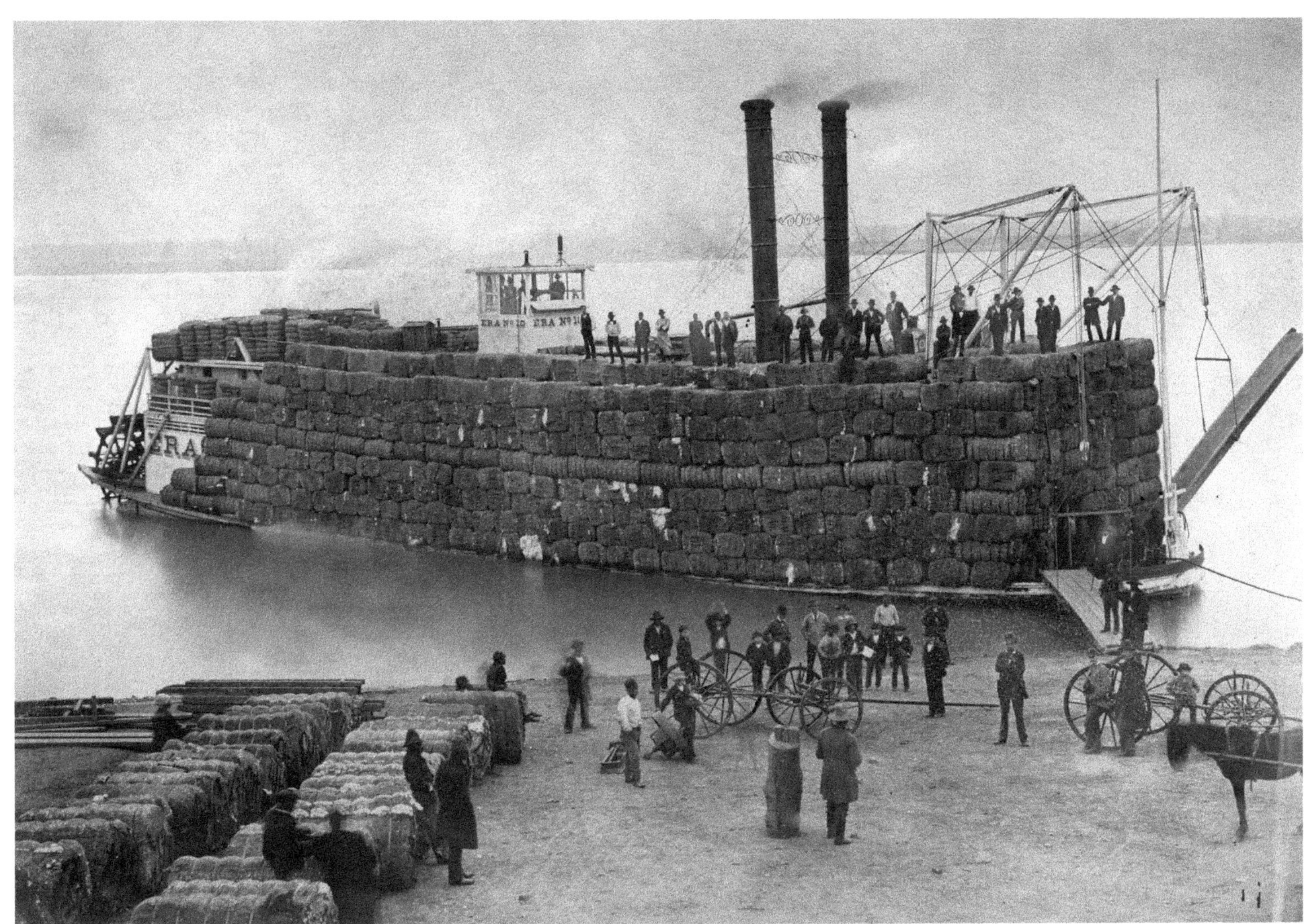

Cotton and other agricultural crops had always been important to the economy of the lower Mississippi Valley. Well into the late 1800s, cotton remained an important commodity. The *Era No. 10,* seen anchored off Baton Rouge around 1900, is so fully loaded with cotton bales that it has no freeboard.

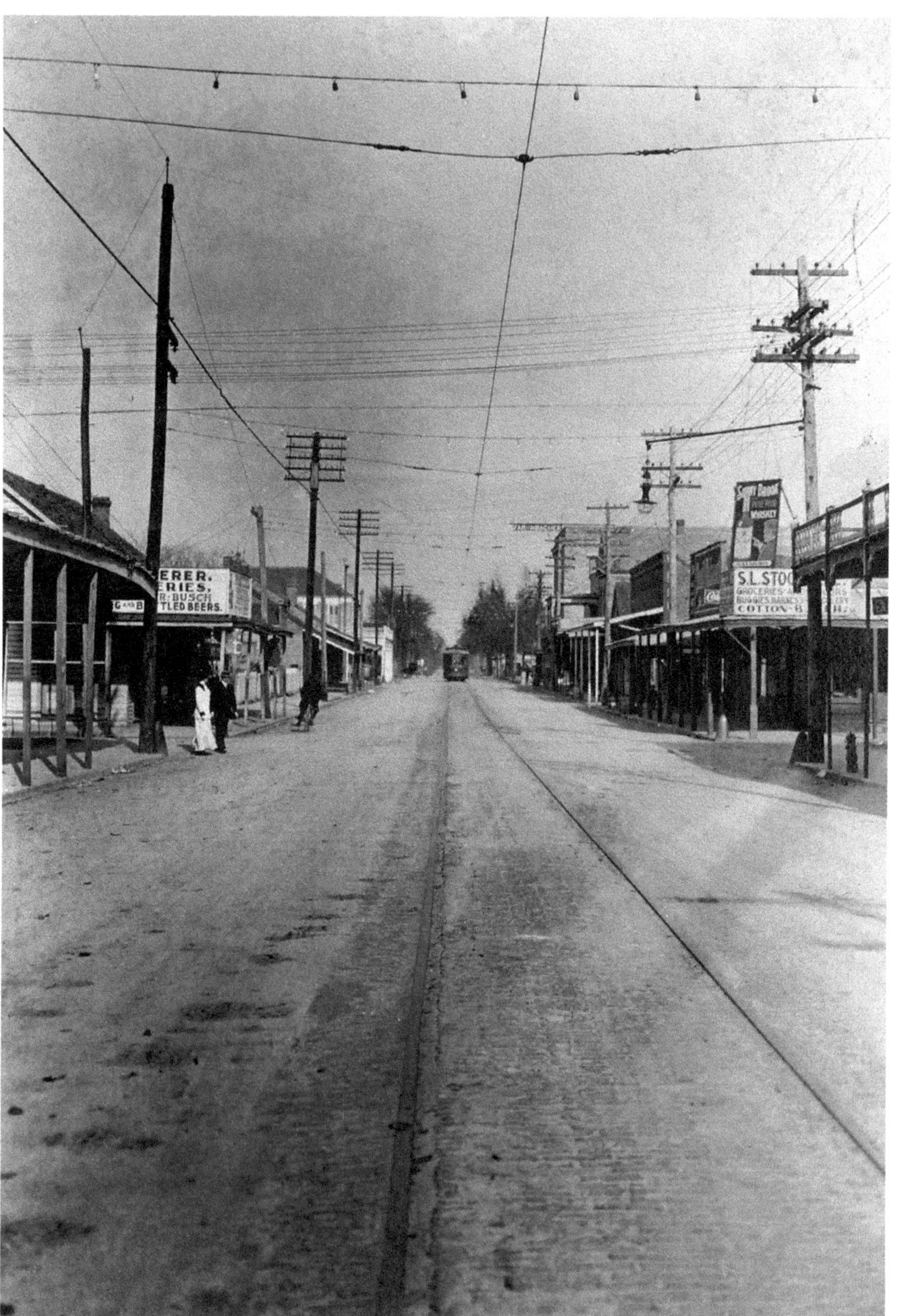

Looking from the intersection of Main and Fifth streets around 1910, Samuel T. Dupuy's Pharmacy, 522 Main, is on the corner at right, diagonally across from William Meyerer's grocery and bar at 601 Main.

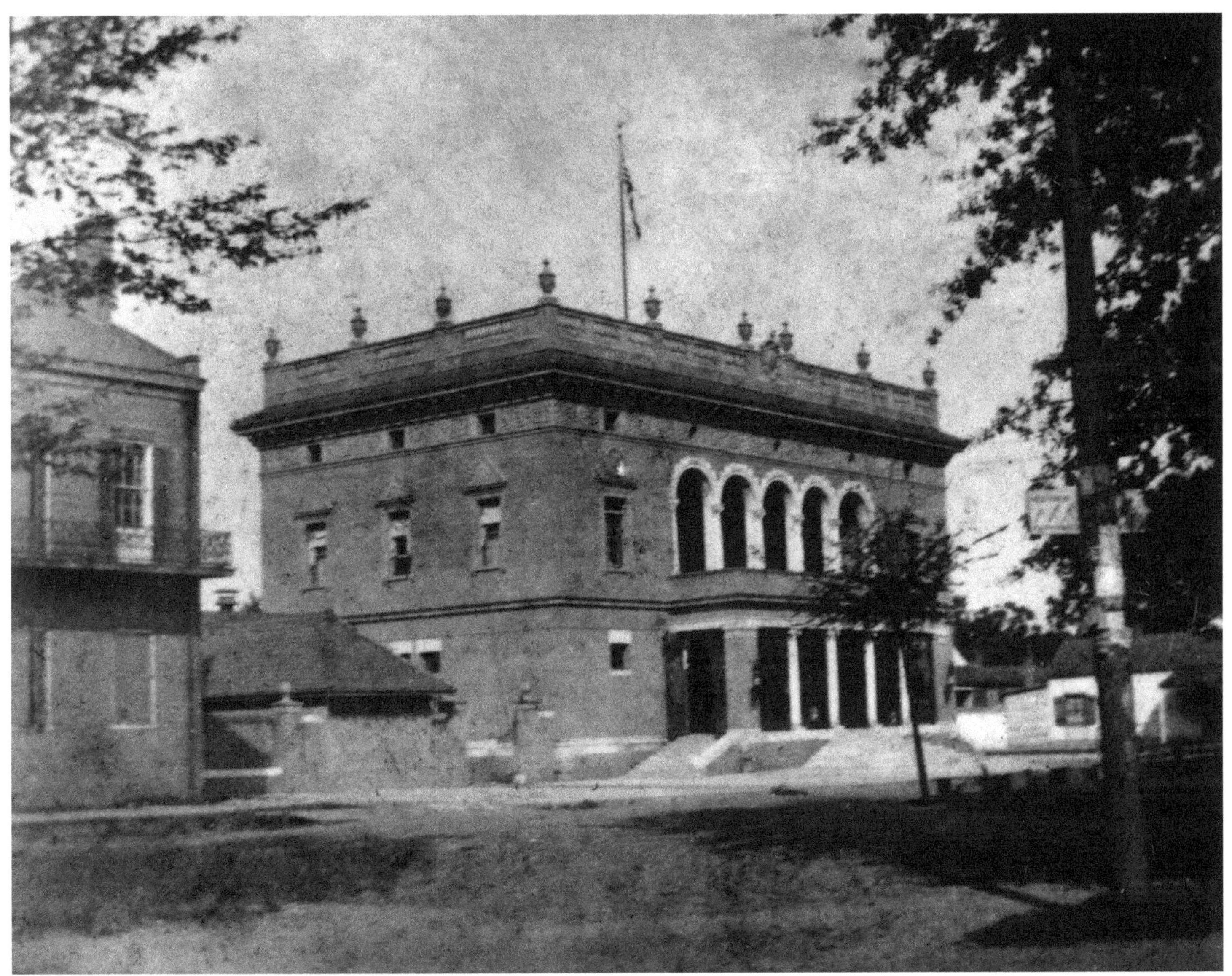

As the seat of parish and state government and an outpost of national governmental agencies, Baton Rouge had good reason to build a new post office and federal building in 1894. This view from the corner of North Boulevard and Fourth Street, around 1901, shows the Italian Renaissance facade.

This is another view of the Baton Rouge Bargain Store, though without the banner proclaiming it the "cheapest store in town."

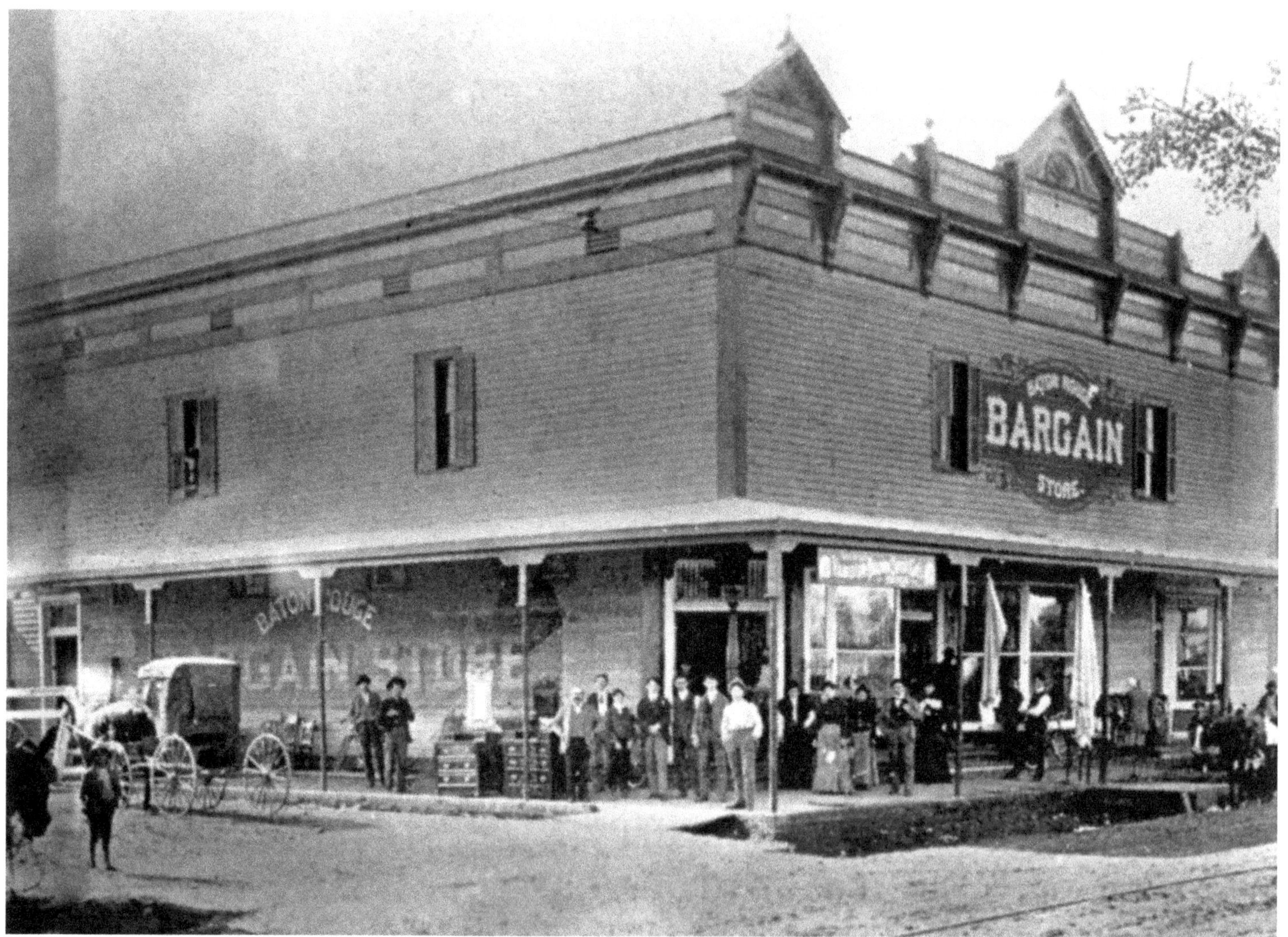

Andrew M. Jackson established his fancy grocery, cotton brokerage, and plantation-supply business at 504 Main Street in this cement-block building with 90 feet of frontage on the street. The Armstrong Furniture Company occupied the corner, 500–502 Main, in 1906. This image was published in 1901.

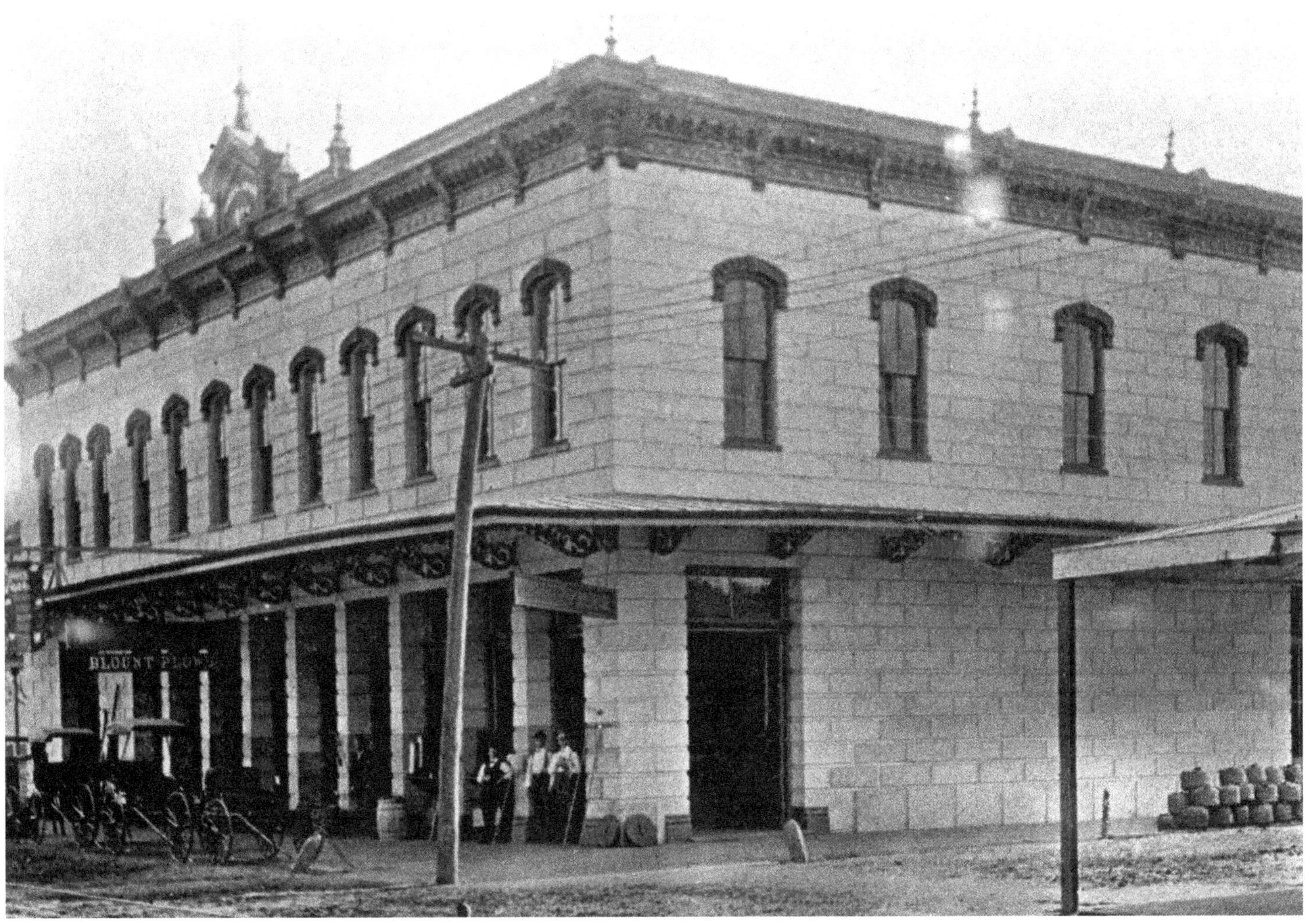

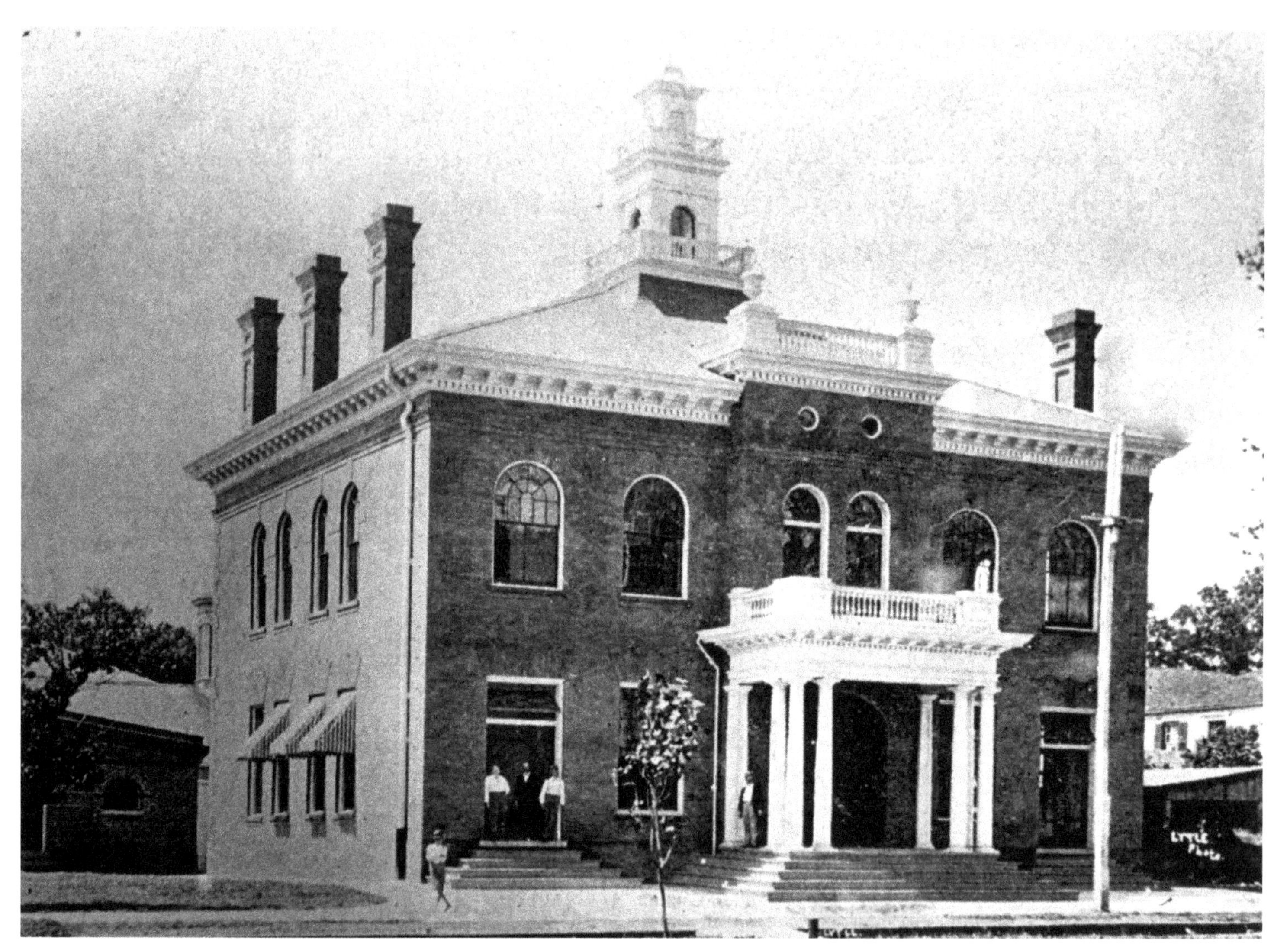

Newly constructed in 1900, the City Hall was a source of civic pride when photographed here not long after its completion.

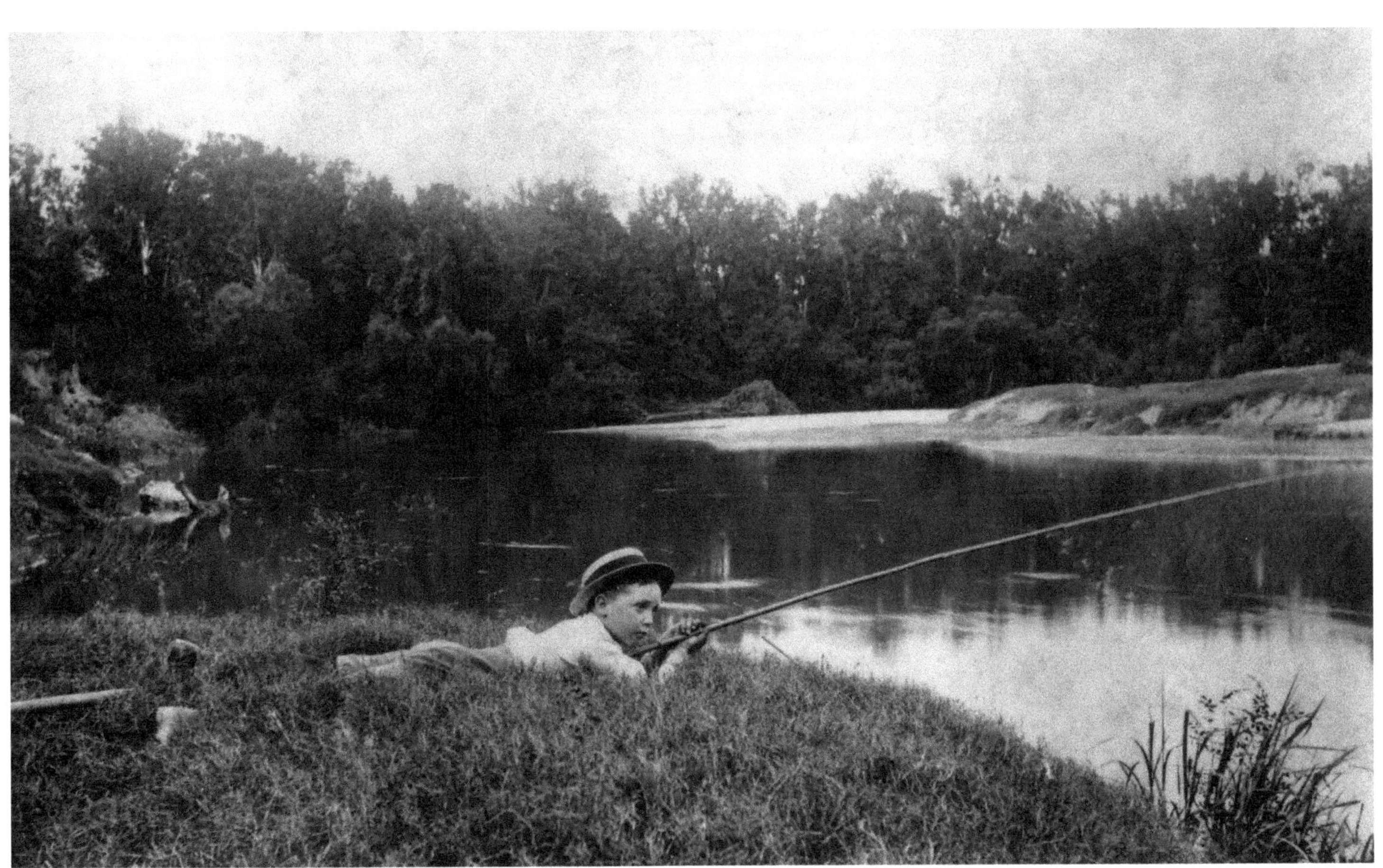

The natural beauty of Baton Rouge and its environs was often commented upon. In this idyllic view of the Amite River on the eastern edge of East Baton Rouge Parish, the hopeful fisherman is Andrew D. Lytle, Jr., photographed around 1900 by Howard Lytle, son of the senior Andrew D. Lytle and partner in his Lytle Studio.

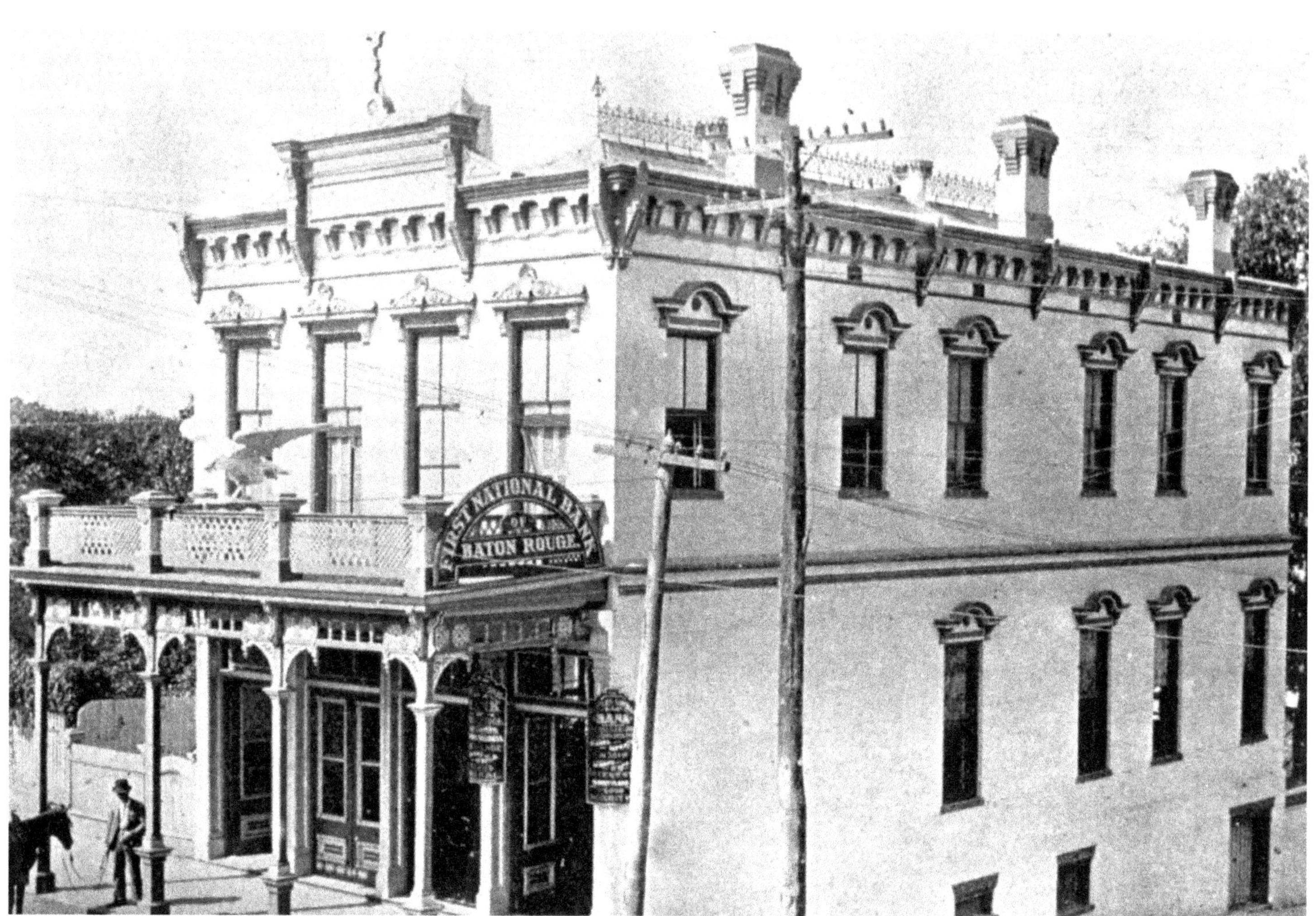

Established June 1889, the First National Bank, located on the corner of Laurel and Lafayette streets, enjoyed a sound financial reputation. This 1901 view shows the facade of the building with its back toward the river.

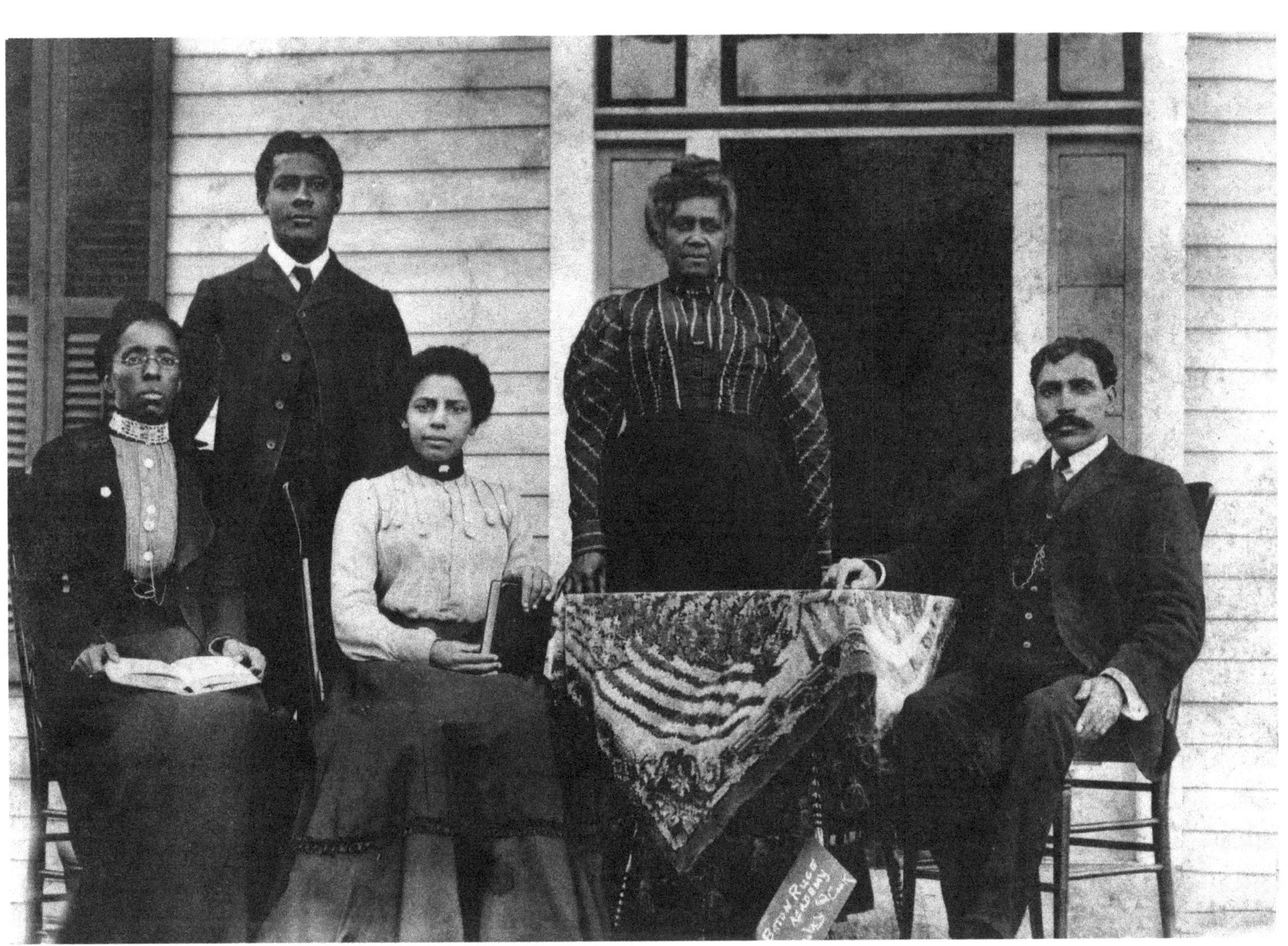

The Baton Rouge Academy was one of five private schools and colleges for African American citizens of Baton Rouge. Here, members of the faculty pose for a group portrait on the porch of the academy, located at 125 Middle Highland Road, around 1910.

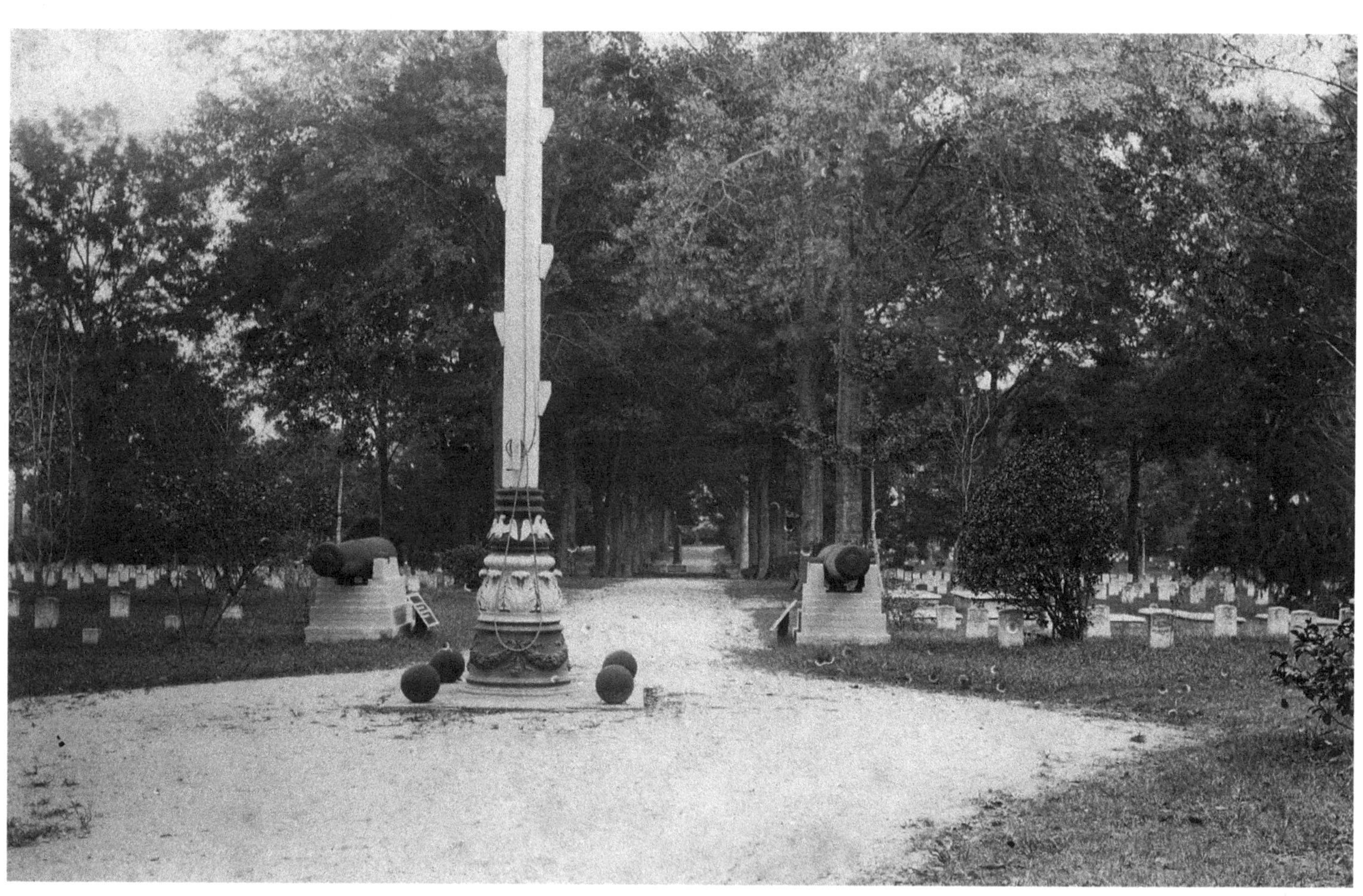

Baton Rouge, occupied by Federal forces in 1862, was the site of a pitched battle in August of that year. Slain soldiers and sailors were buried near Magnolia Cemetery on the outskirts of town. Fifty years after the Civil War ended, the National Cemetery in Baton Rouge began to receive monuments to Northern soldiers and sailors. This image of the National Cemetery from around 1910 shows one such monument.

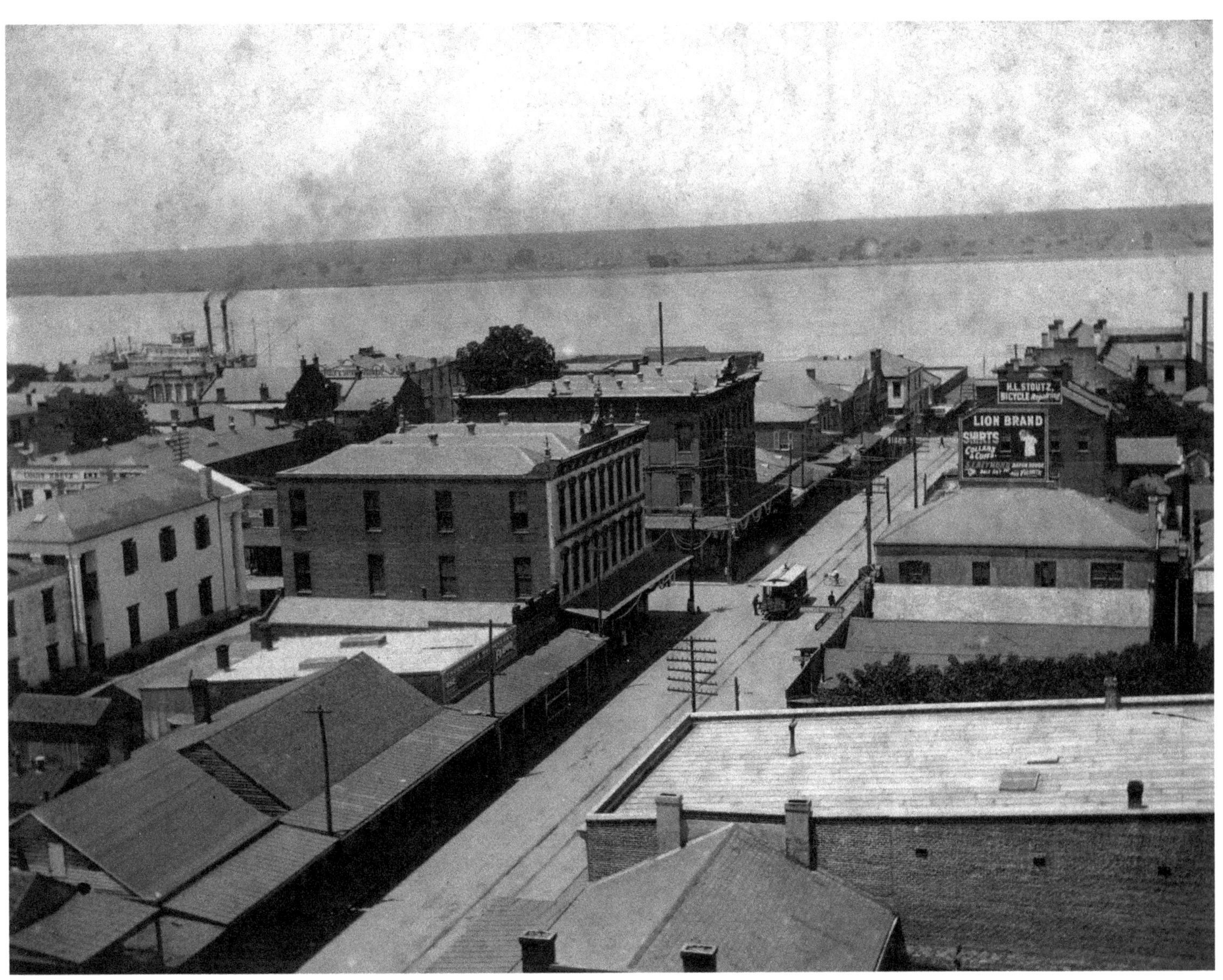

The first four blocks of Main Street as it runs east from the river can be seen in this image by John B. Heroman, which he titled "My home town" for submission to a photo contest around 1910.

As this scene suggests, the Audubon Sugar School played a major role in research and development for the sugar industry in Louisiana. Making sugar from cane juice requires separating the sugar from the water carrying it; traditionally, this was accomplished by boiling off the water in open pans or kettles. Here, classmen stand around an experimental evaporator operating under vacuum, thereby saving energy by allowing the water to evaporate at temperatures below 212 degrees Fahrenheit.

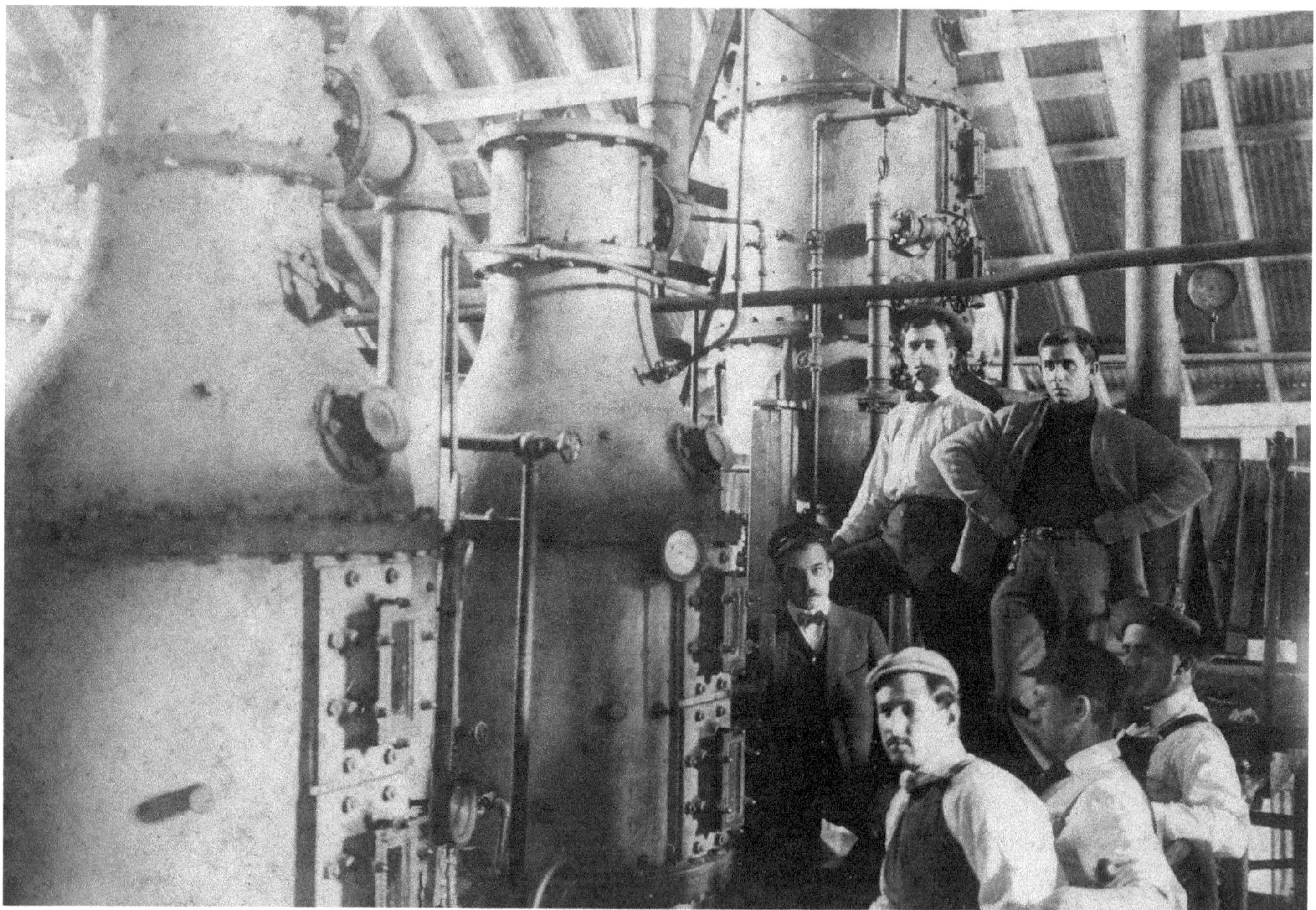

Seen around 1900, this trestle bridge is across the Amite River, which forms the eastern boundary of East Baton Rouge Parish.

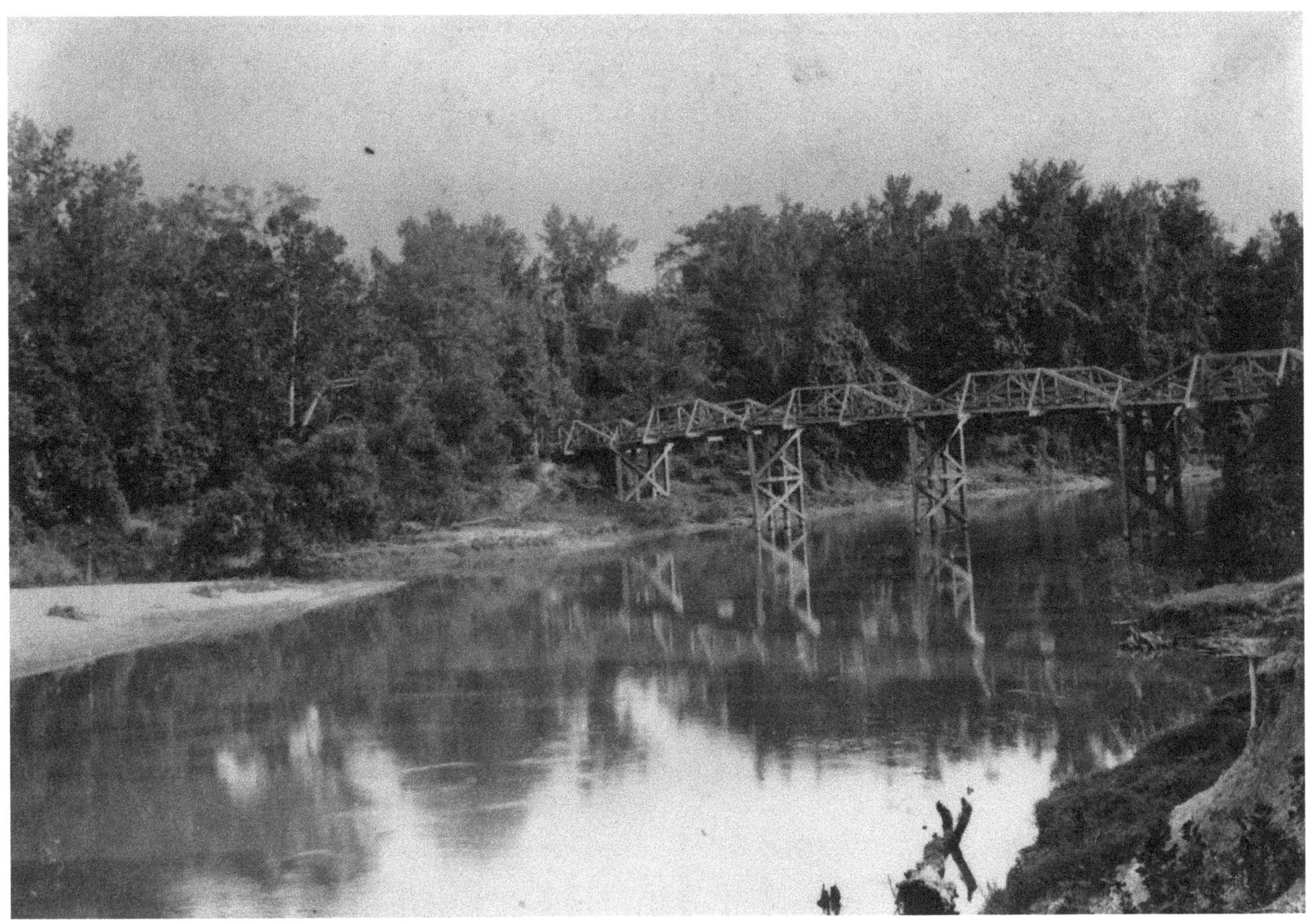

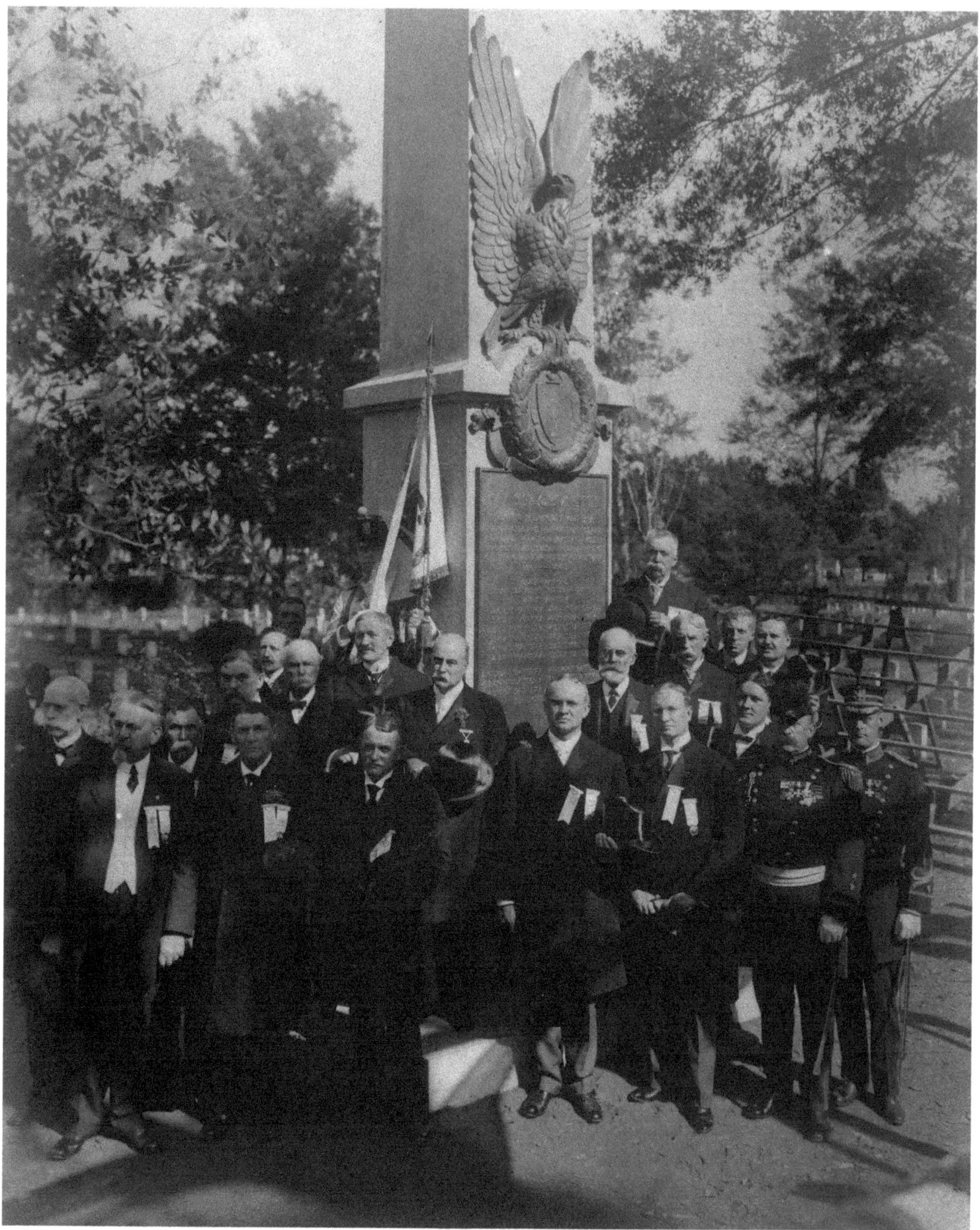

A delegation from Massachusetts came to Baton Rouge for three days in November 1909 to dedicate the monument Massachusetts had erected in the National Cemetery to honor soldiers from that state who lost their lives in the battle of Baton Rouge and were buried here. This image, created by Teunisson Studio of New Orleans, shows the delegation at the monument.

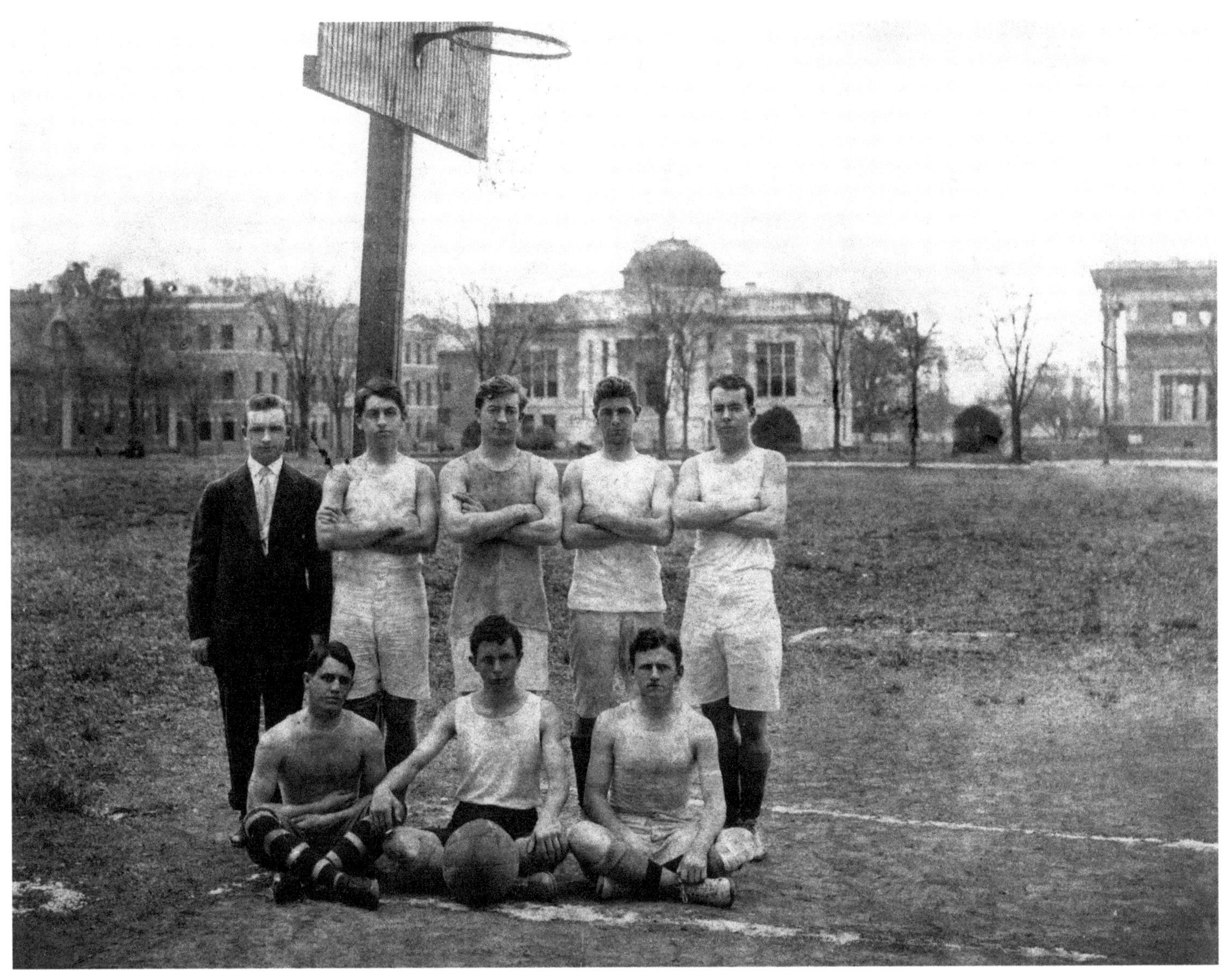

The 1909 Louisiana State University basketball team posed for this group portrait on the athletic field of the old Arsenal campus downtown. Immediately behind the team is Hill Memorial Library.

A warship lies off shore in the Mississippi River around 1910. The river remains navigable to oceangoing craft as far inland as the Mississippi state border.

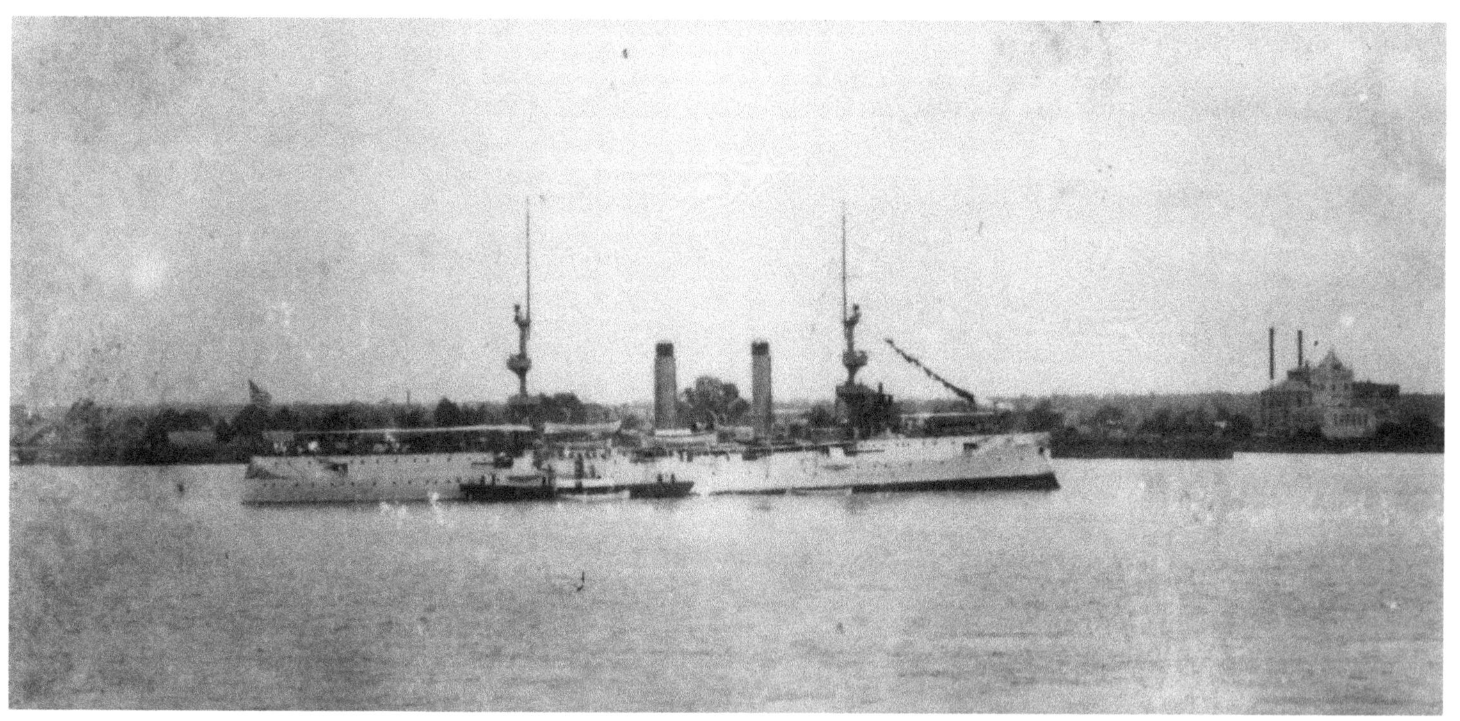

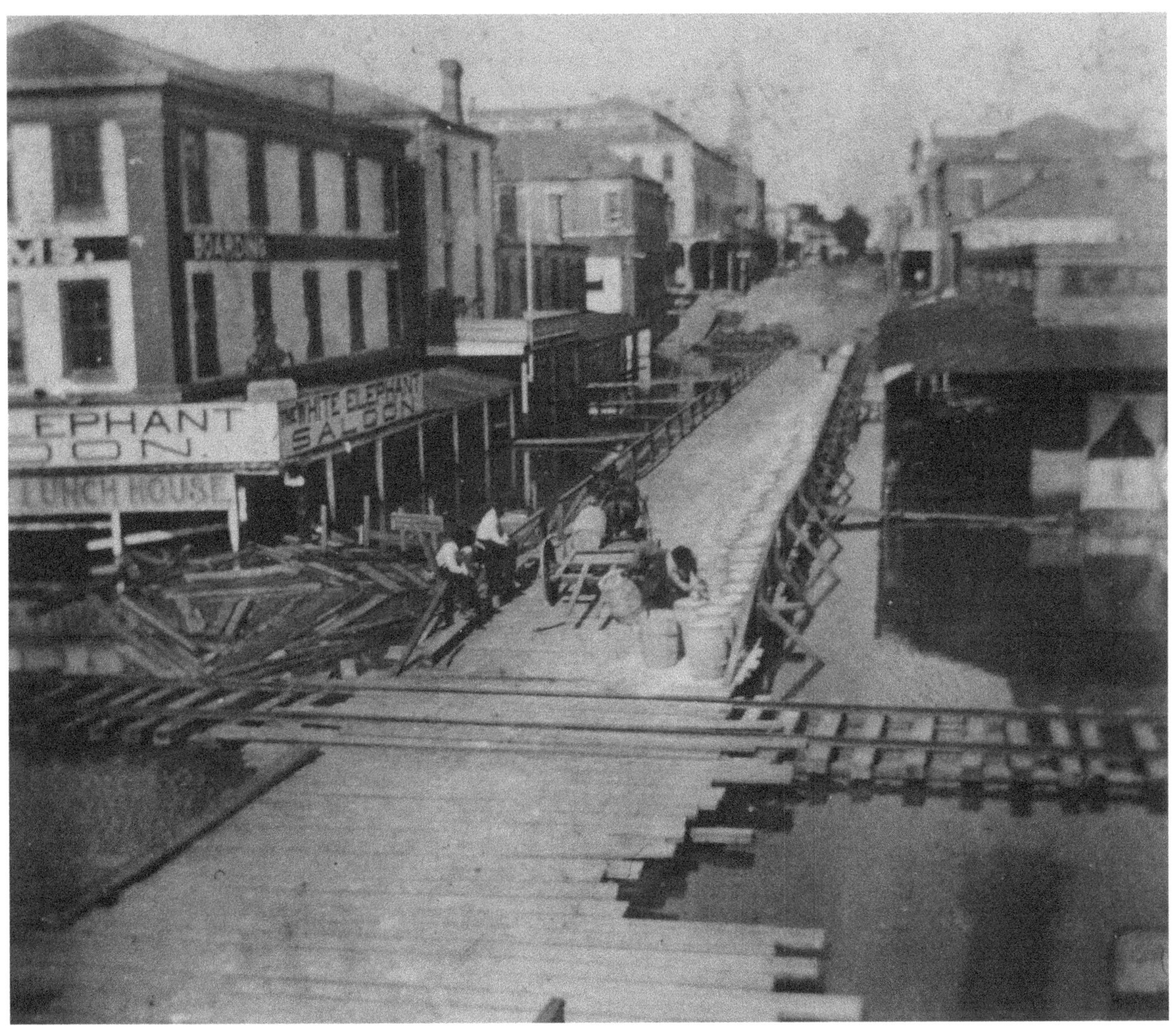

Before the levee was built to protect Baton Rouge, town citizens, through hard-won experience, created innovative, temporary structures to accommodate high-water episodes, such as occurred in both 1915 and 1917. This scene demonstrates the townspeople's skills.

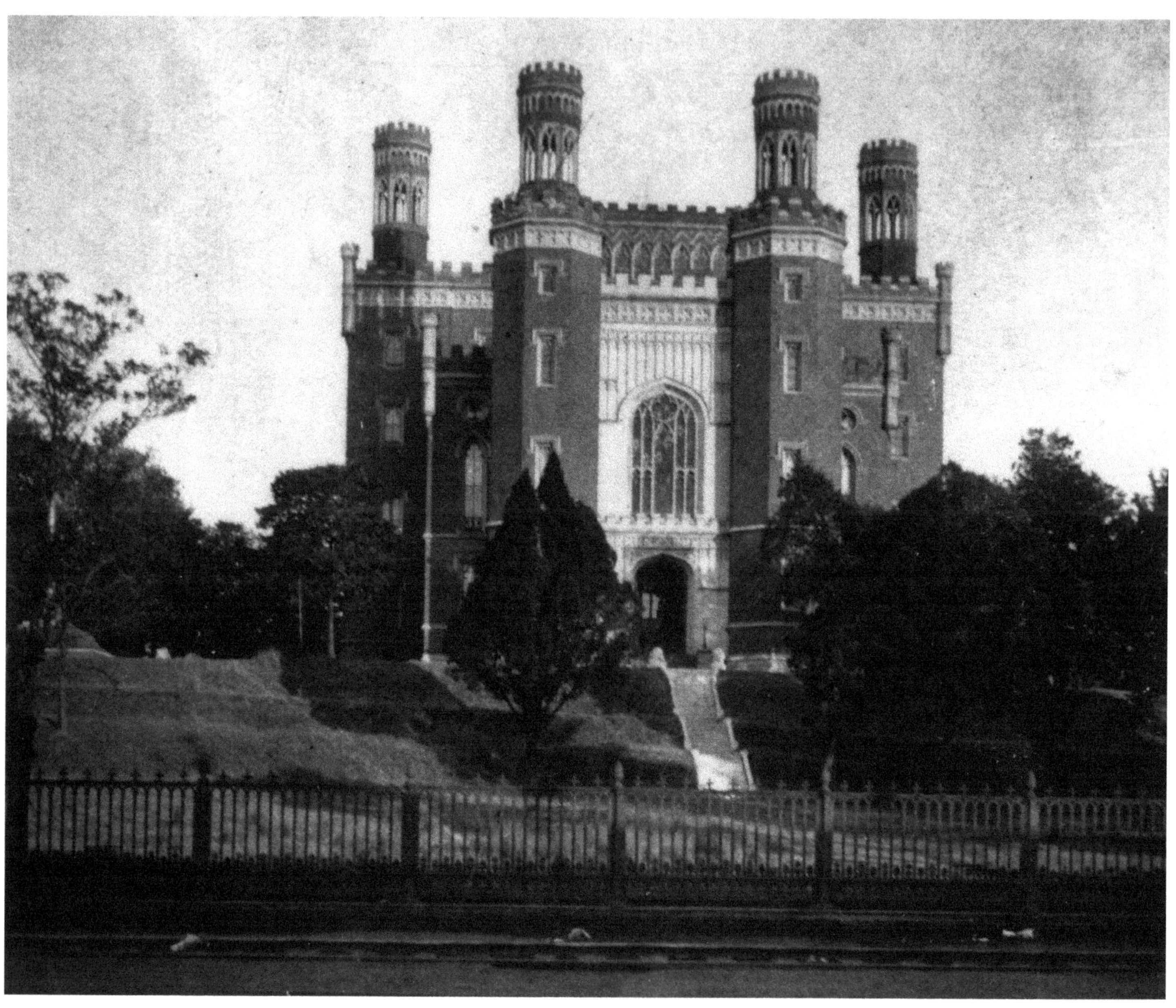

Cast-iron turrets, added during the Capitol's reconstruction under the direction of William A. Freret in the 1880s, added a new dimension to Dakin's castellated Gothic style. The turrets would be removed in 1917 following their partial destruction by a tornado.

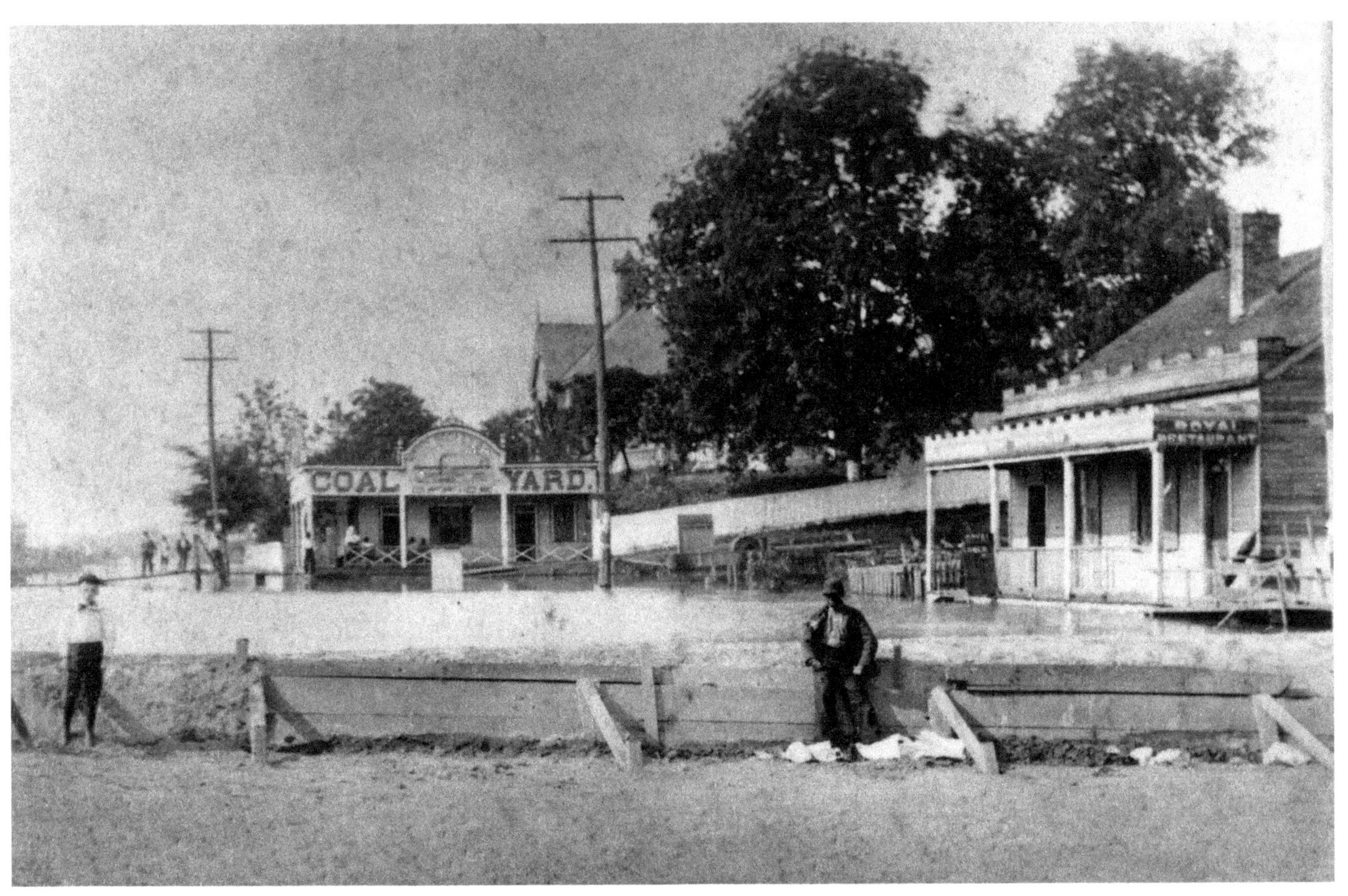

Despite periodic flooding by the Mississippi River, Baton Rouge businesses were built right down to the river's edge. Here, during the flood of either 1915 or 1917, temporary measures were taken to limit the spread of floodwaters.

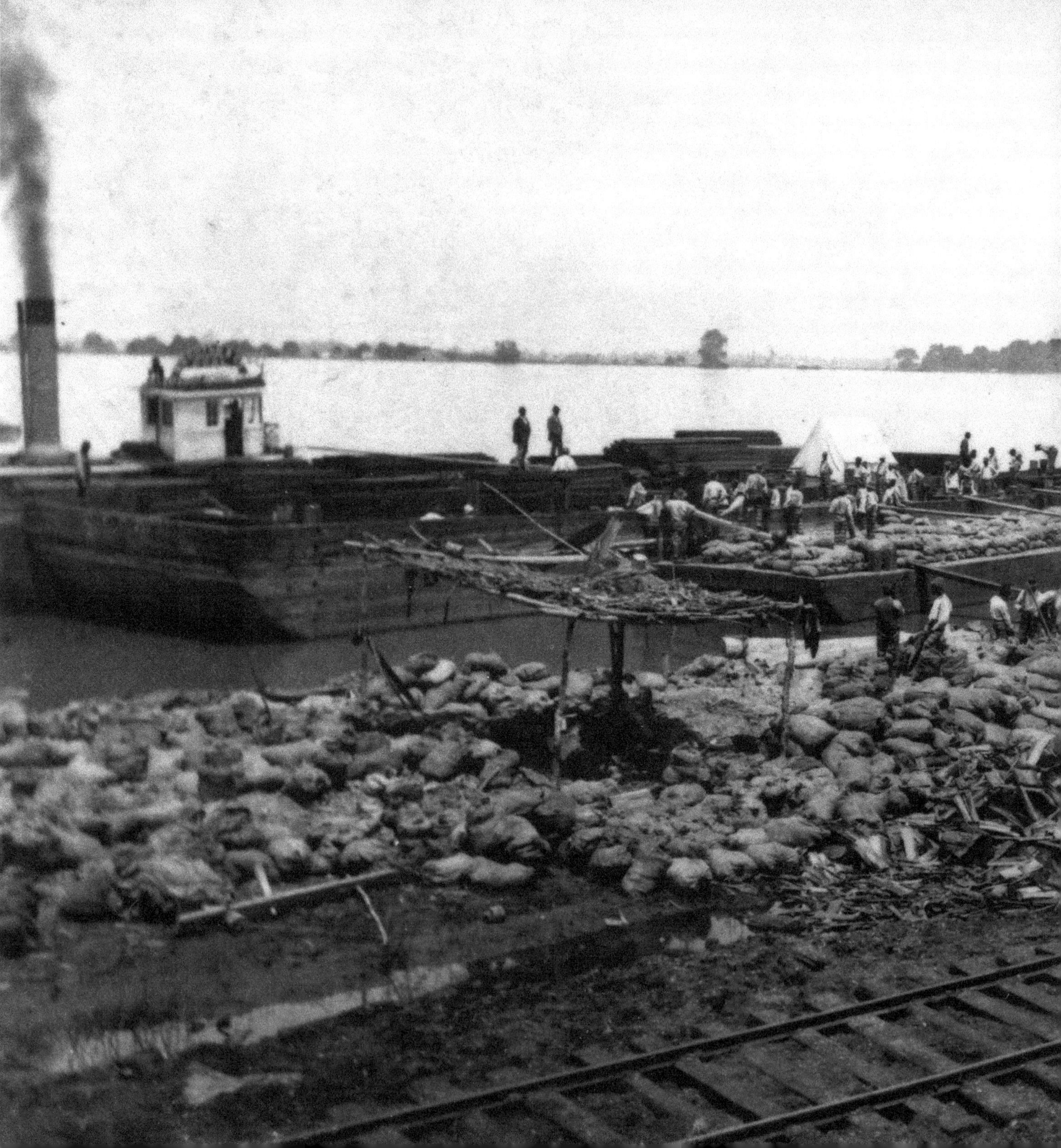

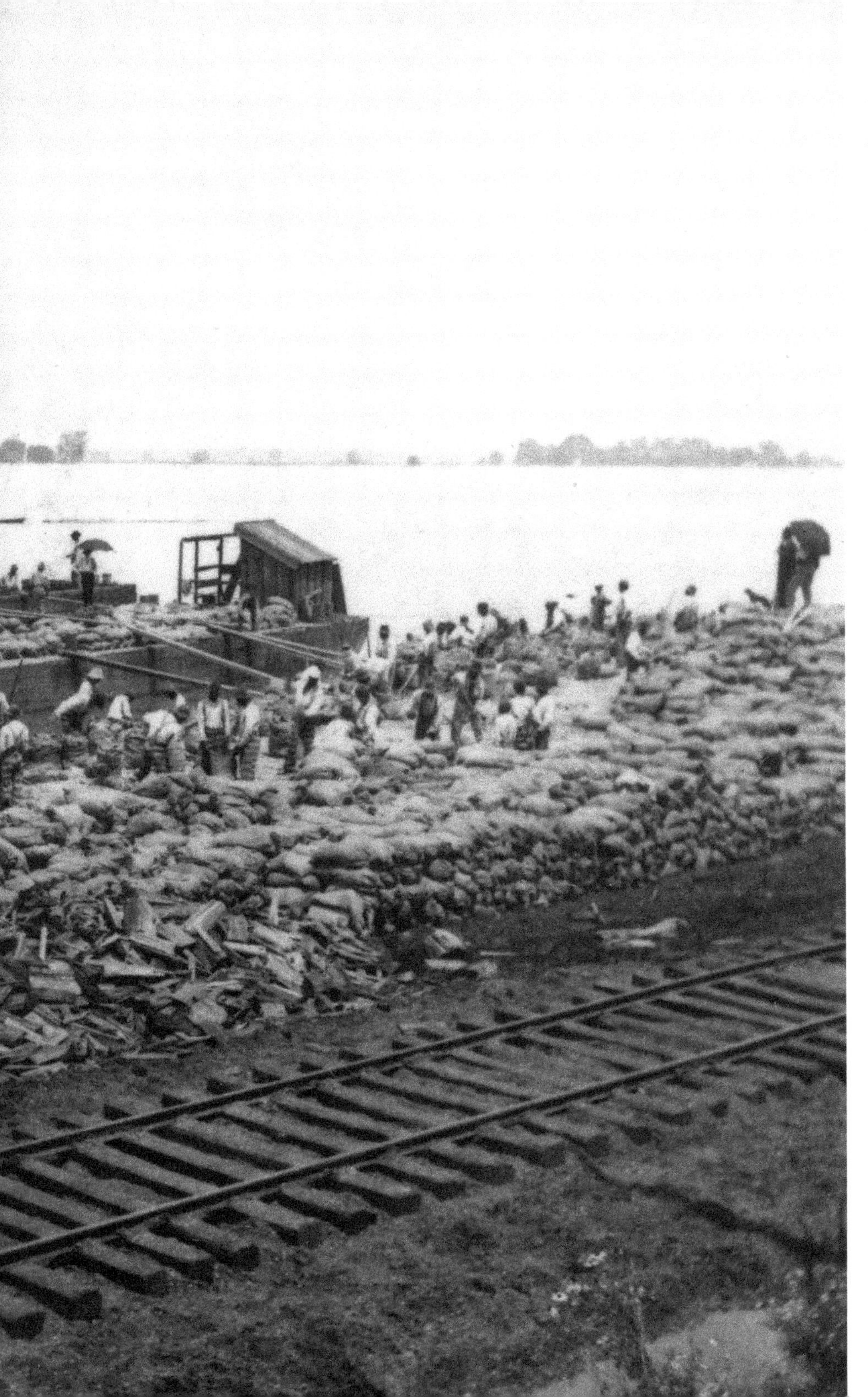

Using state penitentiary inmates to lay sandbags during flood events was a common practice in Baton Rouge. In this scene from 1915 or 1917, the flood was attacked from both land and water.

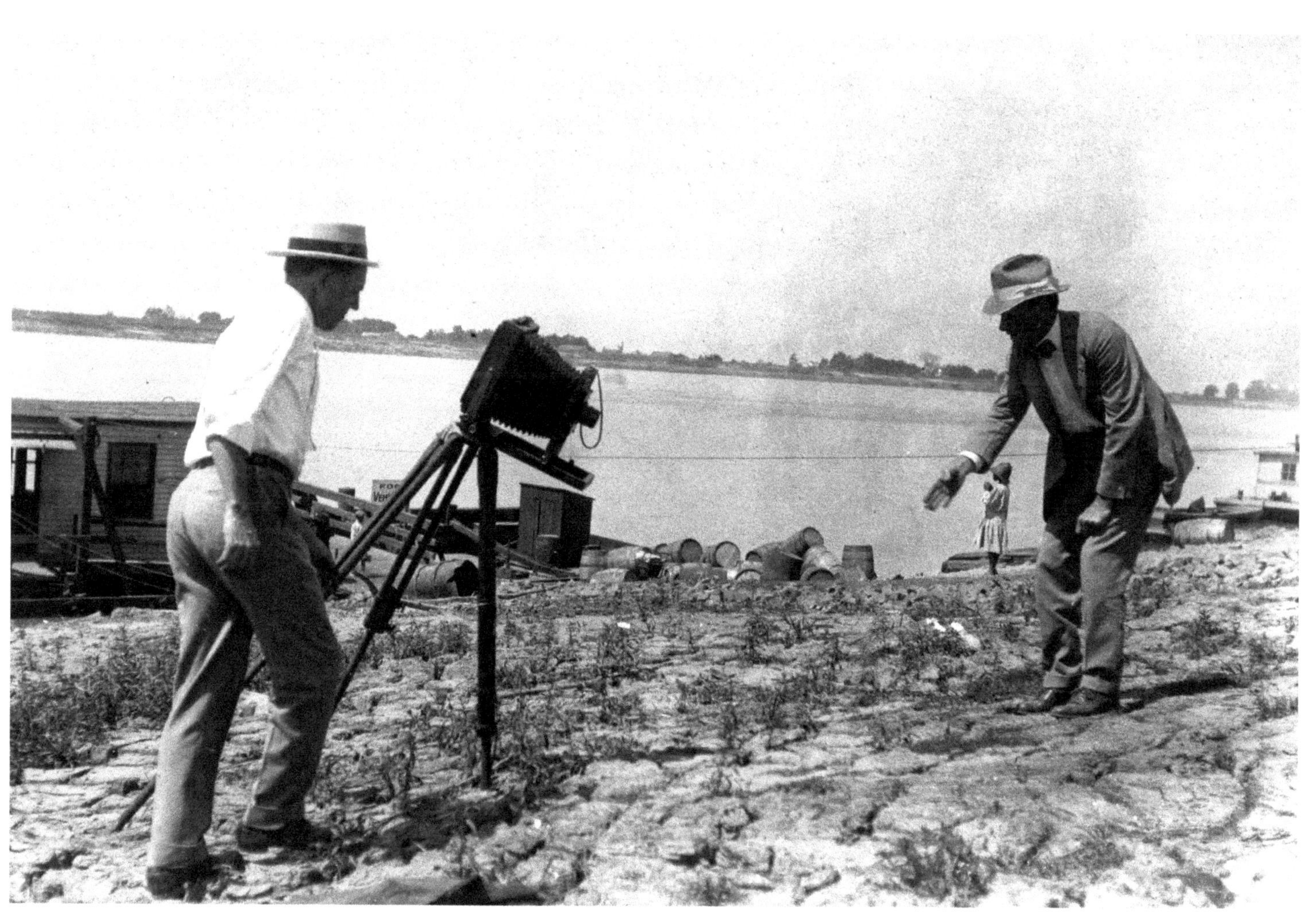

Photographer Jasper Ewing, at left, started his Baton Rouge studio in 1912, four years before this scene of him photographing cracks in the levee along the Mississippi River.

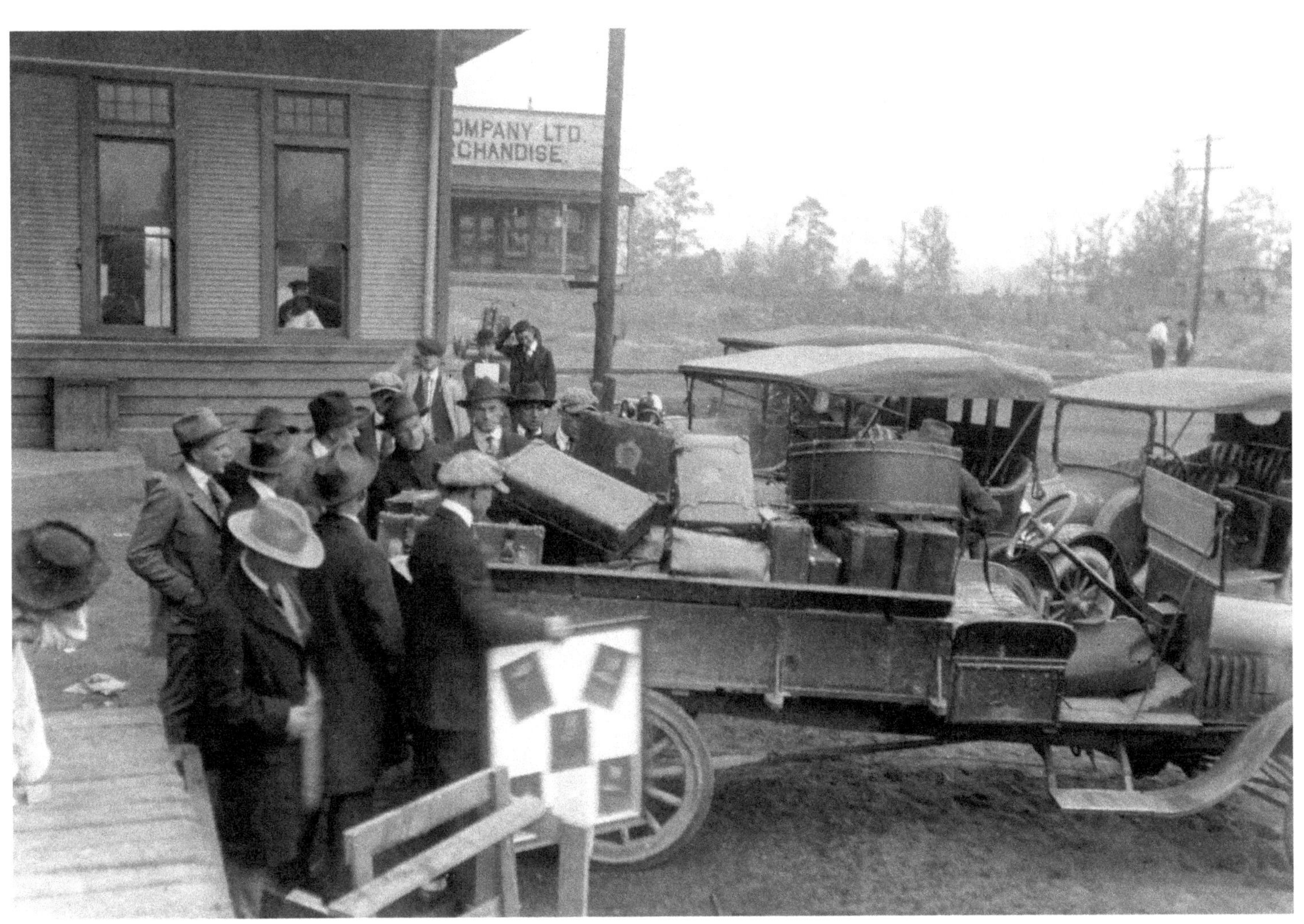

The Louisiana State University Men's Glee Club loads baggage into a truck at the train station in Baton Rouge in either 1916 or 1917. They had been in Lafayette for an event of some kind.

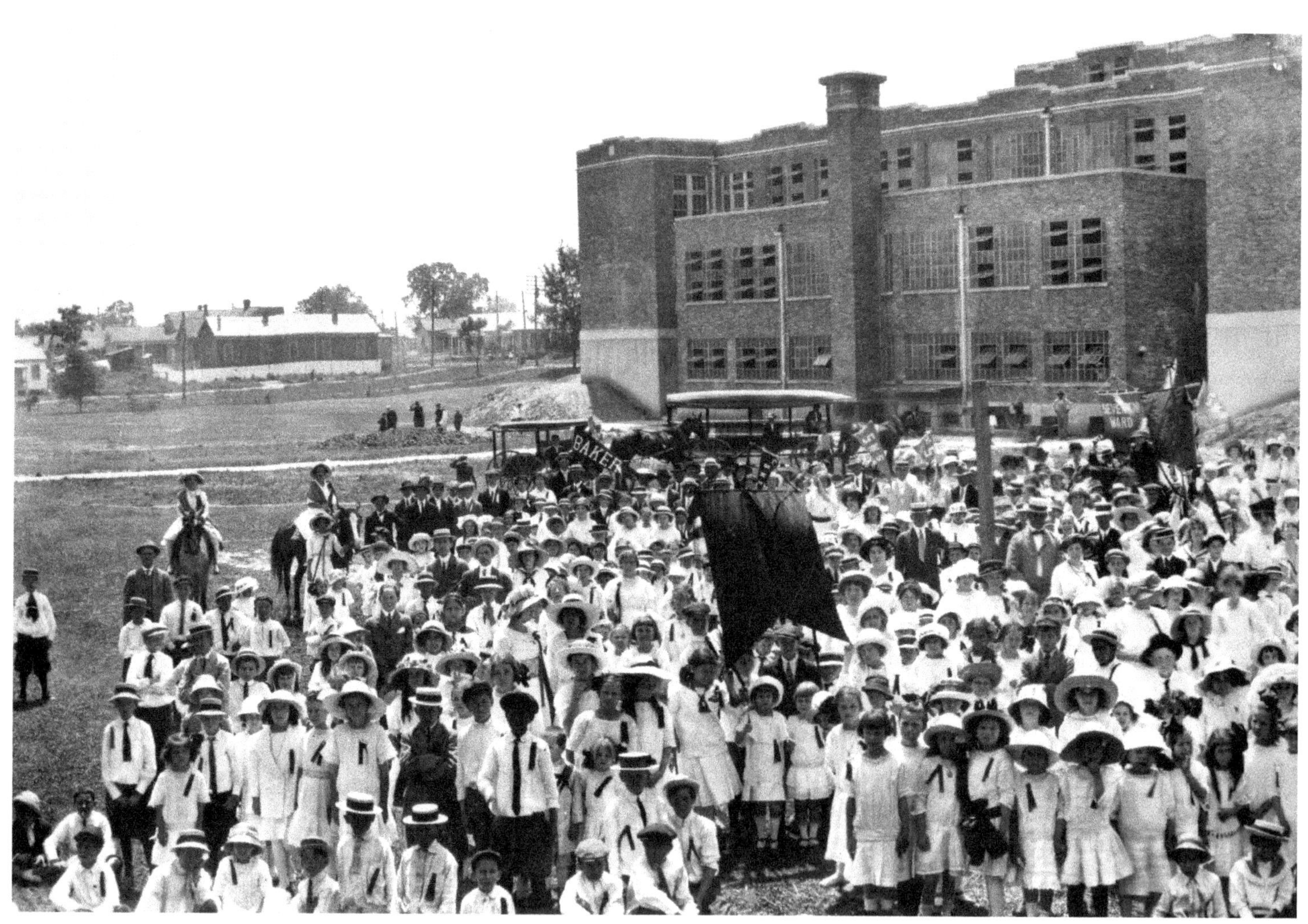

This gathering of schoolchildren, around 1917, included students from both public and private schools in Baton Rouge.

During the Mississippi River flood of May 1912, workers created a temporary levee to protect the Yazoo & Mississippi Valley Railroad lines running along the riverfront in Baton Rouge.

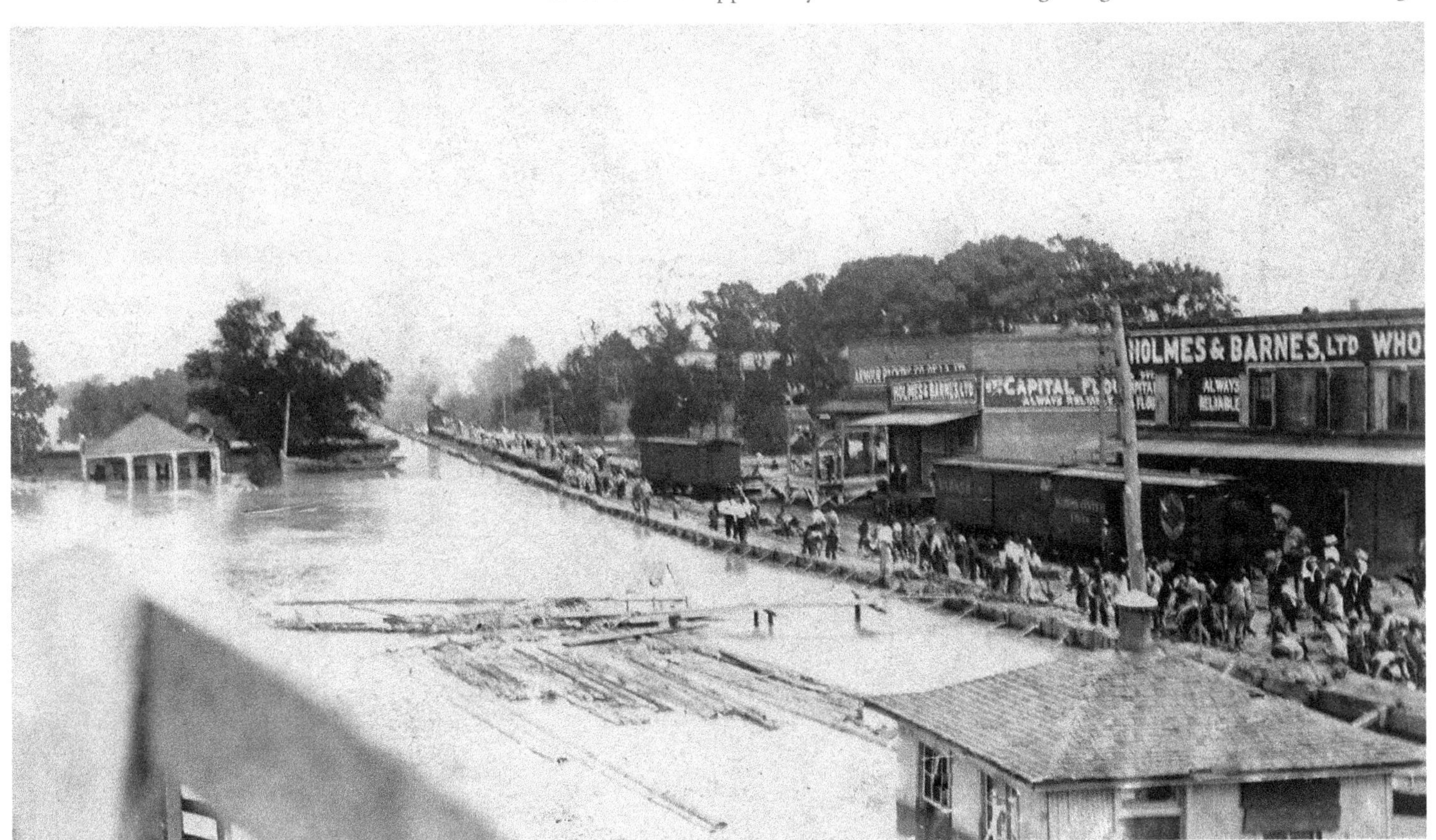

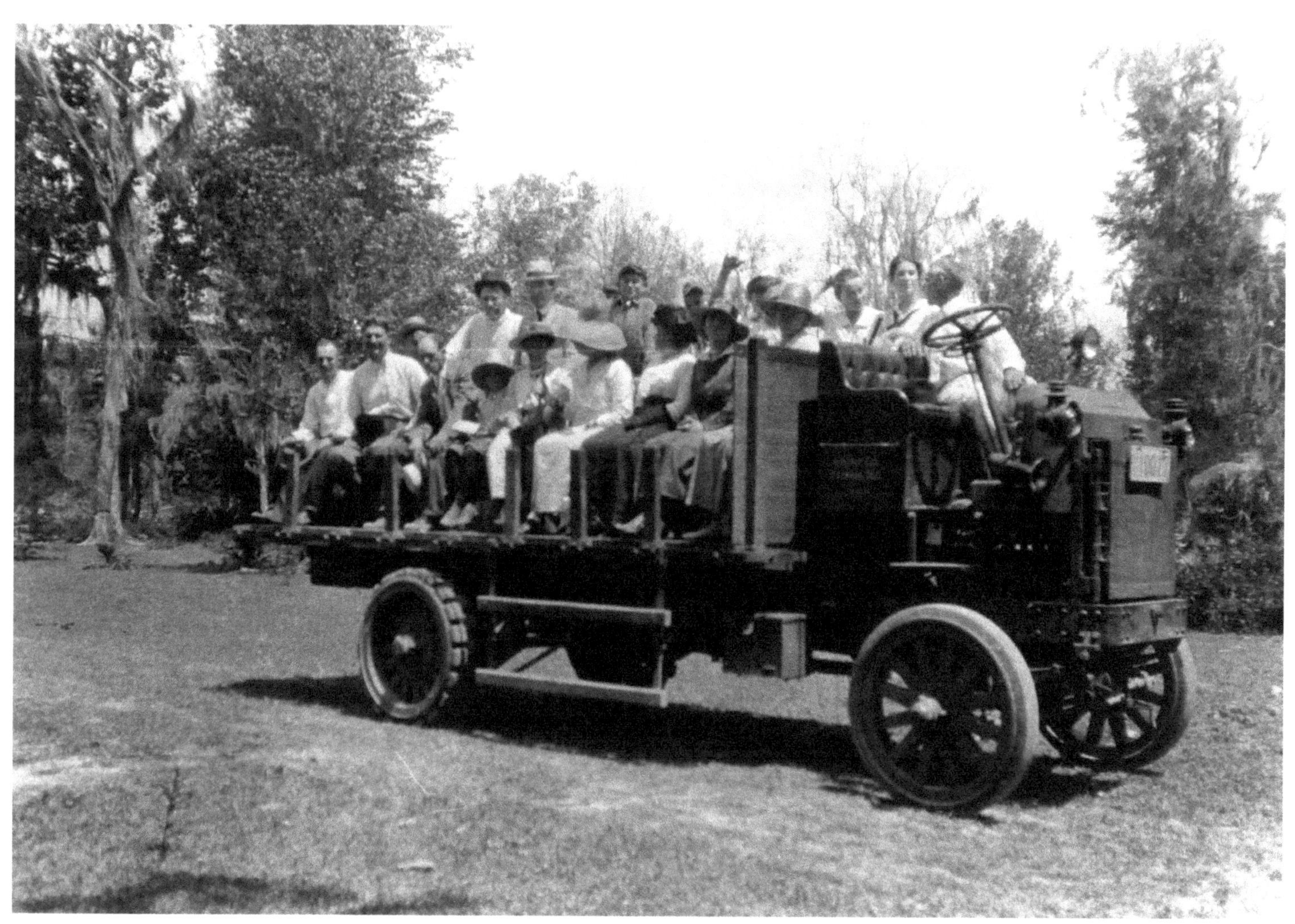

Faculty members from Louisiana State University enjoy a ride to pick blackberries in 1917.

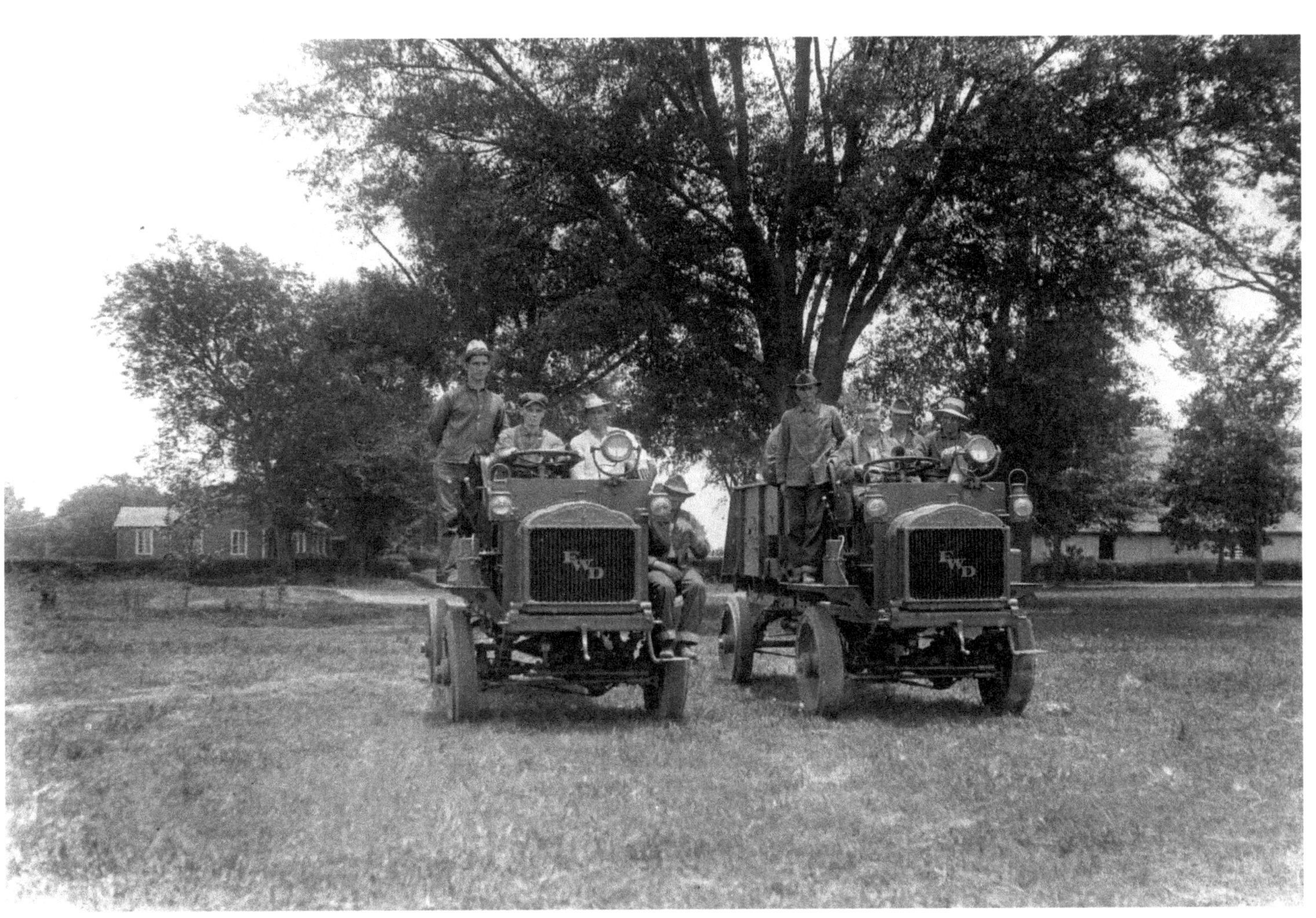

Given Baton Rouge's long history as a military outpost, it is no surprise the area served in that capacity again during World War I. These two vehicles were used as Army ammunition trucks.

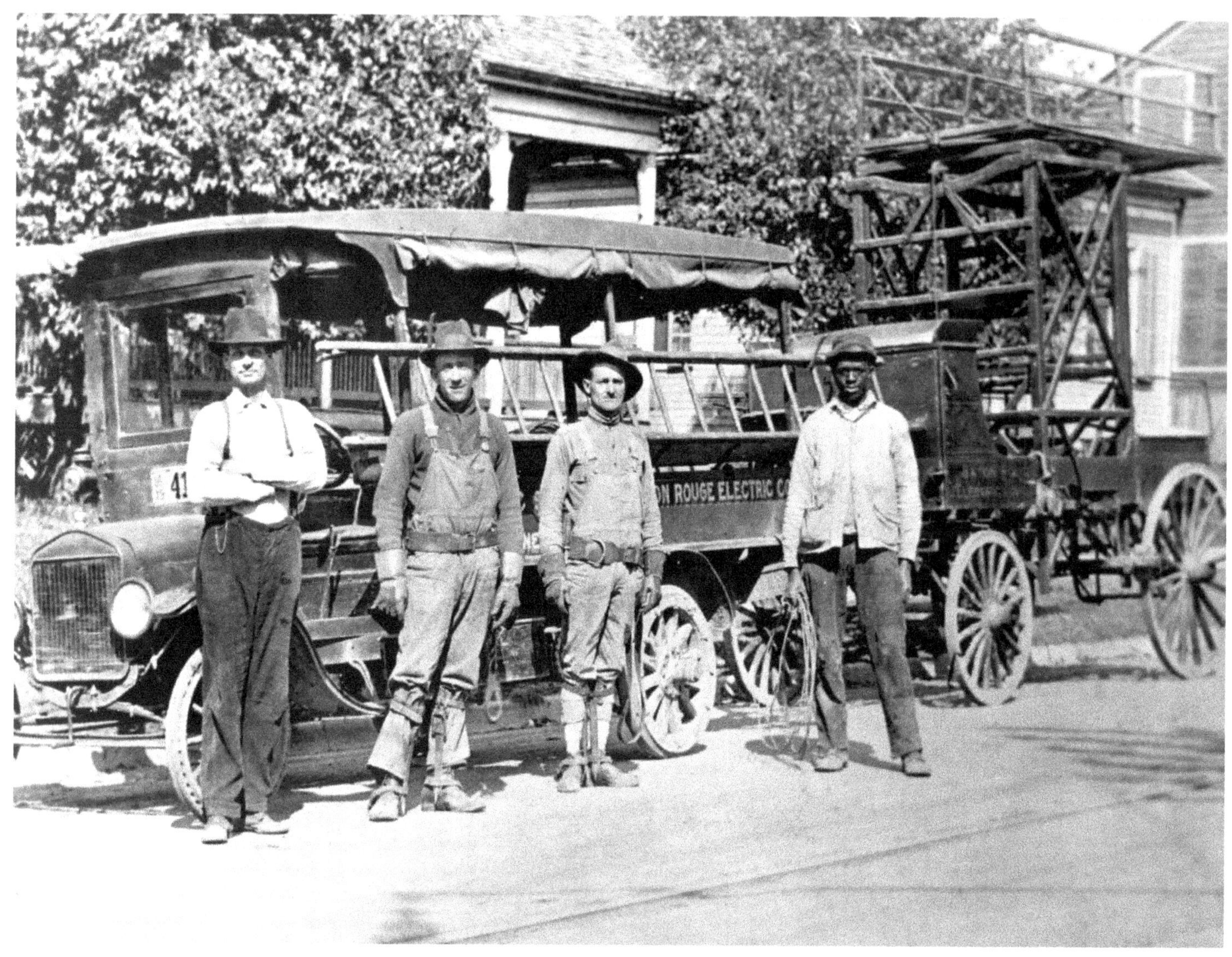

The Baton Rouge Electric Company, established in 1907 following the purchase of the Baton Rouge Electric & Gas Company by Stone & Webster Engineering Corporation, provided service to the Baton Rouge area until the late 1930s when it became part of the Gulf States Utility Company. Repair crew members Cap Denham, Cecil Collins, F. F. "Blondie" Gaines, and Lee Brown pose by their truck around 1918.

A New Campus and a Terrible Flood

(1920–1929)

Baton Rouge enjoyed moderate growth following the arrival of Standard Oil. Petroleum proved an economically stabilizing element for the city of Baton Rouge and East Baton Rouge Parish. Crime remained uncommon, the courts were relatively quiet and largely unused, and the public school system continued to expand and improve for both white and black citizens. Improvements to the city's waterworks and sanitary sewer system curtailed the worst sort of disease outbreaks that had been all too common throughout the previous century.

The biggest disturber of local tranquility proved to be an up-and-coming politician from Winn Parish in rural north Louisiana. Huey Pierce Long entered the political scene in 1918, serving on the state railroad commission. As a commissioner, he fought for the poorer citizens in their conflicts with utility companies, the railroads, and Standard Oil, none of which made him popular in Baton Rouge. In 1924 he ran for governor and lost. Four years later he ran for governor and won. In 1929, after he'd been a year in office, the state legislature tried but failed to impeach Long. Until his assassination in 1935, the local population always had something to talk about and often react against in the form of the radical, populist actions taken by Long.

The year Long lost his bid for governor, LSU moved from its campus downtown to a wholly new campus south of downtown. Southern University expanded its course-offering to include four-year degrees. Under the supervision of Southern University, the State School for the Blind and Deaf for Blacks became two schools: the School for the Blind and the School for the Deaf.

In 1927 the Mississippi River flooded catastrophically. As a misguided strategy to prevent the destruction of New Orleans, levees were dynamited upstream in areas populated largely by poor black sharecroppers. These acts displaced thousands of citizens, destroyed countless lives, and ultimately led to expansion of the levee system.

As the decade closed, the national economy suffered the hammer blow of the Great Depression. Baton Rouge fared better than most cities in the nation, in part due to Standard Oil and its recession-proof qualities; the refinery remained open, so local employees remained at work. However, of the five banks in town, only one survived intact.

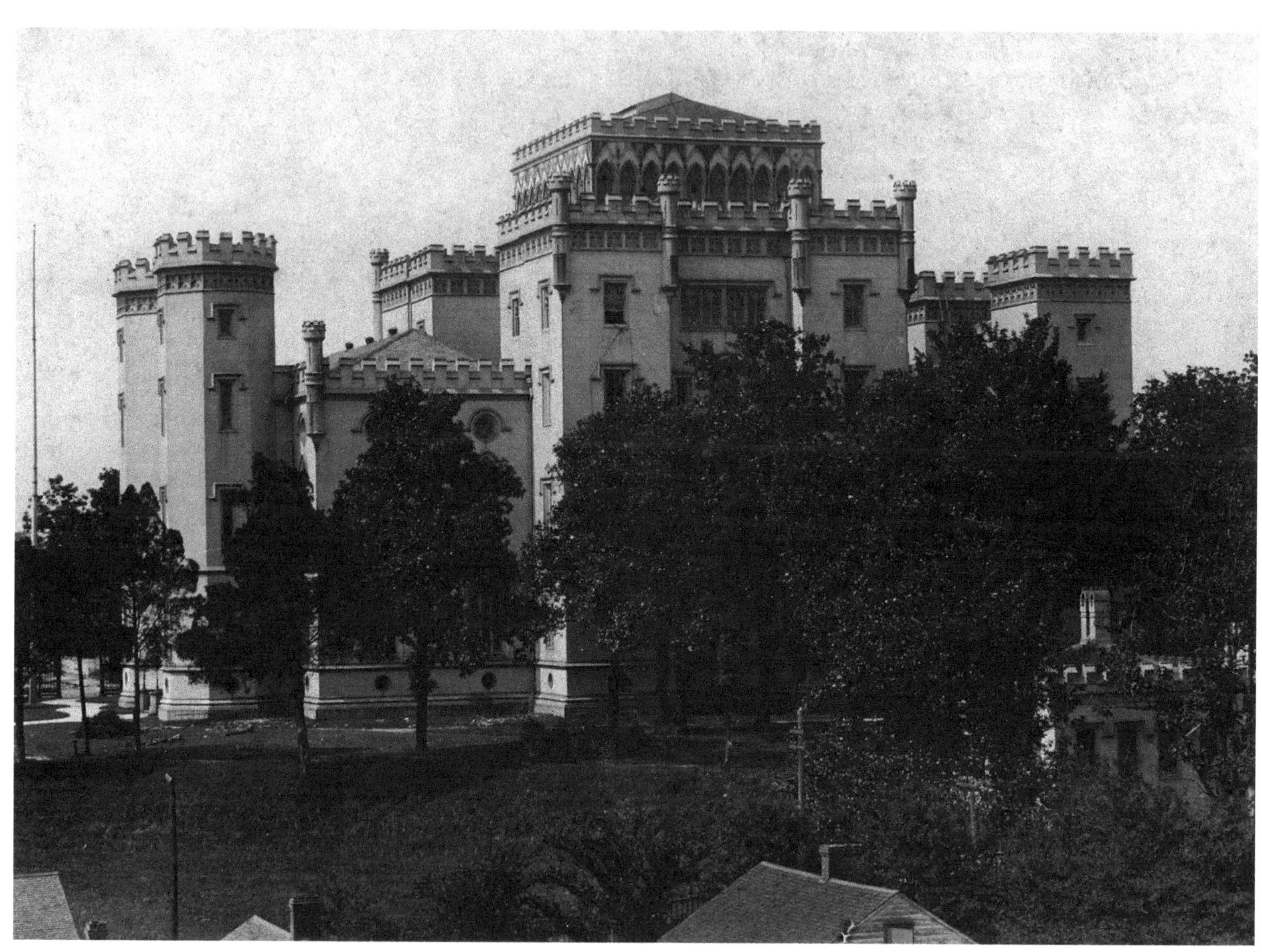

The capitol served as an anchor for the Beauregard Town neighborhood. Originally laid out in 1809, Beauregard Town was intended to be the center of state government, though that plan was never realized. Sited on the northwest corner of the district, the capitol stood surrounded on its east and south sides by the homes of Beauregard Town residents, as this view of the east facade around 1920 shows.

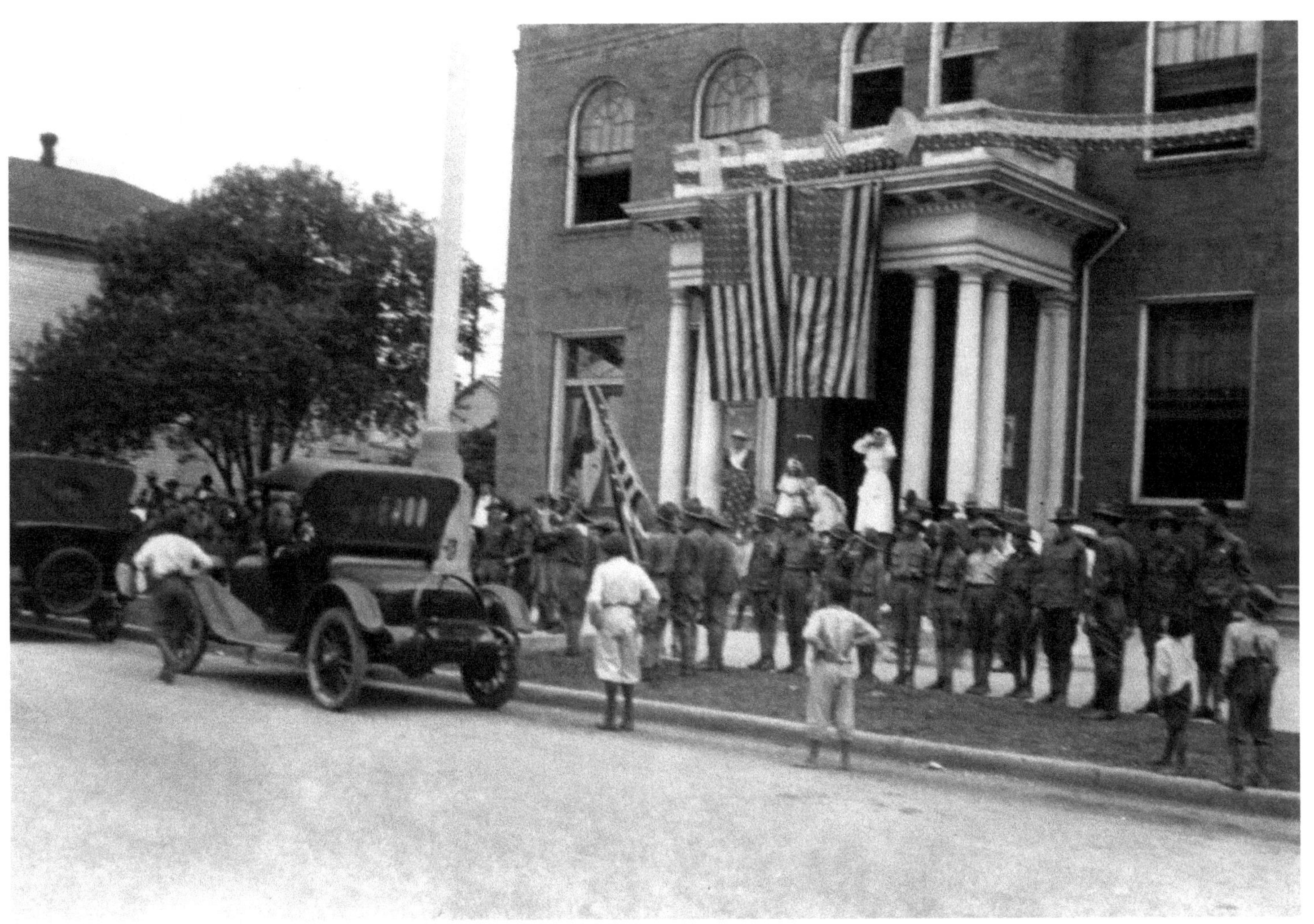

A Boy Scout troop stands in formation outside the front of Baton Rouge City Hall around 1920.

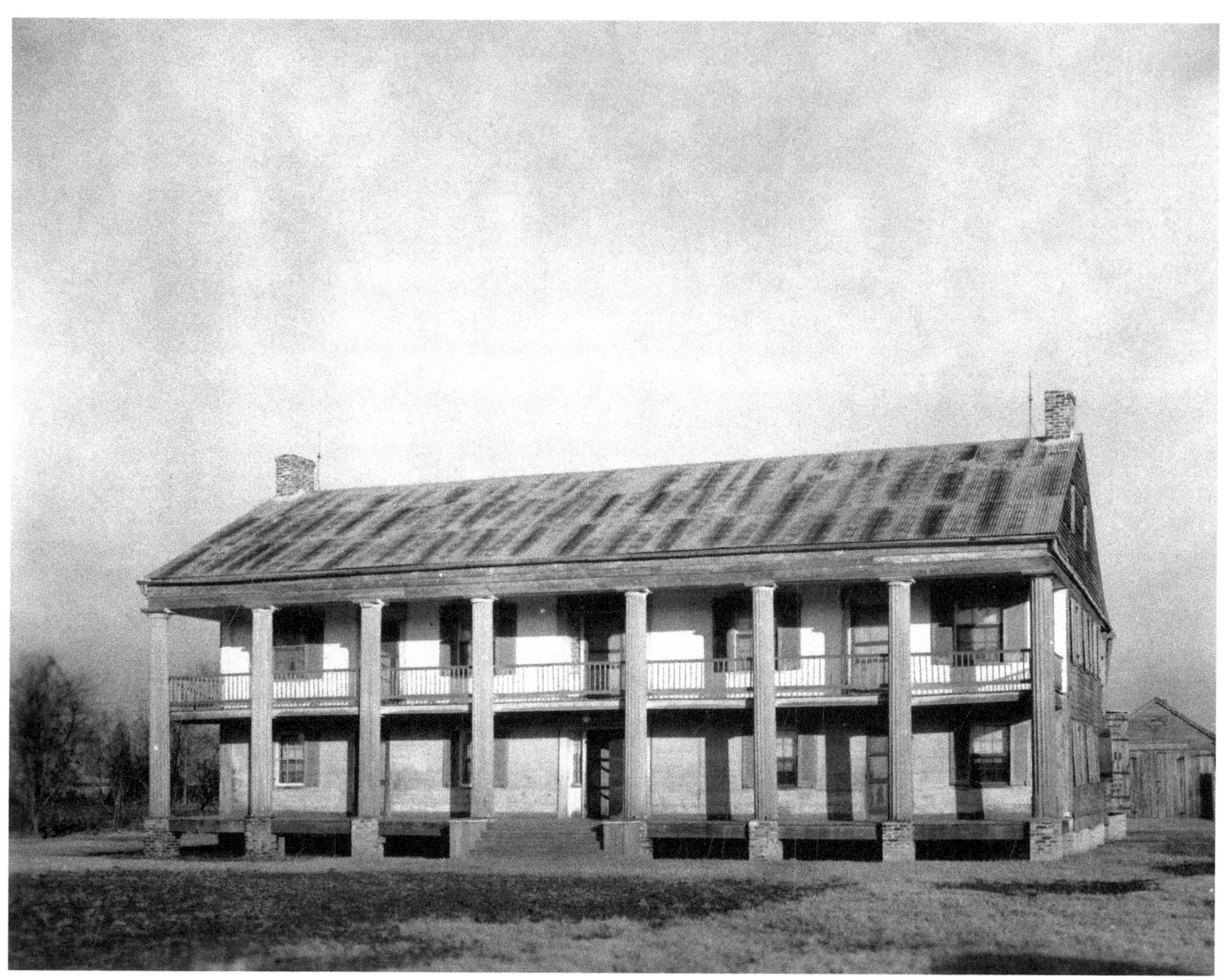

As Louisiana developed over the centuries, the Mississippi River, its tributaries, and its distributaries provided the surest access to the interior. The rich deltaic soils, built up over the centuries by regular flooding, proved rich and profitable to plantation owners, who would construct large homes for their families. Over time, with shifting fortunes, these homes often fell into disrepair. The Becnel Place plantation home, seen here around 1925, is one such example.

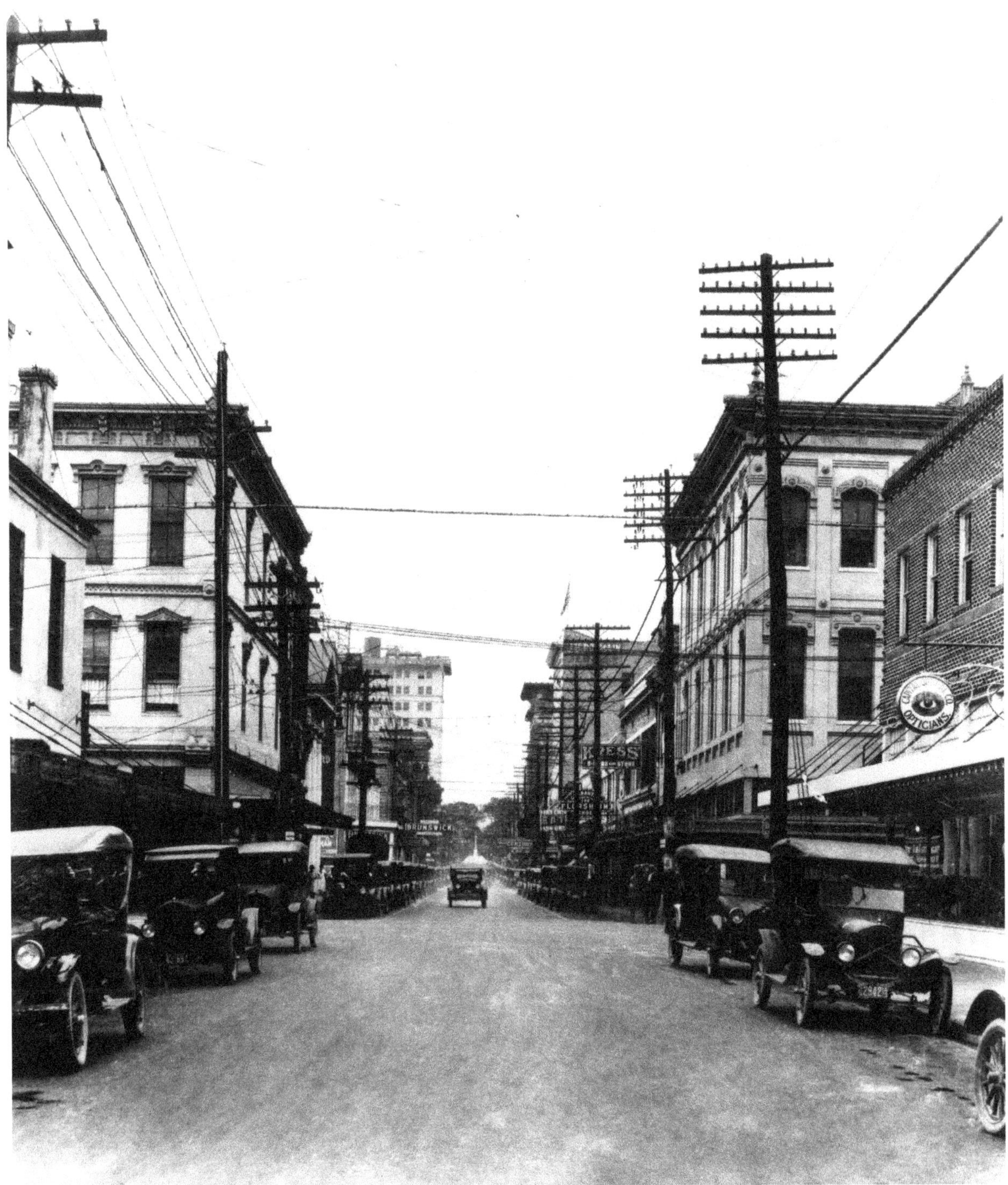

As Baton Rouge experienced tremendous growth in the early twentieth century, Third Street became the center of activity, with businesses, a movie theater, banks, and many other attractions. Looking south on Third from the intersection with Main, this view, about 1925, shows the sign for Capital Optical Company, 511 Third, on the right. Further down the street is the S. H. Kress store at 439 Third.

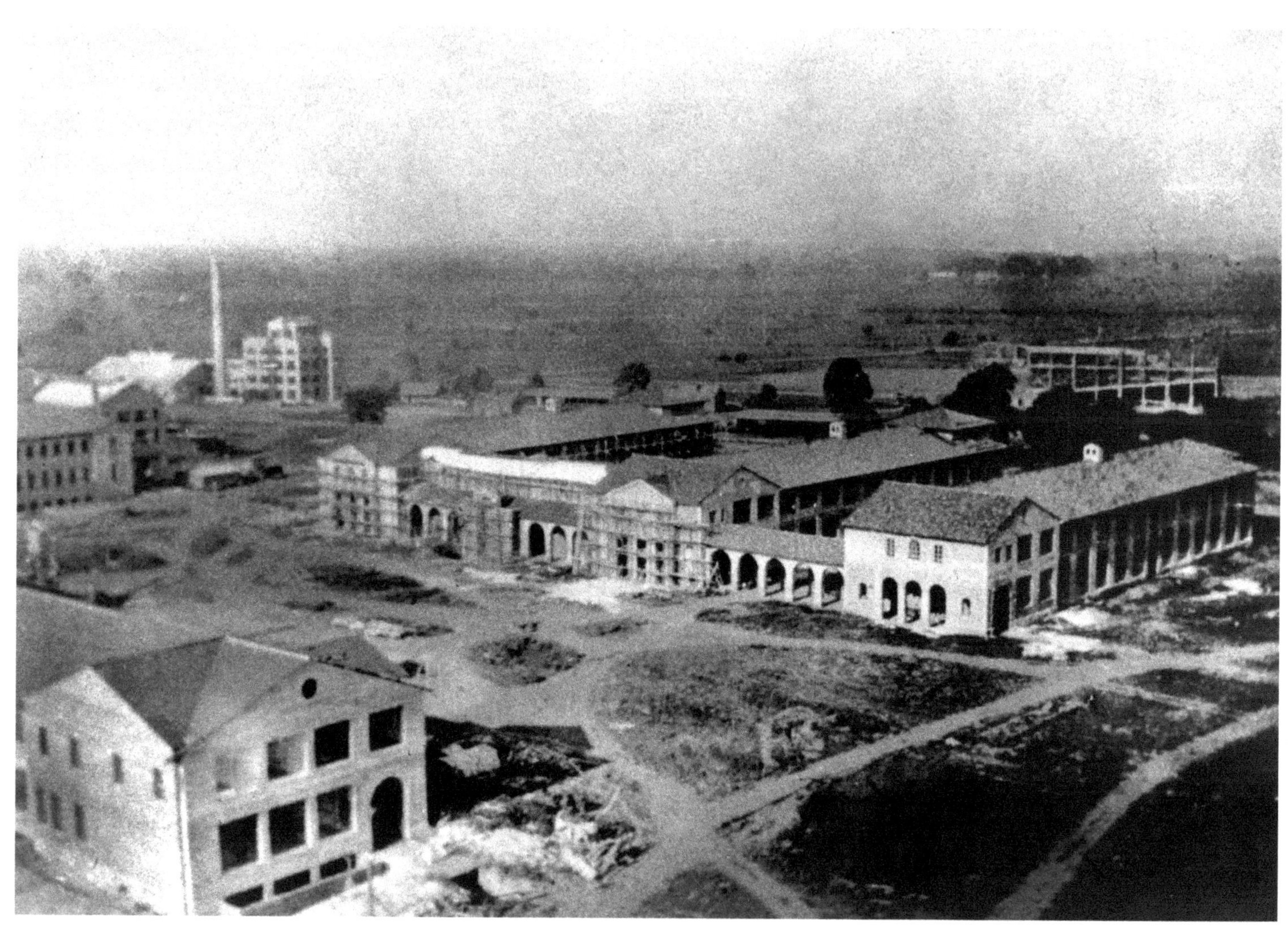

Part of Baton Rouge's growth involved building a new campus for Louisiana State University south of town. In this view, created around 1925, the quadrangle is taking shape. In the left foreground stands Himes Hall. Across the quad are Prescott Hall, Stubbs Hall, Dodson Auditorium, and Audubon Hall.

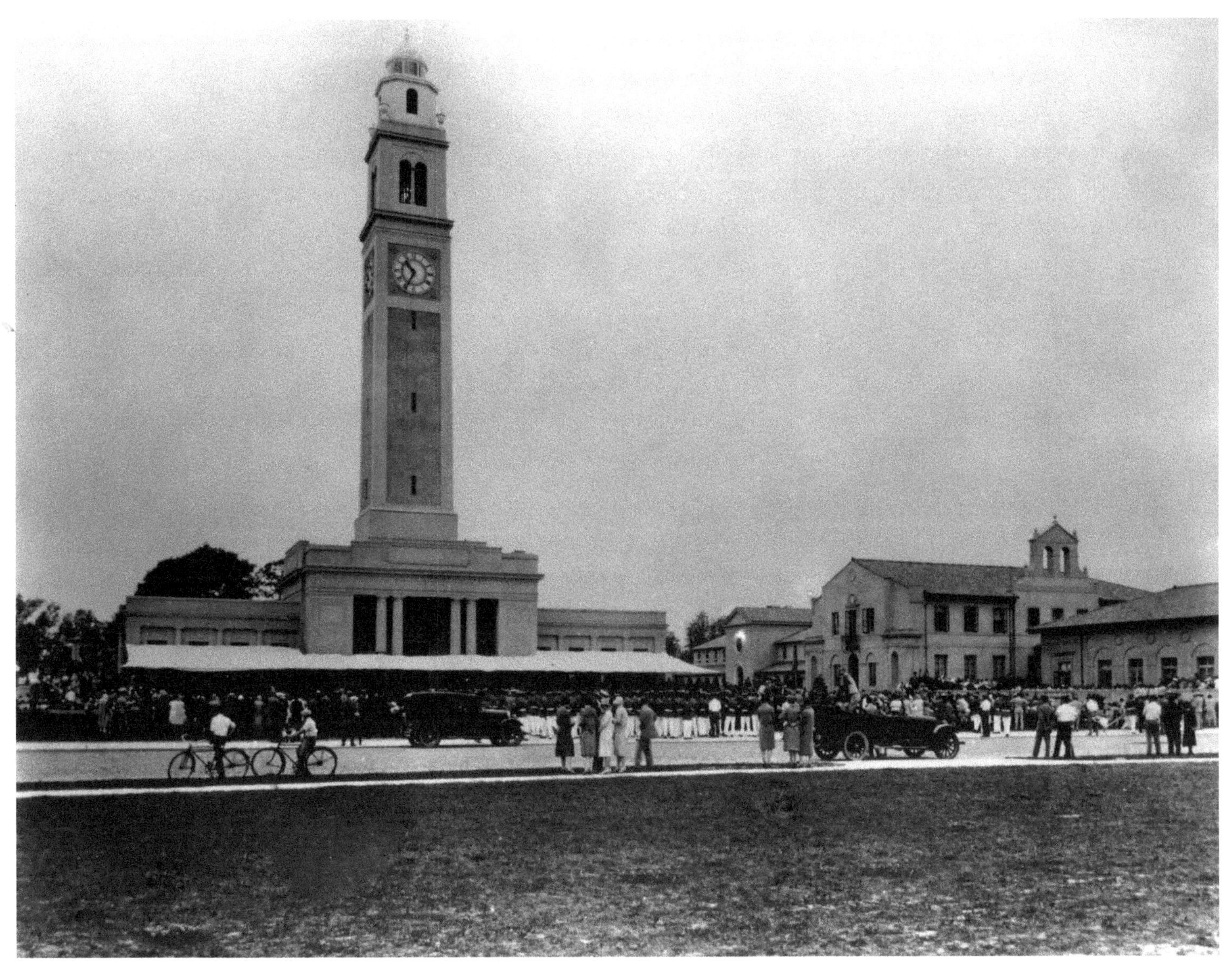

Jasper Ewing took this photograph of the dedication ceremony for LSU's new campus in 1926. The Memorial Tower, commemorating the university's military dead, stands to the left. Boyd Hall can be seen on the right.

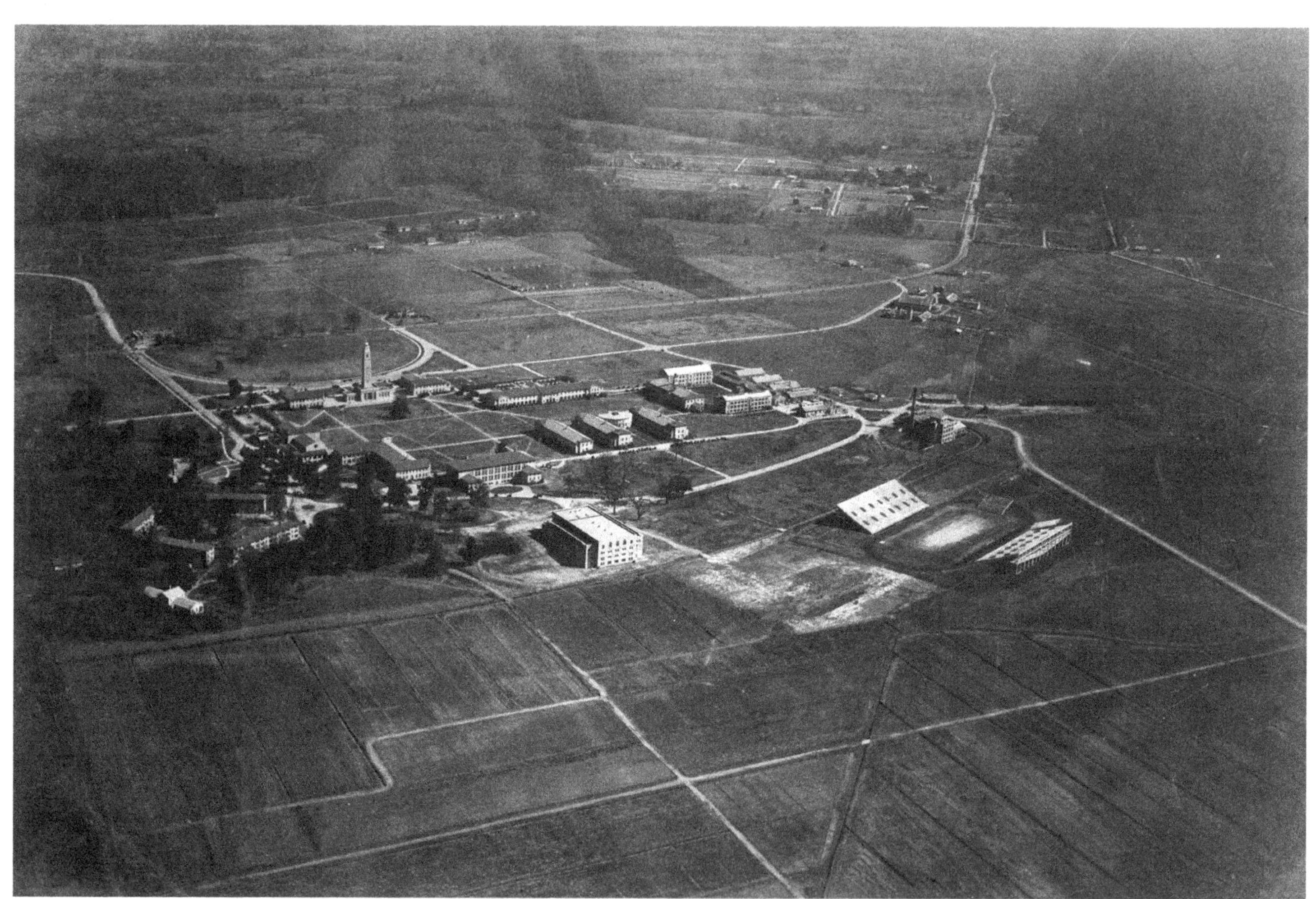

When Louisiana State University moved to its new site south of Baton Rouge, one of the structures included in the first phase of construction was the football stadium. In this phase, completed in 1924, only the east and west stands were finished. Initially seating around 12,000, Tiger Stadium would expand over the years. This aerial photo of the campus provides an excellent overview of the original layout and design.

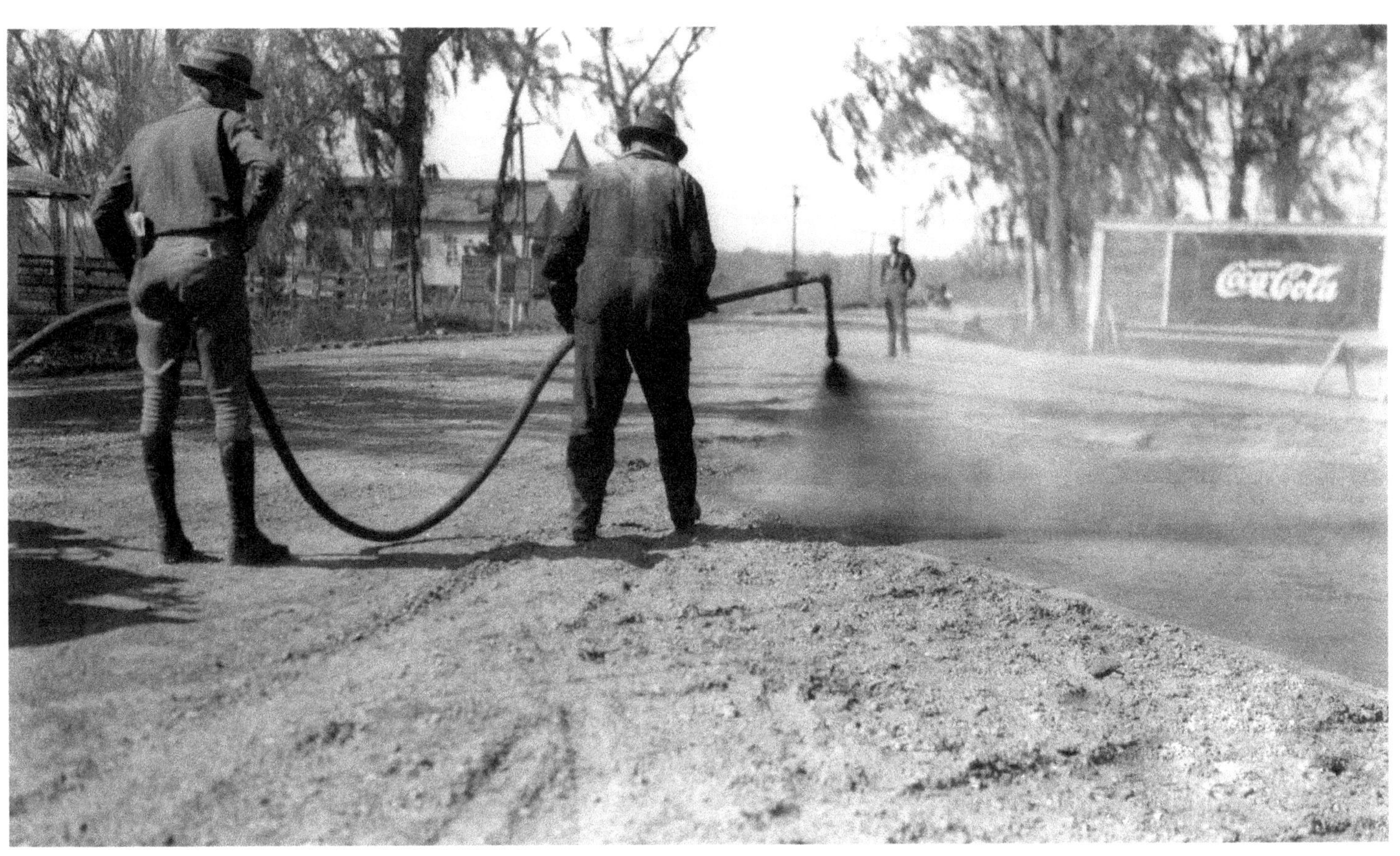

Louisiana had very few paved roads in the middle 1920s. This scene from February 1926 shows one step in the paving process, tarring the dirt road surface.

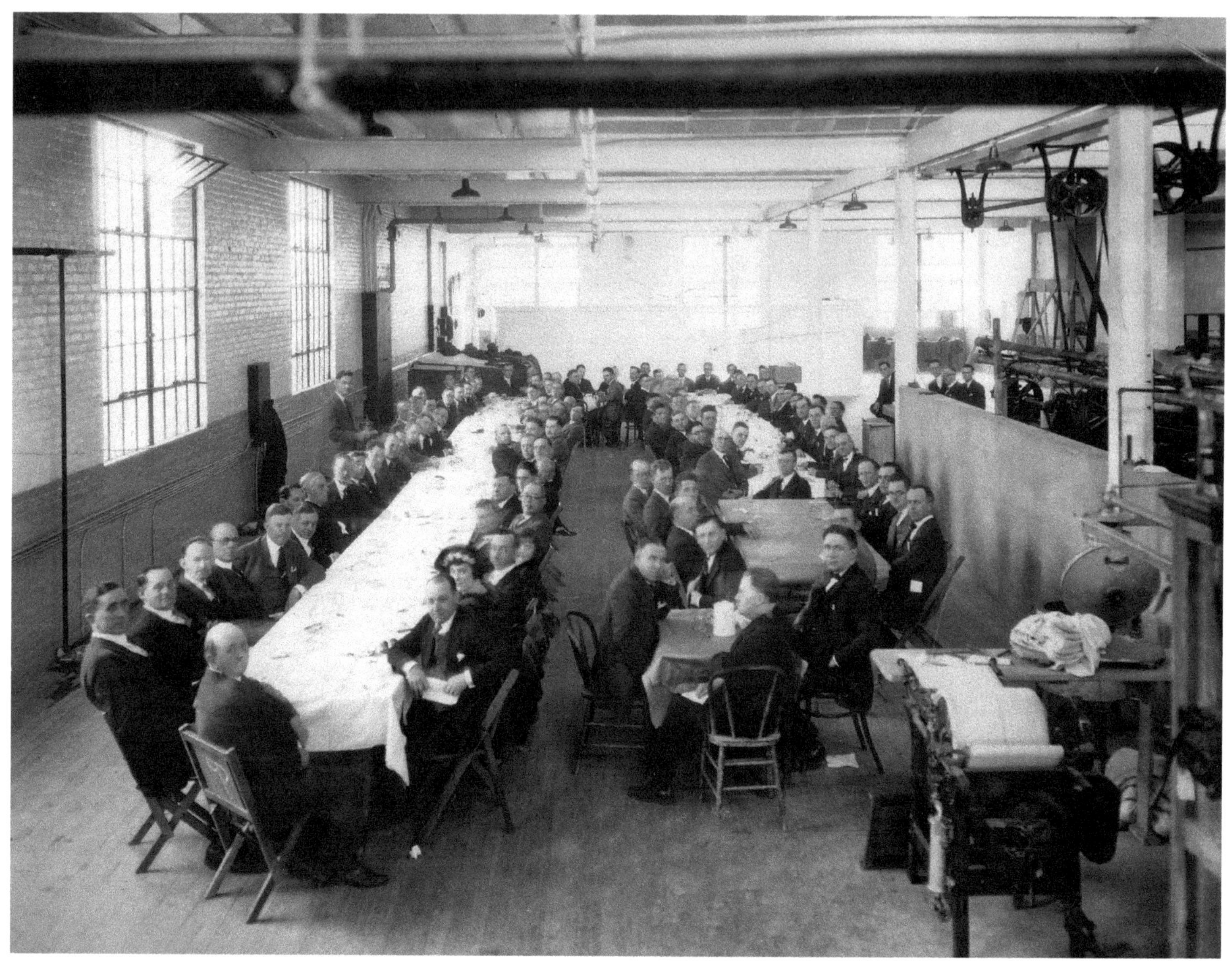

The Rotary Club of Baton Rouge, founded on October 1, 1918, and the Kiwanis Club, founded on April 24, 1919, held a joint meeting January 21, 1925, at the Southern Steam Laundry, 216 Third Street, owned and operated by brothers, J. Selby and Frank H. Kean.

In September 1927, construction of the Heidelberg Hotel was drawing to a close at the corner of Lafayette and Convention streets, overlooking the Mississippi River. The hotel basement holds a "secret" entrance to a tunnel running under the street. Huey P. Long was rumored to have used this tunnel to sneak in and out of the Heidelberg unseen.

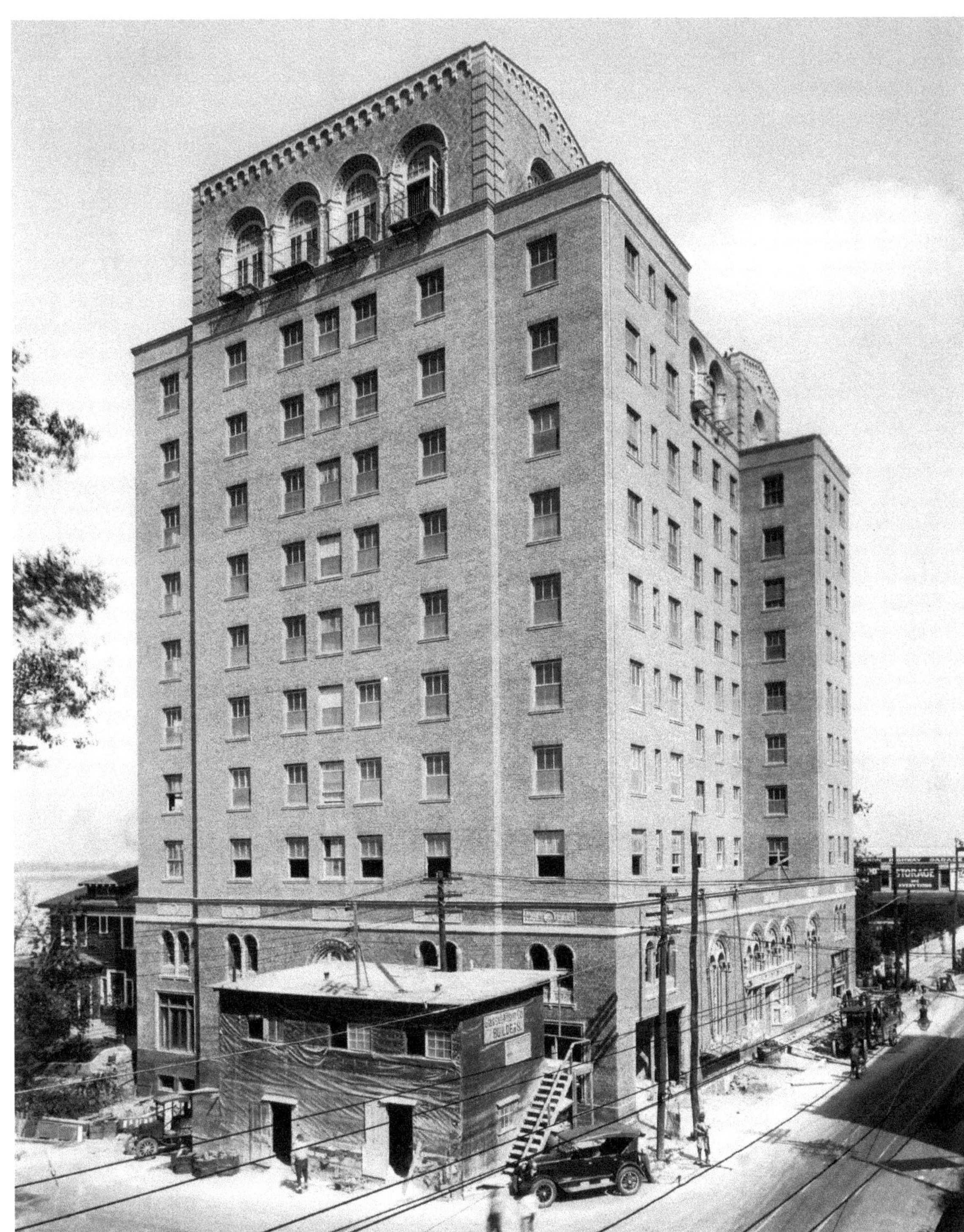

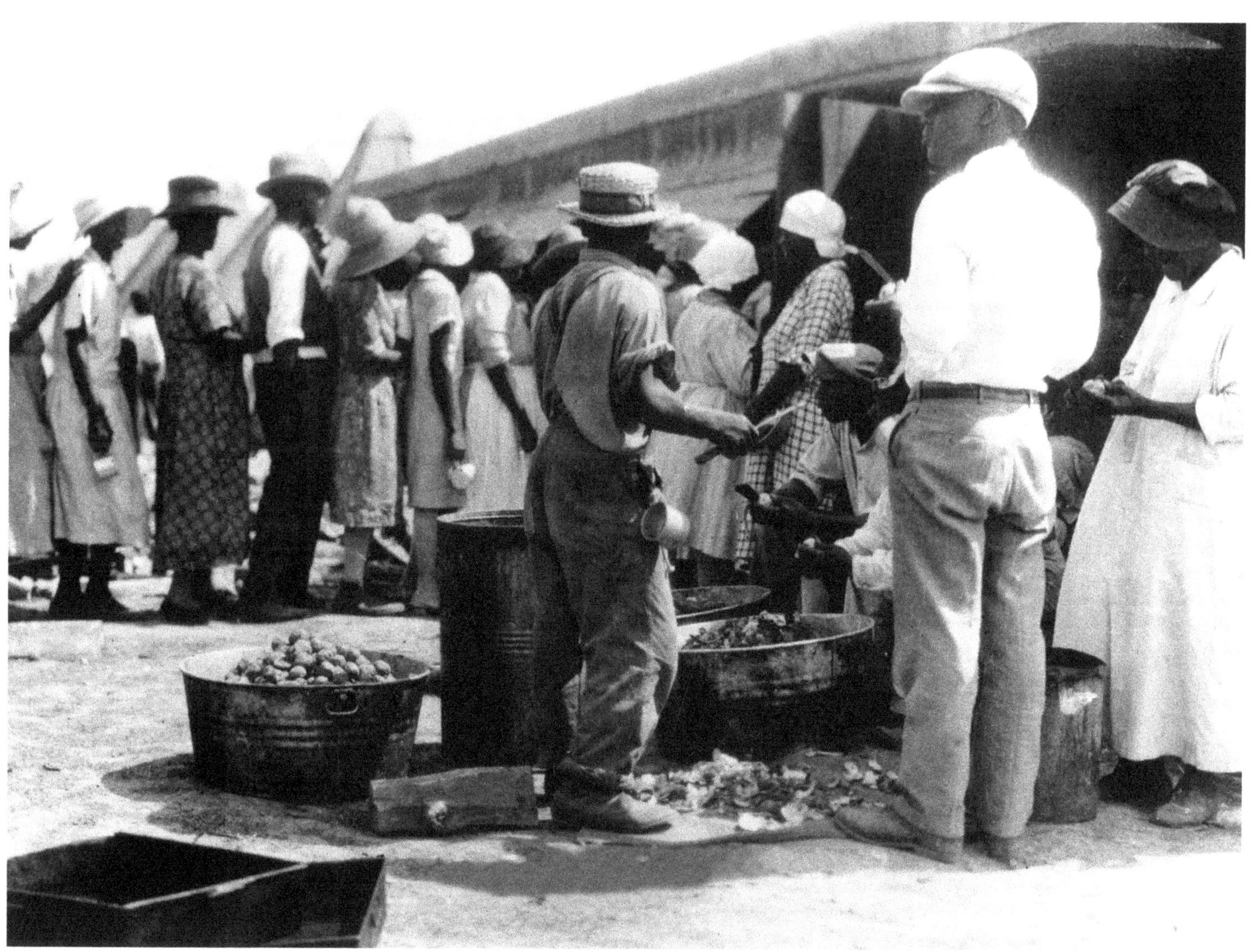

The Mississippi River flood of 1927 had a huge and devastating impact on the people living along the river and for miles inland. African Americans, in particular, suffered, especially after the levees were dynamited upriver of New Orleans in an effort to protect that city. In this scene, food is distributed at a refugee camp near Baton Rouge.

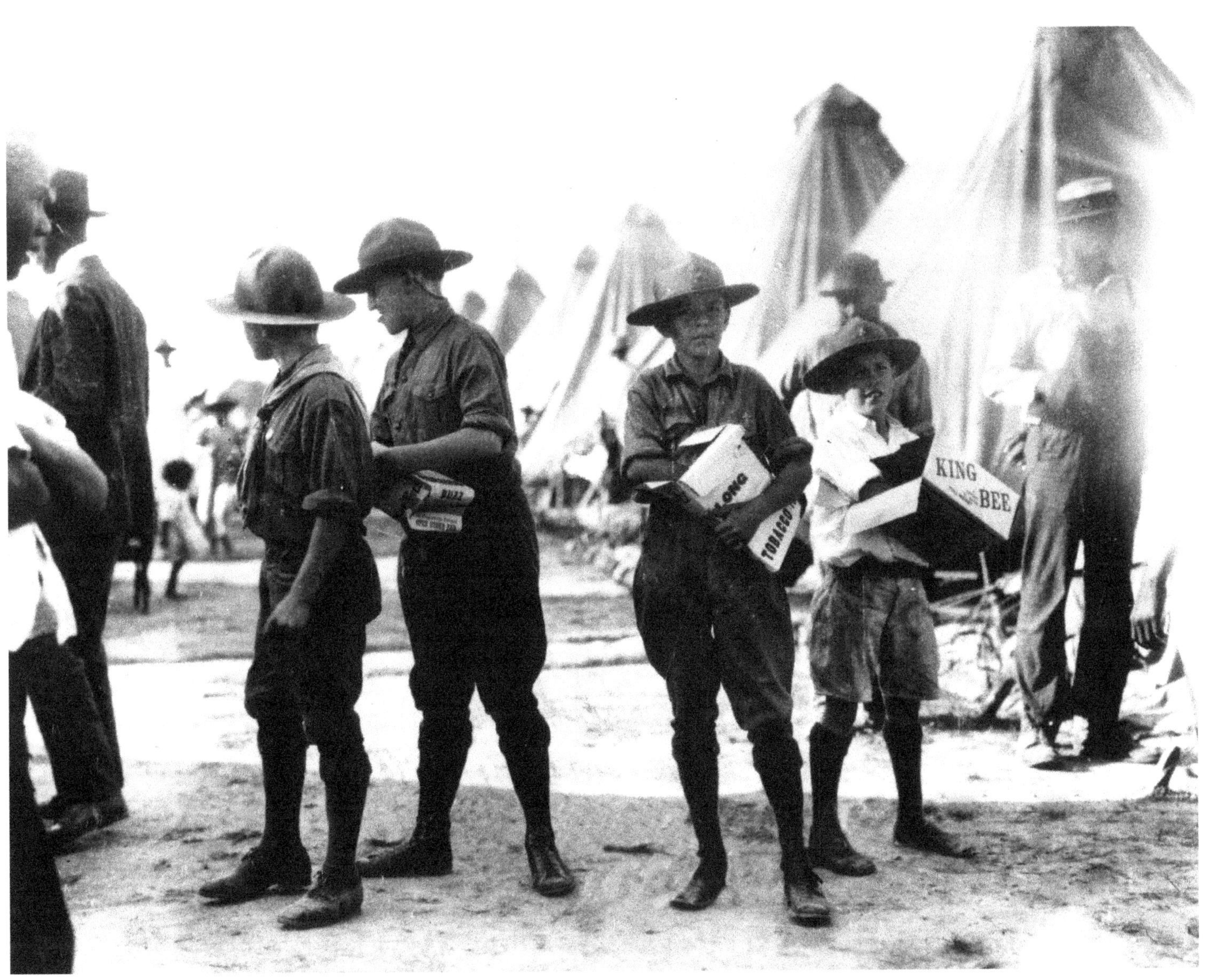

The widespread devastation caused by the flood of 1927 mobilized all manner of people to assist in the refugee camps. In this image, Boy Scouts help with distribution of tobacco at a camp near Baton Rouge.

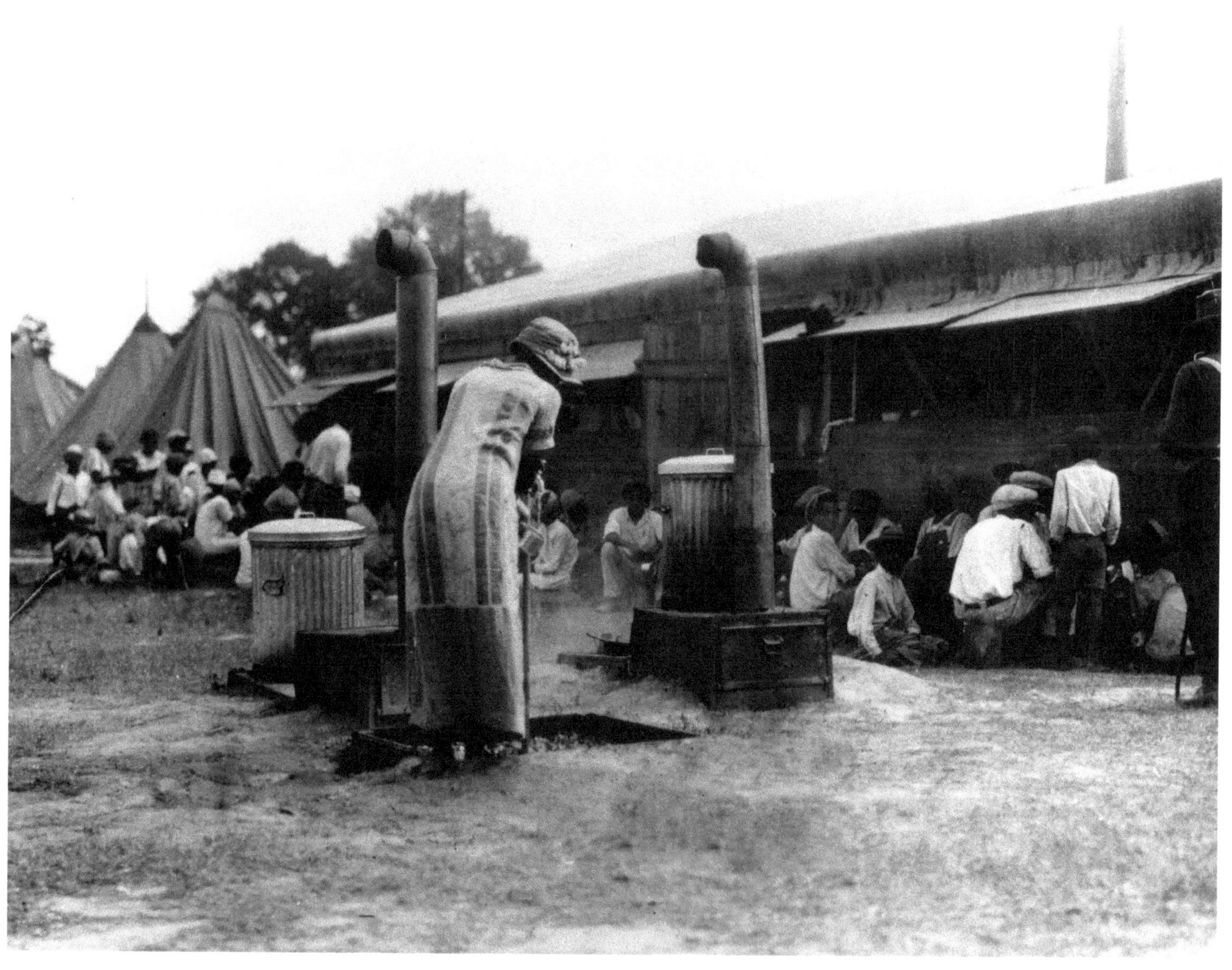

Conditions were harsh in the refugee camps filled with African Americans displaced by the Mississippi River flood of 1927. Photographer Jasper Ewing documented this cooking facility in the camp on Jackson Road north of Baton Rouge.

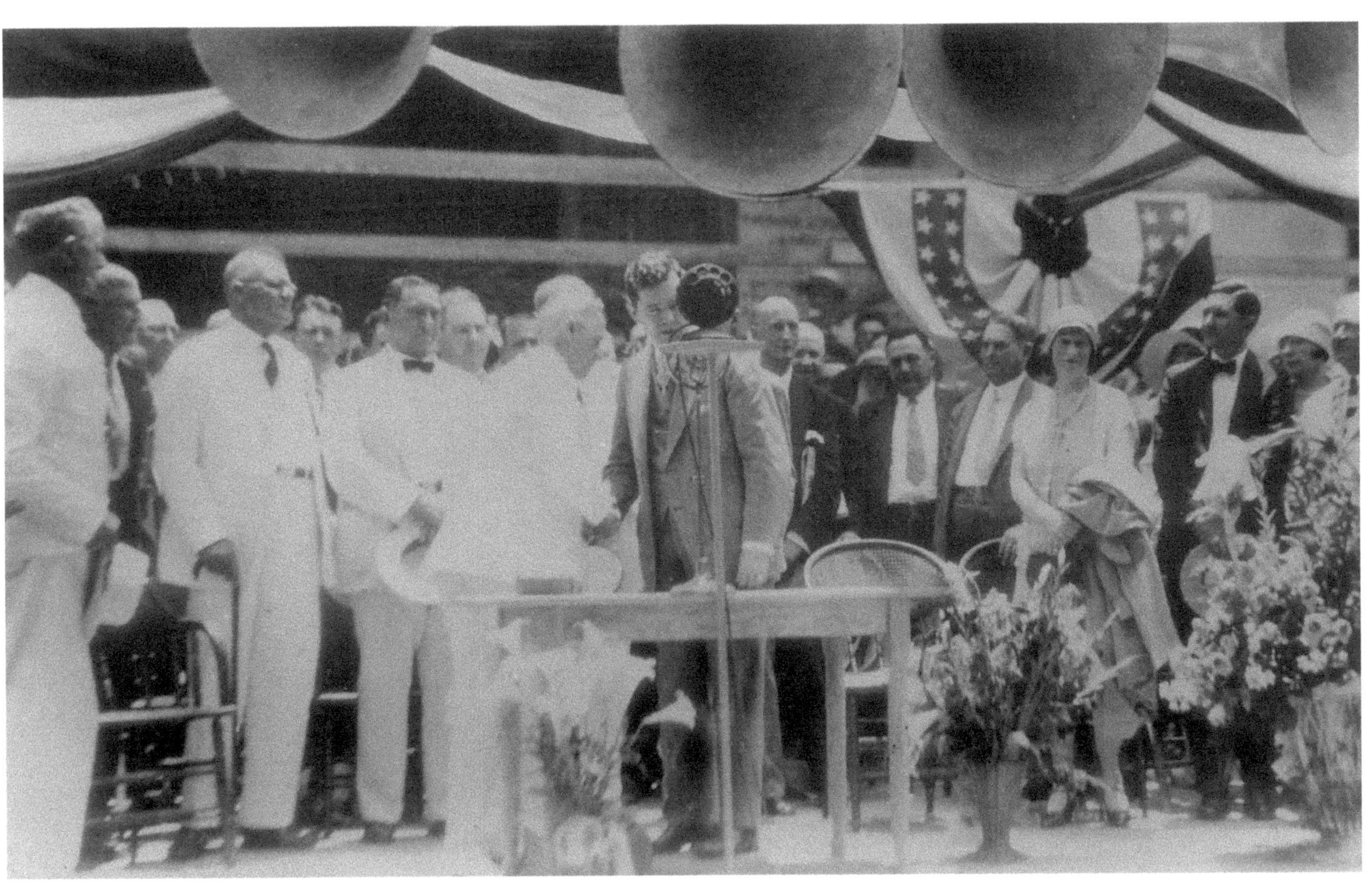

Huey P. Long was elected governor of Louisiana in 1928 after campaigning with the slogan "Every man a king, but no one wears a crown." On Inauguration Day, May 21, 1928, he was sworn into office in Baton Rouge. Partly obscured by the microphone, Long can be seen shaking hands with another official.

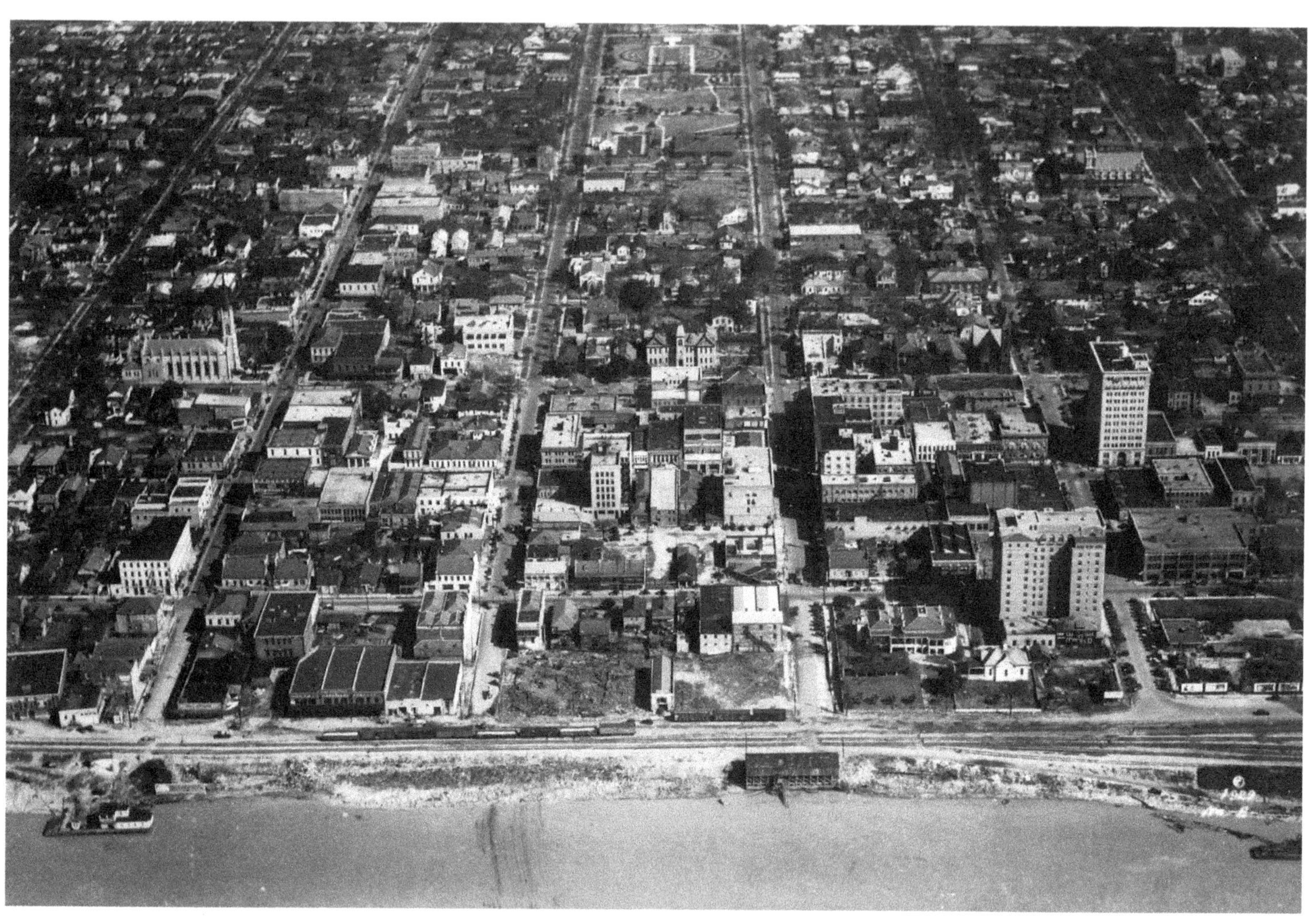

This 1929 aerial photograph of Baton Rouge shows the core of downtown. In the foreground, the railroad runs beside the Mississippi River, as yet without its levee. Saint Joseph's Cathedral, middle left, the Heidelberg Hotel and Auto Hotel, right foreground, and the 12-story Louisiana National Bank, right middle ground, all stand out.

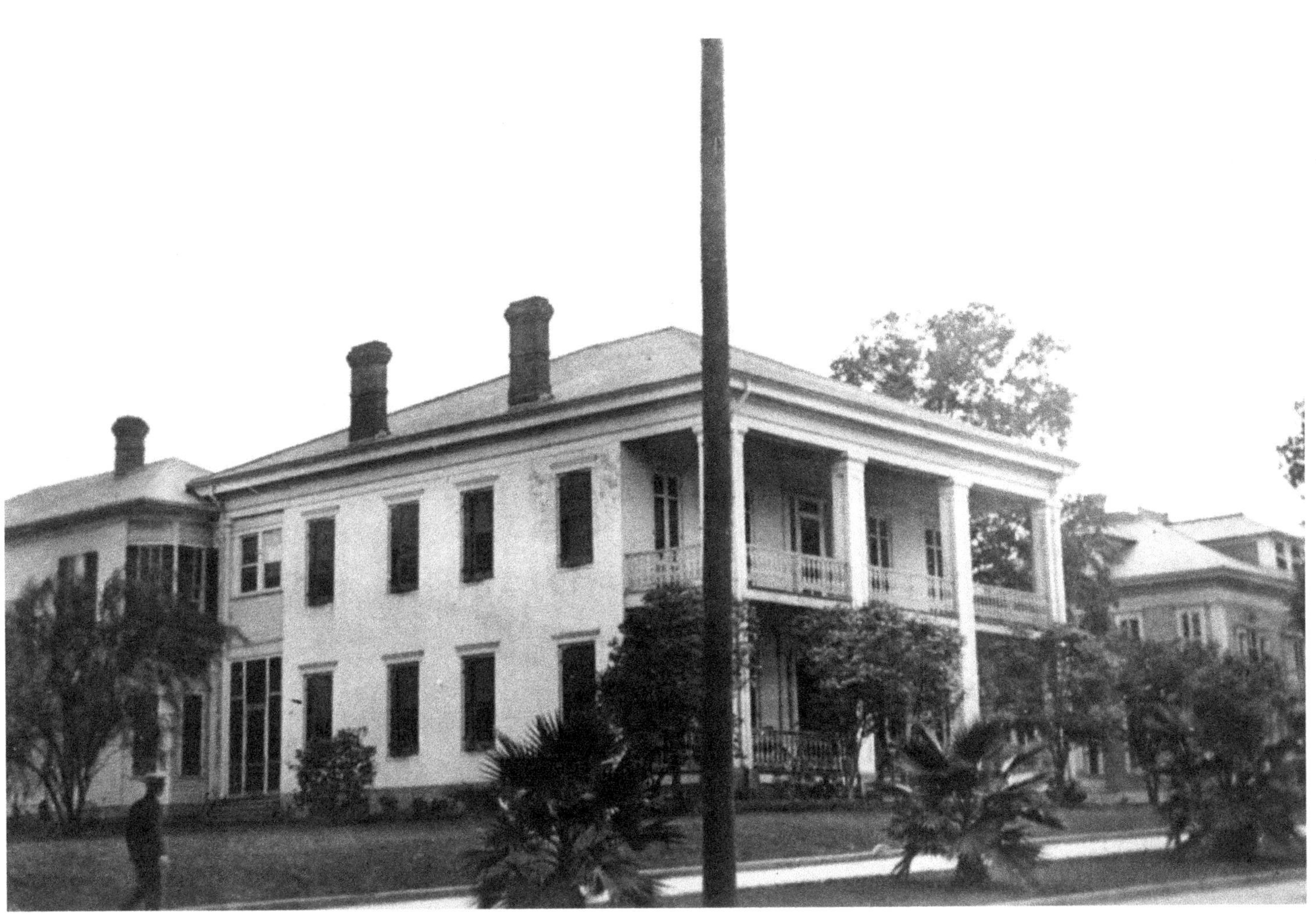

Located on North Boulevard between Royal and Saint Charles streets, this large frame house built for Baton Rouge businessman Nathan King Knox served as the official residence of Louisiana governors from 1887 until 1929, when it was razed on orders from Huey Long. In its place, Long ordered built a stucco Georgian mansion resembling the White House.

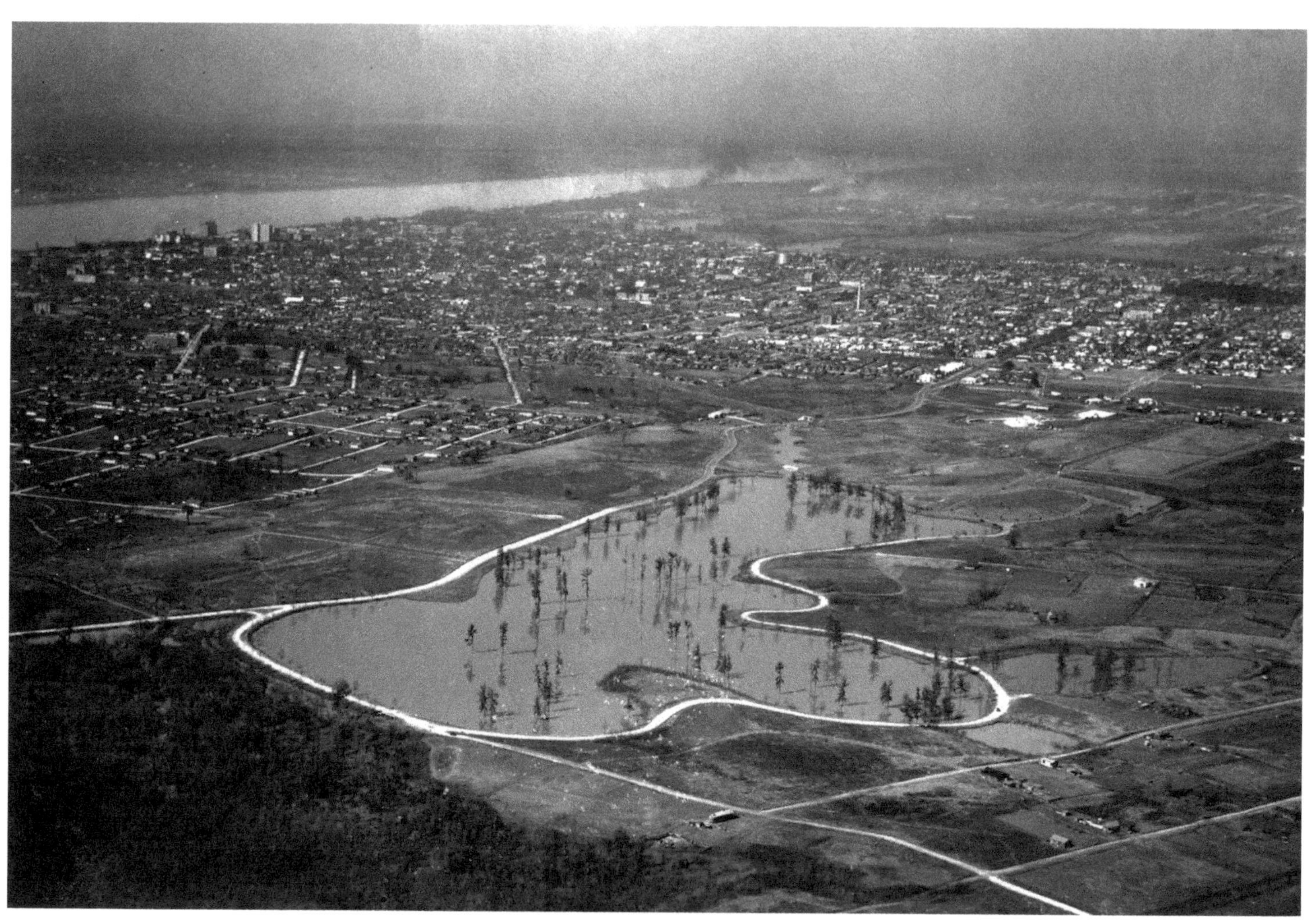

When Louisiana State University moved south from its downtown campus on the old Arsenal grounds in 1925, the campus occupied what had been plantation lands. One improvement made was to transform a part of the low-lying ground into a small lake, seen in this aerial photograph from 1929.

The Huey P. Long Legacy

(1930–1939)

As the Great Depression deepened, Baton Rouge adapted: citizens turned lawns into food gardens, 200 local unemployed persons established the Unemployed Workmen's Association, and those who had led a domestic life of luxury learned to keep house, cook, and sew for themselves. Still, more than 2,000 properties were sold in the first four years of the decade for nonpayment of taxes. Baton Rouge had by no means gone unscathed.

The Federal Emergency Relief Administration helped blunt the force of the Depression through creation of many public projects. Employing thousands of locals, these federal projects built concrete sidewalks on the campuses of LSU and Southern University, built and repaired roads, expanded the City Park lakes, and began construction of a bridge crossing the Mississippi River and of a new air transportation facility that would come into full use the following decade. The petroleum industry also helped blunt the Depression's worst effects when three new processing facilities were established in the capital city.

Huey P. Long, now governor and soon to be senator, took a very personal interest in LSU. He wanted to create a premier educational institution and took pains to funnel funds to the university, sometimes in unique ways. Wanting to expand the football stadium but finding no support in the state or national legislatures, he had a new dormitory built that happened to have stadium seating attached to the back side of the building.

In 1935, shortly before Senator Long's assassination in the new State Capitol (completed 1932), 200 armed members of an anti-Long paramilitary organization, the Square Deal Association, seized the parish courthouse. Long had Governor Oscar K. Allen declare marshal law. The association left the courthouse without bloodshed. A few months later, Huey P. Long would not be so lucky.

On September 8, 1935, Dr. Carl A. Weiss, Jr., approached Senator Long in a hallway of the Louisiana Capitol. No one knows with certainty what transpired next, but Huey P. Long received two bullet wounds that caused his death two days later. Dr. Weiss died immediately of the 30 wounds he suffered at the hands of Long's bodyguards. More than 100,000 Louisianans attended Long's funeral at the Capitol.

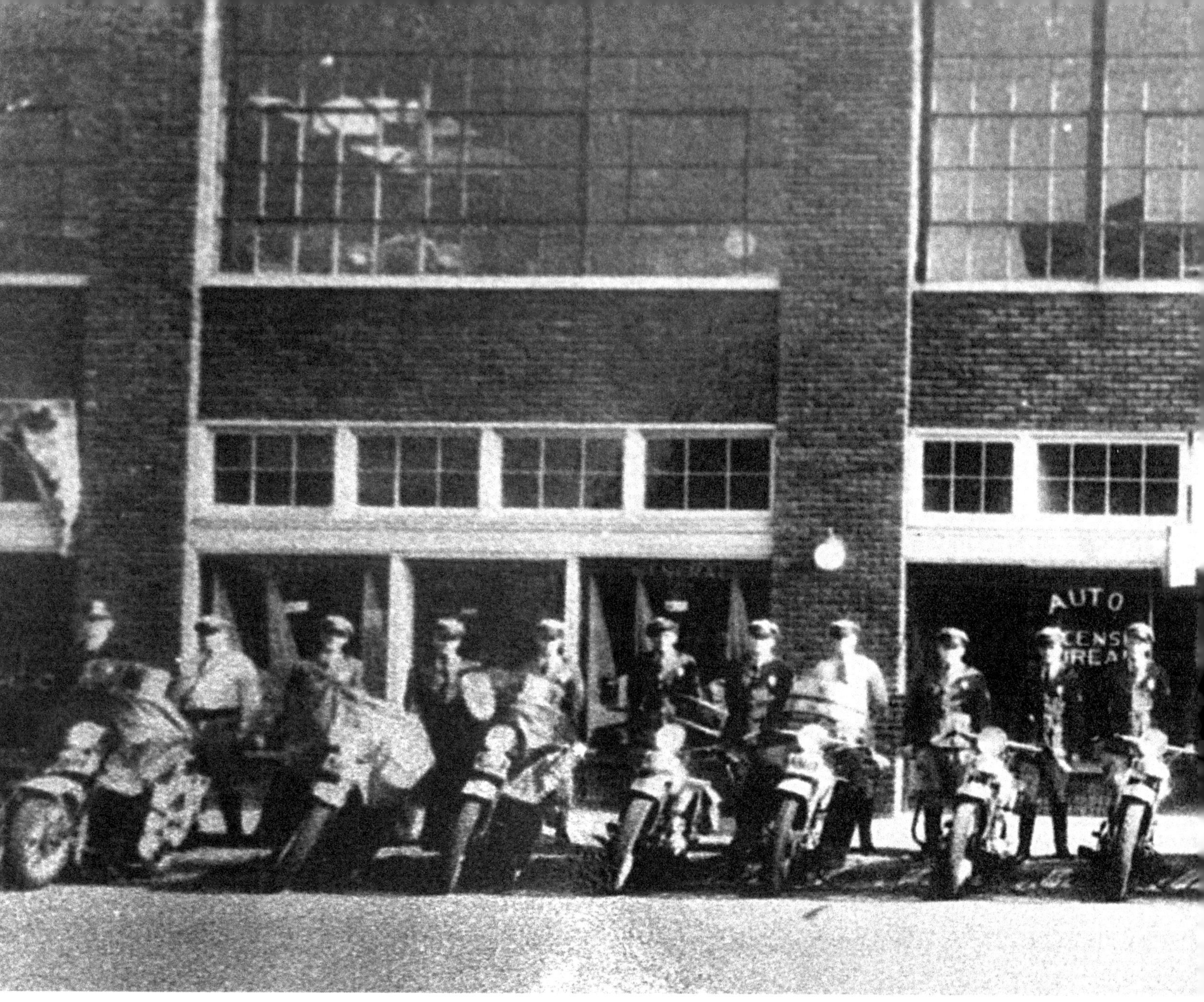

On July 28, 1936, the Louisiana Bureau of Criminal Investigation and the State Highway Patrol were combined to form the Louisiana Department of State Police. In this image, Louisiana State Police motorcycle troopers pose in front of the Auto Hotel, Baton Rouge's first parking garage.

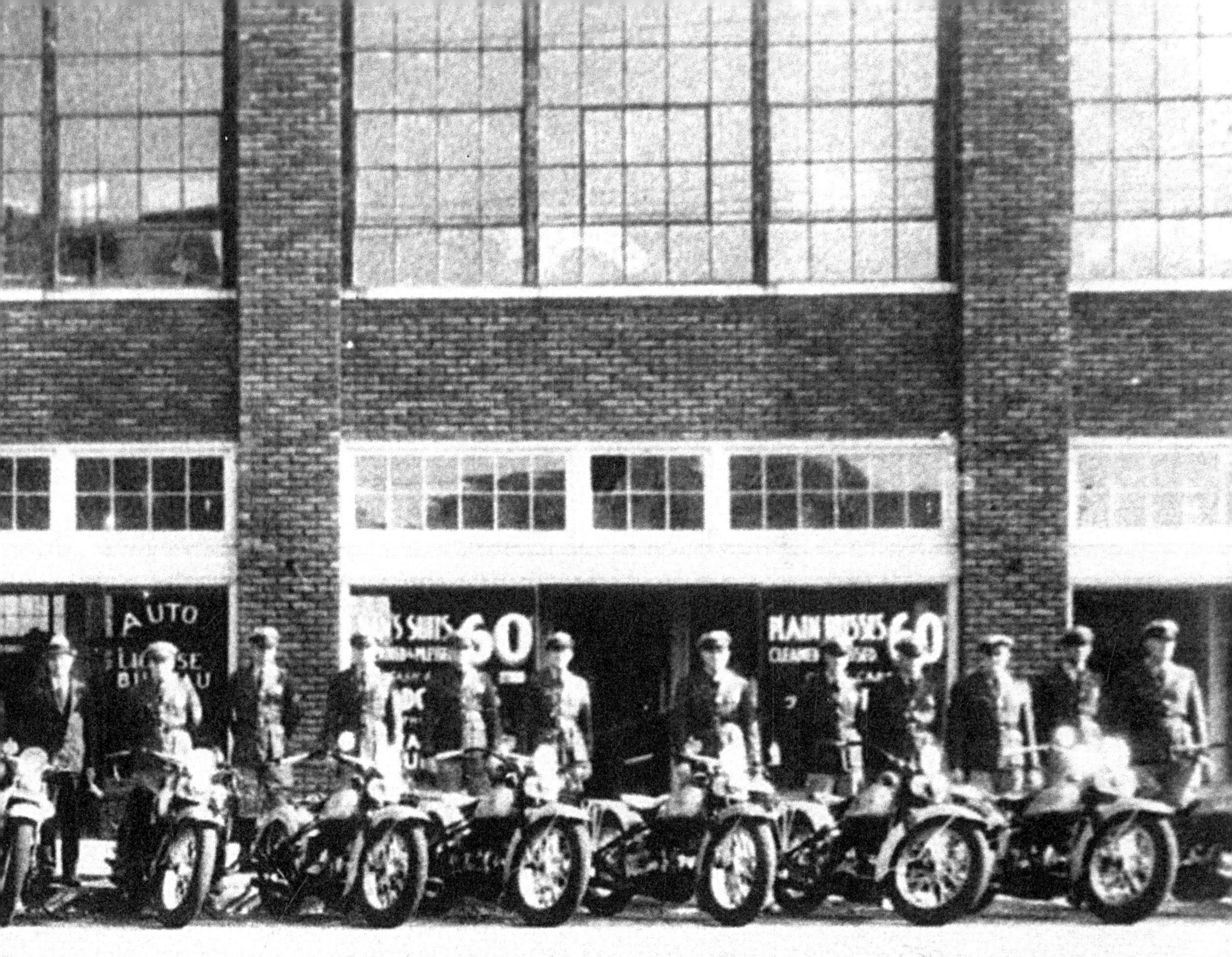
AUTO
PLAIN DRESSES 60

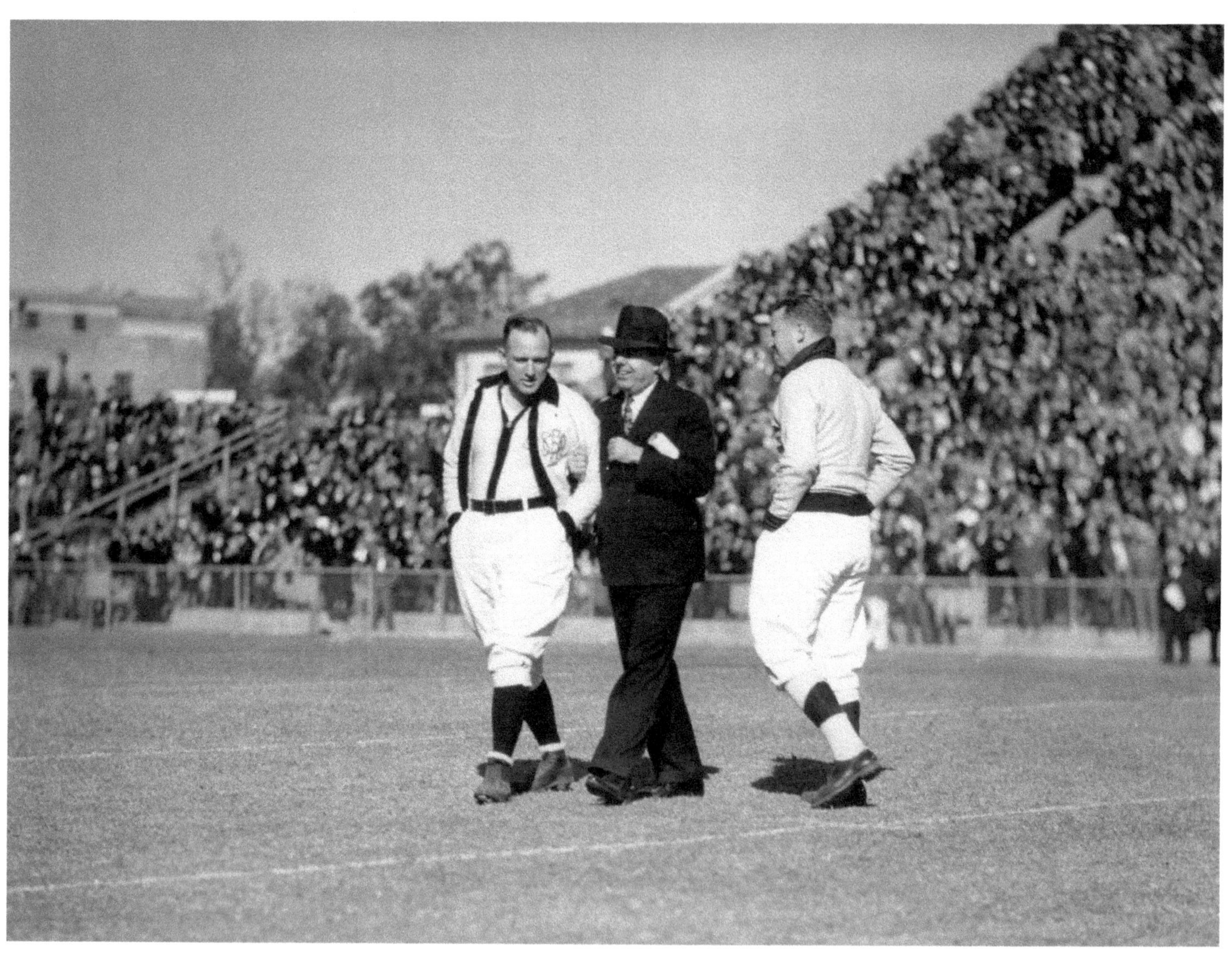

Football had long been an institution at Louisiana State University when Huey P. Long was elected governor. Always in the public eye, Long did not hesitate to confer with the referees during a game, even if it meant walking onto the field with them, as in this scene from around 1930.

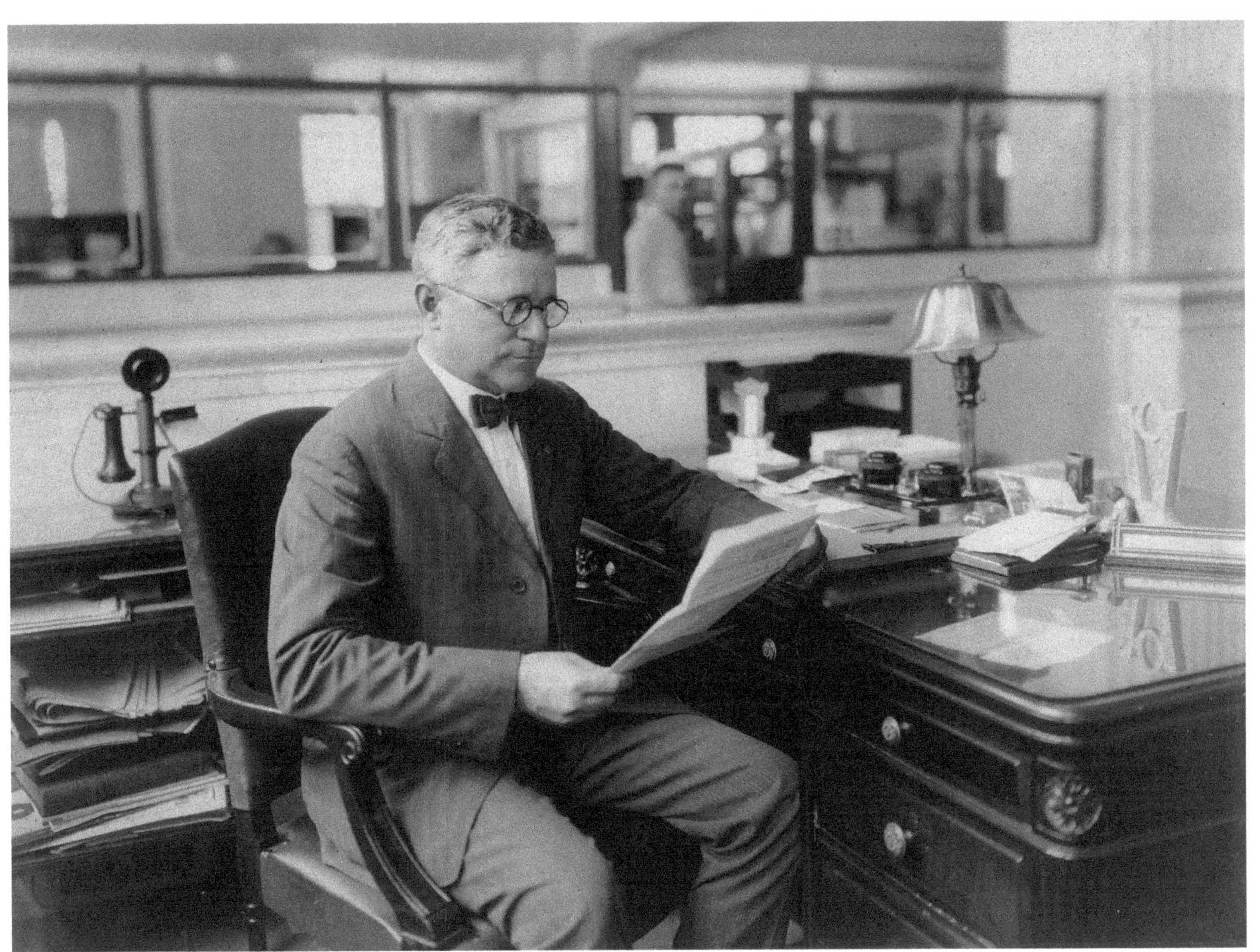

John B. Heroman, Sr., sits at his desk at the First National Bank, around 1930.

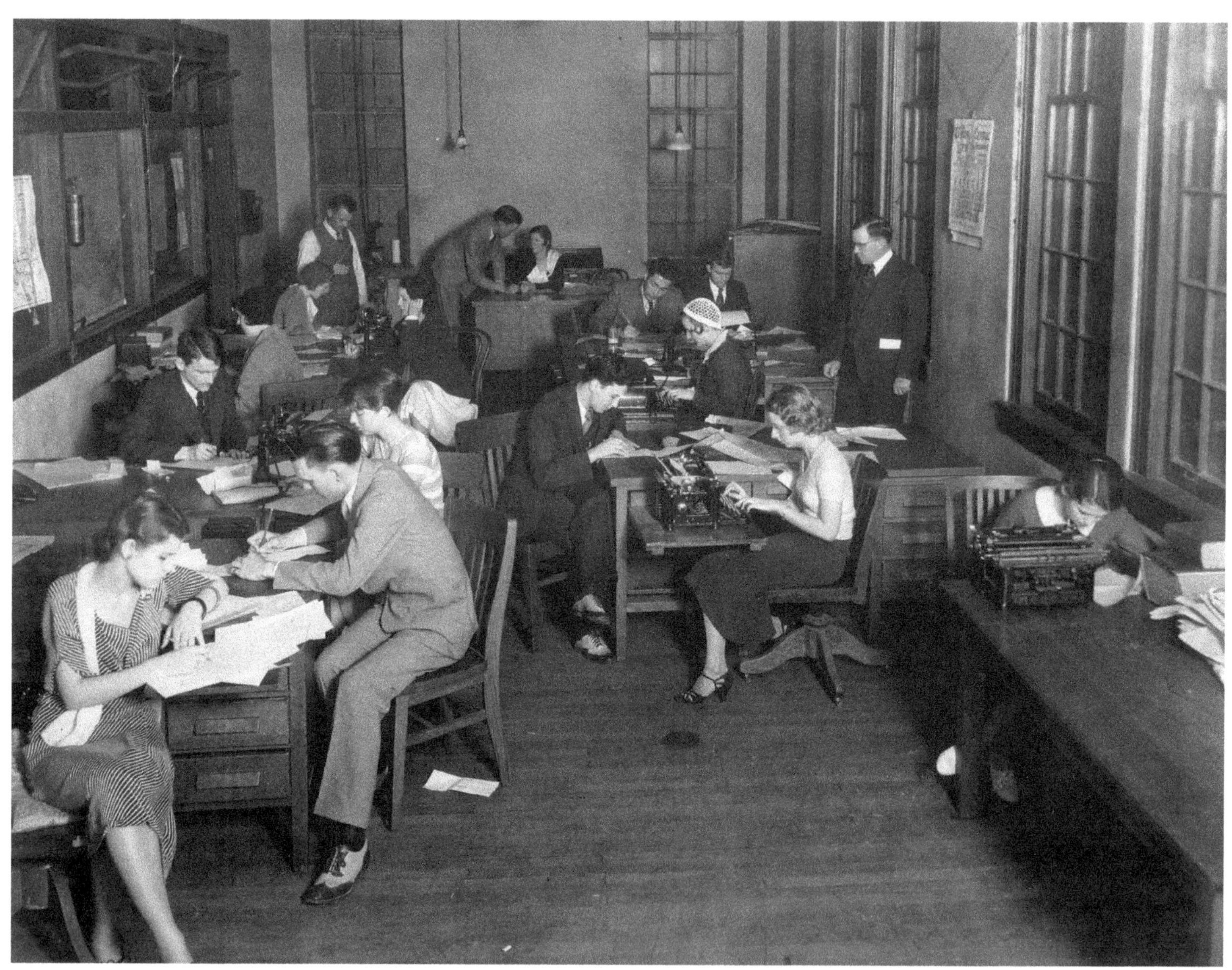

Baton Rouge has a long history with its newspapers. Capital City Press, founded in 1909 by Charles P. Manship, Sr., and James Edmonds, purchased the *State-Times*, an afternoon paper, that year. Capital City Press created the *Morning Advocate* in 1925 to provide the town's growing population with an early edition of the news. Here, around 1930, staffers of the *Morning Advocate* work under somewhat crowded conditions in the newsroom downtown.

During his 1928 gubernatorial campaign, Huey P. Long advocated for construction of a new Capitol to replace the old Louisiana State Capitol built in 1847. Ground-breaking for the new Capitol took place in 1930; construction ended 27 months later. The new Capitol—the tallest in the United States—cost $5 million to complete. Three years later, Huey P. Long would be assassinated in an interior hallway on his way out of the building.

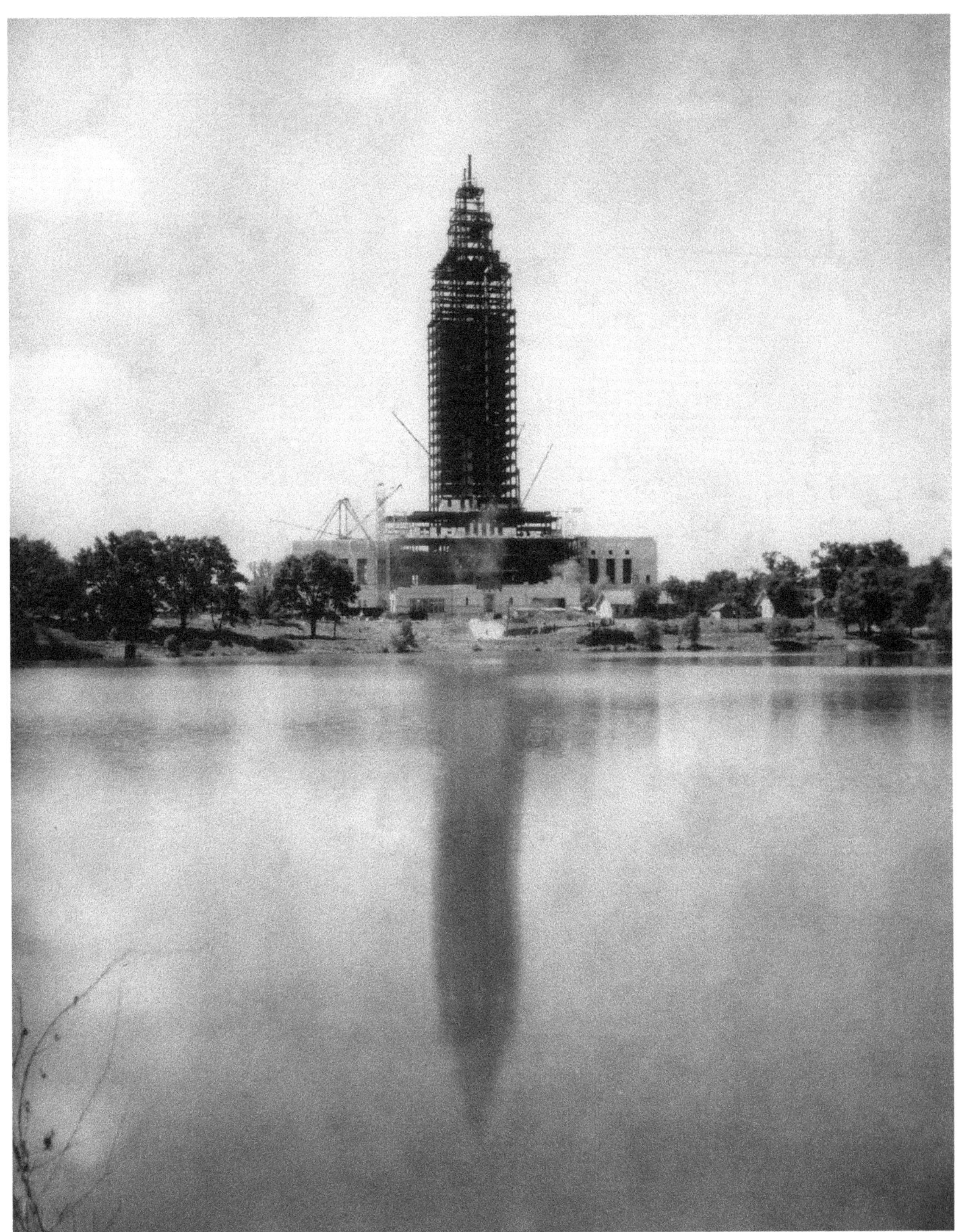

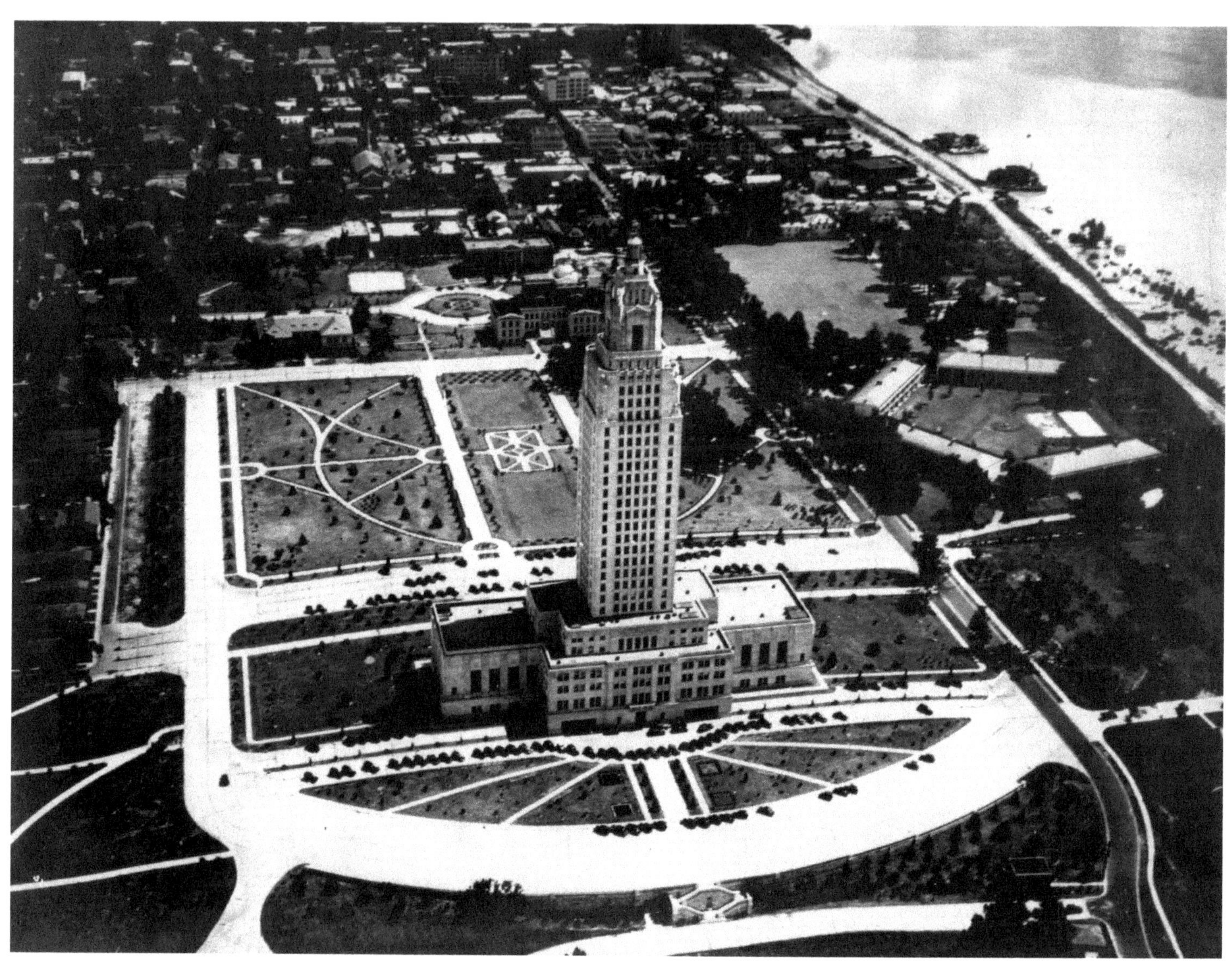

Sitting squarely on what had been the old Arsenal grounds and the Louisiana State University campus, the new State Capitol rose high above Baton Rouge. The Pentagon Barracks can be seen at right of the Capitol. At this point, around 1937, the Huey P. Long memorial had not yet been erected at his grave site in the formal garden on the south side of the Capitol.

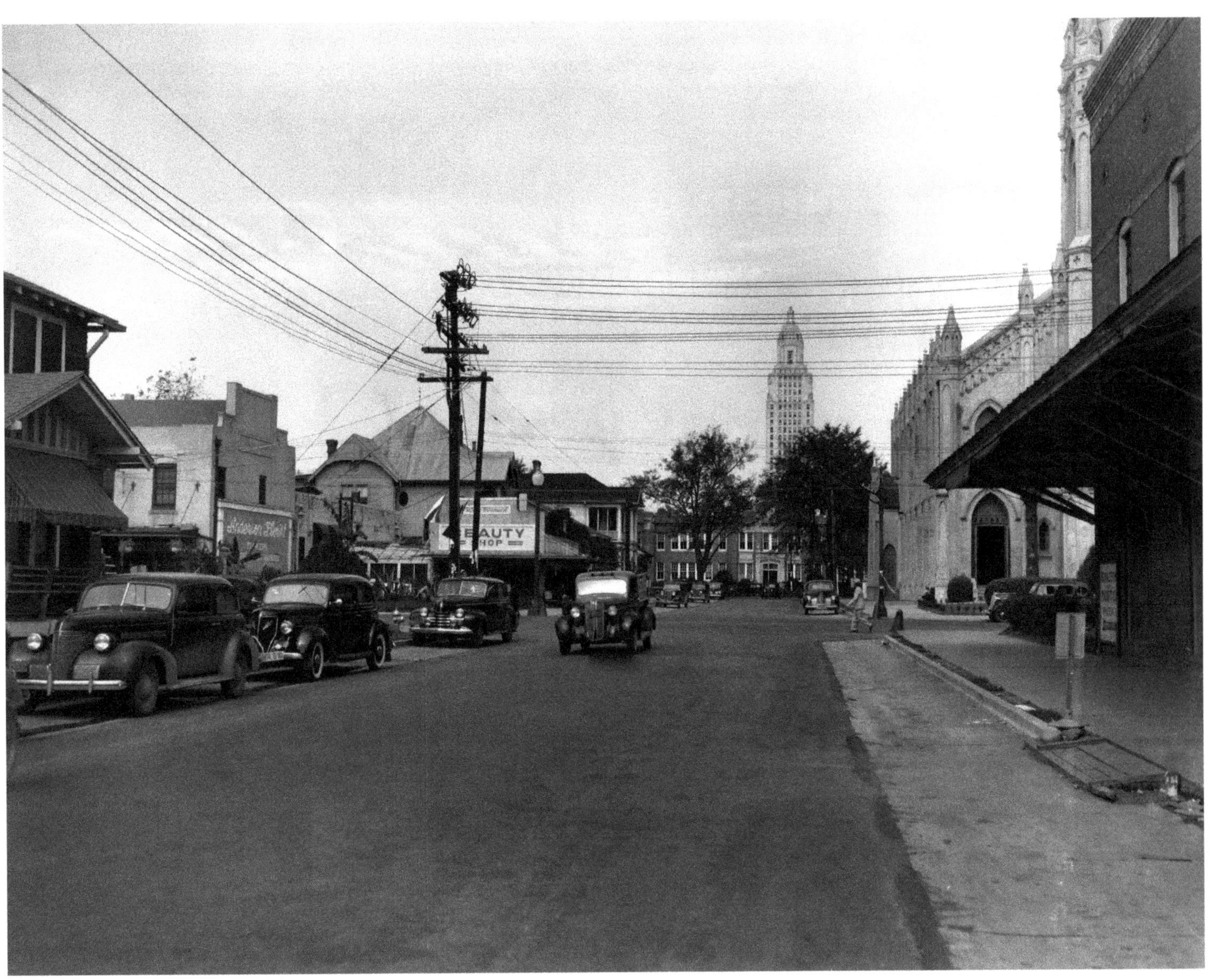

In this view looking north on Church Street toward the new State Capitol, around 1935, part of Saint Joseph Catholic Church can be seen at middle-right.

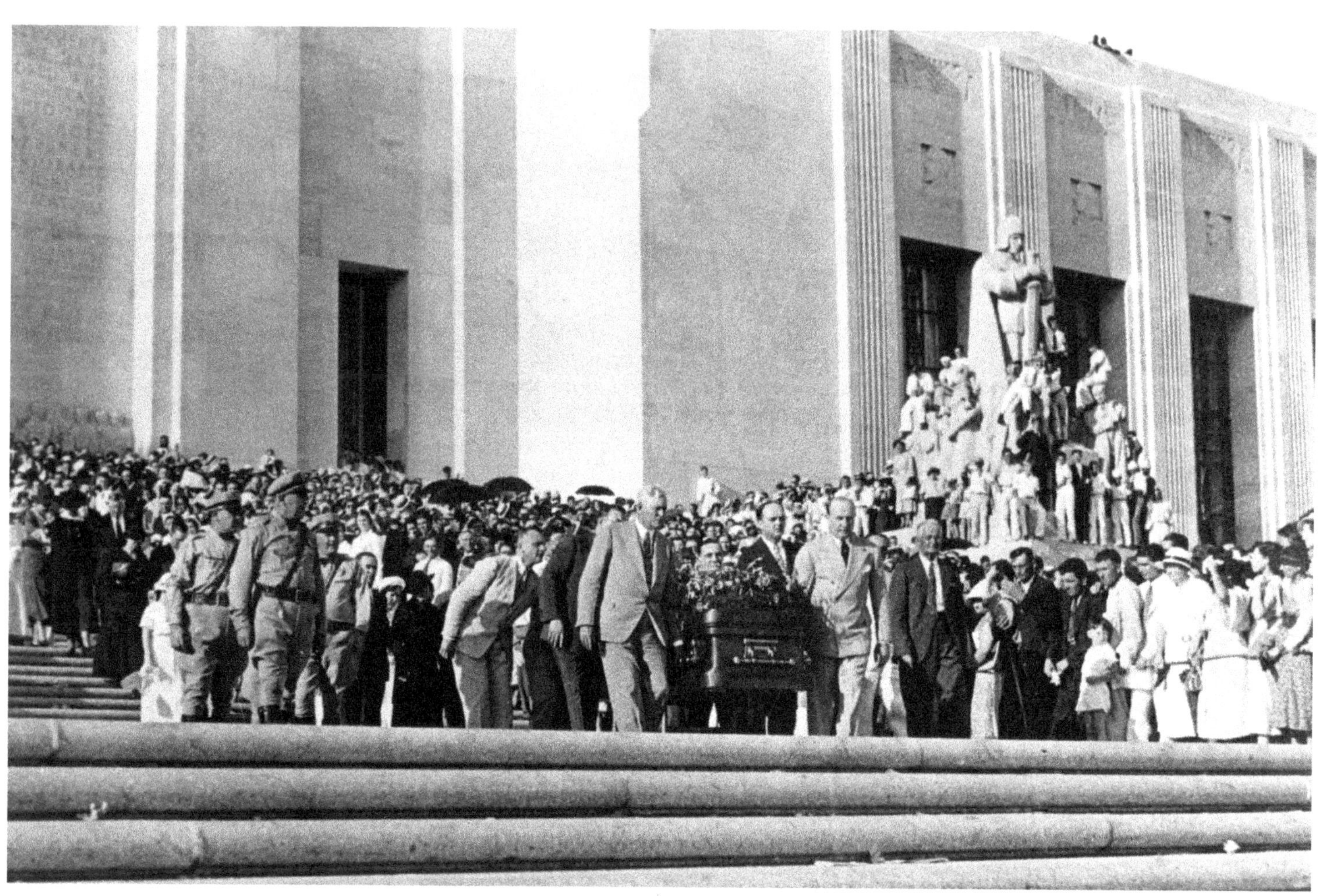

Following Huey P. Long's assassination, a public funeral was held on the grounds of the new State Capitol, September 12, 1935. After the public viewing of his body, Long's casket was carried to his grave site in front of the building.

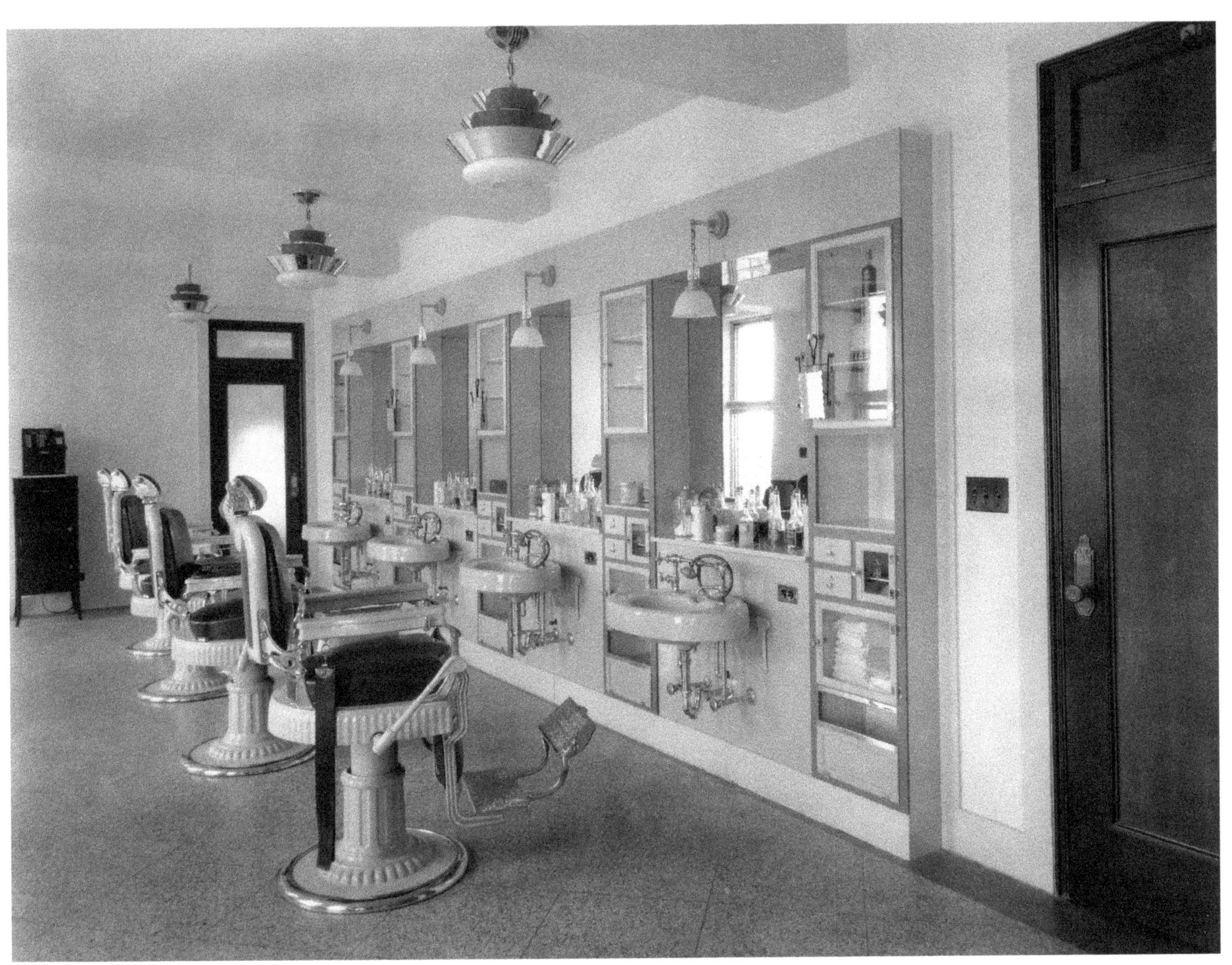

The new State Capitol held all the modern conveniences for state legislators, including this well-equipped barber shop on the seventh floor, seen in 1932.

As the state police force modernized in the mid-1930s, troopers received specialized training in all manner of equipment, including this .45-caliber Thompson submachine gun, popularly called the "Tommy gun."

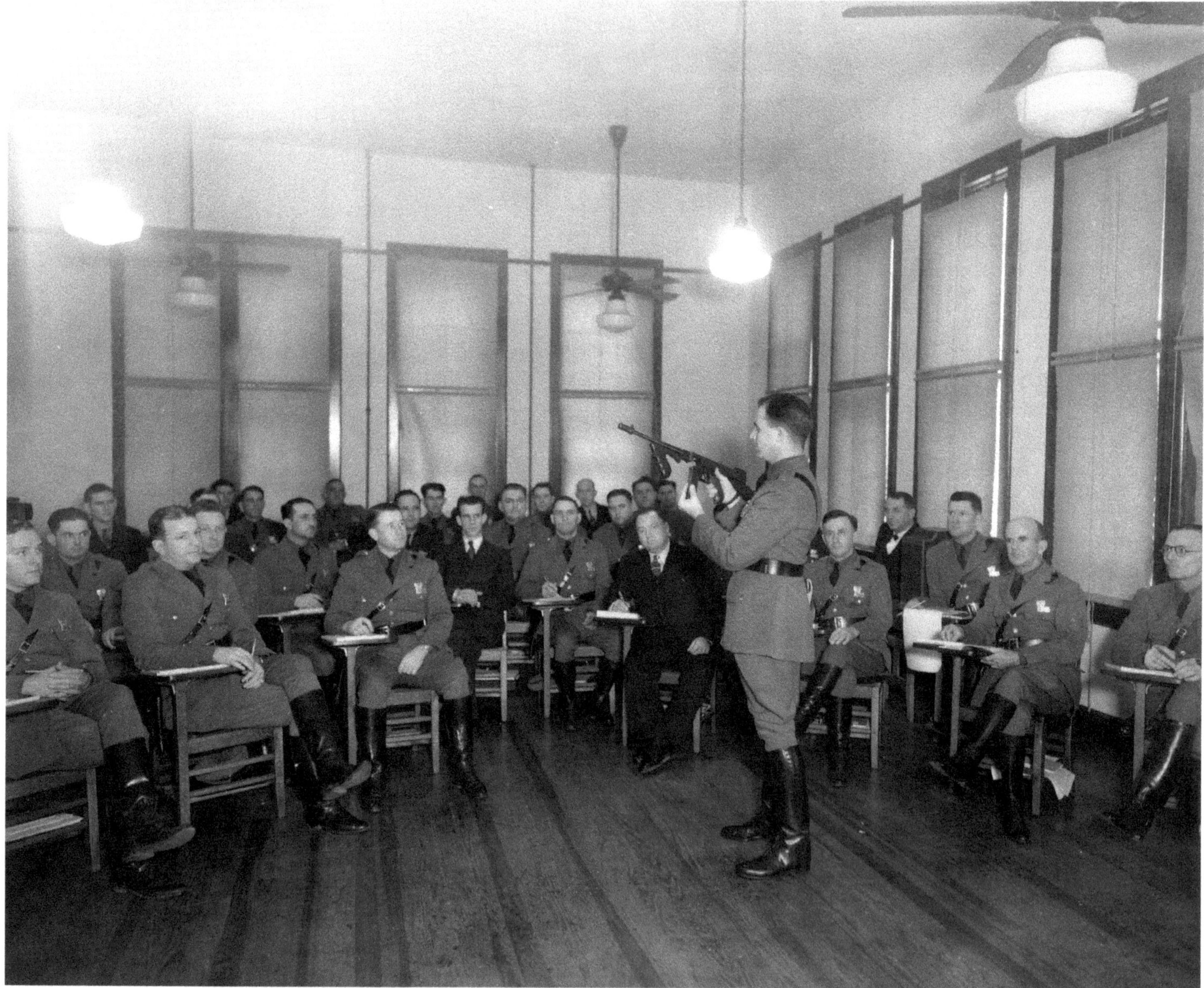

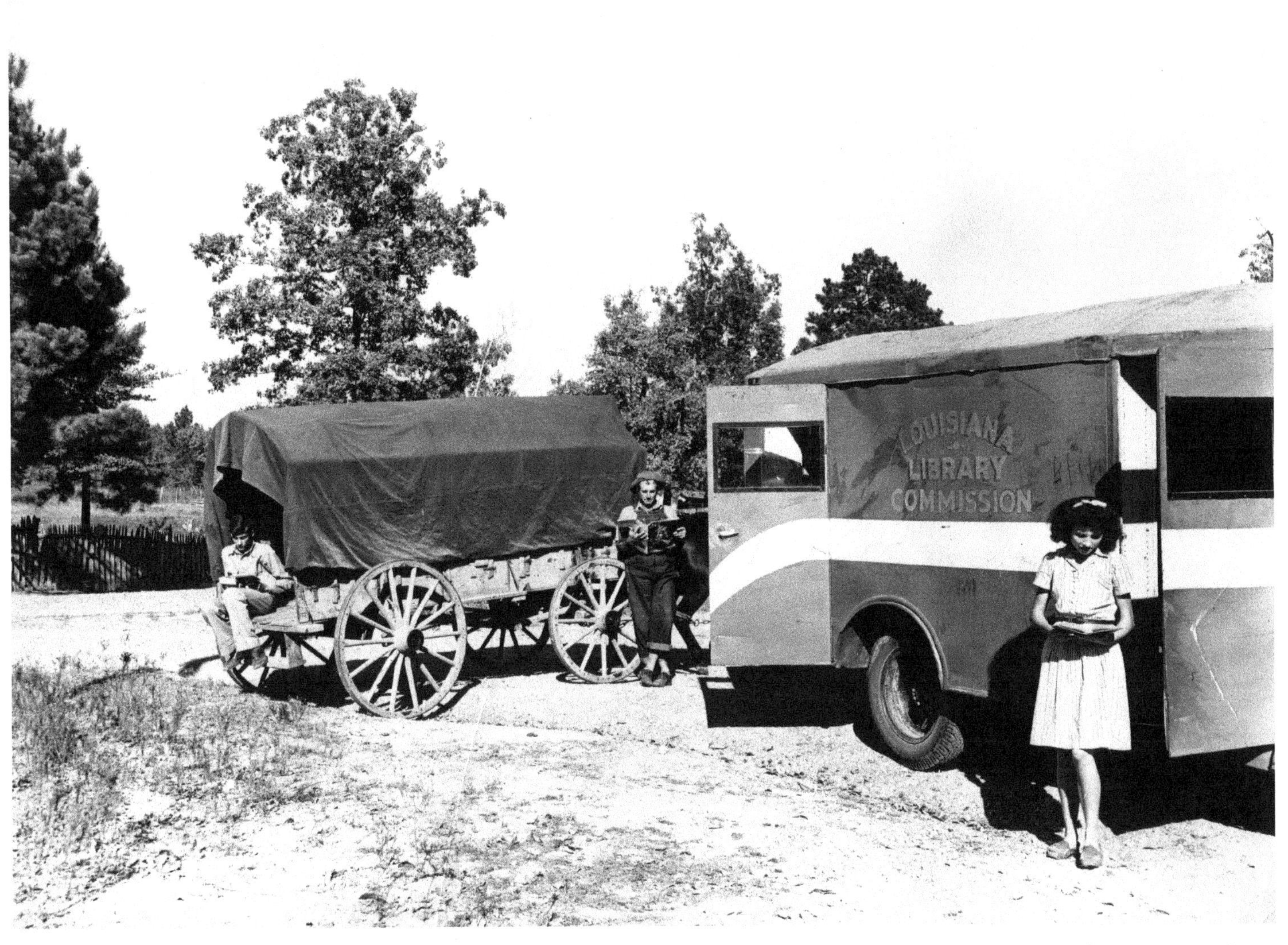

Life in largely rural and dirt-poor 1930s Louisiana could be harsh. The Louisiana Library Commission, established in 1920, partnered with the Carnegie corporation to establish a network of libraries throughout the state. Here, around 1935, a rural family traveling in a covered wagon meets the Library Commission's bookmobile near Baton Rouge.

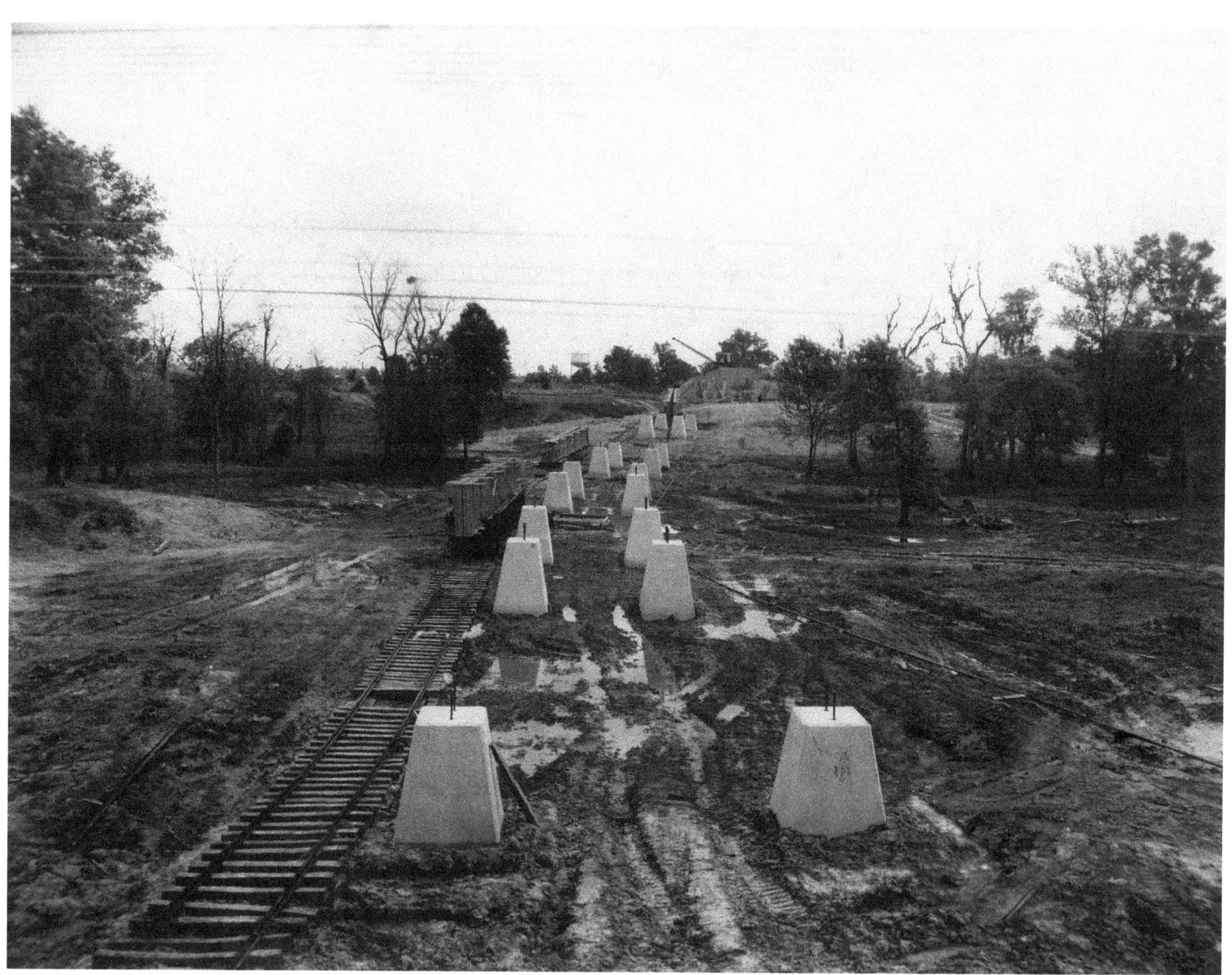

The second bridge across the Mississippi River to be named after Huey P. Long linked Baton Rouge on the east bank with Port Allen on the west bank. Though it was built largely as a railroad bridge, two narrow lanes for motor-vehicle traffic run along either side of its central railroad track. This image from April 11, 1938, shows the east-side approach under construction.

Downtown was the center of Baton Rouge activity; this 1935 scene shows its diversity of business. In the first block on the left are Stroube Drug Store, the Book Shop, Grand Beauty Parlor, the Rembrandt photography studio, and Sears, Roebuck. Businesses on the right include Orange Delight, National Jewelry & Optical Company, Coney Island Sandwich Shop, City National Bank, and the Western Union Telegraph Company, among others.

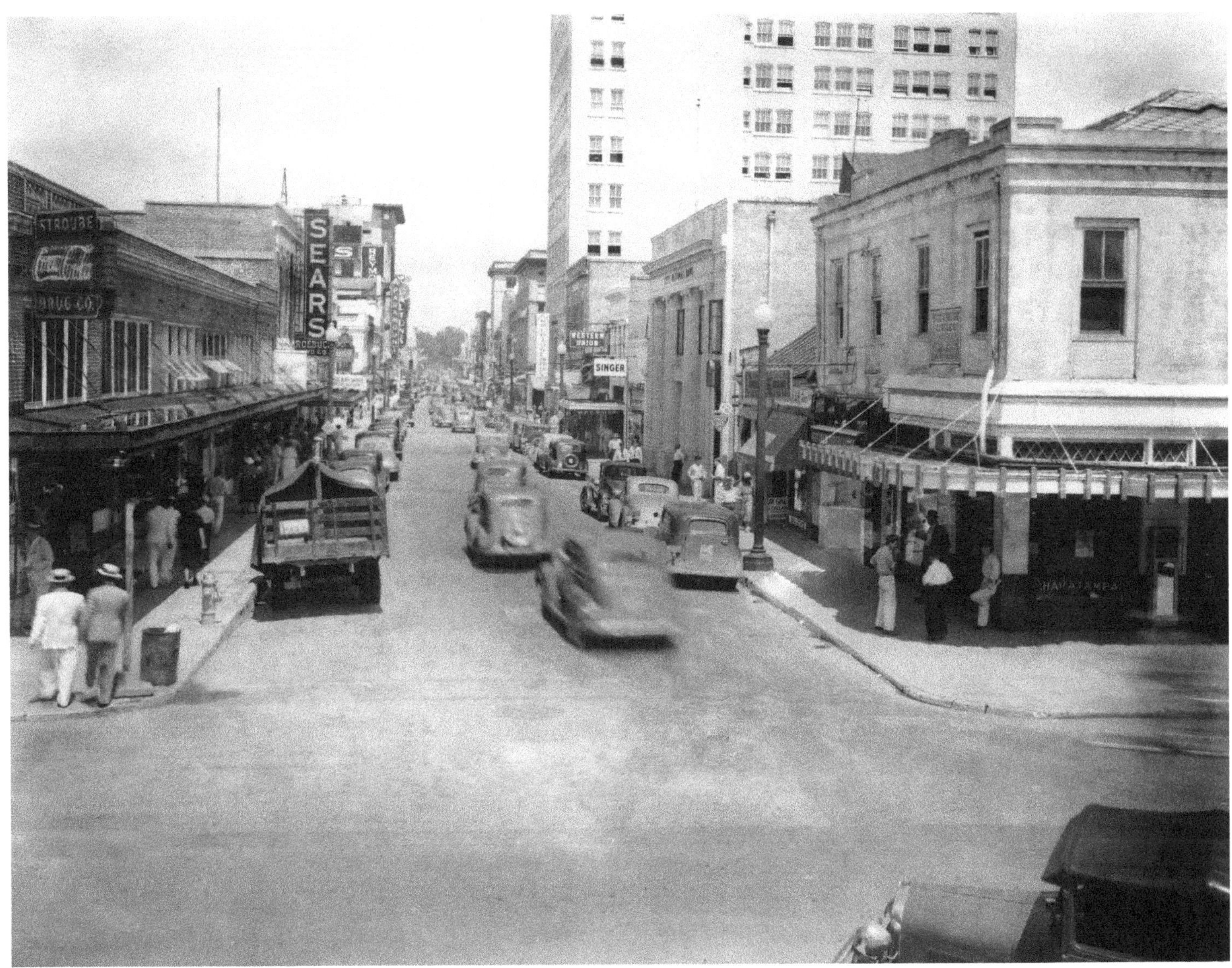

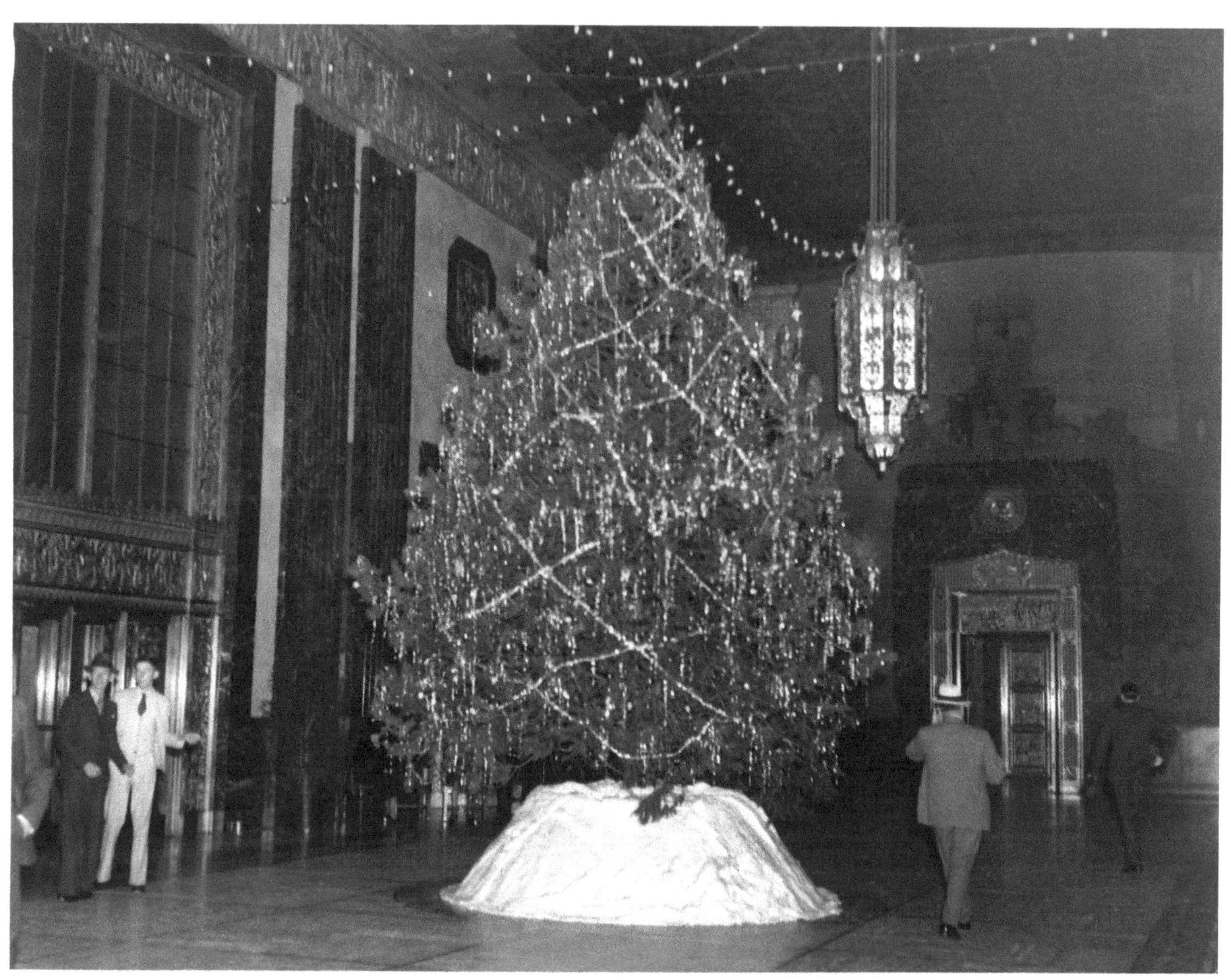

Here, the lobby of the new Capitol is decorated for a mid-1930s Christmas season.

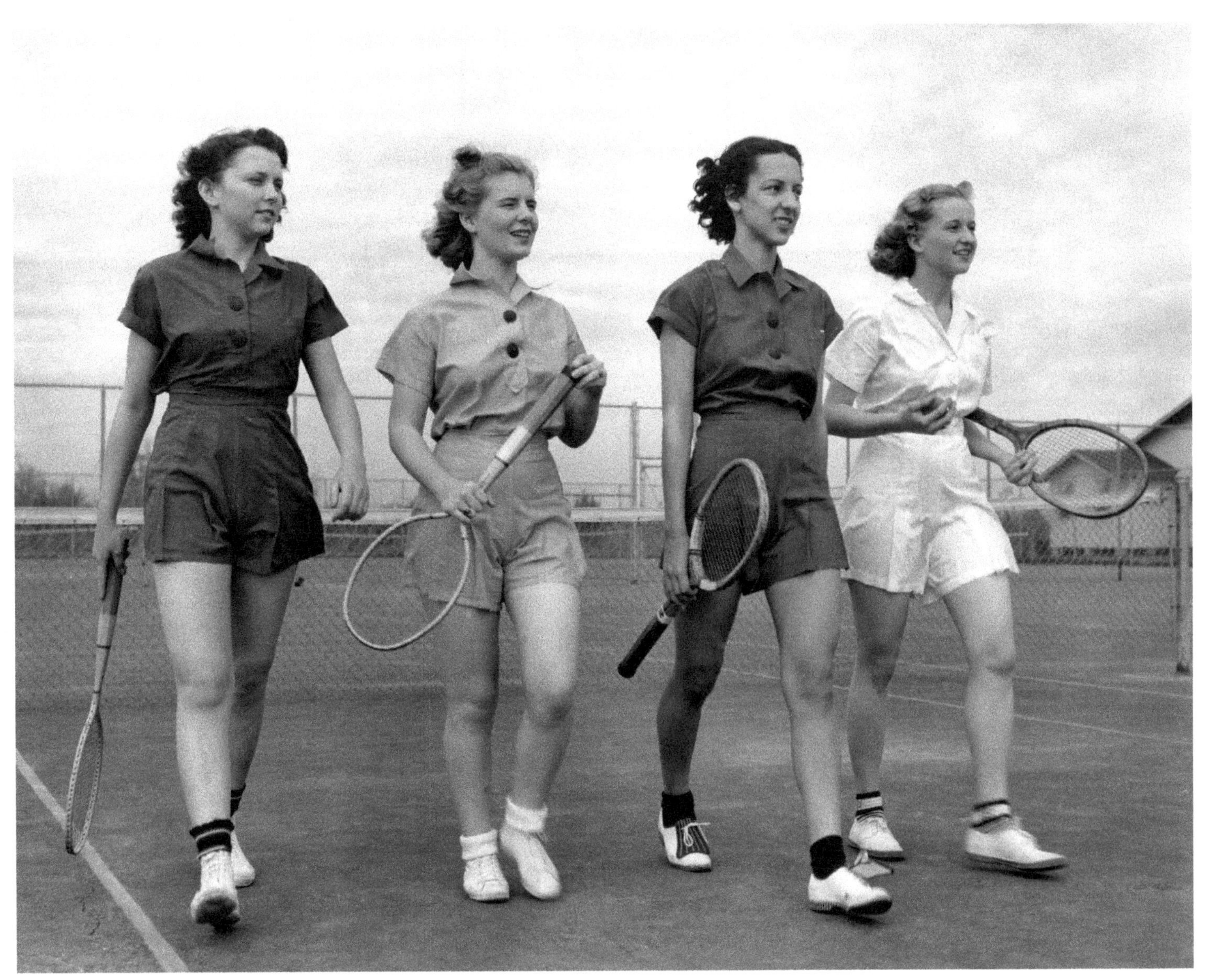

Olivia Davis became the first female student at Louisiana State University in 1904. Three decades later, these four young women are walking on the campus tennis court.

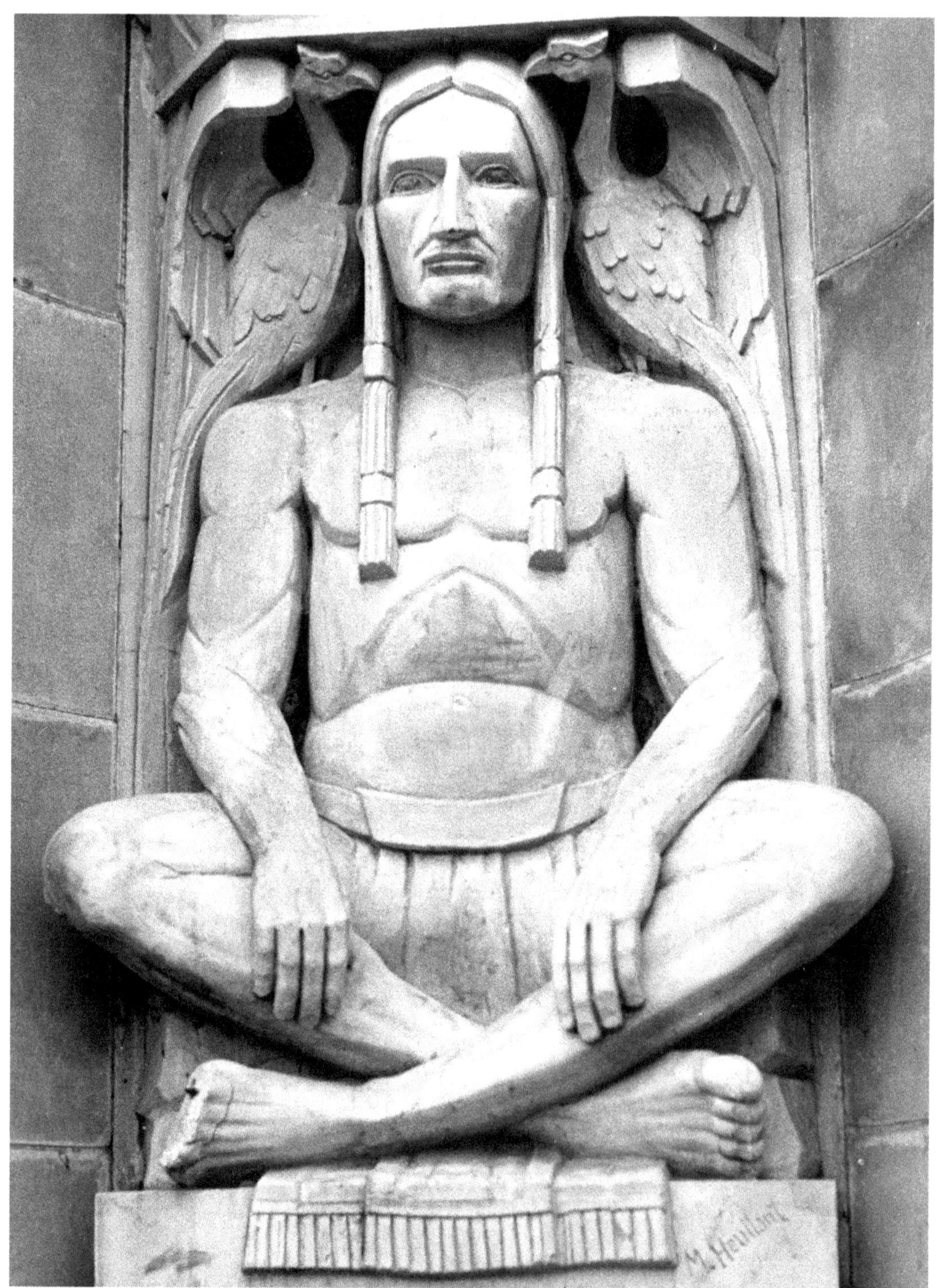

The State Capitol built under the Huey P. Long administration includes a number of art-deco details. One detail, set into the stairs between two parking areas behind the building, is this fountain designed as an American Indian sitting in contemplation with a phoenix perched on either shoulder.

The War Years and Beyond

(1940–1949)

As the Depression eased and the world stood on the brink of the Second World War, Baton Rouge continued to expand. Suburbs sprang up in the northern part of town to accommodate petroleum workers needed to staff that growing and increasingly important industry. Other suburbs were created to house the growing faculty and staff of LSU, which had expanded to meet demand for trained petroleum engineers and other professionals. The massive state government created under Huey P. Long added more demand for housing.

With the declaration of war, Baton Rouge provided two essentials of the war effort: soldiers and petroleum products. LSU, with its long military history, had been called the "Old War Skule" for years and had helped mold many military leaders. One of the most noted was Troy H. Middleton, who at his highest rank served as lieutenant general in the European theater and later served as one of the most effective leaders of LSU. Standard Oil vastly expanded its facilities to produce aviation fuel, so critical to the war effort, and synthetic rubber to replace the natural rubber that had fallen under the control of the Japanese empire in the East. Harding Air Field, constructed north of Baton Rouge under a Federal Emergency Relief Administration program, became a flight-training facility for the Army Air Corps. Munitions-storage facilities sprang up near the airfield, since Baton Rouge was far enough from the coast to make enemy attack highly unlikely. These factors created a boom in Baton Rouge; military personnel, new employees at the refineries, and their families needed homes, food, clothing, and other essentials.

Following the war, Baton Rouge maintained its growth. Harding Field reverted to civilian control in August 1948 and would be renamed Ryan Field, in honor of Captain William Joseph Ryan, in 1954. LSU and Southern University expanded their campuses to keep up with the huge increase in their student enrollments caused in large part by the GI Bill. The city moved quickly toward the turbulence, continued growth, and reshaping that the next decade would bring.

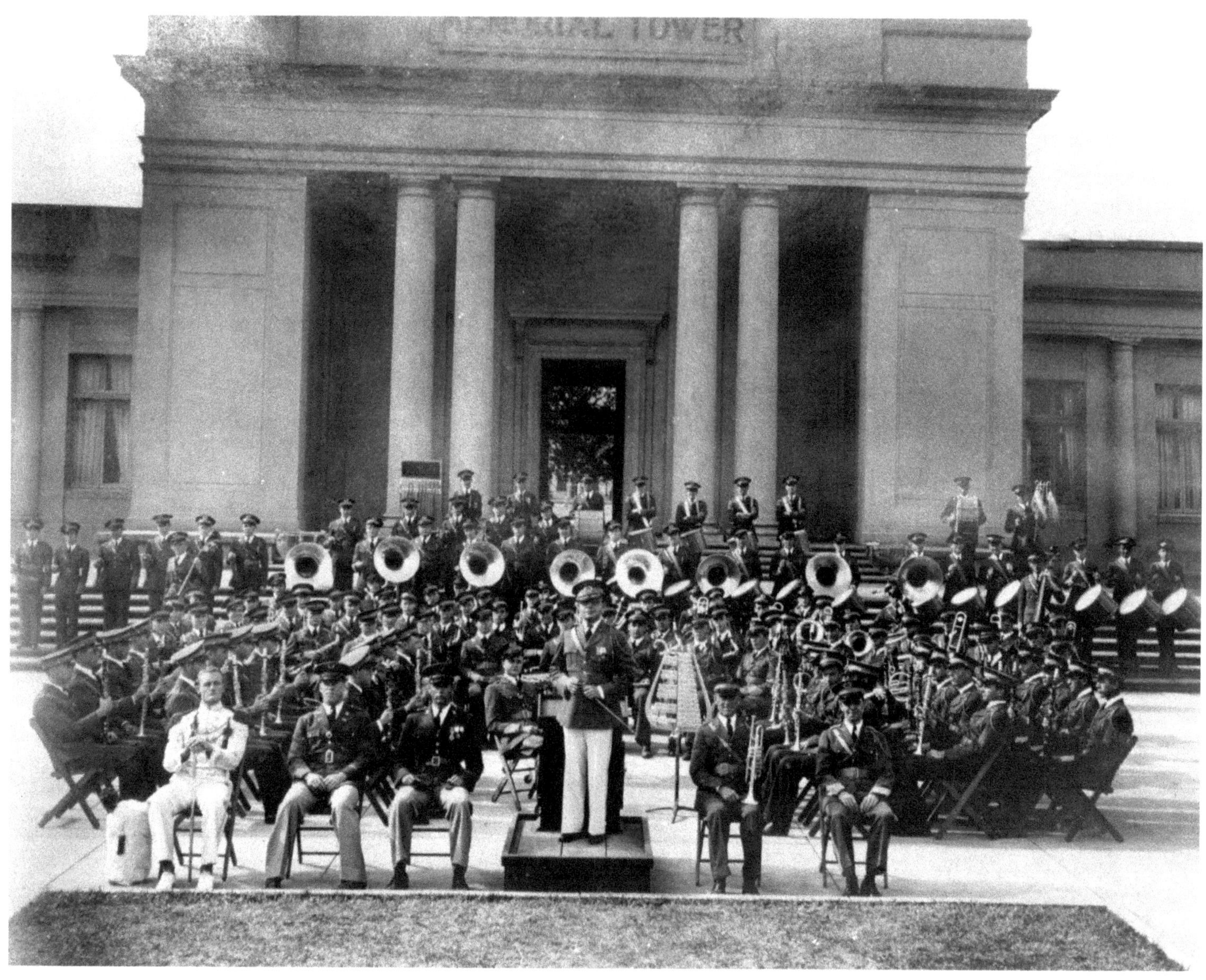

Governor Huey P. Long's personal interest in Louisiana State University extended to the marching band, for which he hired Castro Carazo, orchestra leader at the Roosevelt Hotel in New Orleans, and with whom he co-wrote a number of LSU songs. Here, around 1940, the Tiger Band poses in front of Memorial Tower on the LSU campus.

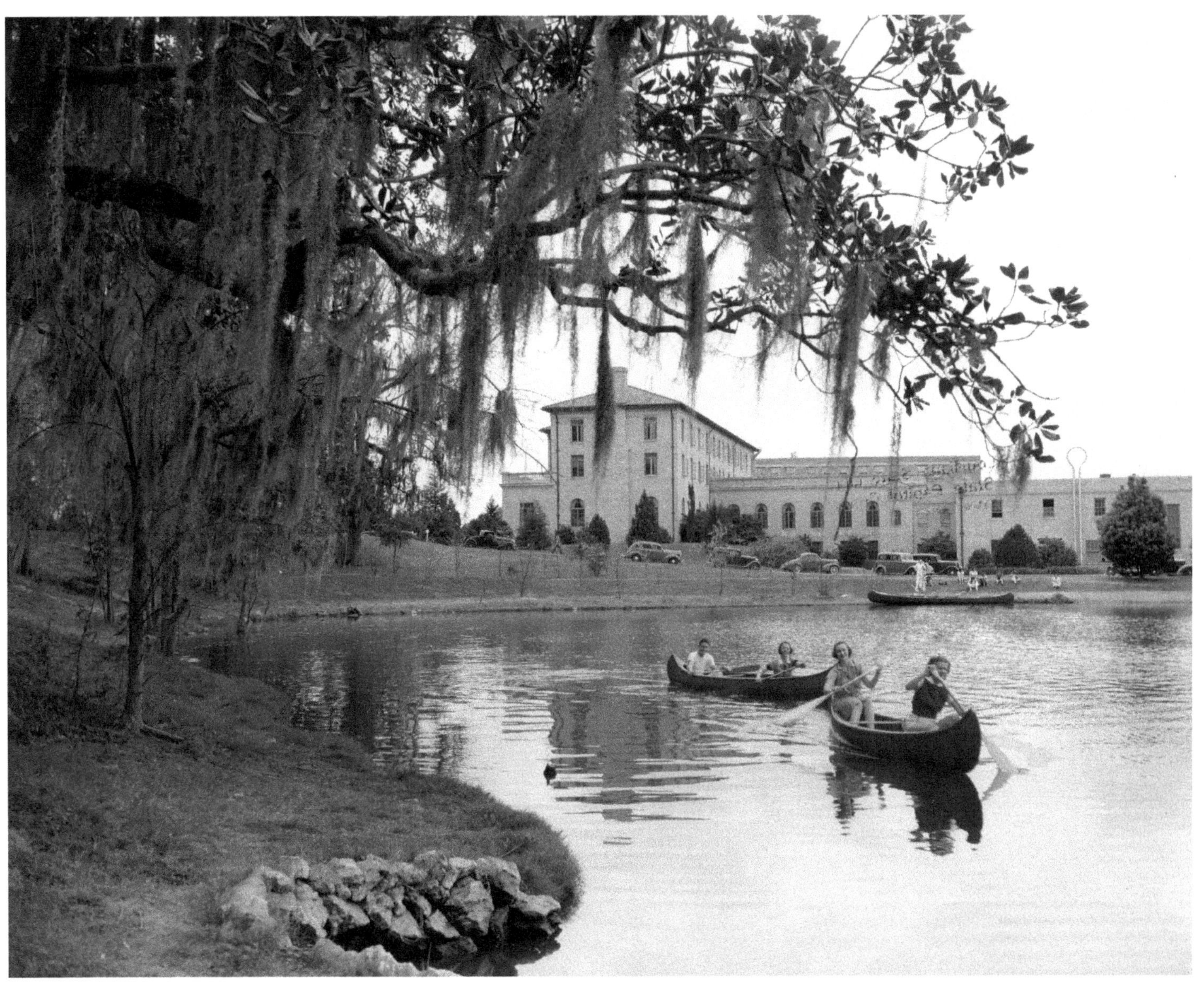

Students enjoy canoeing on the recently expanded City Park lakes near the campus of Louisiana State University, about 1940.

Opening for business in 1931, Baton Rouge's "downtown" Municipal Airport was located a few miles east of the river on the edge of town. In May 1940, the parish Police Jury took title to 1,000 acres of land approximately eight miles north of town and secured Works Project Administration approval of plans for a new airport. The new facility, Harding Field, opened in February 1941. This image is from the initial stage of construction in 1940.

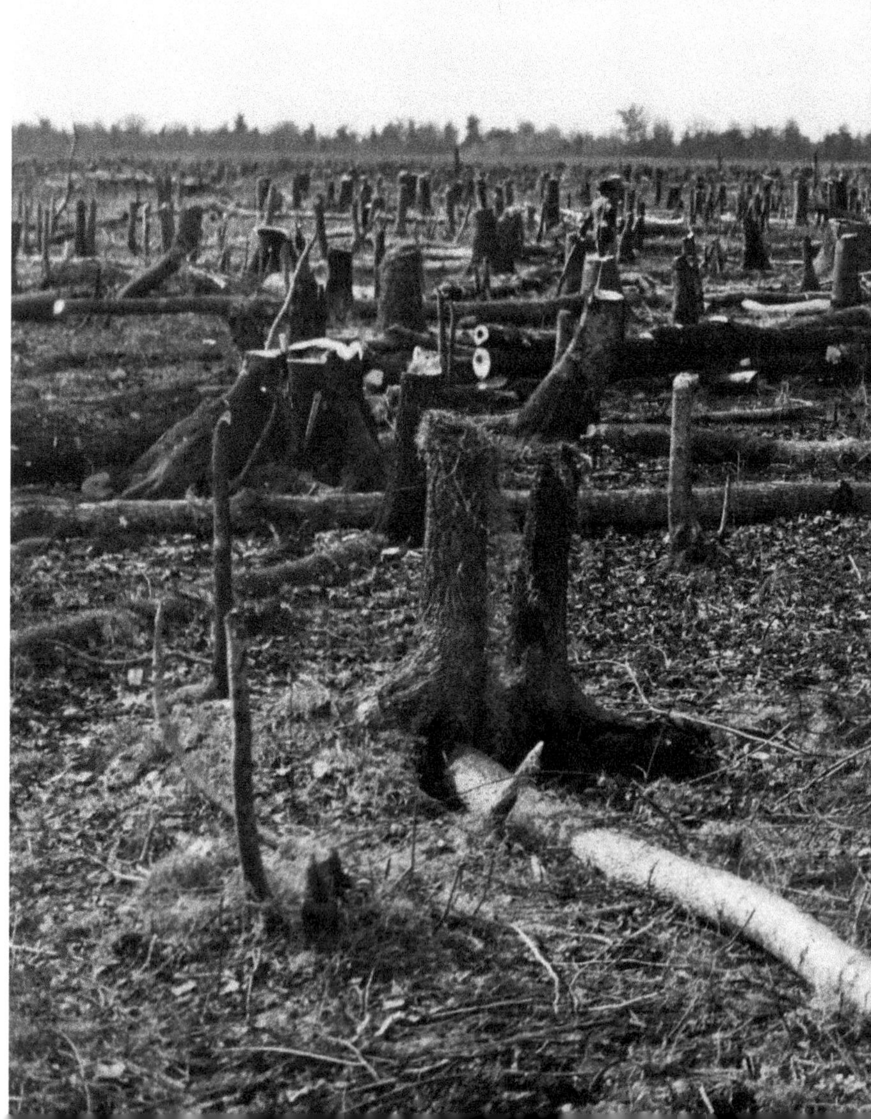

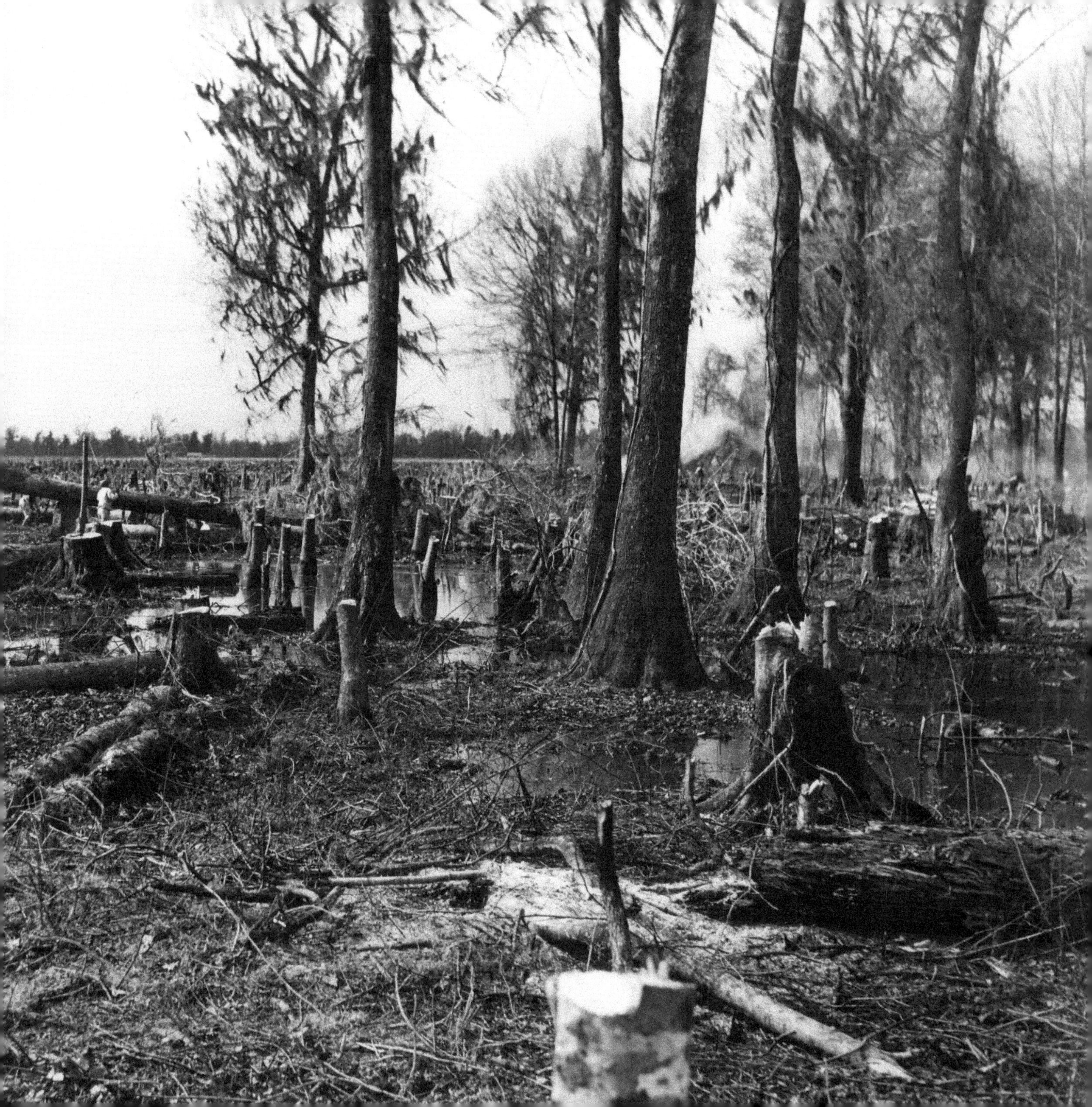

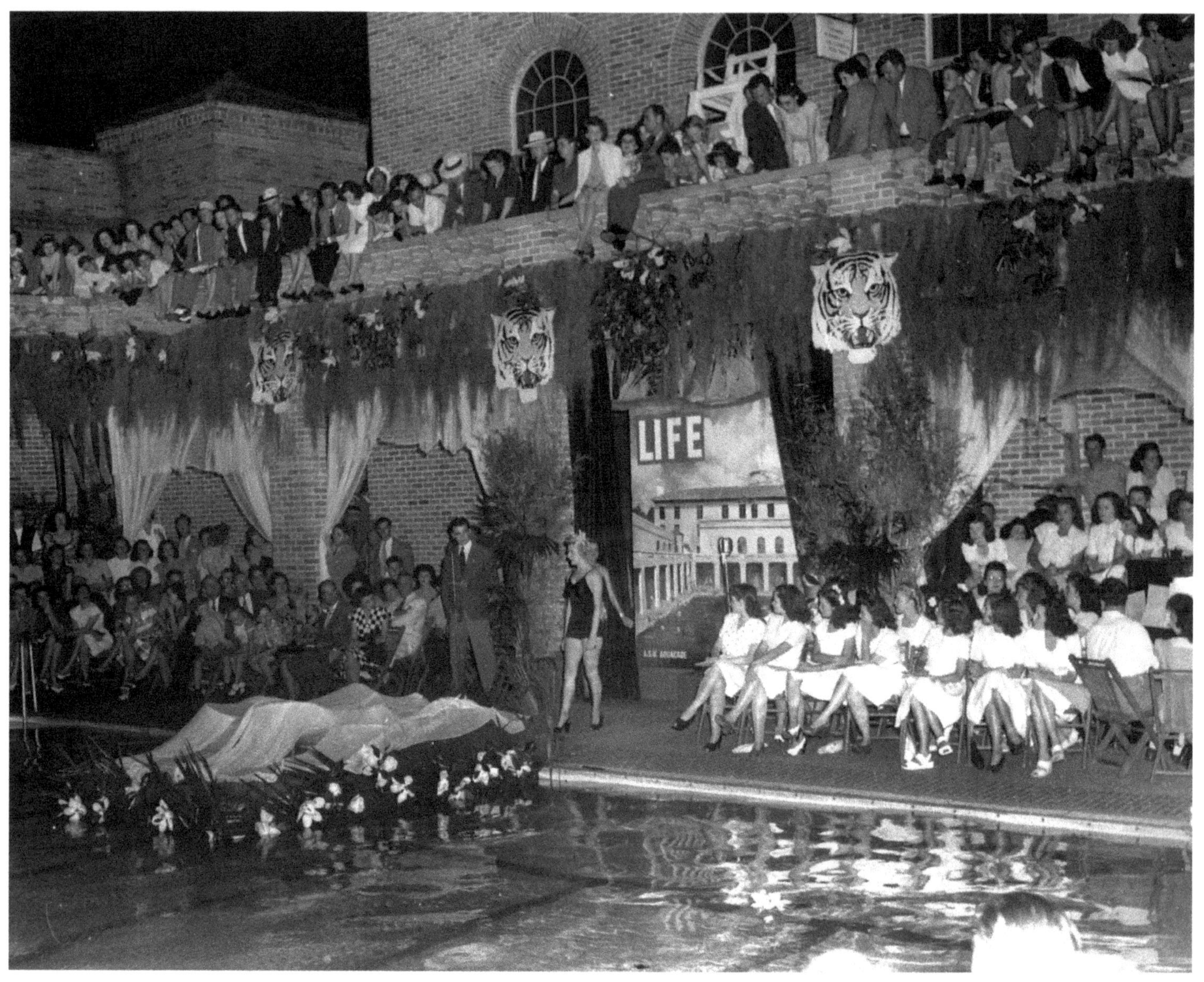

This Aquacade held at the LSU Natatorium around 1940 was one of many on-campus entertainments for students during homecoming. Here, a crowned beauty approaches the floating throne.

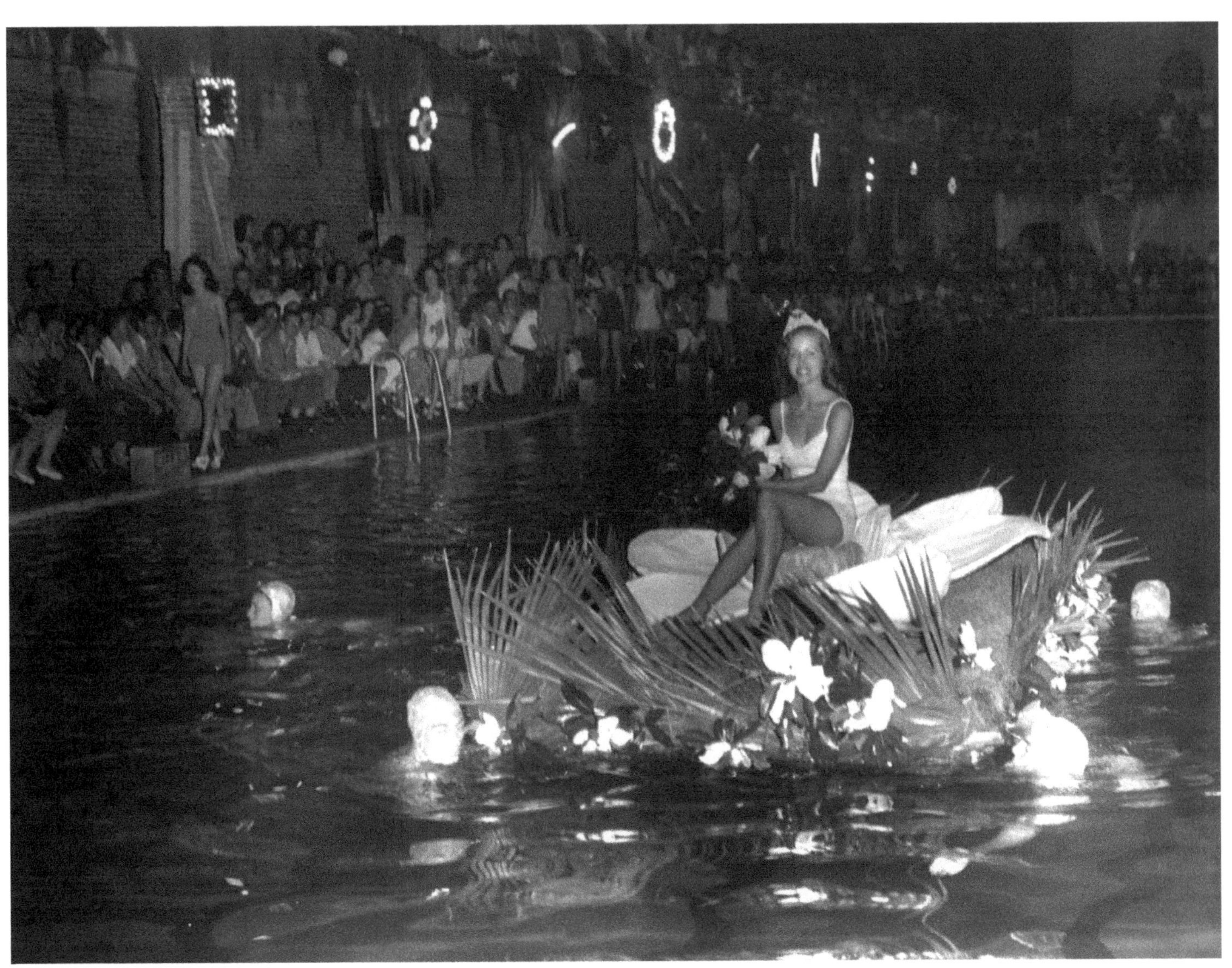

Perhaps the newly crowned homecoming queen, this young woman enjoys a quick spin around the pool on her floating throne. Her attendants provide the necessary motive power.

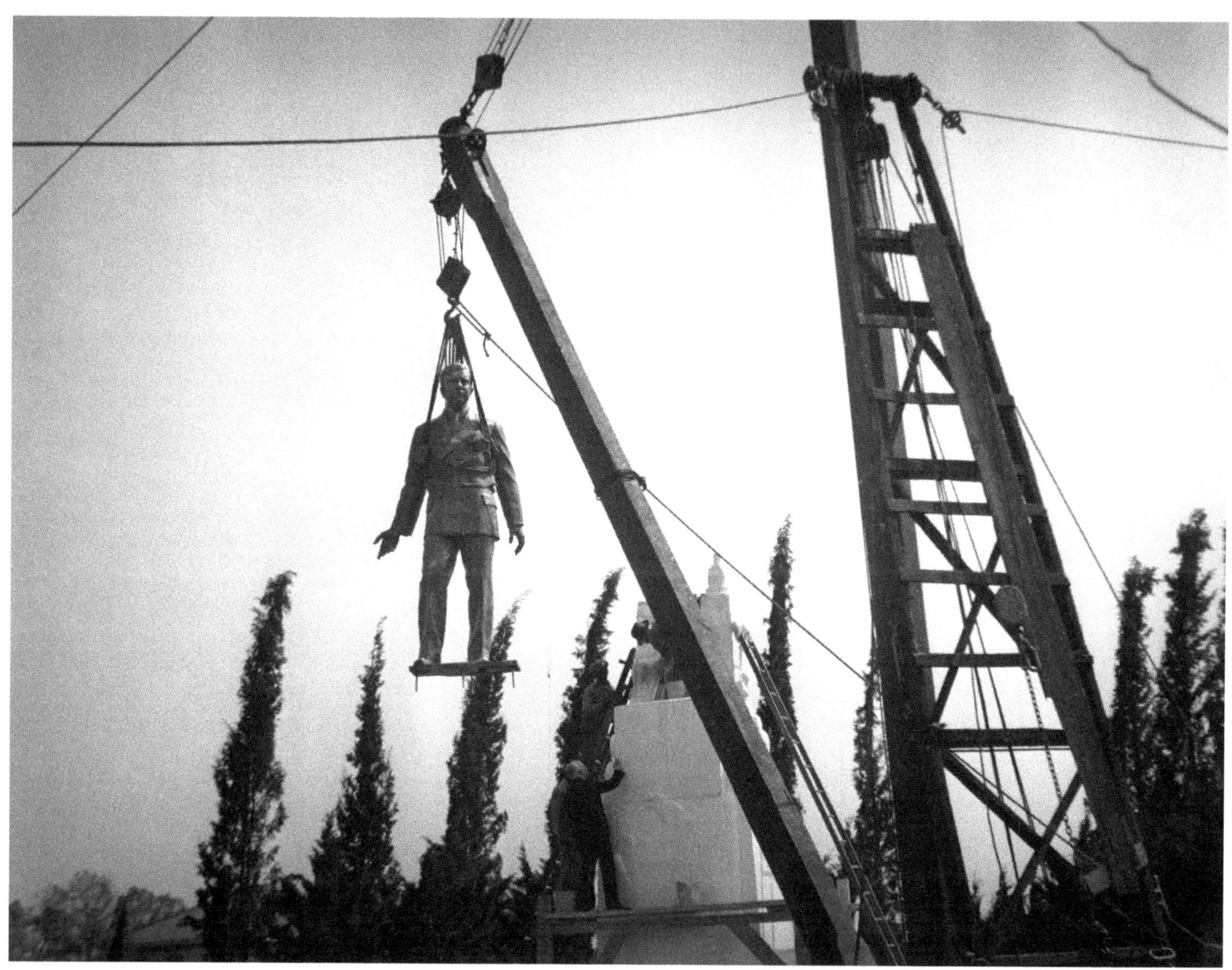

Five years after Huey P. Long's assassination, his remaining supporters in the state legislature earmarked funds to have this statue erected over his grave in front of the Capitol. In this view, workers stand ready by the marble plinth upon which the memorial still stands.

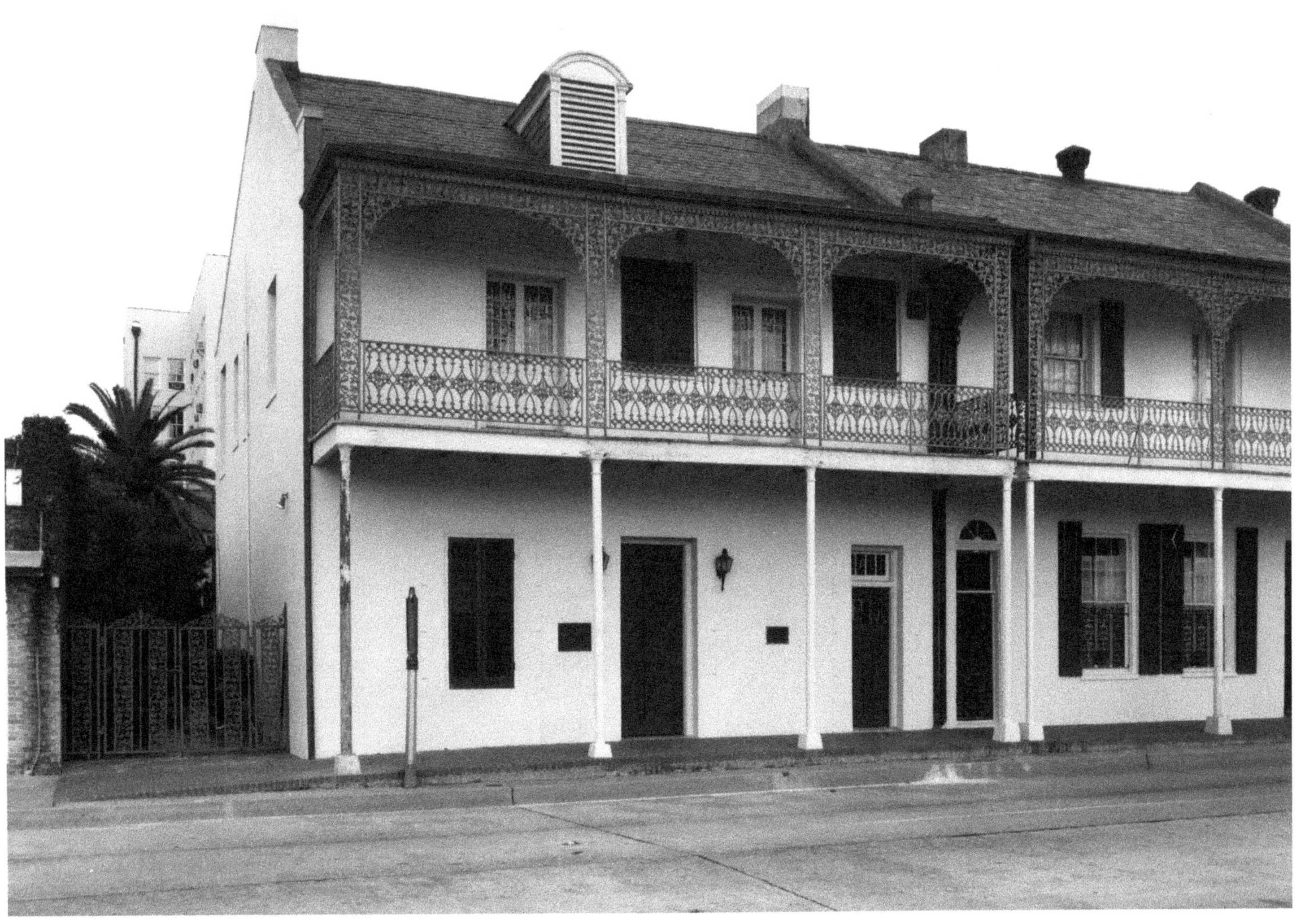

The Historic American Buildings Survey (HABS) was begun in 1933 as a joint program of the American Institute of Architects, the Library of Congress, and the National Park Service. Its purpose was, and is, to document America's architectural heritage. This photo of the Tessier Building, constructed in 1800 on Lafayette Street in downtown Baton Rouge, was taken around 1940 as part of the survey.

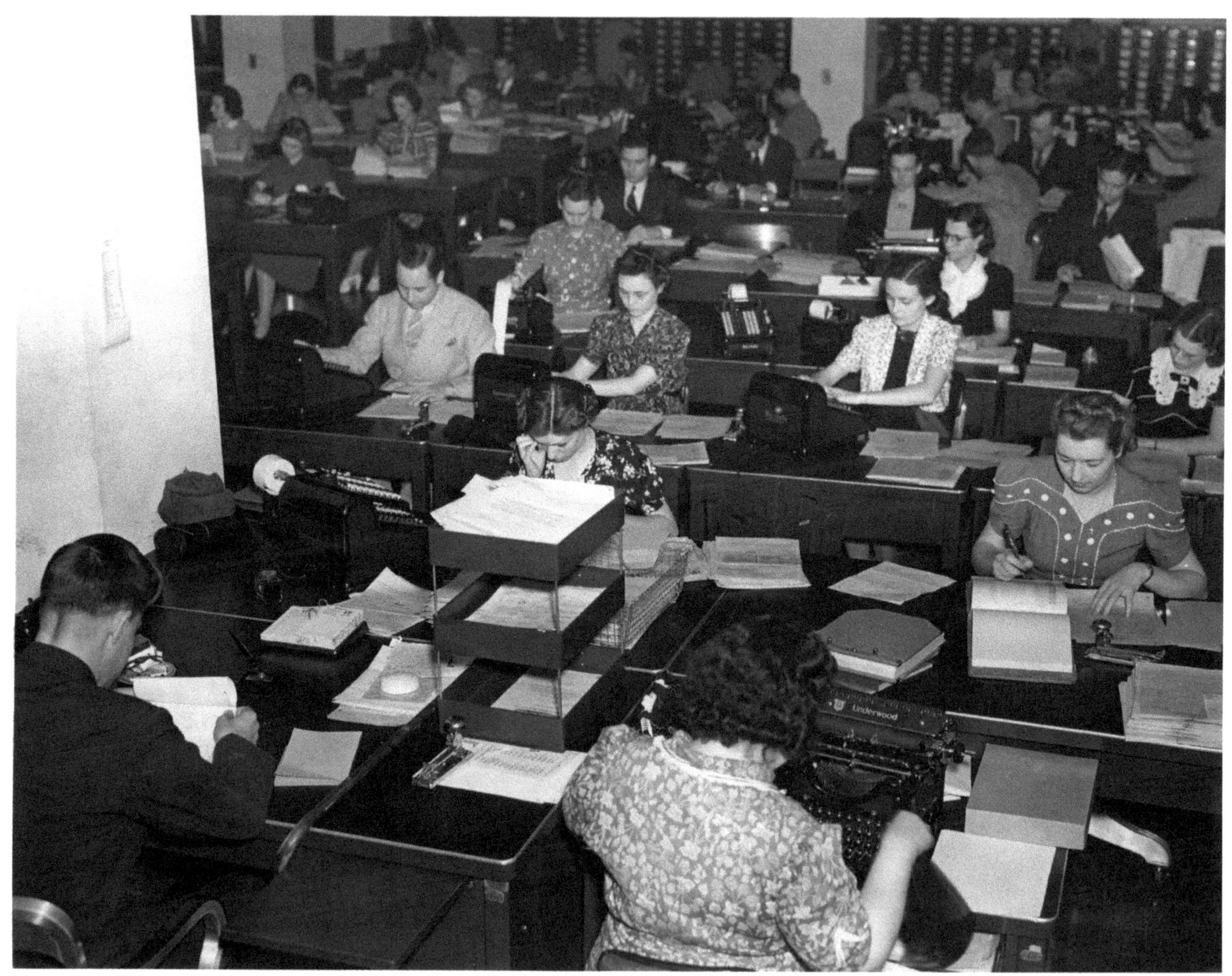

Employees of the Louisiana Department of Commerce and Industry work under crowded conditions in this photograph from around 1940.

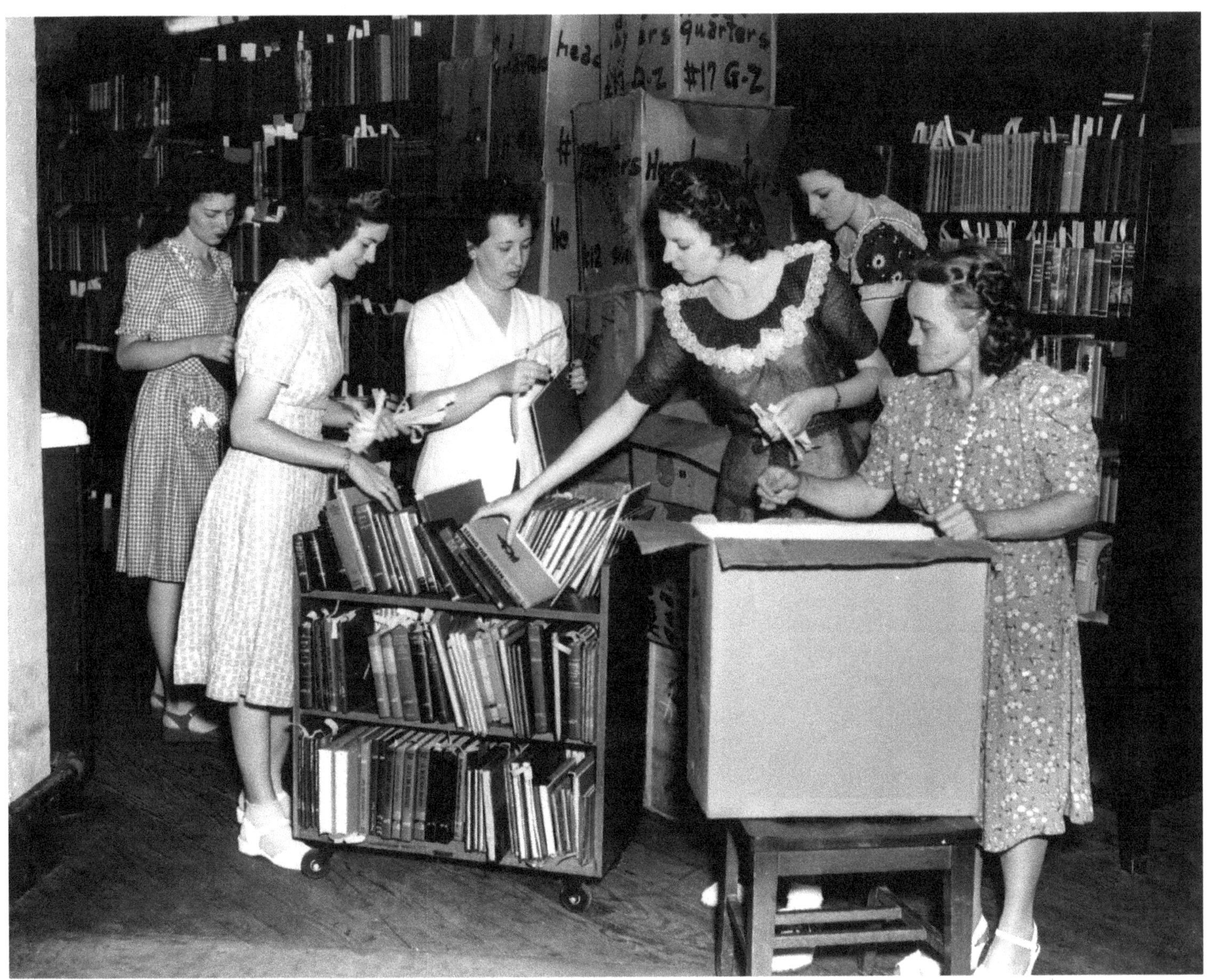

As the Depression eased, the State Library of Louisiana expanded its services. Here, in the 1940s, a group of Extension Department employees pack up a shipment of books destined for the Saint Helena Parish Demonstration Library.

By the time of this 1940s photo, Baton Rouge had long been the seat of state services to blind citizens. The state library played a large role in those services by providing works printed in Braille for the reading pleasure of the visually impaired.

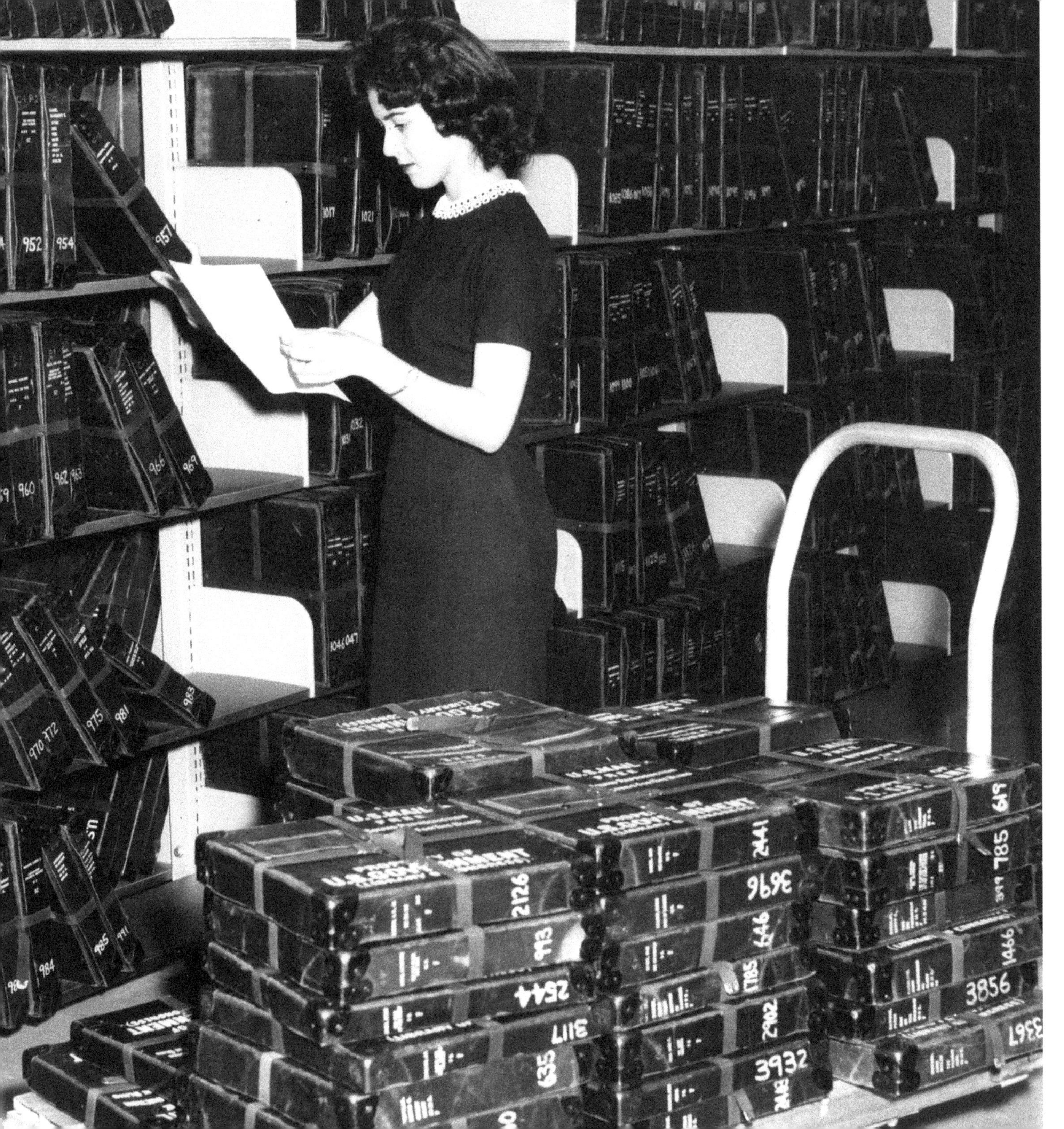
952
954
957
960
966
969
975
981
983
984
985
2126
2441
3696
913
646
2544
3117
635
2902
3932
619
785
1466
3856
3367

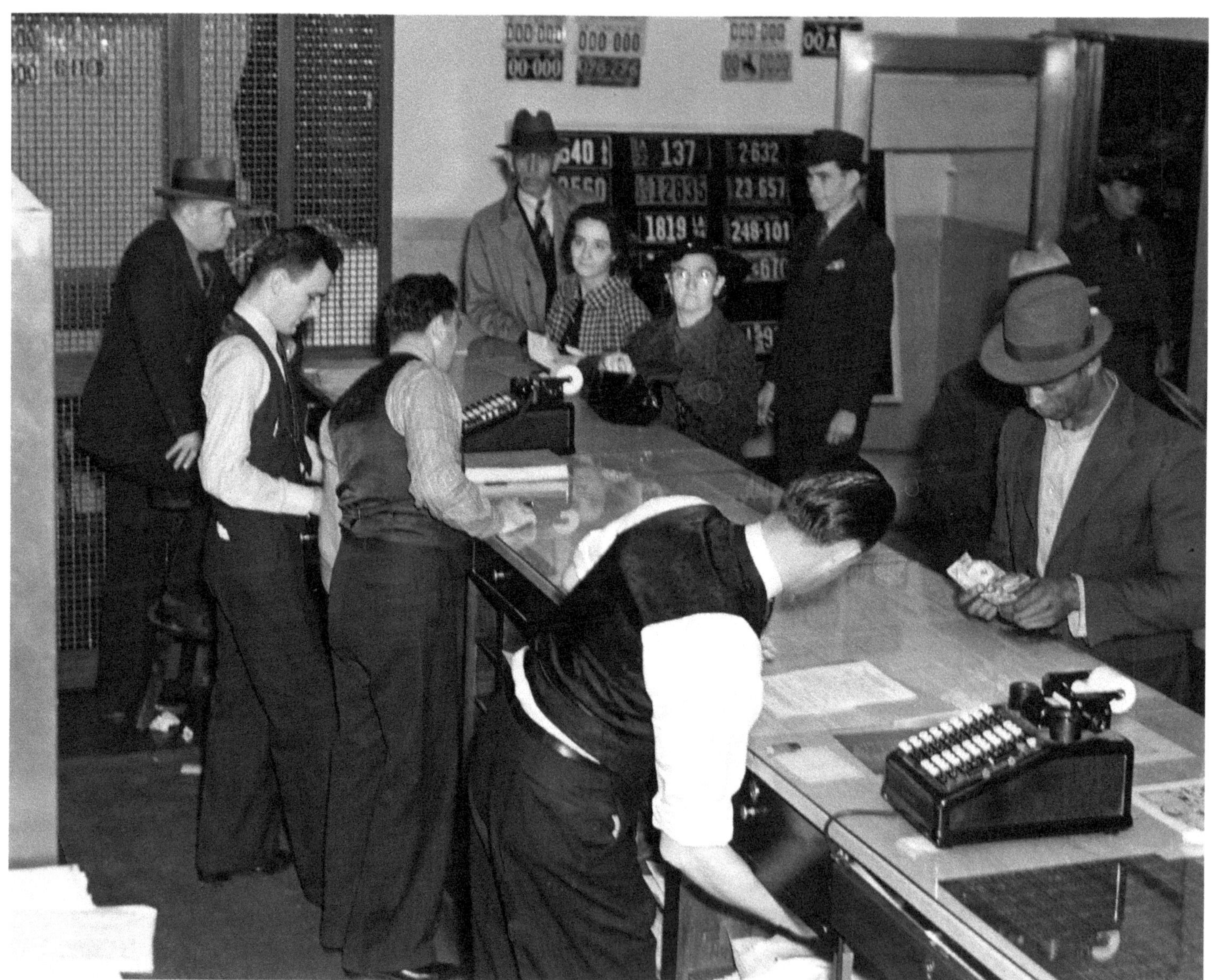

The Louisiana Department of Commerce and Industry was responsible for running and maintaining the Motor Vehicle Bureau in the 1940s. In this image from that period, bureau workers serve citizens in search of new licenses and motor vehicle tags.

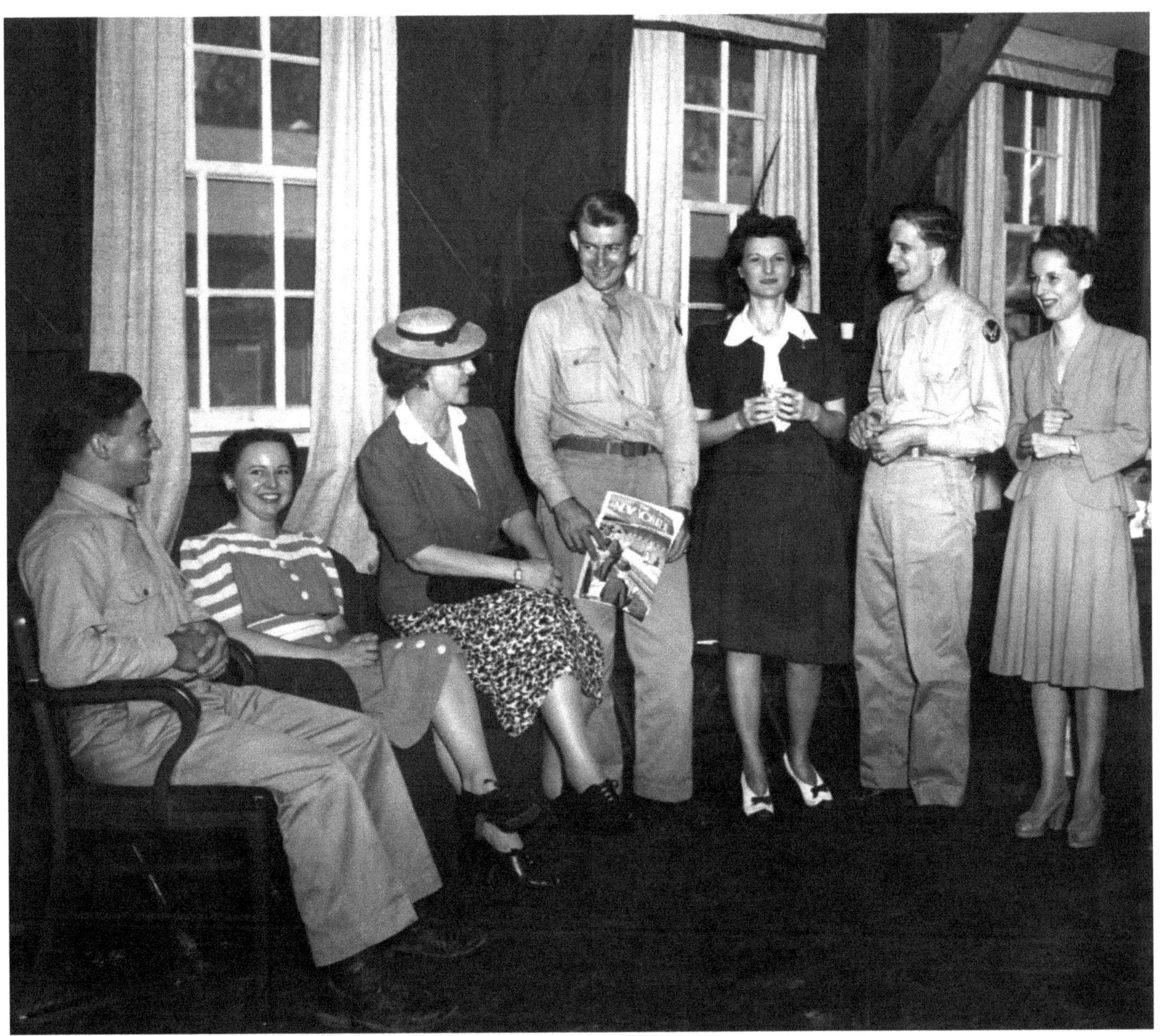

With the advent of World War II, Harding Air Field north of Baton Rouge became a training base that would house thousands of nascent airmen. When not flying, the Army Air Corps men could relax and enjoy the latest magazines, as well as the company of civilian women, at the base library.

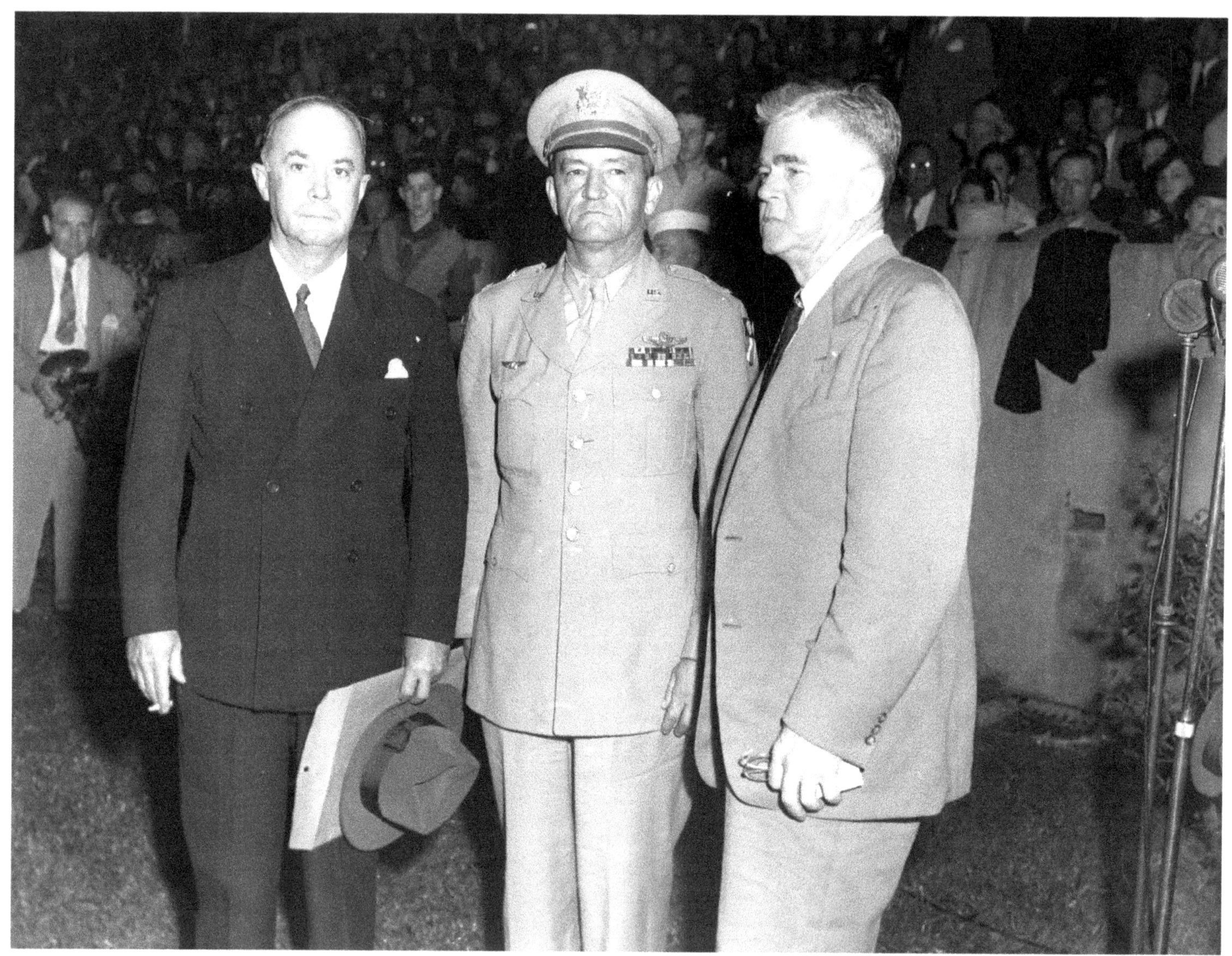

Born in Commerce, Texas, and raised in Waterproof, Louisiana, Claire Lee Chennault attended LSU briefly. During World War I he learned to fly while in the Army. After resigning from the Army in 1937, he volunteered with the Chinese, training airmen. In August 1941, Chennault established the Flying Tigers, a group of volunteer American airmen who fought the Japanese in Southeast Asia. Here, around 1947, General Chennault, at center, visits with LSU President William B. Hatcher, at right.

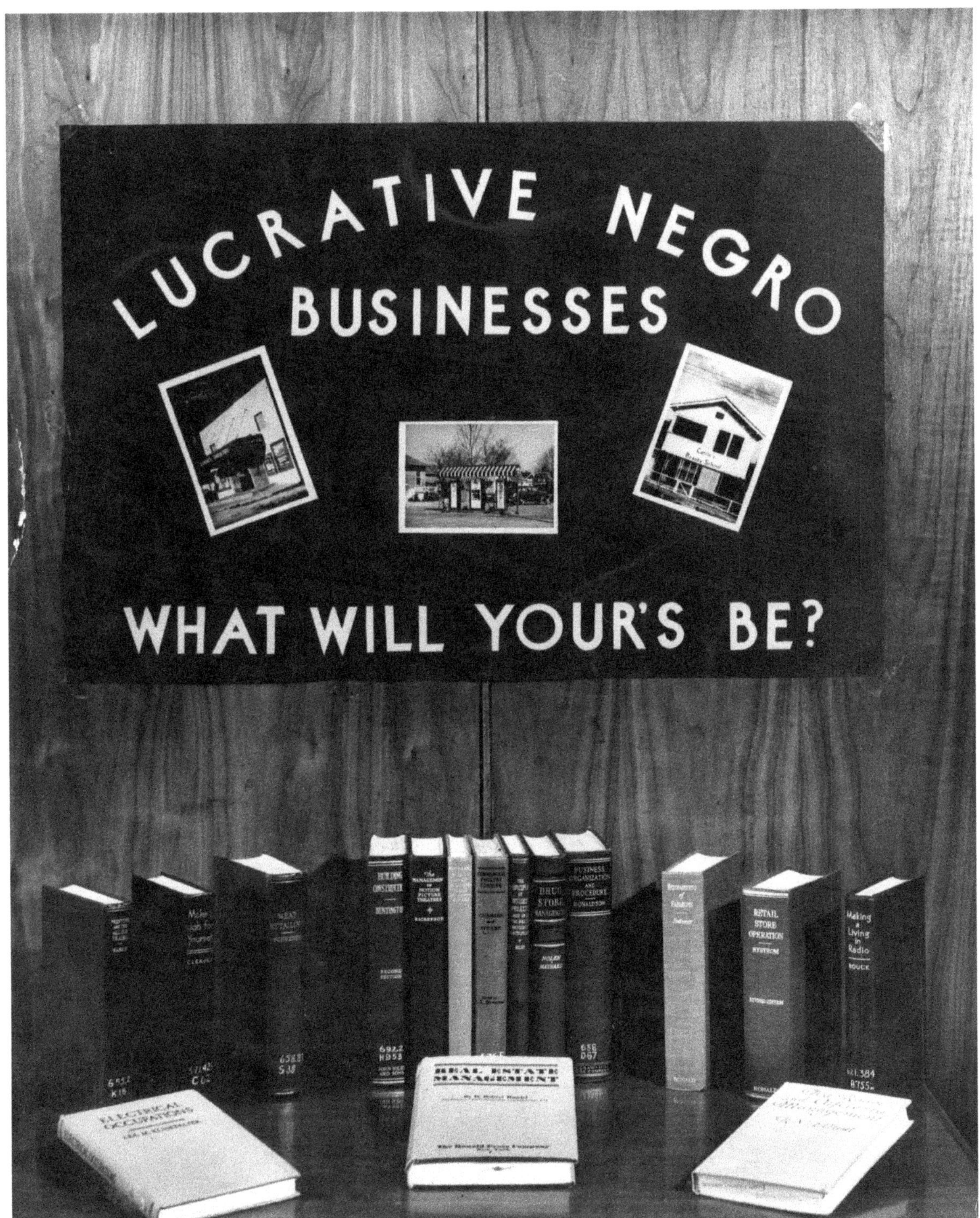

The State Library of Louisiana, working with Southern University and A&M College, put together a display for the Negro Services Department of the university in 1948. The library and the university worked together to aid the improvement of African American businesses in Baton Rouge.

LSU's mascot, Mike the Tiger, arrived on campus in 1936 due in large part to the efforts of athletic director T. P. Heard, trainer Chellis Mike Chambers, swimming pool manager and intramural swimming coach William G. Hickey Higginbotham, and LSU law student Ed Laborde. This image of Mike the First was taken around 1945 at his cage near "Death Valley," the LSU football stadium.

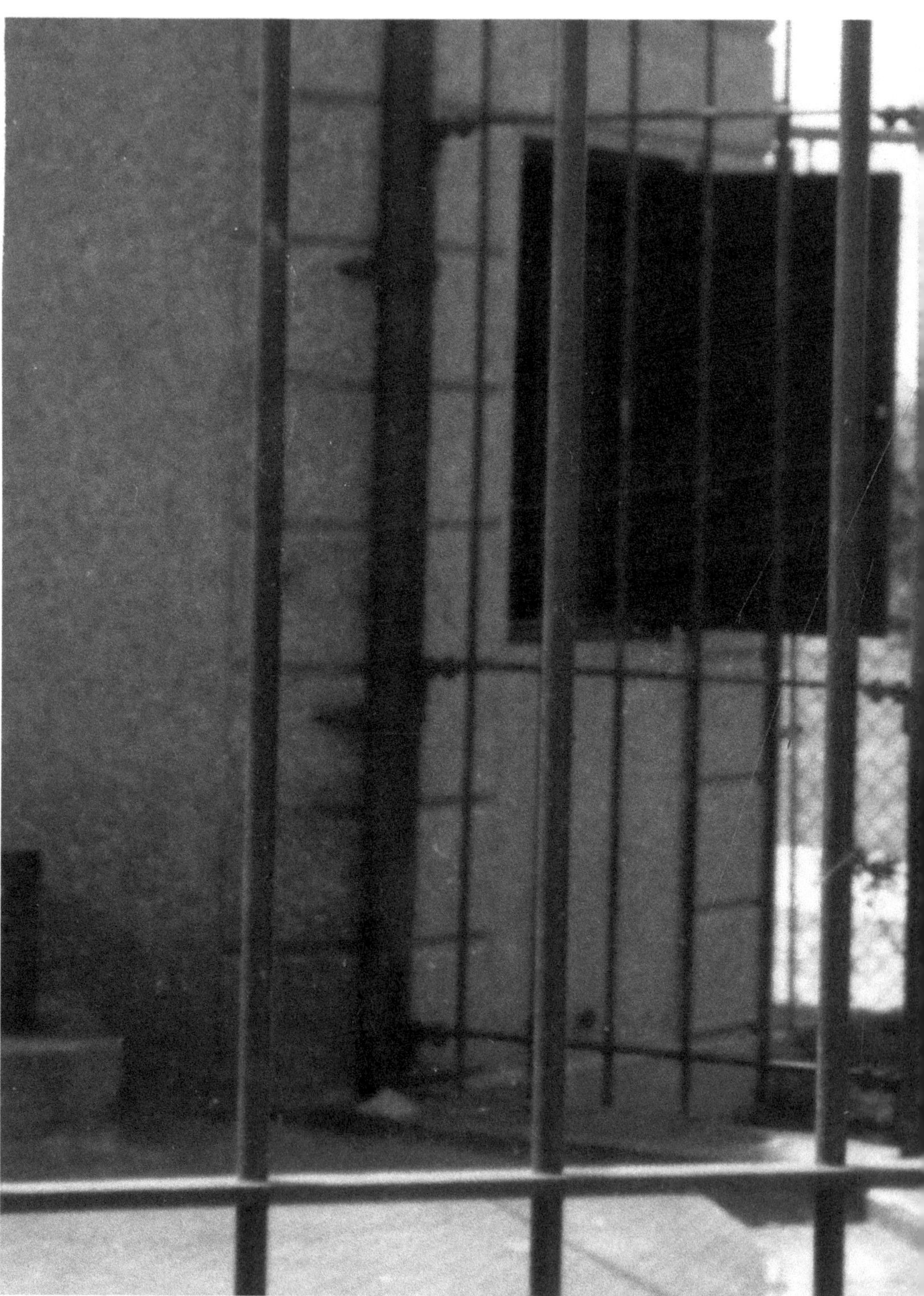

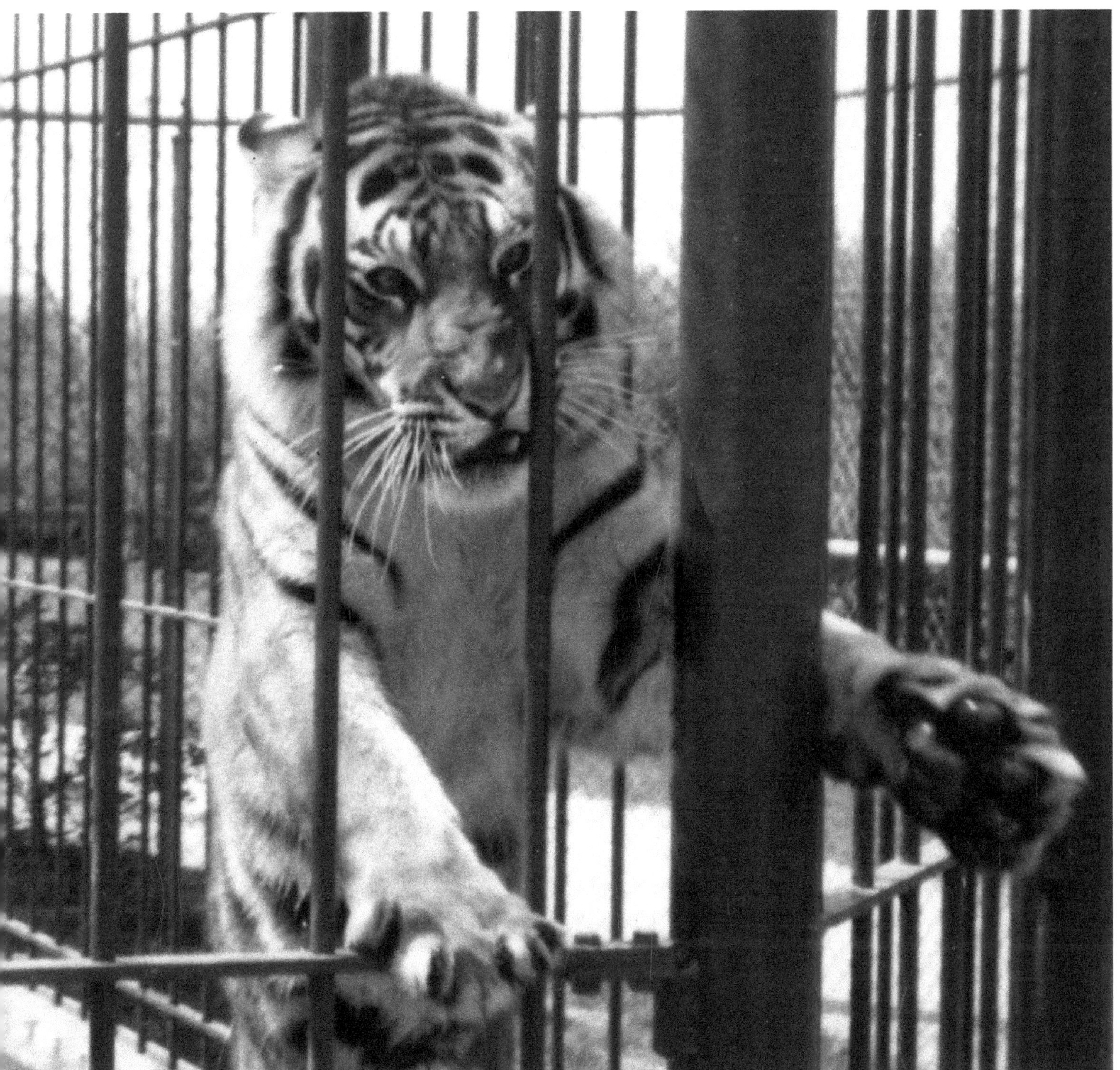

By the time of this February 1945 scene at the Humble Oil & Refining Company's refinery hospital, the city's many refineries were the source of aviation fuel, synthetic rubber, and a host of other products created for the war effort.

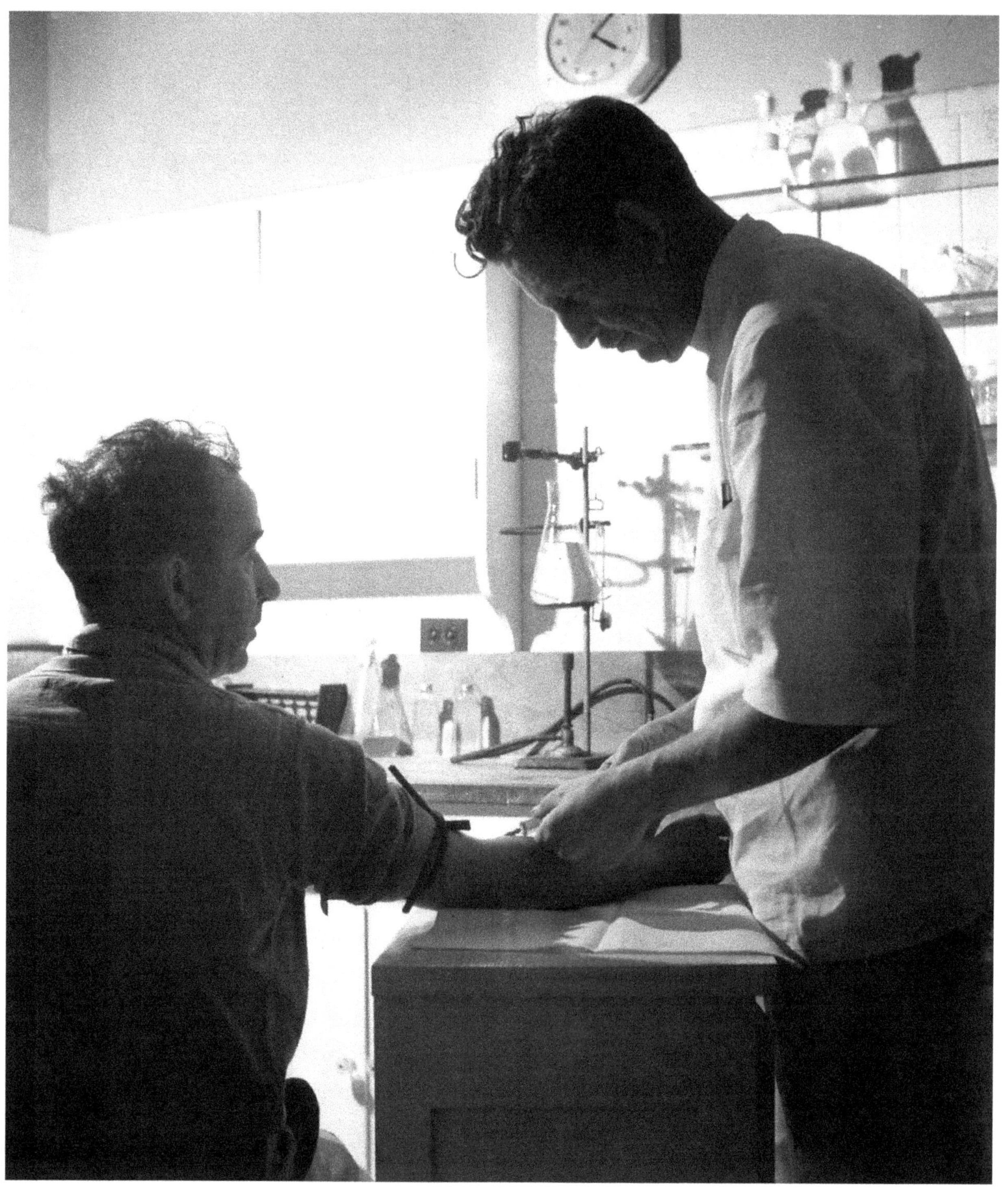

Postwar Baton Rouge

(1950–1959)

Postwar Baton Rouge experienced continued growth. The city's suburban expansion accelerated as the industrial base grew and city, parish, and state governments swelled. The 1947 vote to consolidate the city and parish governments into one entity with a mayor-president heading the system and working with, or in spite of, the Metro Council led to many challenges in this decade. A new war in Korea drew LSU graduates into battle once again.

Not only did existing industry expand, but new industries became established and transportation systems improved to handle this new demand. The petroleum industry, already well established, brought the need for railroad tank cars to carry raw materials into the plants and finished products out of the plants. In 1958 the Union Tank Car Company built the largest freestanding circular building in the world, using Buckminster Fuller's geodesic dome principals. The Mississippi River, long the nation's highway, had made Baton Rouge an inland port of some note. Following the creation of the Greater Baton Rouge Port Commission in 1952, ever more cargo and commodities flowed into and out from the city.

Civil rights took a front seat, literally, in the city in 1953 during the bus boycott. African American riders had been banned from sitting in the front of city buses from the bus system's inception. The Metro Council voted to end the practice at a March meeting, but bus drivers went on strike in retaliation. The drivers returned to work in June following a ruling in favor of segregated seating by the state attorney general. Later that month, African American riders organized a boycott that ultimately forced the hand of white leadership, resulting in an agreement to desegregate seating.

Public schools, including LSU and Southern University, also struggled with integration. African American parents sued the public school system to end segregation in 1956, but the suit remained unsettled until 2003. Southern University opened a graduate program in 1957. In the coming decade more and more aspects of the city would come under pressure to desegregate, with varying degrees of success.

As new media technology develops, public libraries provide these media to their patrons. In February 1950, Vivian Cazayoux and an assistant at the State Library of Louisiana inspect a reel of motion picture film before sending it out on loan.

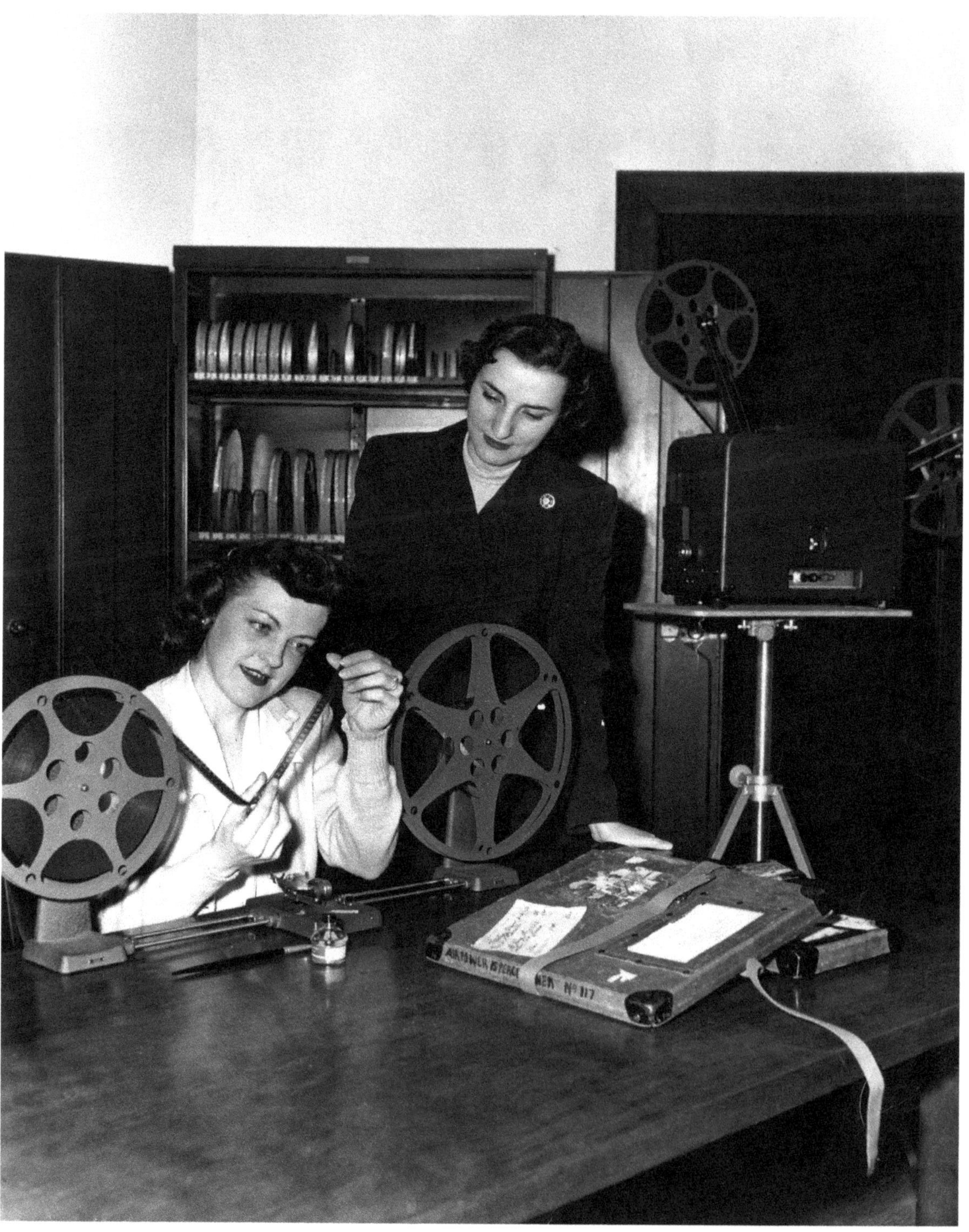

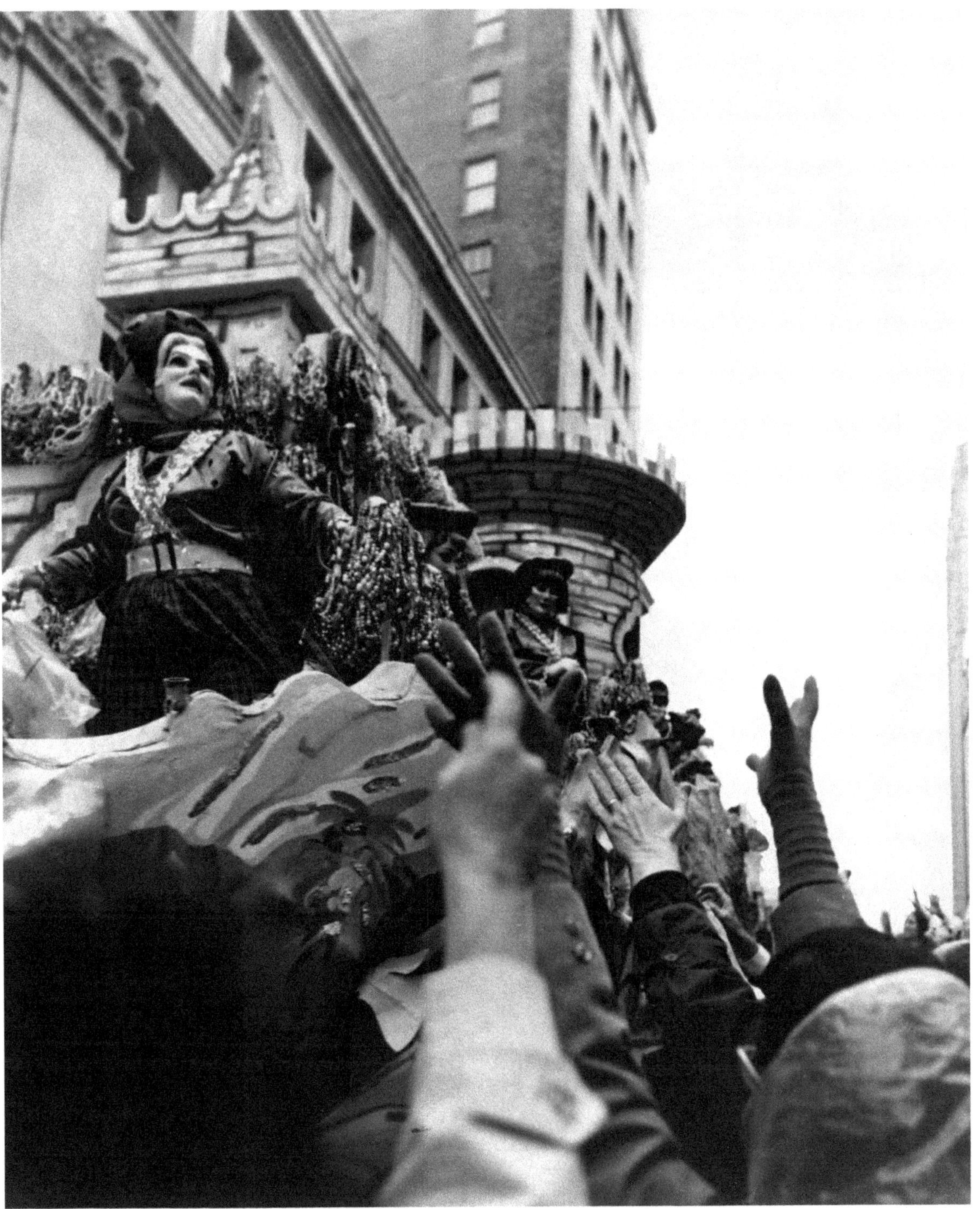

Following a few decades' decline during which neither the Firemen's Parade nor the Mardi Gras Parade took place in Baton Rouge, Fat Tuesday made a comeback with the establishment of the Krewe of Romany in 1949. The return of the Mardi Gras Parade meant the return of downtown scenes such as this one from the 1950s.

Before the days of corporate, big-box bookstores, Baton Rouge had a number of privately owned-and-operated book dealers. One such store, the Shortess Book Shop, kept the people of Baton Rouge in reading material. Here, around 1955, Helen and Melvin Shortess speak with journalist and author Harnett T. Kane.

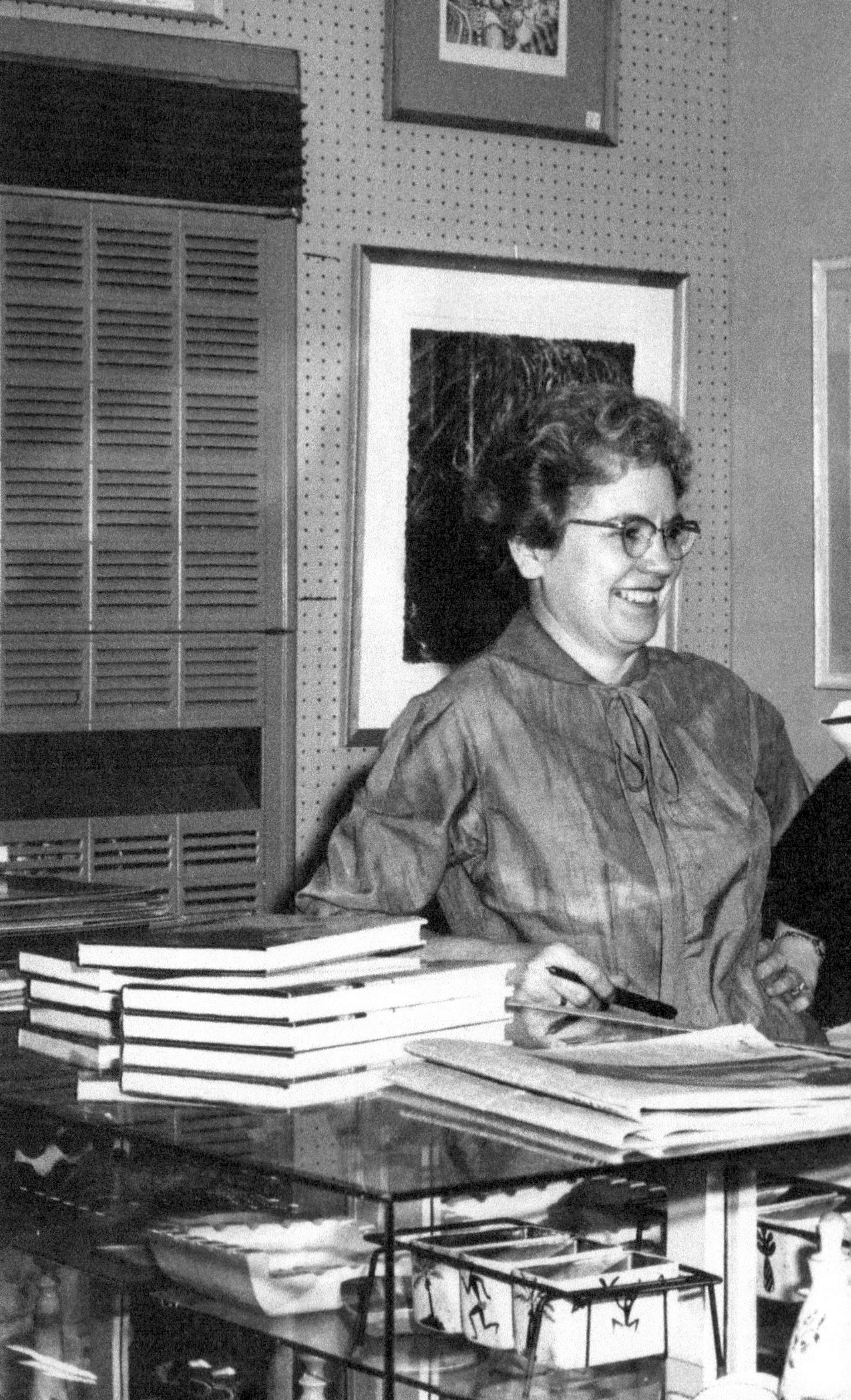

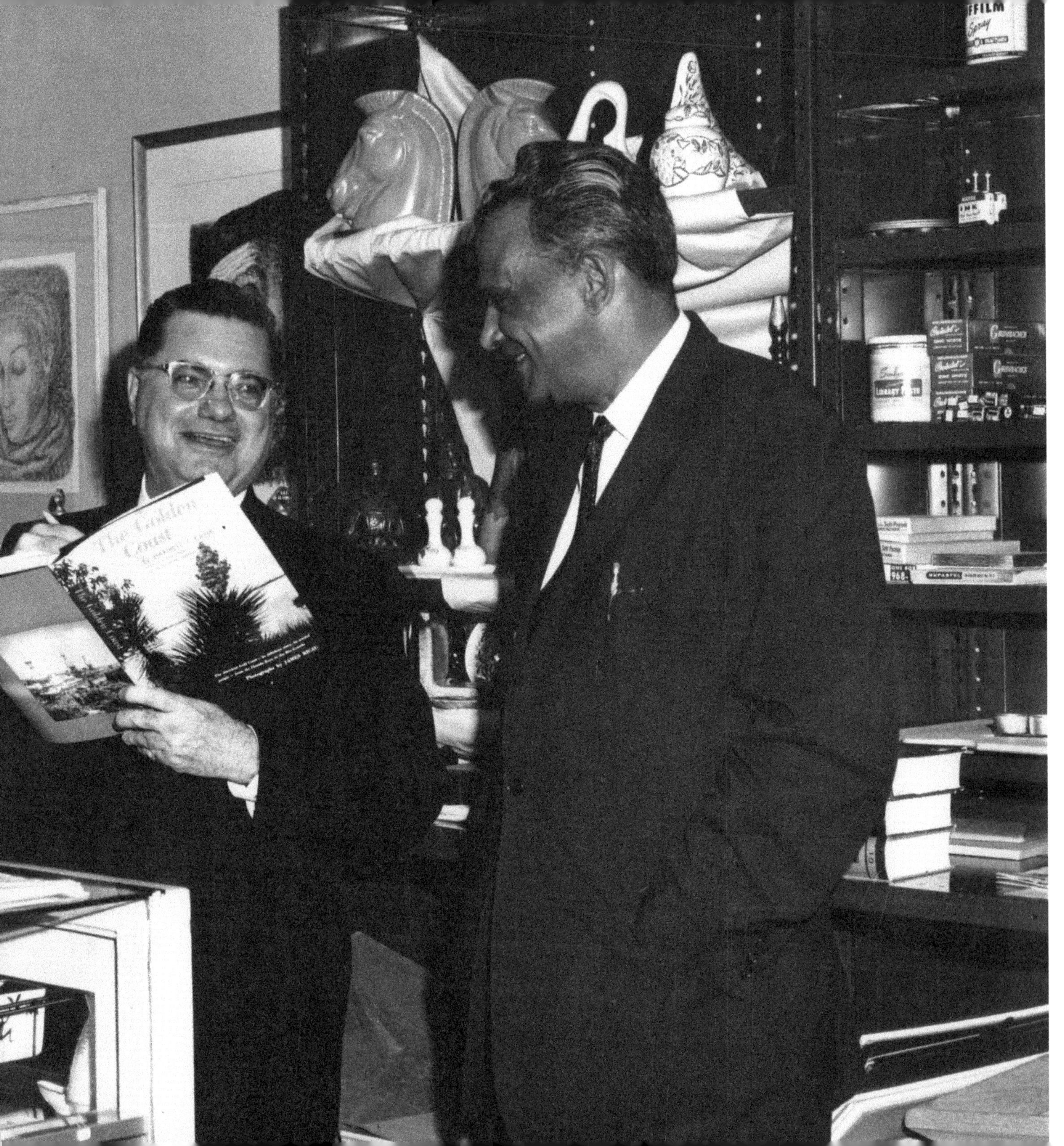
The Golden Coast
NUPASTEL

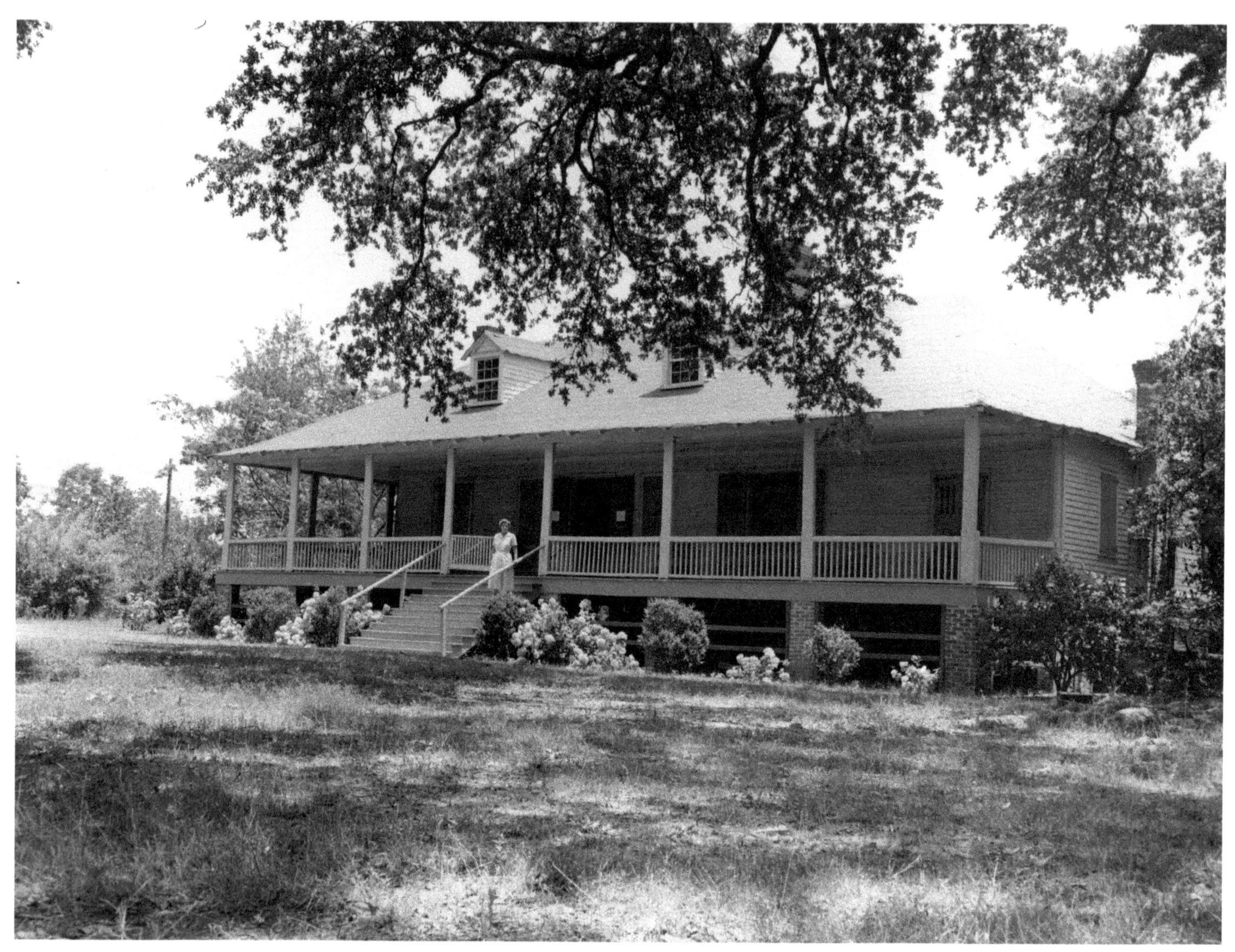

The main house at Magnolia Mound Plantation was constructed around 1791. Mrs. Blanche Duncan acquired the property after it had passed through numerous hands. In 1951, about the time of this photo, Mrs. Duncan hired a local architectural firm to create numerous alterations and additions to the house. In 1966 Magnolia Mound became a Baton Rouge Recreation Department property.

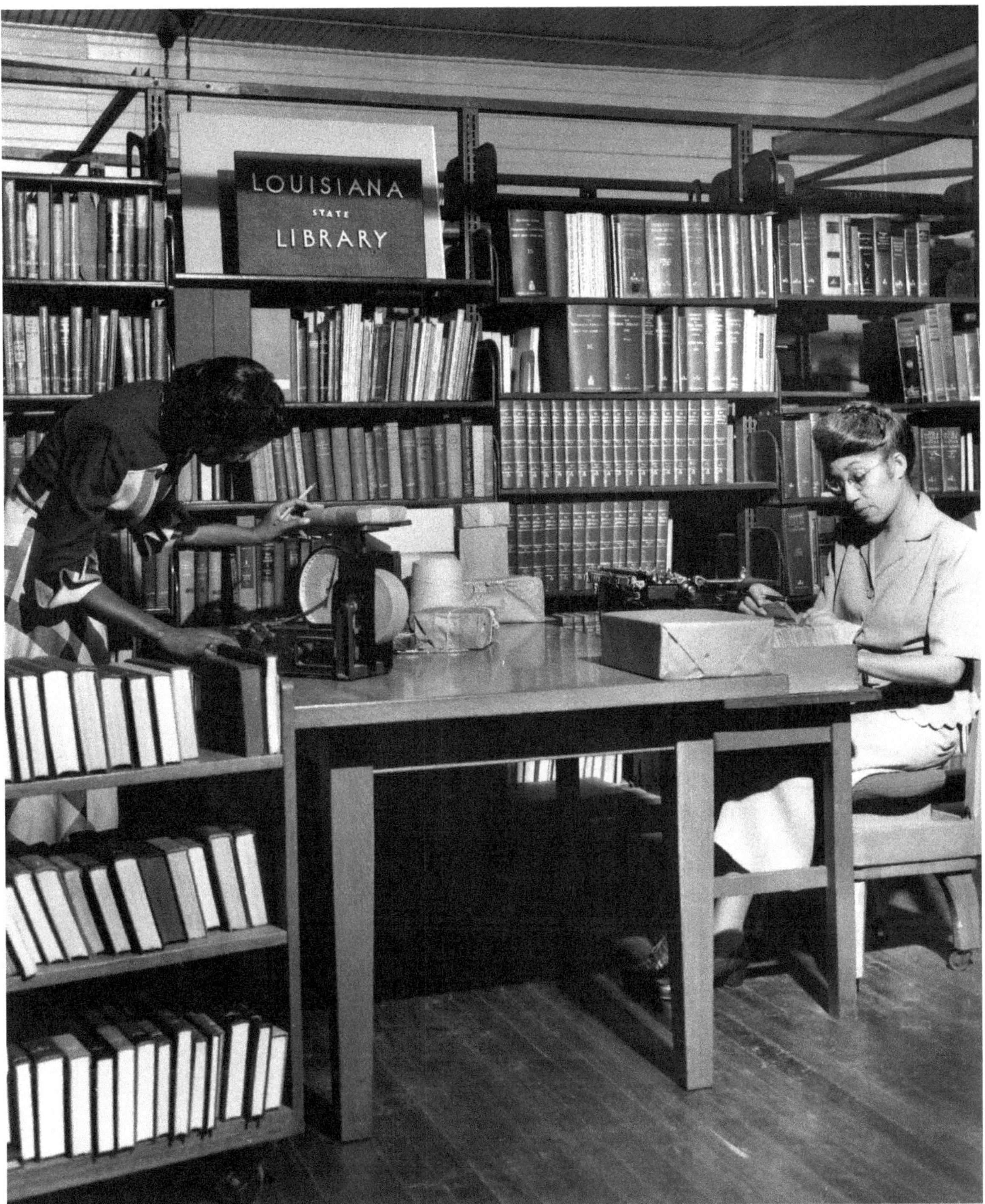

The State Library of Louisiana maintained a branch library, the Negro Services Department, at Southern University and A&M College. In this scene from the early 1950s, Mrs. Murray, seated, and an assistant work with library materials.

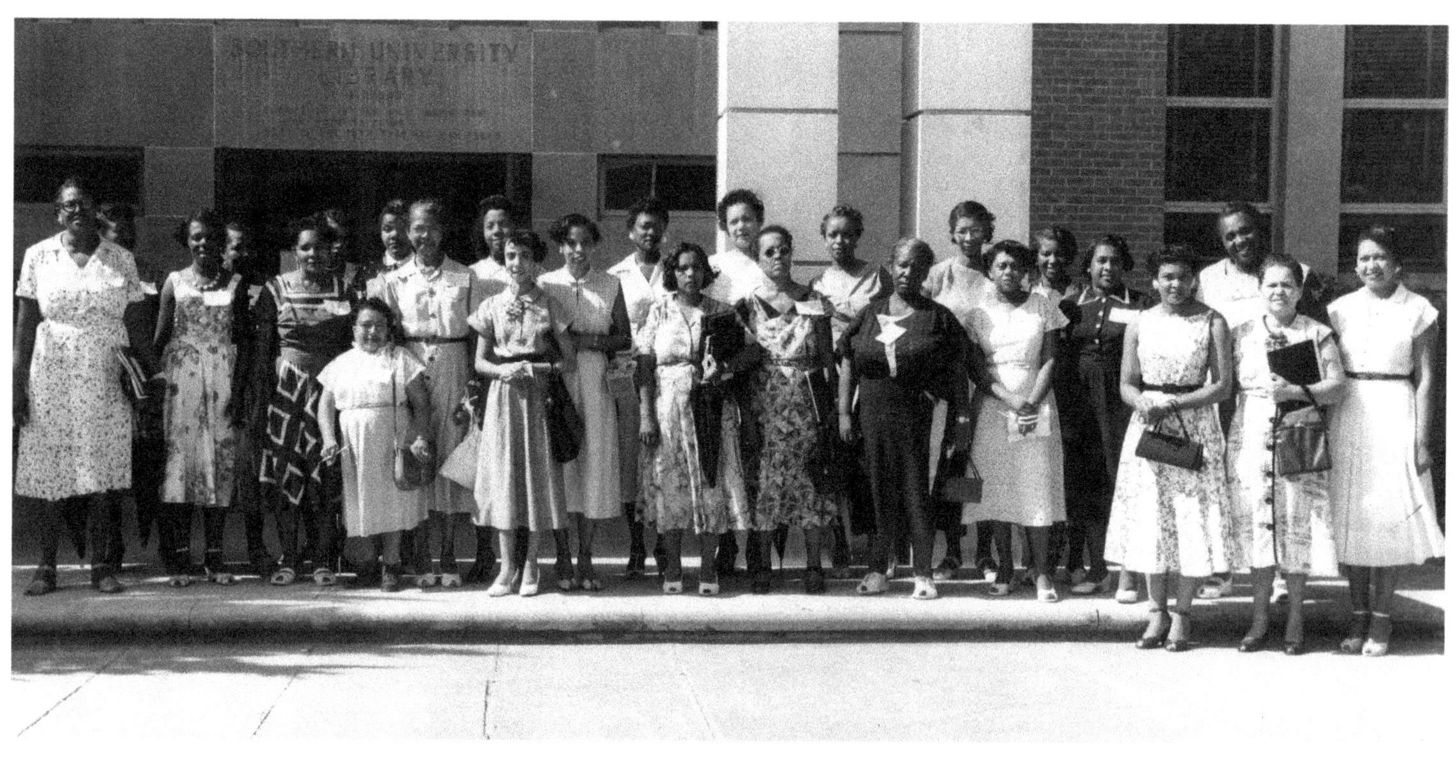

Participants in a Negro Librarians Conference held in the 1950s stand in front of the Southern University Library. Attendees arrived in Baton Rouge from all over the state.

A Turbulent Decade

(1960–1969)

As more and more change took place in Baton Rouge, the citizens began to look to the past. Urban renewal, increased motor vehicle activity in the old town, and spreading suburbs introduced even more traffic, and the national urge to modernize led to the destruction of many historic structures. Efforts begun in the 1930s to preserve historic buildings continued into the 1960s, but with only limited success.

Racial integration of Baton Rouge continued into the 1960s and introduced a great deal of turbulence, as had similar efforts nationwide. The Ku Klux Klan and other white-supremacist groups held countermarches protesting integration. The city's park and recreation department closed one swimming pool rather than integrate. Both LSU and Southern University moved forward with their integration efforts. The public school system remained embroiled in its integration lawsuit. White flight created a growing demographic shift as middle- and upper-class whites left the city for neighboring parishes.

LSU, with its long history as a military school, dropped its requirement that all males enroll in ROTC. At the same time, increased United States involvement in the Vietnam War drew more and more LSU men and women into the conflict. Antiwar demonstrations would begin to appear on campus, an unheard-of event in the history of the university.

And yet, the city continued to grow. The recently organized Greater Baton Rouge Port Commission increased its business to become one of the top 10 ports in the United States, and rail connections expanded. A new bridge built across the Mississippi River in the latter years of the decade provided another transportation access point, tying Baton Rouge even more tightly to the rest of the nation through the interstate highway system.

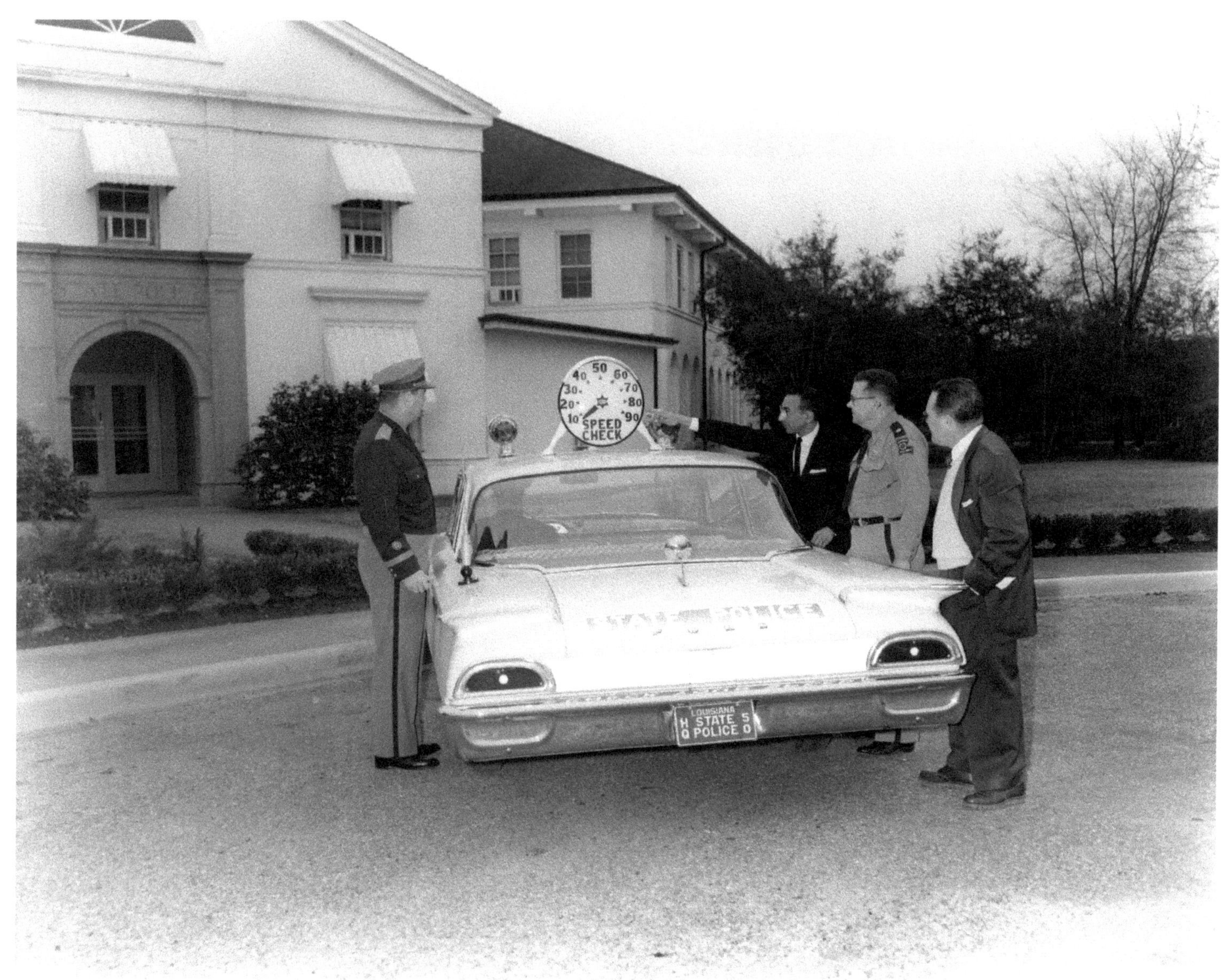

Enforcing traffic laws has always been a primary mission of the Louisiana State Police. This patrol car, photographed in front of the State Police Headquarters in Baton Rouge around 1960, has the latest in speed-checking devices installed on its roof.

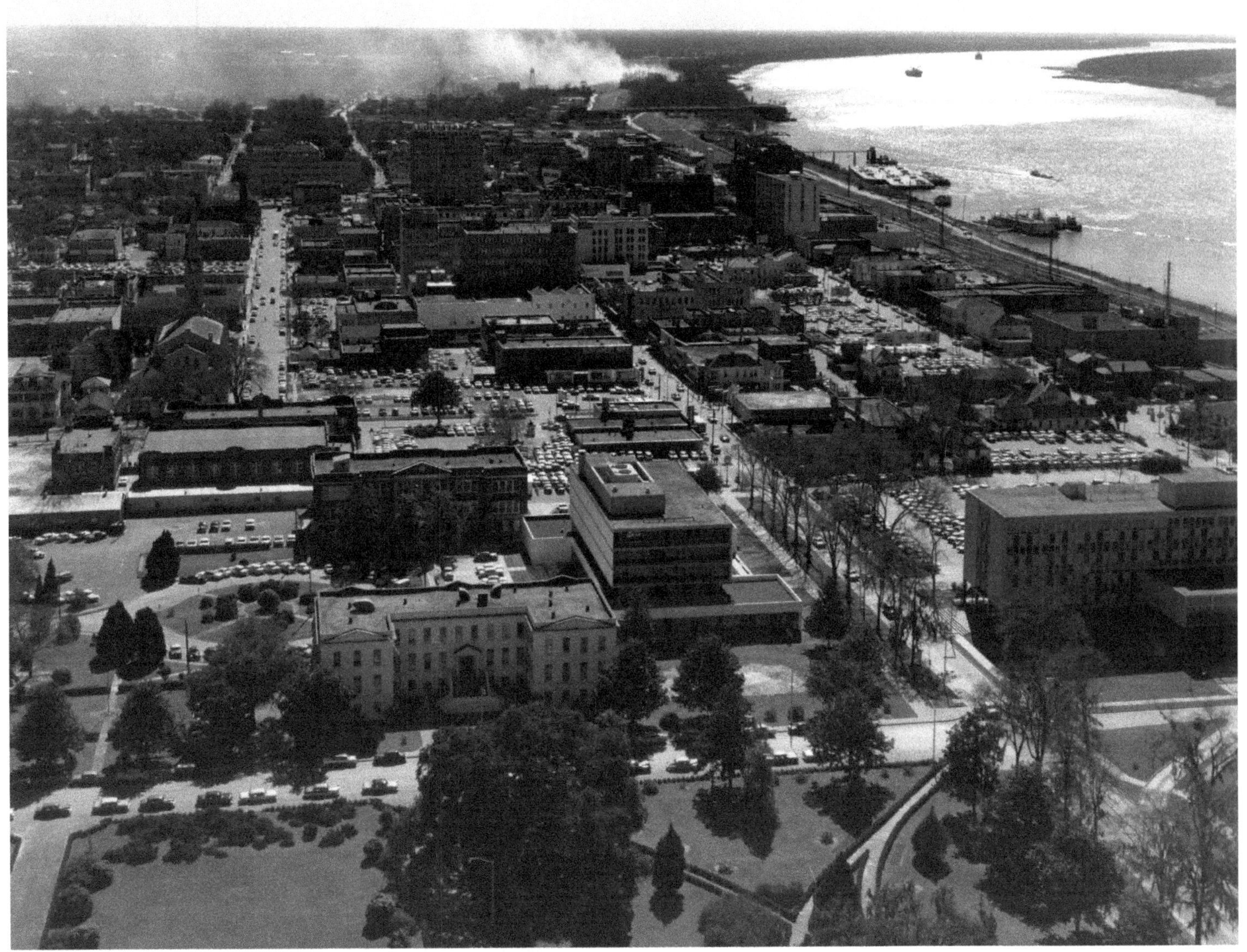

Looking south from the observation deck of the new State Capitol in 1960, this bird's-eye view of Baton Rouge shows many buildings in the foreground that have been demolished over time to make room for newer state buildings.

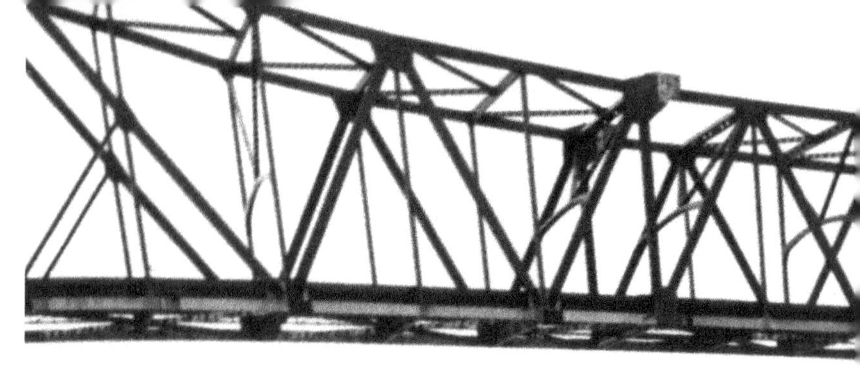

A new bridge crossing the Mississippi River was built in the 1960s. Construction, completed in 1968, was still underway when this shot of the span, as yet without its roadbed, was taken.

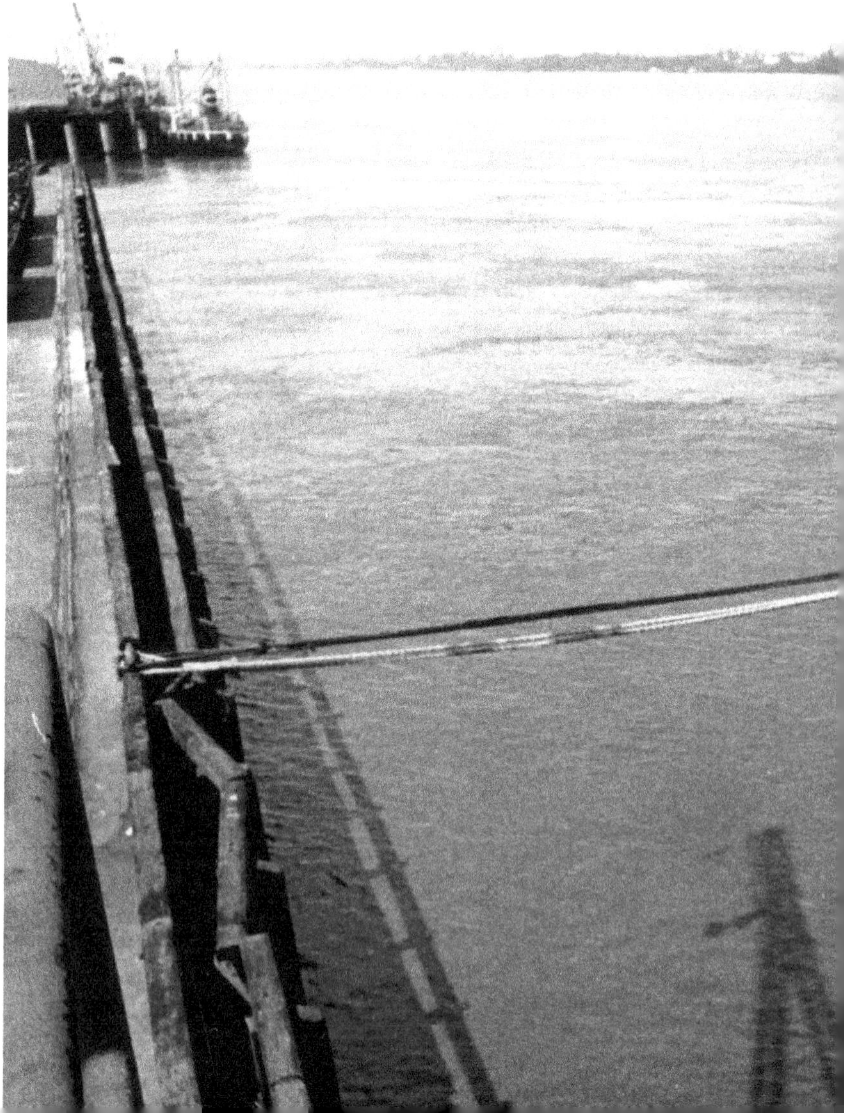

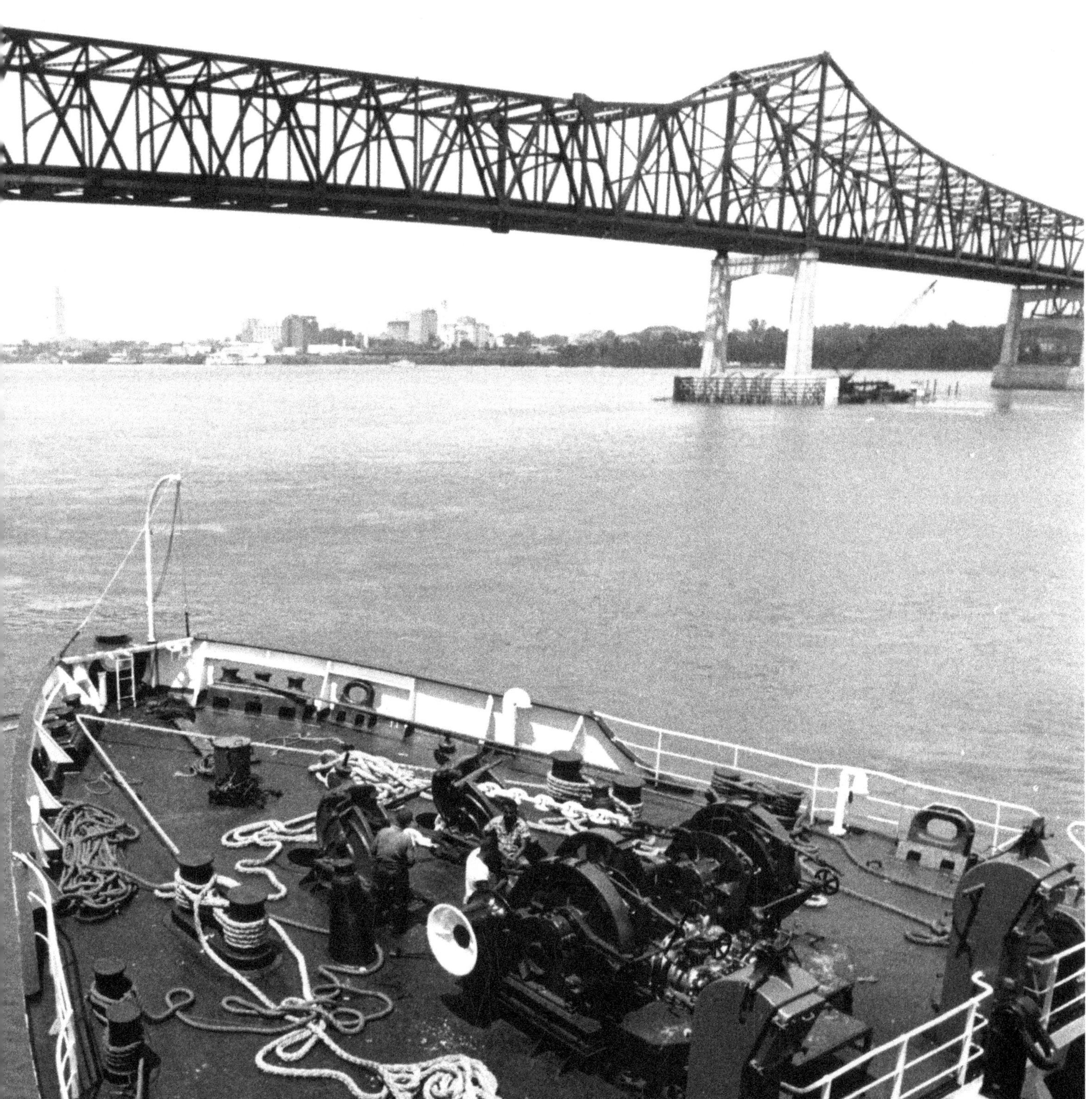

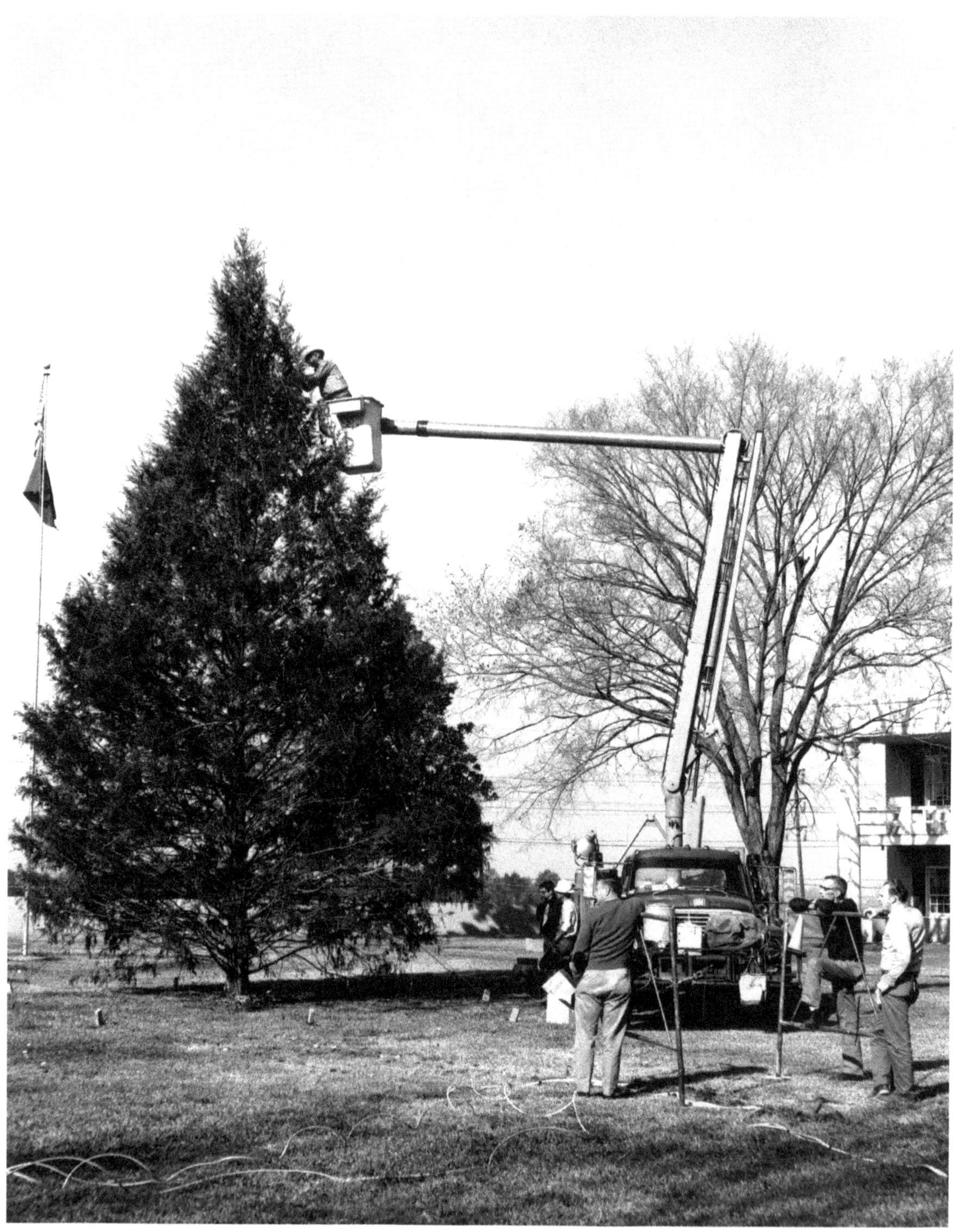

The new Capitol, erected on the site of the old military base that LSU occupied from the 1870s through the 1920s, maintained a few of the old structures. Among them were the Pentagon Barracks, now used for state offices, legislators' apartments, and a tourist center. In this scene from 1969, state workers erect a Christmas tree in the Barracks courtyard.

This aerial view of Baton Rouge, created around 1960, is looking east from the observation deck of the new State Capitol. The old Arsenal building can be seen at center, just past the formal garden. Behind the Arsenal, a recently built roadway connects to Interstate 110, part of which is visible in the upper-right corner.

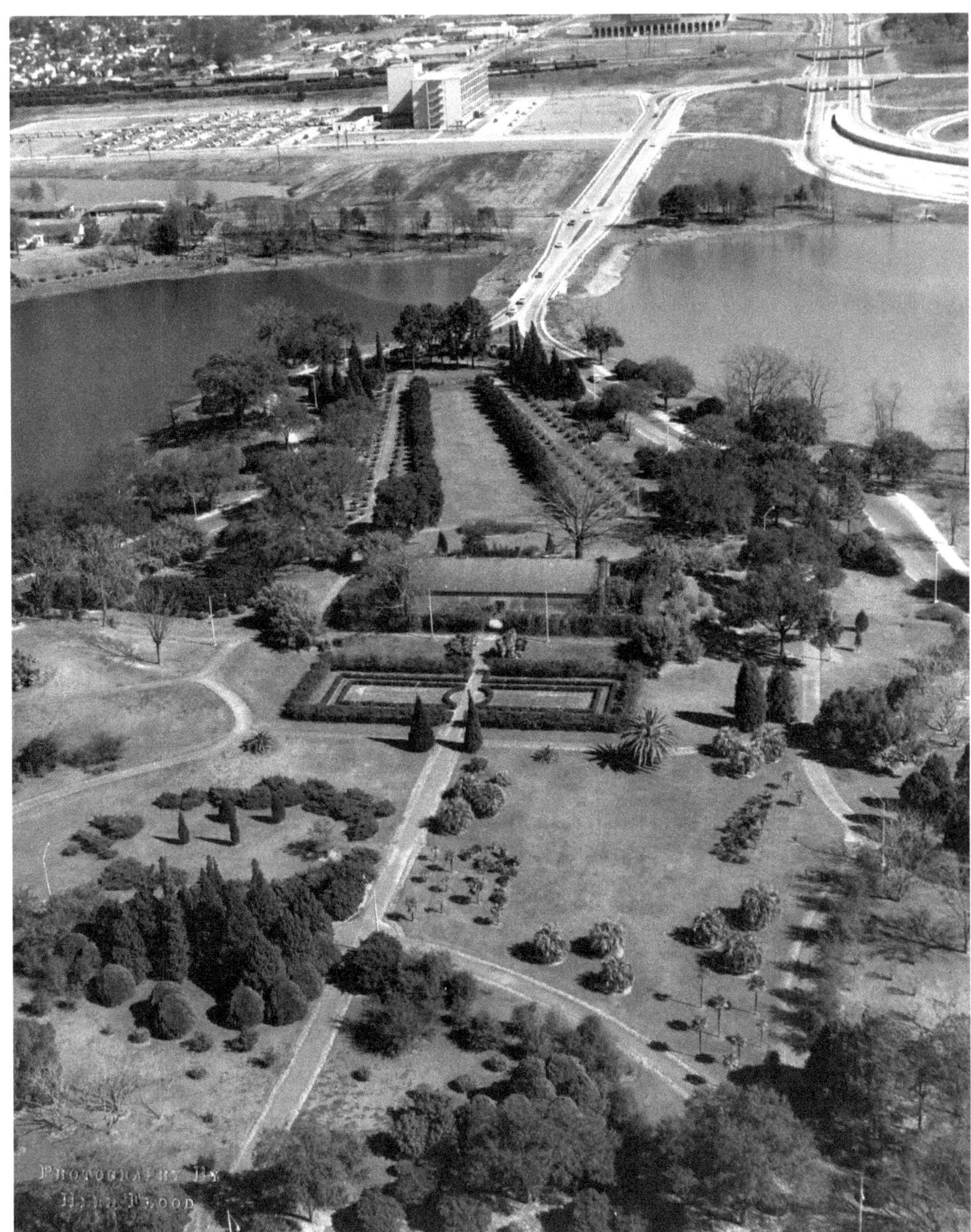

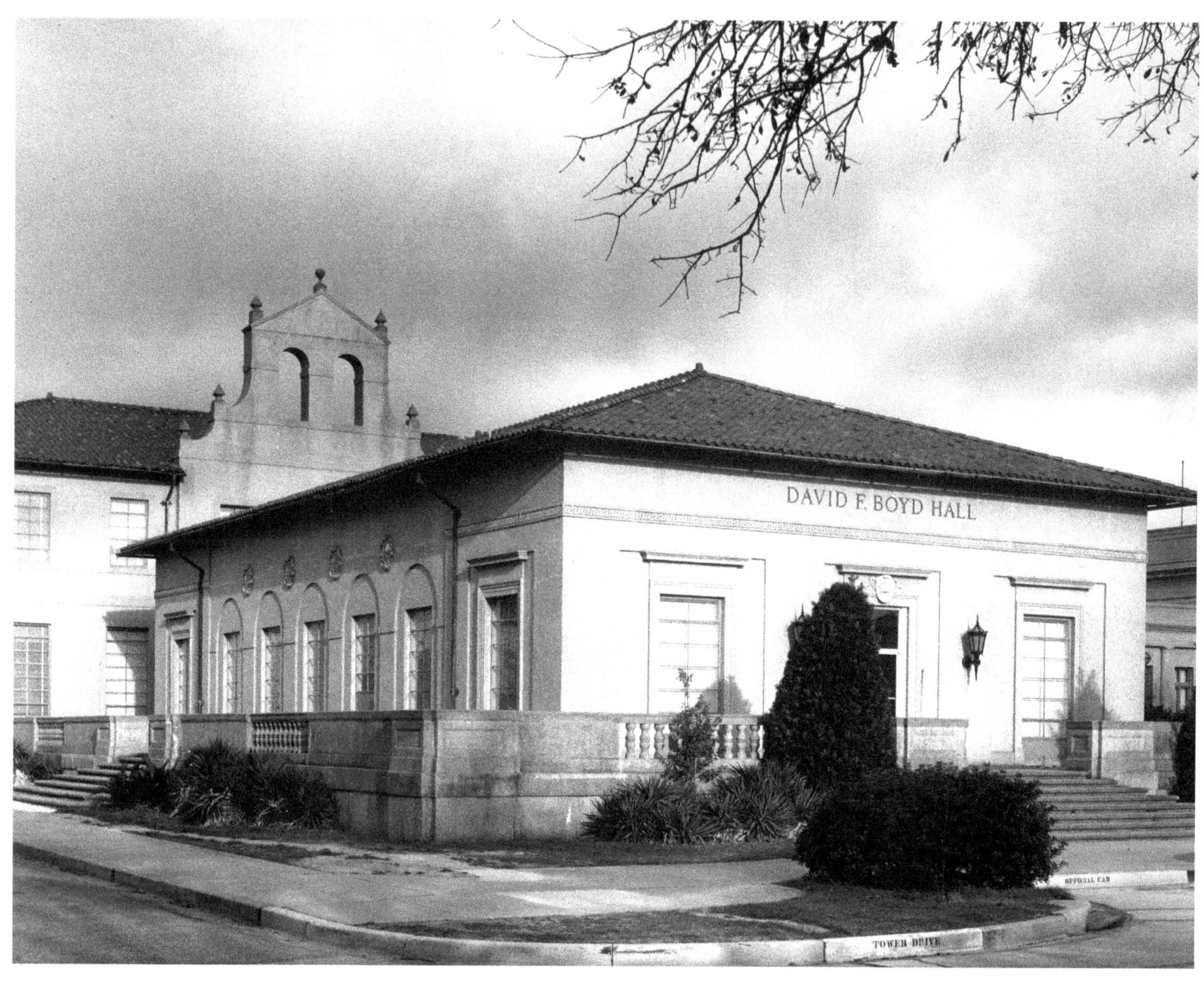

The LSU campus, nearly 40 years old here around 1965, continued to grow through the years. The David F. Boyd Hall was constructed to serve as administrative offices.

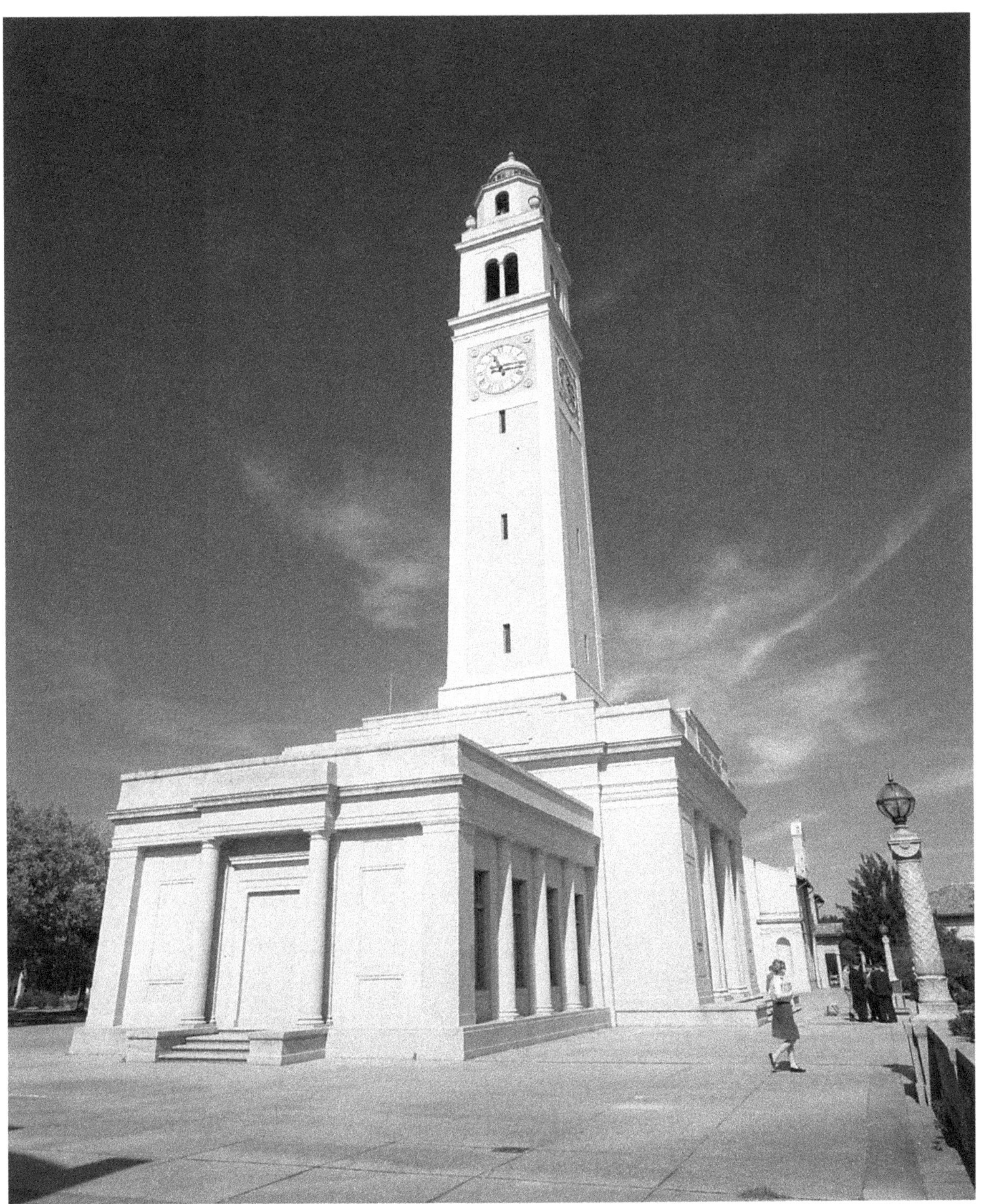

The Campanile and Memorial Tower anchored the eastern arm of the central LSU campus when the university grounds were first laid out. This scene from around 1965 provides an excellent view of the structure.

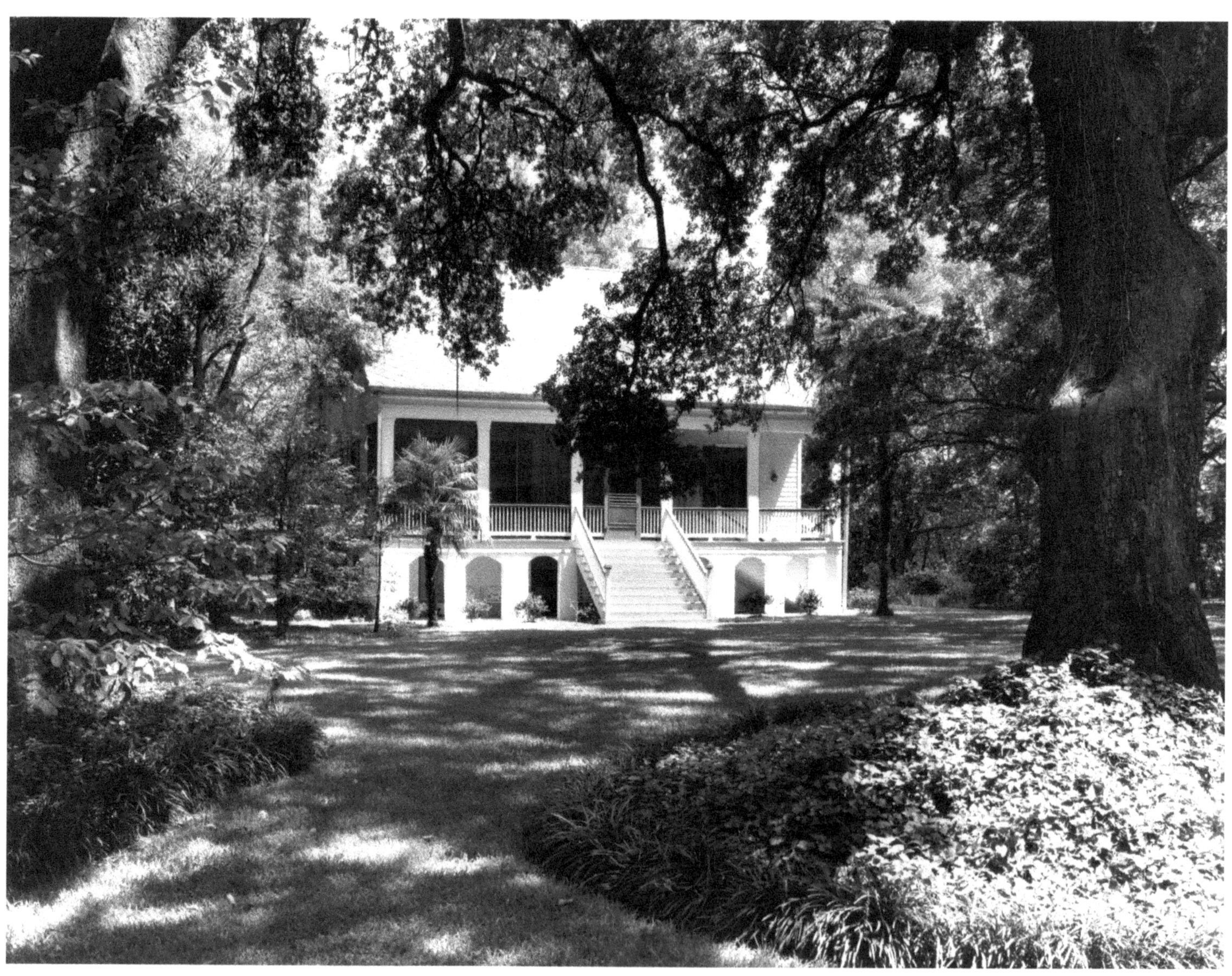

Seen here around 1965 is the southwest facade of the Santa Maria Plantation house, built in 1877. Located on Perkins Road south of town, the home is listed on the National Register of Historic Places.

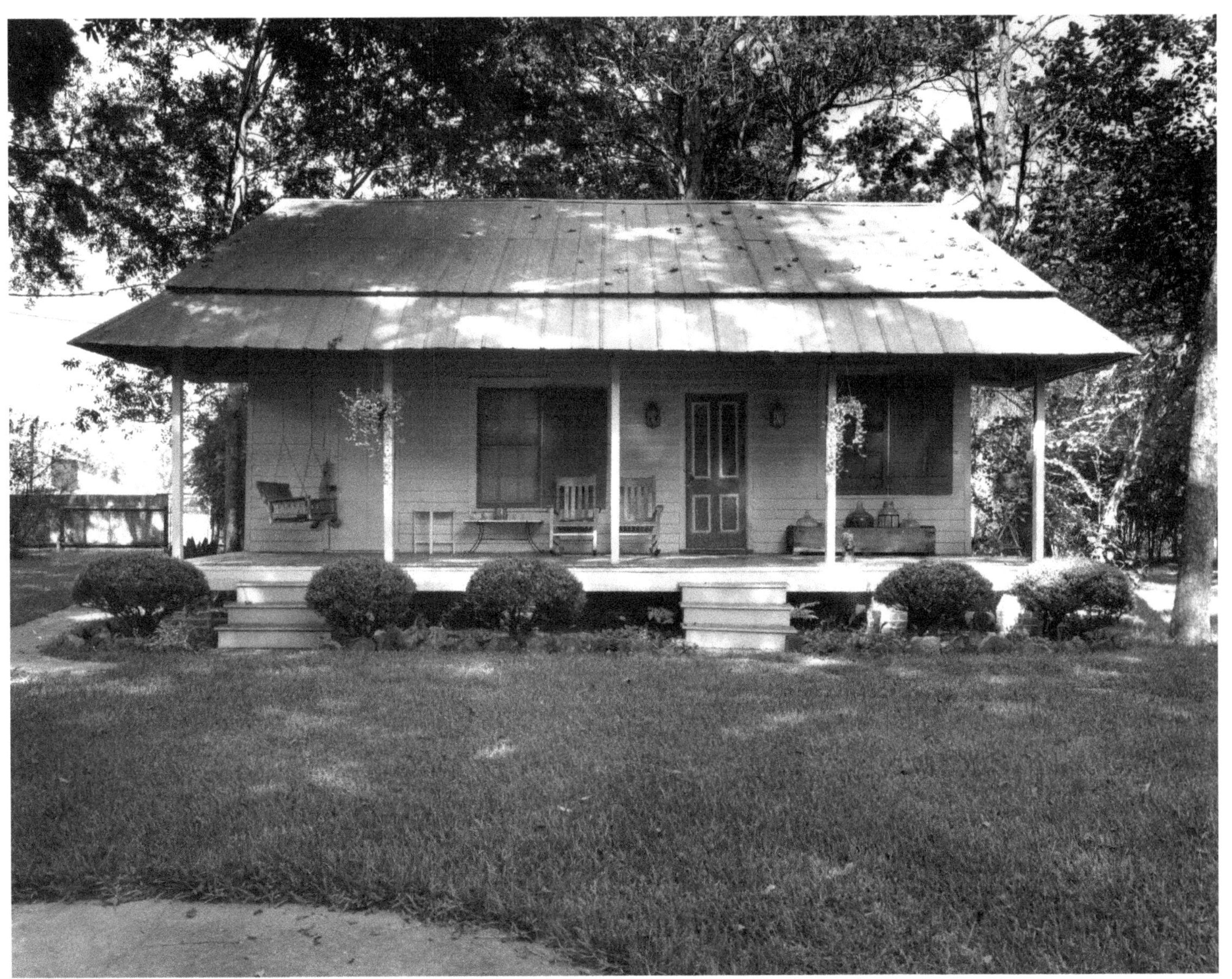

This cabin on the grounds of Santa Maria Plantation, complete with porch swing, also was photographed around 1965.

This image of the Santa Maria Plantation provides researchers using the Historic American Buildings Survey a view of its interior construction.

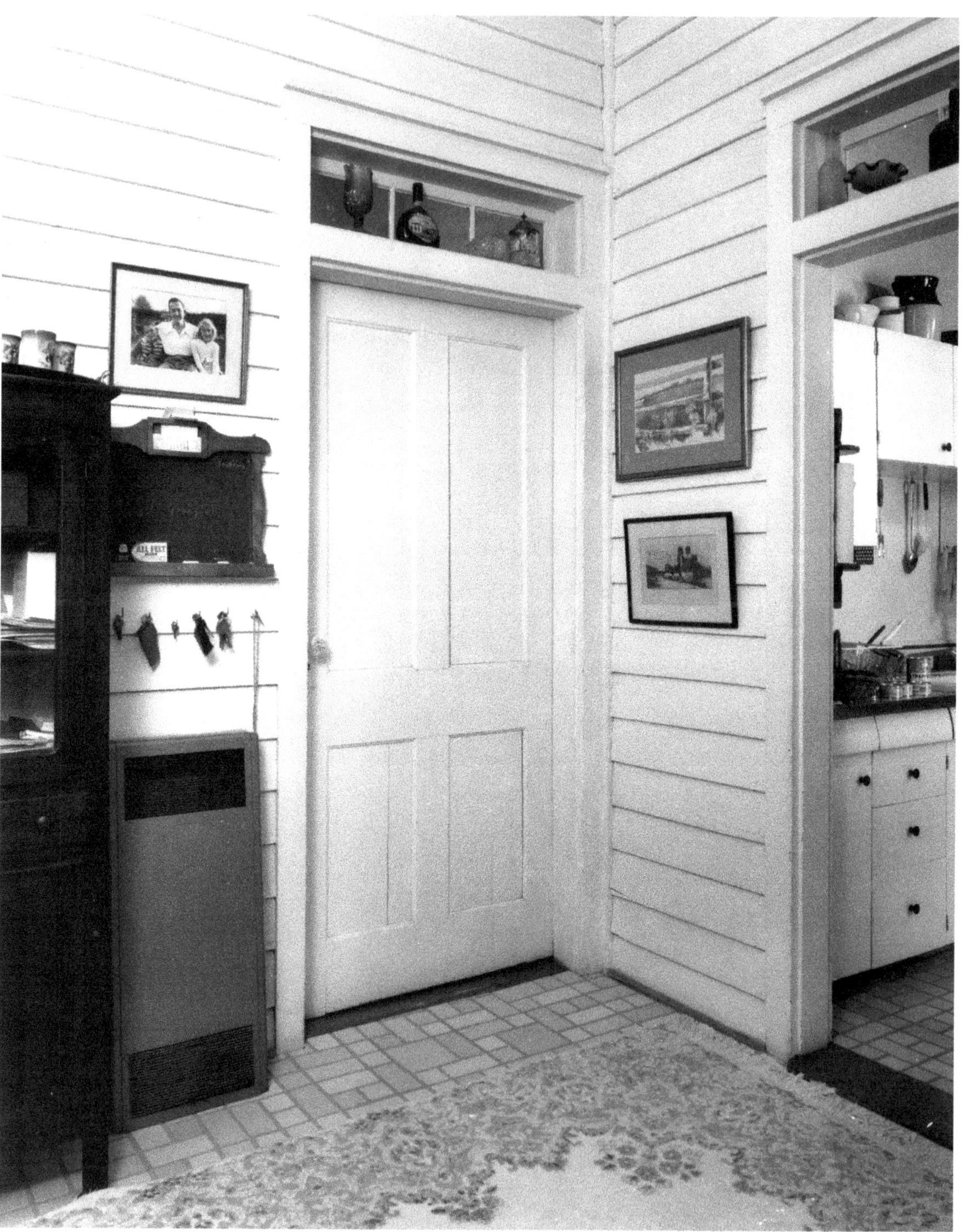

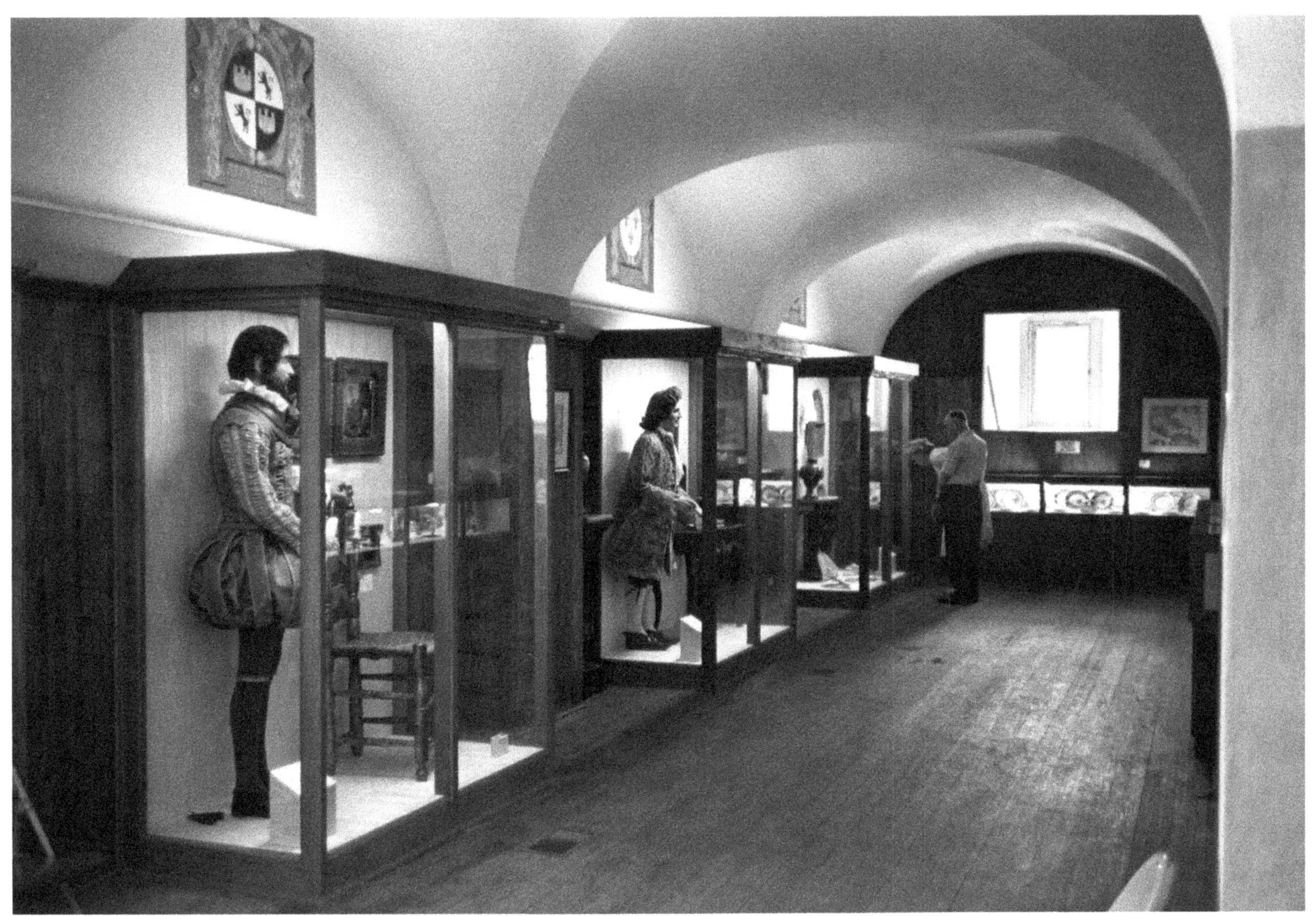

The Old Arsenal Powder Magazine, constructed around 1838, was the third structure on its site to be used as a magazine by the military base that once surrounded it. It survived not only the test of time but also the plans of Huey P. Long and others who wanted to use the site for other purposes. This 1960s interior view shows its current use as a museum.

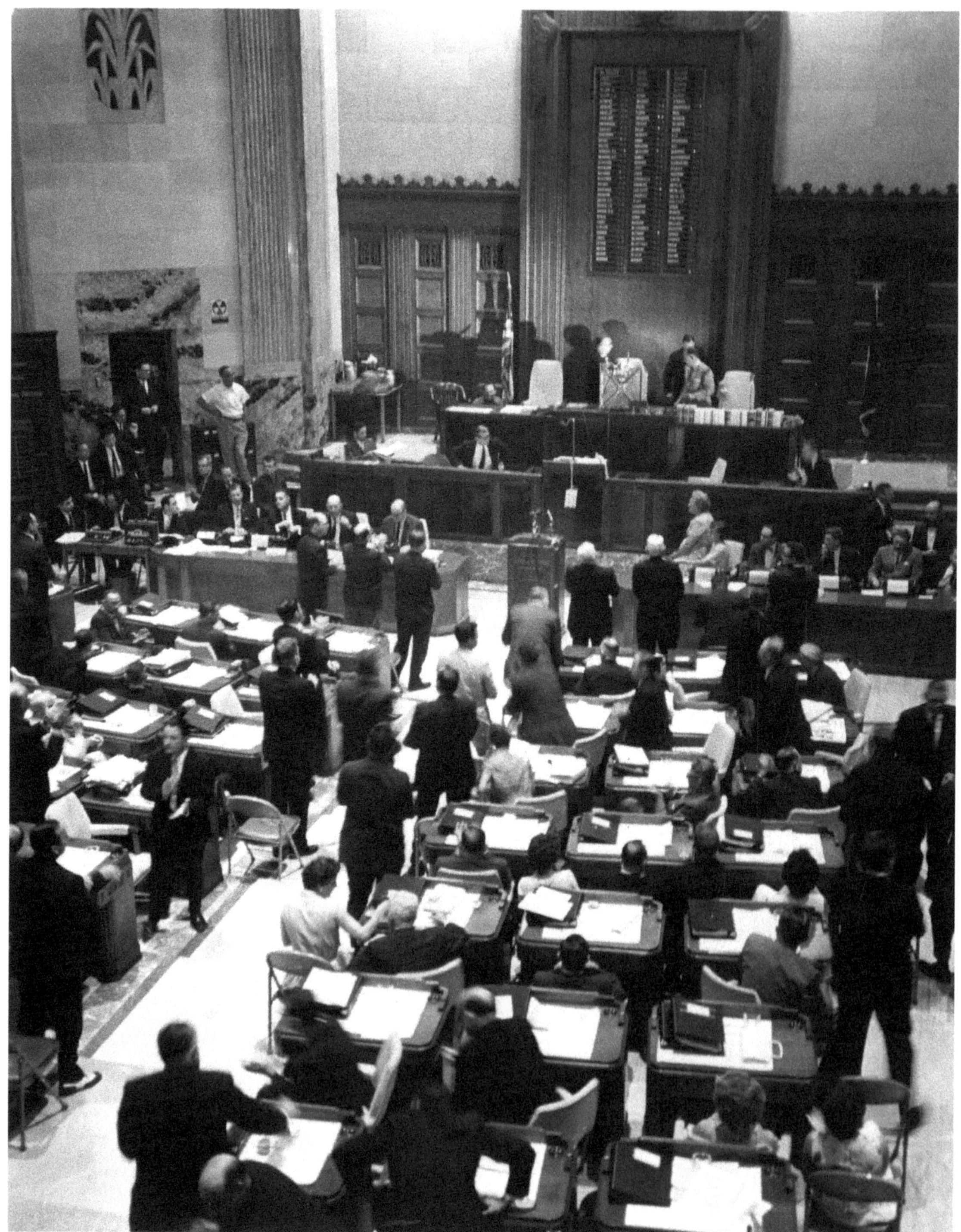

The House Chamber of the Louisiana State Capitol has been the site of many spirited debates during its nearly 90-year history. Here in the mid-1960s there was much to debate.

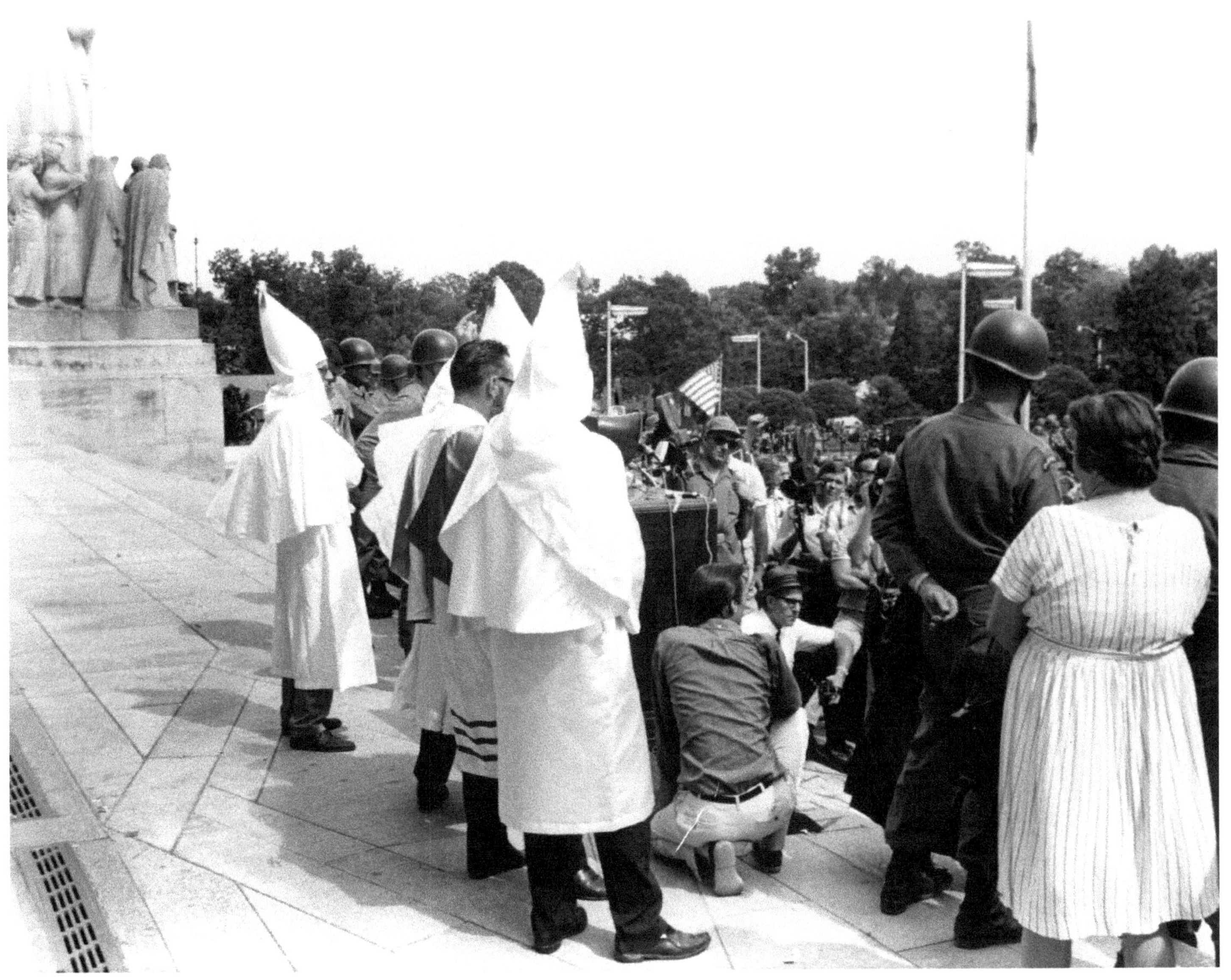

The turbulent 1960s were marked by demonstrations and counterdemonstrations nationwide; Louisiana was no exception. In the early 1960s, civil rights workers, white and black working together, held a demonstration on the Capitol steps. The Ku Klux Klan held a counterdemonstration, with state troopers and National Guard troops forming a barricade between the rival groups.

At University Terrace Elementary School in March 1967, students in the school library use one of the library's tape recorders while Mrs. Marie D. Brewer, the librarian, looks on. From left to right, the students are Joan Earle, Bruce Retamal, Cathy Walker, Wayne Welch, and Cathy Snellings. The school library had just been awarded the Louisiana Library Association Modisette Award for showing the greatest improvement over the past year.

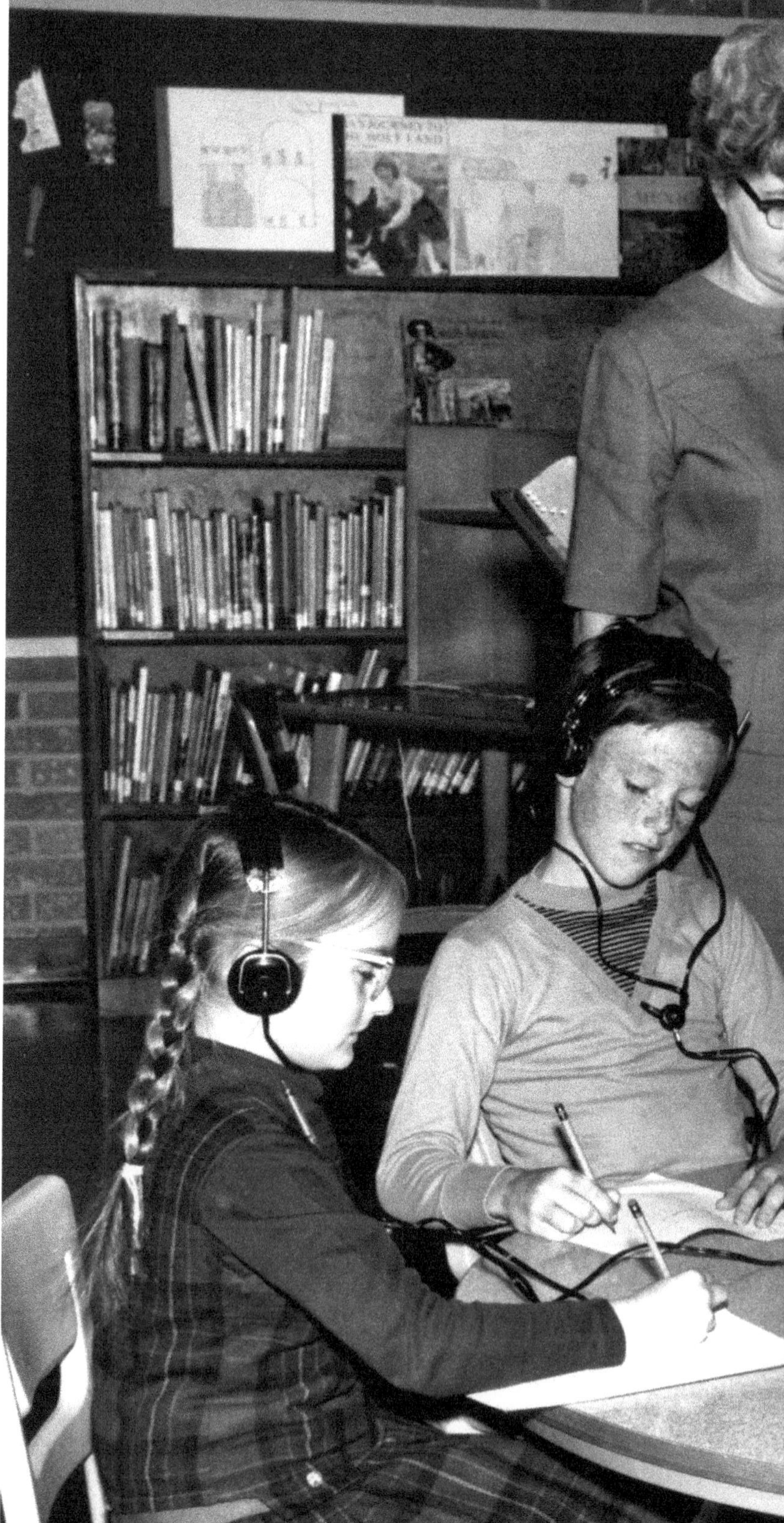

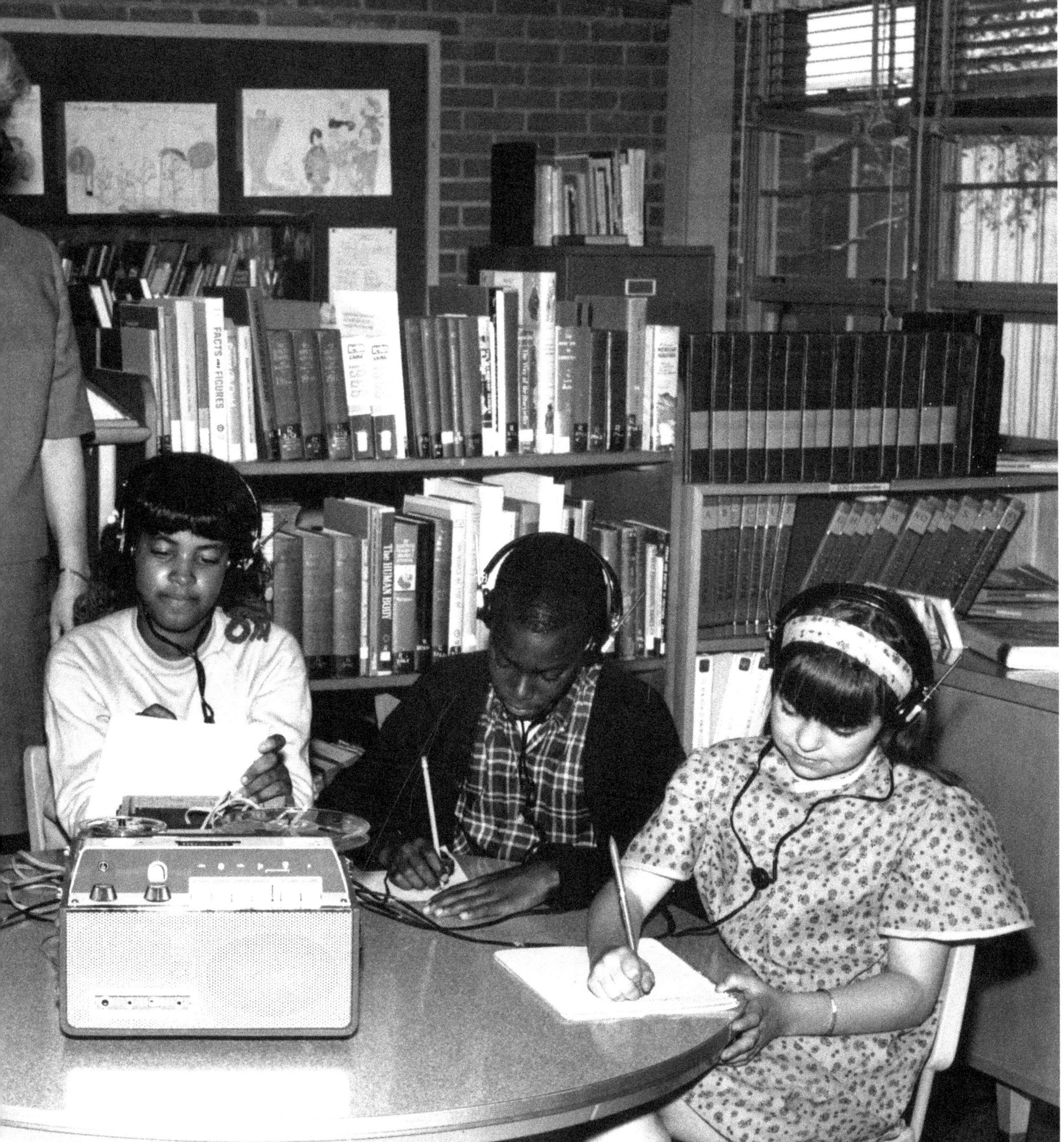
FACTS and FIGURES
The HUMAN BODY

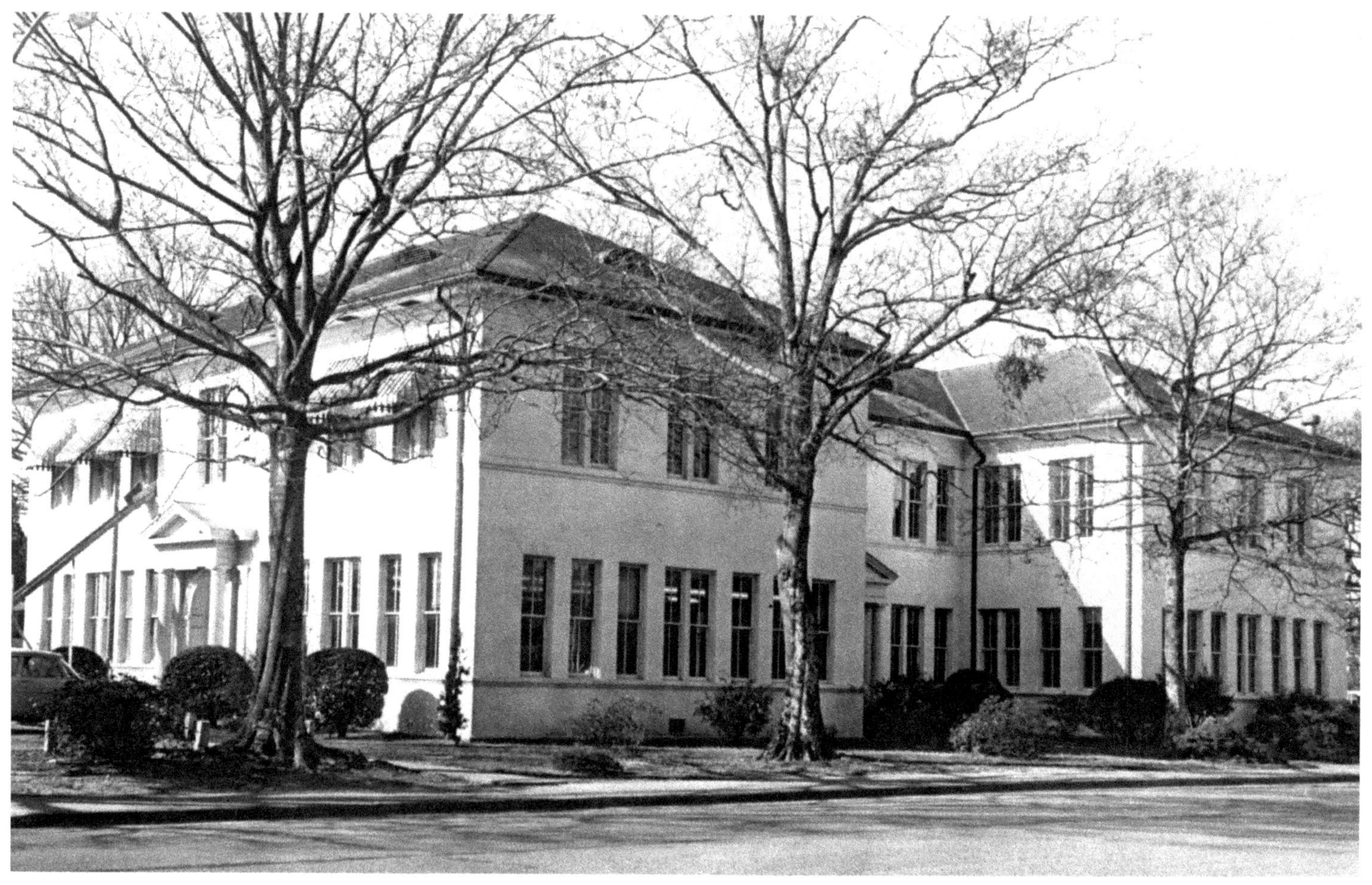

One testament to the importance of oil and gas and associated industries to Louisiana's economy is the Louisiana Oil and Gas Building in Baton Rouge. Shown here around 1965, the simple but massive state building is dedicated to this vital component of the state's economy.

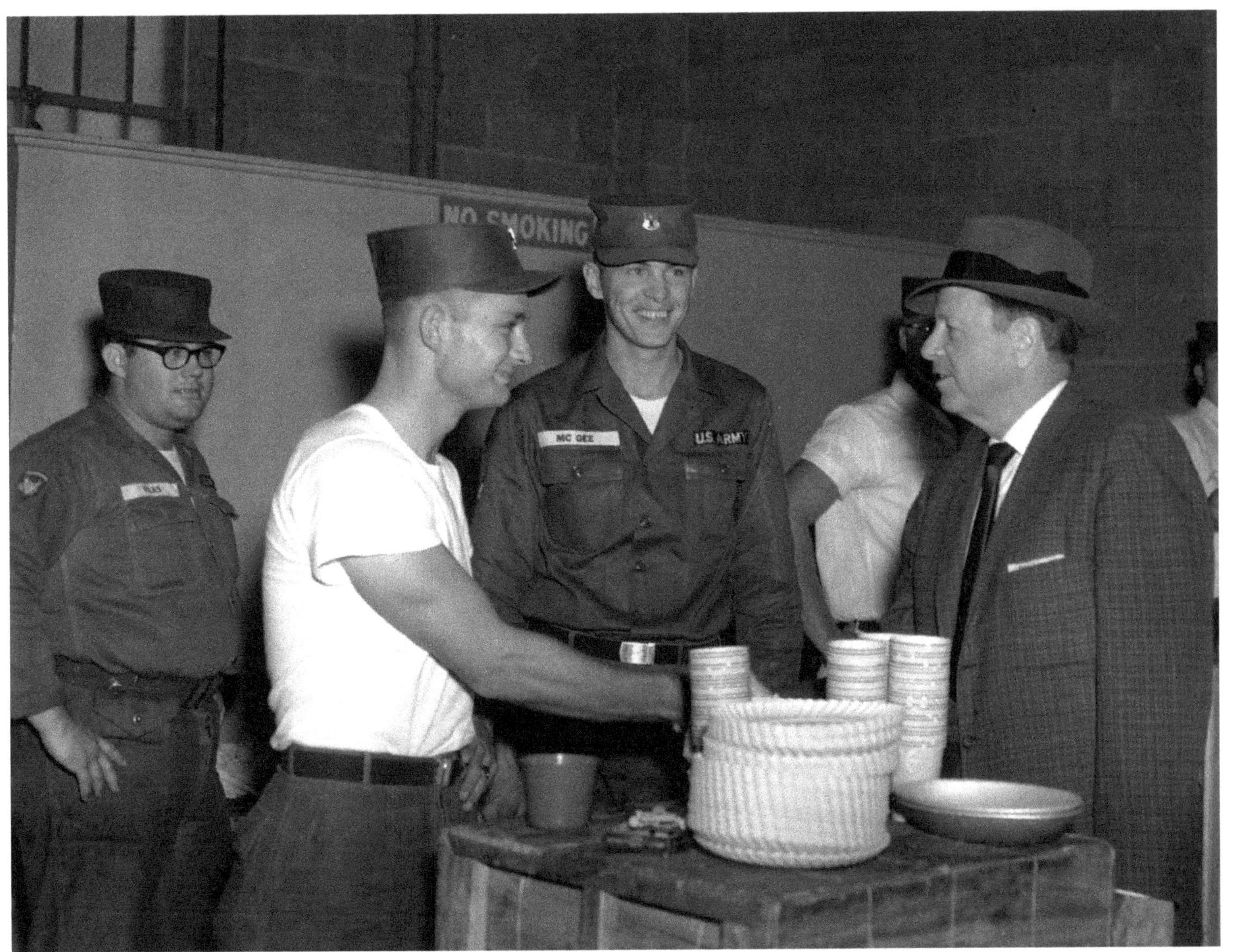

Jimmie Davis, perhaps best known for popularizing the song "You Are My Sunshine," served as governor of Louisiana twice: 1944–1948 and 1960–1964. Here he engages in friendly banter with Army personnel sometime in the 1960s.

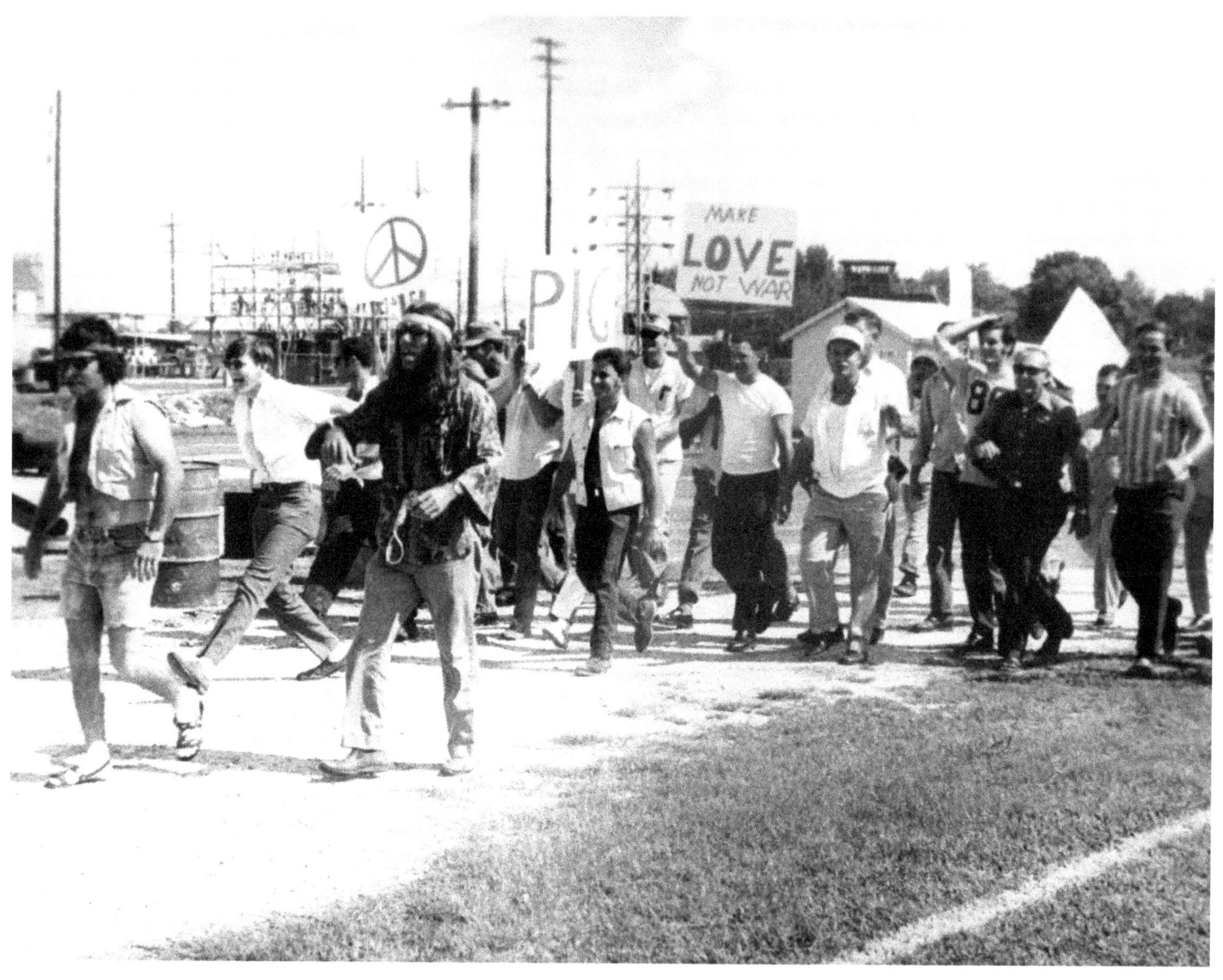

Antiwar protesters march near one of Baton Rouge's many chemical plants in 1967. In largely blue-collar Baton Rouge, such marches were not particularly well attended nor supported within the larger community.

Changes by the River

(1970–1979)

Despite the 1973 and 1978 oil embargoes, Baton Rouge benefited greatly from its association with the petroleum industry. As the domestic oil boom advanced, so too did Baton Rouge's efforts with urban renewal. An area of the southwest corner of downtown bordered by Government Street on the south, Saint Louis Street on the east, North Boulevard on the north, and River Road on the west became the Riverside Centroplex. Its combination of government offices and civic buildings, including a library, arena, theater, and parking garages, completely remade the face of downtown.

Two new television stations, an NBC affiliate and a PBS affiliate, began broadcasting events of the day to the community in 1971 and 1975, respectively. Harding Field, renamed Ryan Field in 1954, became the commercial air traffic hub for the metropolitan area when the old Municipal Airport closed in 1976. A new mall at the intersection of Florida Boulevard and Airline Highway opened the same year. Baton Rouge also joined in the national Bicentennial celebrations by sprucing up downtown then holding a week-long party in July. Two years later the historic Paramount Theater on Third Street downtown showed its last feature film; within a year the site became a parking lot.

While parts of town were being pulled down, other areas were gaining recognition for their historic qualities. The entire Spanish Town neighborhood, first laid out in 1805, was placed on the National Register of Historic Places in 1978. Within a few years the Beauregard Town district would join Spanish Town on the list.

The coming decades would bring petroleum industry–based recession and recovery, more downtown buildings being replaced by parking lots, a new and larger mall to serve the increasing number of sprawl communities on the eastern edge of the parish, more television and radio stations, and a number of hurricanes. Baton Rouge continues to change with the times.

The Louisiana State Capitol, decorated for Christmas during the 1970s, is reflected in the waters of Capitol Lake immediately to the north of the building.

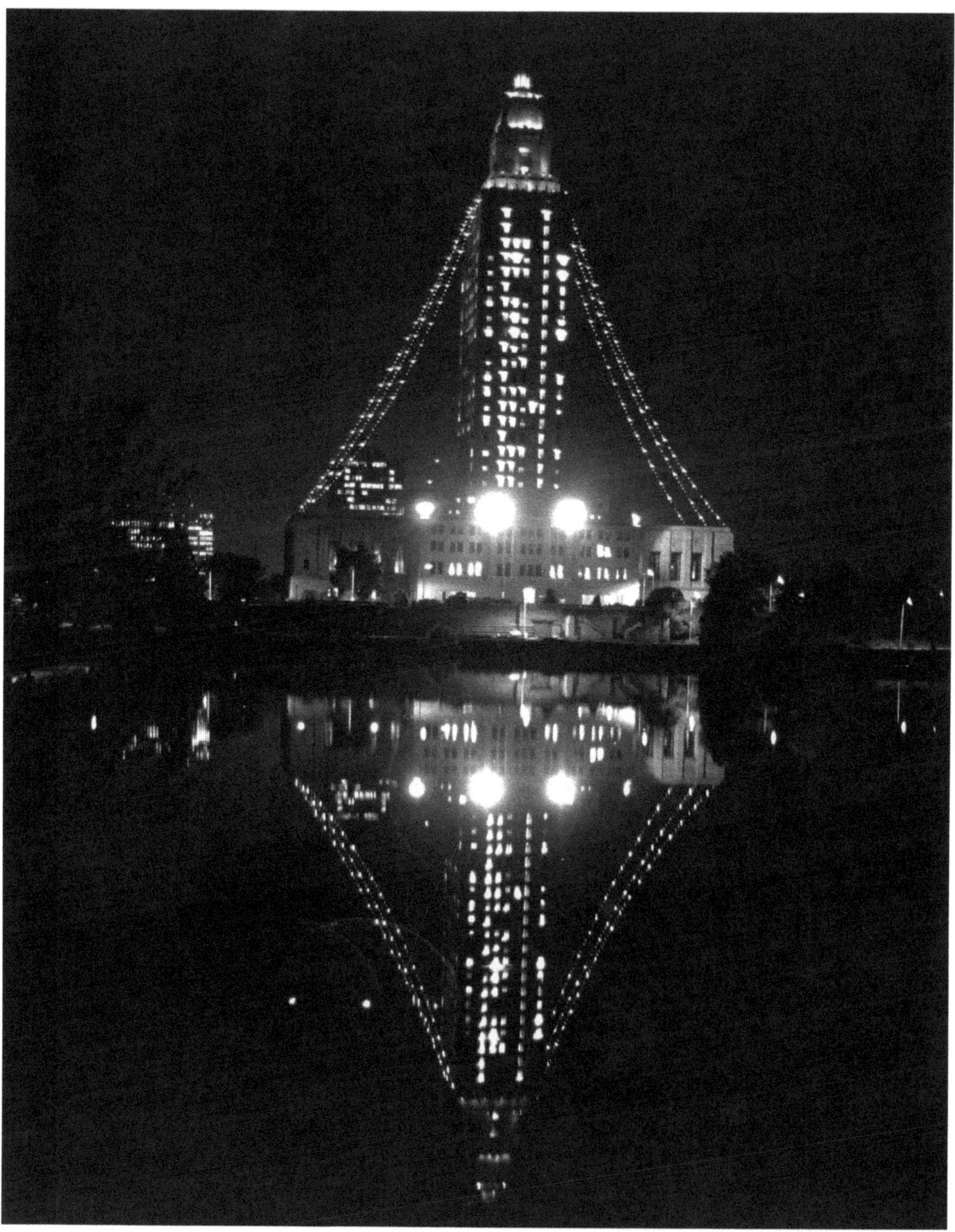

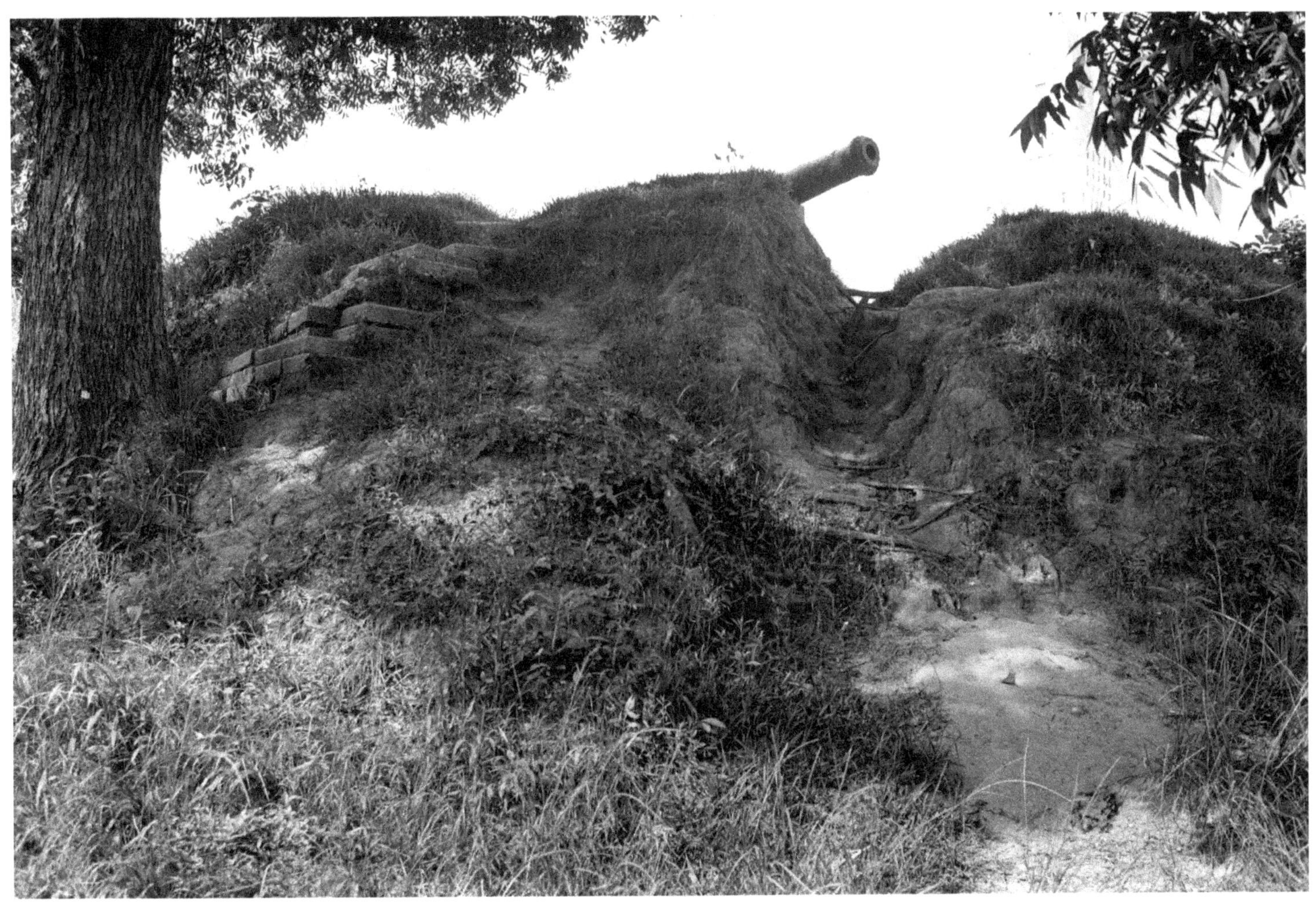

The area named Baton Rouge by French explorers in the eighteenth century had been home to Native Americans for centuries. Part of the mound-building culture distributed from the Great Lakes to the Gulf of Mexico, these local peoples constructed a number of mounds in the area. One of them, located on what became the Army garrison grounds and seen here as it was in the mid-1970s, had been used as the garrison's officer cemetery in the early nineteenth century.

Students on the LSU campus in the early 1970s did protest the Vietnam War. Free Speech Alley, an area in front of the Student Union, became the site of many rallies—both antiwar, as seen here, and prowar.

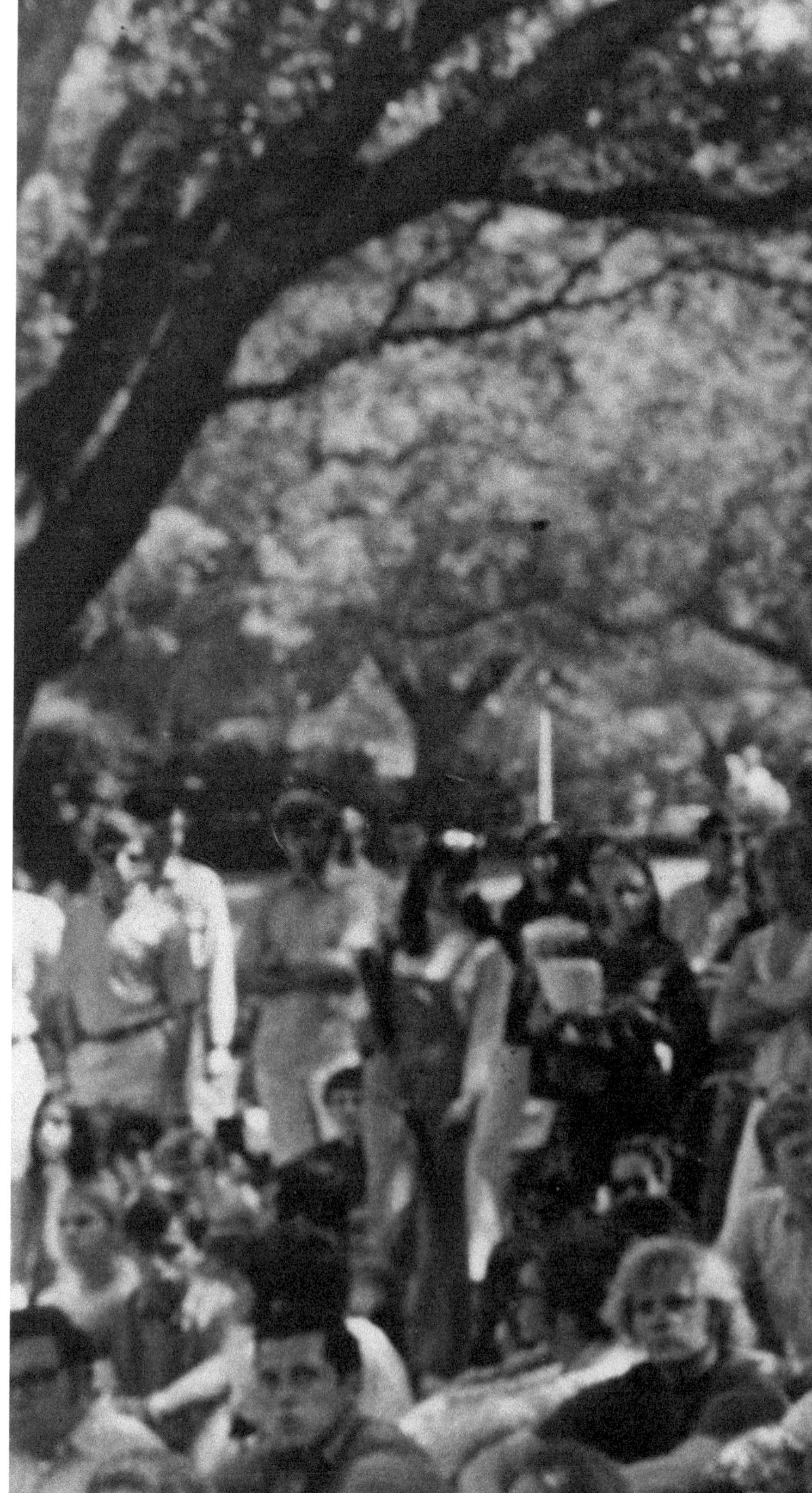

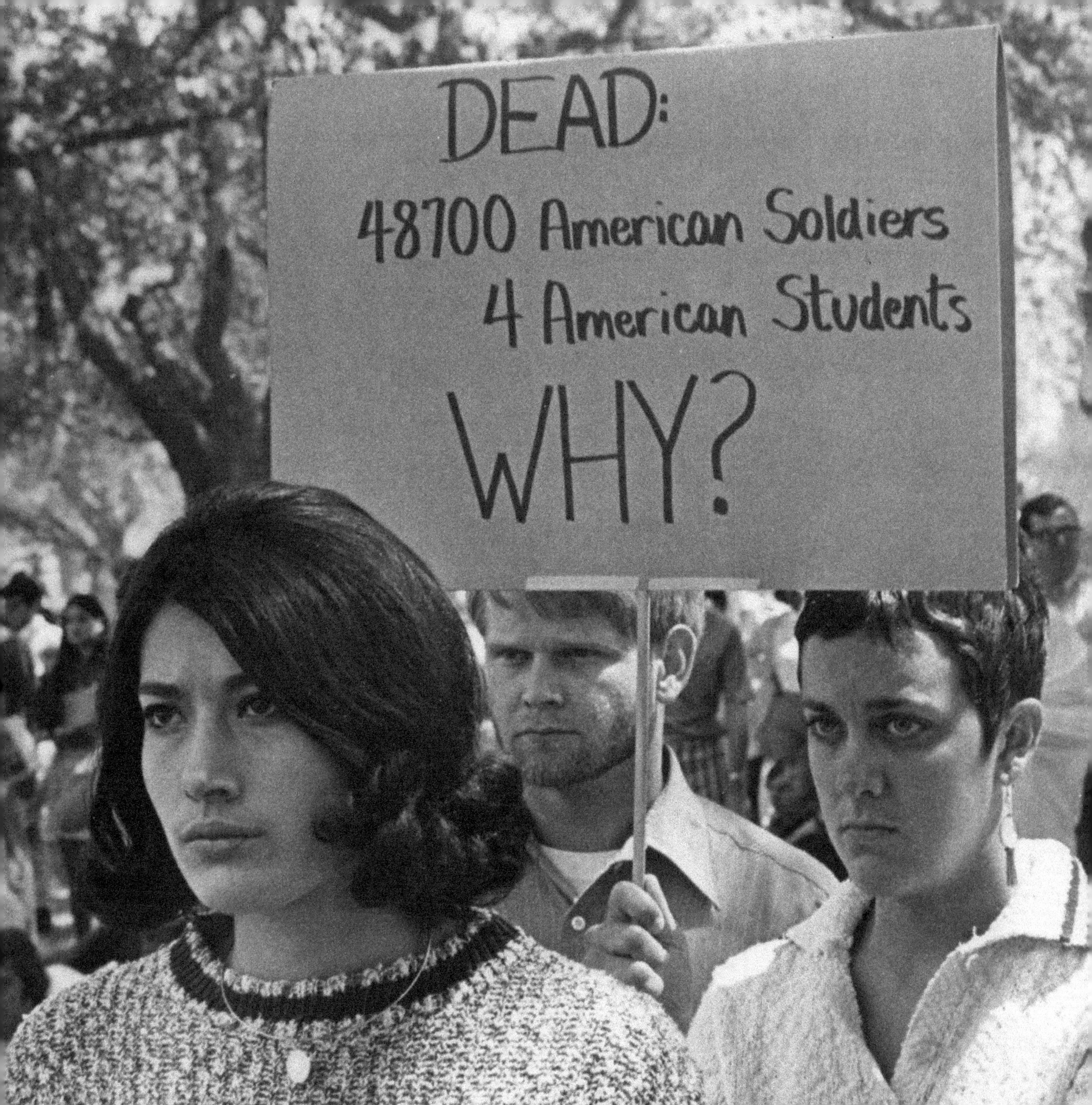
DEAD:
48700 American Soldiers
4 American Students
WHY?

Downtown Baton Rouge changed in many ways over the years. In the nineteenth century, Church Street, running parallel to and four blocks east of the Mississippi River, earned its name for the number of religious houses built along its length. By the mid twentieth century, this road had been renamed Fourth Street and was becoming more and more integrated into the economic and governmental life of the city.

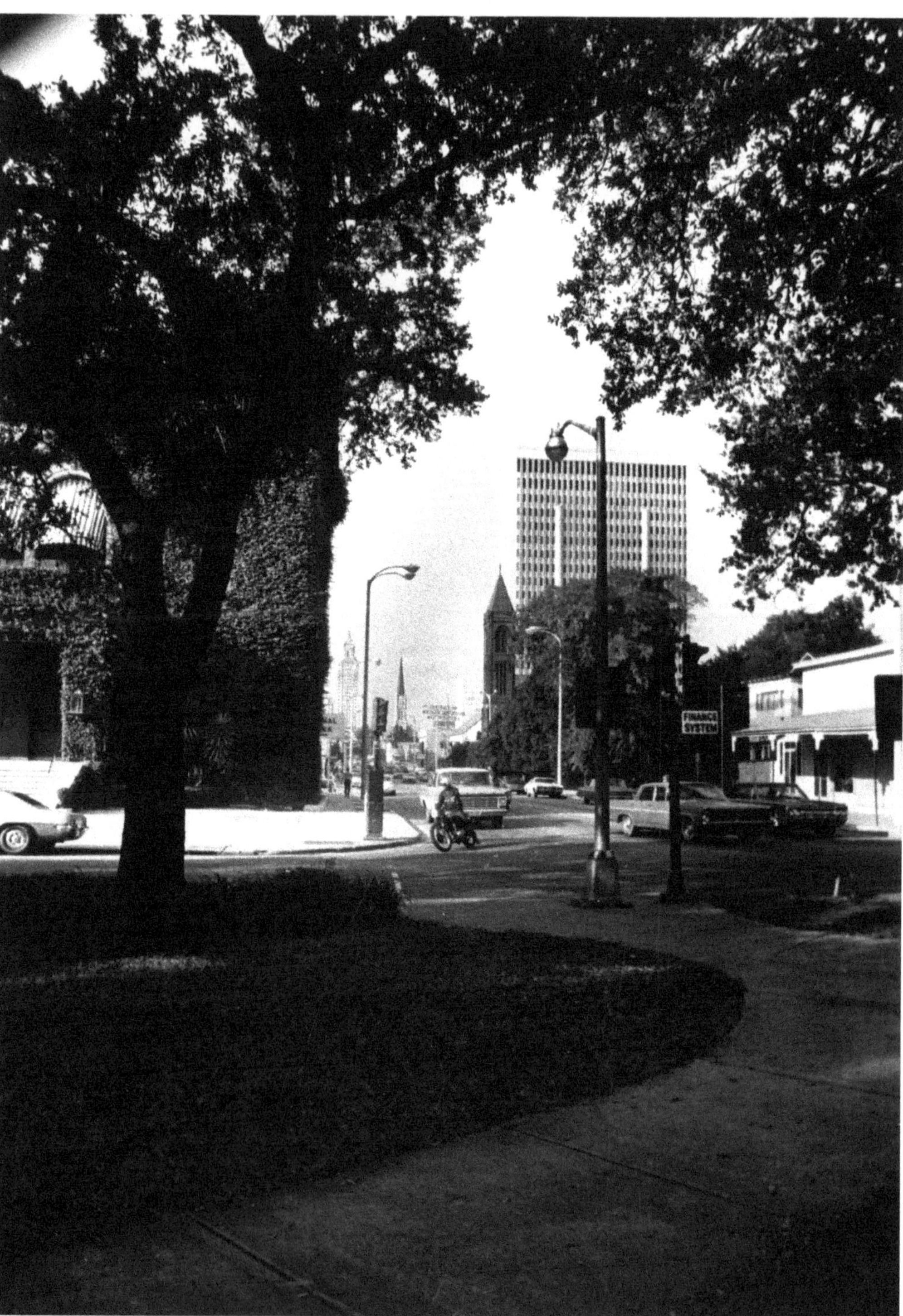

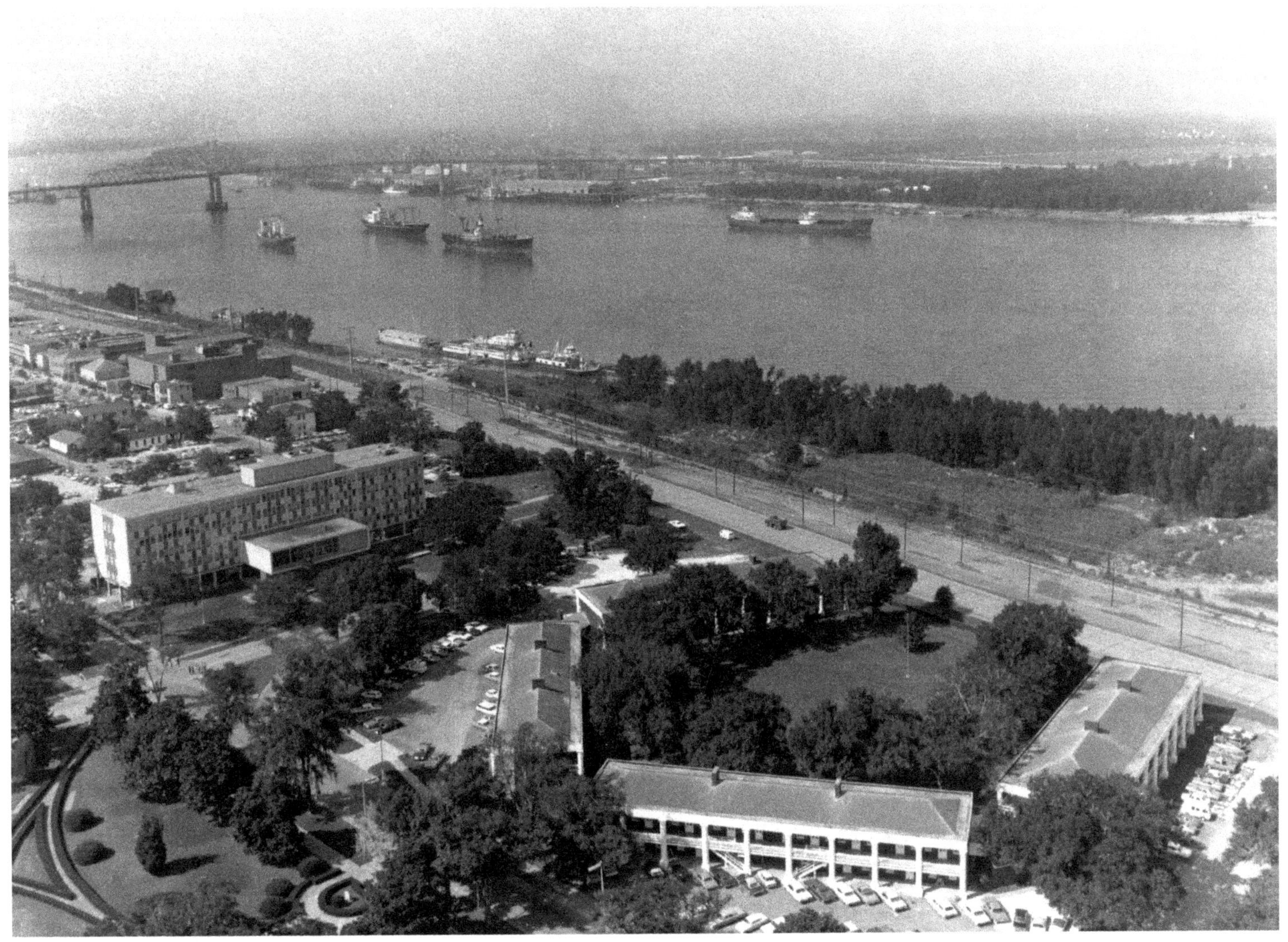

This mid-1970s image of the riverfront, the Mississippi River bridge, and the port of Baton Rouge shows the city's capabilities for handling deep-water vessels. These oceangoing ships helped make Baton Rouge one of the top cargo-handling ports in the nation.

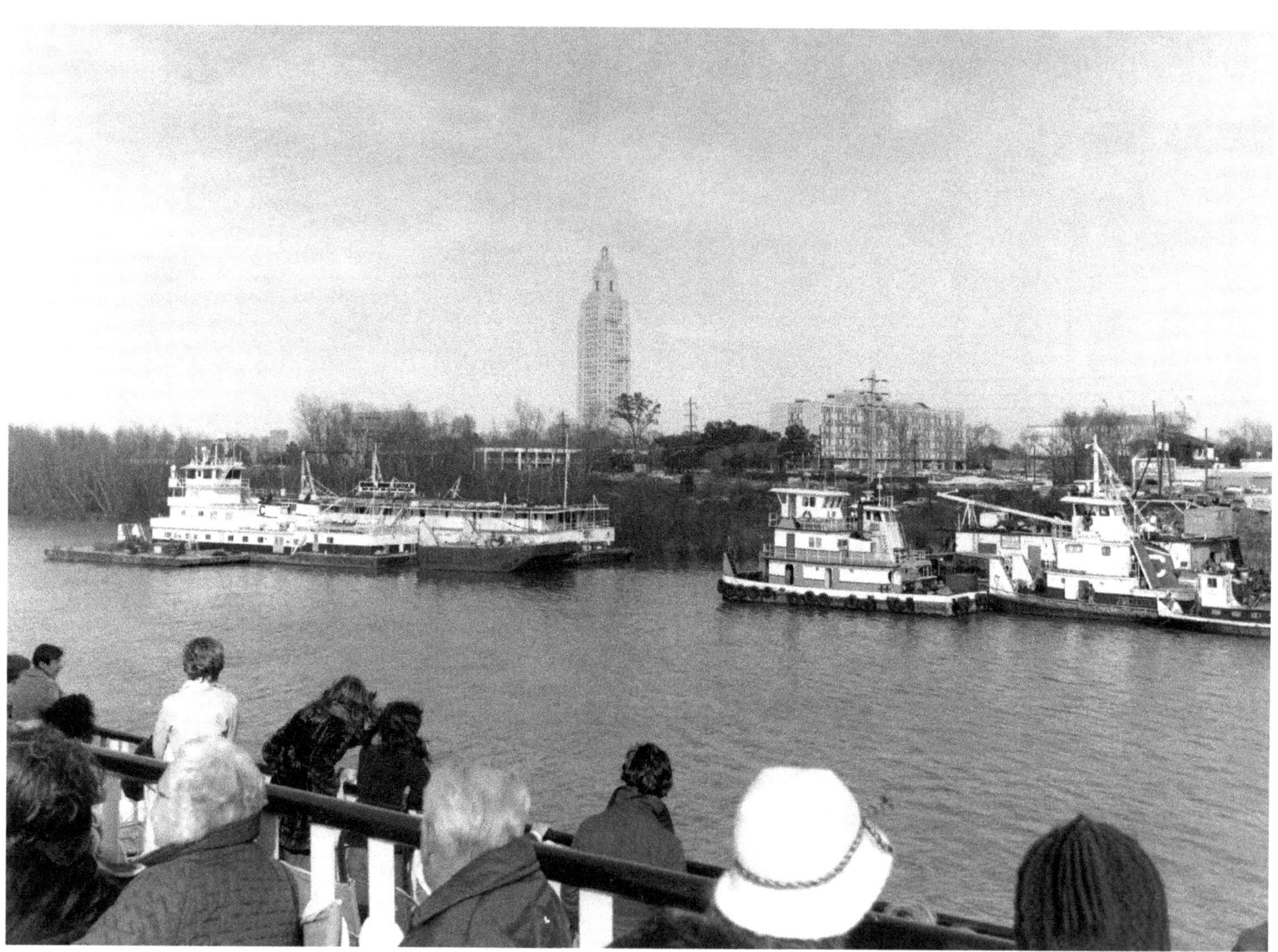

The port of Baton Rouge handles a great deal more than oceangoing vessels. Seen here from the deck of a tourist boat in the mid-1970s, the Baton Rouge riverfront is serving tugboats and push boats, barges, and the tour boat itself.

Notes on the Photographs

These notes, listed by page number, attempt to include all aspects known of the photographs. Each of the photographs is identified by the page number, photograph's title or description, photographer and collection, archive, and call or box number when applicable. Although every attempt was made to collect all available data, in some cases complete data was unavailable due to the age and condition of some of the photographs and records.

II **City Park, 1930s**
State Library of Louisiana
wp002553

VI **Enjoying Watermelon**
Andrew D. Lytle Album Photograph Collection, Mss. 3708, Louisiana and Lower Mississippi Valley Collections, LSU Libraries, Baton Rouge, LA

X **Main Street**
Andrew D. Lytle Photograph Collection, Mss. 2600, Louisiana and Lower Mississippi Valley Collections, LSU Libraries, Baton Rouge, LA

2 **Old State Capitol in Baton Rouge**
State Library of Louisiana
Hp004089

3 **Baton Rouge Market**
State Library of Louisiana
Hp002569

4 **Riverside Social Event**
Andrew D. Lytle Collection, Mss. 893, 1254, Louisiana and Lower Mississippi Valley Collections, LSU Libraries, Baton Rouge, LA

5 **Militia Groups Meeting in Town**
Andrew D. Lytle Collection, Mss. 893, 1254, Louisiana and Lower Mississippi Valley Collections, LSU Libraries, Baton Rouge, LA

6 **Camp of General Christopher Colon Augur's 19th Army Corps**
G. H. Suydam Collection, Mss. 1394, Louisiana and Lower Mississippi Valley Collections, LSU Libraries, Baton Rouge, LA

8 **Baton Rouge Arsenal**
Marshall Dunham Photograph Album, Mss. 3241, Louisiana and Lower Mississippi Valley Collections, LSU Libraries, Baton Rouge, LA

9 **Courthouse and Market**
Marshall Dunham Photograph Album, Mss. 3241, Louisiana and Lower Mississippi Valley Collections, LSU Libraries, Baton Rouge, LA

10 **Arsenal Grounds**
Andrew D. Lytle Collection, Mss. 893, 1254, Louisiana and Lower Mississippi Valley Collections, LSU Libraries, Baton Rouge, LA

11 **Segment of the 18th New York Artillery**
G. H. Suydam Collection, Mss. 1394, Louisiana and Lower Mississippi Valley Collections, LSU Libraries, Baton Rouge, LA

12 **Federal West Gulf Blockading Squadron**
G. H. Suydam Collection, Mss. 1394, Louisiana and Lower Mississippi Valley Collections, LSU Libraries, Baton Rouge, LA

13 **Contraband Camp in Baton Rouge**
G. H. Suydam Collection, Mss. 1394, Louisiana and Lower Mississippi Valley Collections, LSU Libraries, Baton Rouge, LA

14 **USS Choctaw**
Andrew D. Lytle Collection, Mss. 893, 1254, Louisiana and Lower Mississippi Valley Collections, LSU Libraries, Baton Rouge, LA

15 **Horses and Buggy at Fourth and Church Streets**
State Library of Louisiana
Hp003858

16 **Asylum for the Deaf and Dumb of Louisiana**
Andrew D. Lytle Photograph Collection, Mss. 2600, Louisiana and Lower Mississippi Valley Collections, LSU Libraries, Baton Rouge, LA

17 **Louisiana State Penitentiary**
Marshall Dunham Photograph Album, Mss. 3241, Louisiana and Lower Mississippi Valley Collections, LSU Libraries, Baton Rouge, LA

18 **Federal Army Encampment**
Andrew D. Lytle Photograph Collection, Mss. 2600, Louisiana and Lower Mississippi Valley Collections, LSU Libraries, Baton Rouge, LA

20 **First Methodist Episcopal Church**
Andrew D. Lytle Photograph Collection, Mss. 2600, Louisiana and Lower Mississippi Valley Collections, LSU Libraries, Baton Rouge, LA

21 **Church Street**
John B. Heroman, Sr., Photograph Collection, Mss. 4951, Louisiana and Lower Mississippi Valley Collections, LSU Libraries, Baton Rouge, LA

22 **Turkish Bazaar**
Andrew D. Lytle Collection, Mss. 893, 1254, Louisiana and Lower Mississippi Valley Collections, LSU Libraries, Baton Rouge, LA

24 **Louisiana State University Campus Interior**
LSU Photograph Collection, RG#A5000, LSU Archives, LSU Libraries, Baton Rouge, LA

25 **Trapeze Act**
Alvin E. Rabenhorst Photograph Collection, Mss. 4110, Louisiana and Lower Mississippi Valley Collections, LSU Libraries, Baton Rouge, LA

26 **Louisiana State University Campus**
Alvin E. Rabenhorst Photograph Collection, Mss. 4110, Louisiana and Lower Mississippi Valley Collections, LSU Libraries, Baton Rouge, LA

27 **Small Church**
Andrew D. Lytle Photograph Collection, Mss. 2600, Louisiana and Lower Mississippi Valley Collections, LSU Libraries, Baton Rouge, LA

28 **Volunteer Fire Fighters**
Andrew D. Lytle Collection, Mss. 893, 1254, Louisiana and Lower Mississippi Valley Collections, LSU Libraries, Baton Rouge, LA

29 **Synagogue of the Hebrew Congregation**
State Library of Louisiana Hp000466

30 **Trolleys**
State Library of Louisiana Hp005880

32 **Old War Skule**
Andrew D. Lytle Collection, Mss. 893, 1254, Louisiana and Lower Mississippi Valley Collections, LSU Libraries, Baton Rouge, LA

33 **Washington Fire Company No. 3**
State Library of Louisiana Hp002524

34 **Leaving Market**
Alvin E. Rabenhorst Photograph Collection, Mss. 4110, Louisiana and Lower Mississippi Valley Collections, LSU Libraries, Baton Rouge, LA

35 **St. Vincent's Academy**
Andrew D. Lytle Glass Plate Negative Collection, Mss. 2600, Louisiana and Lower Mississippi Valley Collections, LSU Libraries, Baton Rouge, LA

36 **Electric Railway Celebration**
State Library of Louisiana Hp007129

38 **Post Office Dray**
Alvin E. Rabenhorst Photograph Collection, Mss. 4110, Louisiana and Lower Mississippi Valley Collections, LSU Libraries, Baton Rouge, LA

39 **Firemen's Parade Float**
Alvin E. Rabenhorst Photograph Collection, Mss. 4110, Louisiana and Lower Mississippi Valley Collections, LSU Libraries, Baton Rouge, LA

40 **Woodstock Plantation**
Andrew D. Lytle Collection, Mss. 893, 1254, Louisiana and Lower Mississippi Valley Collections, LSU Libraries, Baton Rouge, LA

41 **Sandbagging**
John B. Heroman, Sr., Photograph Collection, Mss. 4951, Louisiana and Lower Mississippi Valley Collections, LSU Libraries, Baton Rouge, LA

42 **Decorated Float**
Andrew D. Lytle Collection, Mss. 893, 1254, Louisiana and Lower Mississippi Valley Collections, LSU Libraries, Baton Rouge, LA

43 **Capitol**
John B. Heroman, Sr., Photograph Collection, Mss. 4951, Louisiana and Lower Mississippi Valley Collections, LSU Libraries, Baton Rouge, LA

44 **Pelican Hook and Ladder Company**
Andrew D. Lytle Glass Plate Negative Collection, Mss. 2600, Louisiana and Lower Mississippi Valley Collections, LSU Libraries, Baton Rouge, LA

46 **Chemical Laboratory**
LSU Photograph Collection, RG#A5000, LSU Archives, LSU Libraries, Baton Rouge, LA

47 **New Main Post Office and Federal Courthouse**
Andrew D. Lytle Collection, Mss. 893, 1254, Louisiana and Lower Mississippi Valley Collections, LSU Libraries, Baton Rouge, LA

48 **Levee Construction**
Andrew D. Lytle Collection, Mss. 893, 1254, Louisiana and Lower Mississippi Valley Collections, LSU Libraries, Baton Rouge, LA
1254a14

49 **Cadets of Louisiana State University**
Andrew D. Lytle Collection, Mss. 893, 1254, Louisiana and Lower Mississippi Valley Collections, LSU Libraries, Baton Rouge, LA

50 **Tolbert Doiron's Grocery Store**
Andrew D. Lytle Glass Plate Negative Collection, Mss. 2600, Louisiana and Lower Mississippi Valley Collections, LSU Libraries, Baton Rouge, LA Business

51 **The Stanley & Gore Store**
Andrew D. Lytle Glass Plate Negative Collection, Mss. 2600, Louisiana and Lower Mississippi Valley Collections, LSU Libraries, Baton Rouge, LA
Business

52 **Steamboat Wreckage**
Andrew D. Lytle Collection, Mss. 893, 1254, Louisiana and Lower Mississippi Valley Collections, LSU Libraries, Baton Rouge, LA
1254C88

53 **Brass Band**
Andrew D. Lytle Glass Plate Negative Collection, Mss. 2600, Louisiana and Lower Mississippi Valley Collections, LSU Libraries, Baton Rouge, LA

54 **Demolition**
Joseph St. Clair Favrot Family Papers, Mss. 3317, Louisiana and Lower Mississippi Valley Collections, LSU Libraries, Baton Rouge, LA

55 **State Penitentiary**
Henry L. Fuqua, Jr., Lytle Photograph Collection and Papers, Mss. 1898, Louisiana and Lower Mississippi Valley Collections, LSU Libraries, Baton Rouge, LA

56 **Levee Construction**
Henry L. Fuqua, Jr., Lytle Photograph Collection and Papers, Mss. 1898, Louisiana and Lower Mississippi Valley Collections, LSU Libraries, Baton Rouge, LA

57 **Store Interior**
John B. Heroman, Sr., Photograph Collection, Mss. 4951, Louisiana and Lower Mississippi Valley Collections, LSU Libraries, Baton Rouge, LA

58 **Baton Rouge Water Quality Banner**
John B. Heroman, Sr., Photograph Collection, Mss. 4951, Louisiana and Lower Mississippi Valley Collections, LSU Libraries, Baton Rouge, LA

59 **Electric Trolleys**
State Library of Louisiana
Hp005879

60 **Rainy Day**
John B. Heroman, Sr., Photograph Collection, Mss. 4951, Louisiana and Lower Mississippi Valley Collections, LSU Libraries, Baton Rouge, LA

61 **Washington's Birthday Firemen's Parade**
Alvin E. Rabenhorst Photograph Collection, Mss. 4110, Louisiana and Lower Mississippi Valley Collections, LSU Libraries, Baton Rouge, LA

62 **New Post Office Interior**
Alvin E. Rabenhorst Photograph Collection, Mss. 4110, Louisiana and Lower Mississippi Valley Collections, LSU Libraries, Baton Rouge, LA

63 **Washington's Birthday Firemen's Parade**
Alvin E. Rabenhorst Photograph Collection, Mss. 4110, Louisiana and Lower Mississippi Valley Collections, LSU Libraries, Baton Rouge, LA

64 **Ground-breaking for the Alumni Memorial Hall**
LSU Photograph Collection, RG#A5000, LSU Archives, LSU Libraries, Baton Rouge, LA

66 **Old Arsenal Grounds**
LSU Photograph Collection, RG#A5000, LSU Archives, LSU Libraries, Baton Rouge, LA

67 **The Colony**
LSU Photograph Collection, RG#A5000, LSU Archives, LSU Libraries, Baton Rouge, LA

68 **LSU Woodworking Shop**
LSU Photograph Collection, RG#A5000, LSU Archives, LSU Libraries, Baton Rouge, LA

69 **Agriculture Experiment Station Offices**
LSU Photograph Collection, RG#A5000, LSU Archives, LSU Libraries, Baton Rouge, LA

70 **LSU Foster Hall and Hospital**
LSU Photograph Collection, RG#A5000, LSU Archives, LSU Libraries, Baton Rouge, LA

71 **View of LSU Campus Buildings**
LSU Photograph Collection, RG#A5000, LSU Archives, LSU Libraries, Baton Rouge, LA

72 **Garig Hall**
LSU Photograph Collection, RG#A5000, LSU Archives, LSU Libraries, Baton Rouge, LA

73 **Heard Hall**
LSU Photograph Collection, RG#A5000, LSU Archives, LSU Libraries, Baton Rouge, LA

74 **Hill Memorial Library**
LSU Photograph Collection, RG#A5000, LSU Archives, LSU Libraries, Baton Rouge, LA

76 **Baton Rouge Bargain Store**
Andrew D. Lytle Glass Plate Negative Collection, Mss. 2600, Louisiana and Lower Mississippi Valley Collections, LSU Libraries, Baton Rouge, LA

77 **Digging a Trench**
State Library of Louisiana
Hp000237

78 **Football**
John B. Heroman, Sr., Photograph Collection, Mss. 4951, Louisiana and Lower Mississippi Valley Collections, LSU Libraries, Baton Rouge, LA

80 Riverboat America
Oliver Brice Steele Andrew Lytle Photograph Collection, Mss. 4028, Louisiana and Lower Mississippi Valley Collections, LSU Libraries, Baton Rouge, LA

81 The Era No. 10
Oliver Brice Steele Andrew Lytle Photograph Collection, Mss. 4028, Louisiana and Lower Mississippi Valley Collections, LSU Libraries, Baton Rouge, LA

82 Main and Fifth Streets
John B. Heroman, Sr., Photograph Collection, Mss. 4951, Louisiana and Lower Mississippi Valley Collections, LSU Libraries, Baton Rouge, LA

83 Post Office and Federal Building
State Library of Louisiana Hp000212

84 Baton Rouge Bargain Store
State Library of Louisiana Hp000247

85 Andrew M. Jackson's Store
State Library of Louisiana Hp000248

86 City Hall
State Library of Louisiana Hp000215

87 Amite River
Andrew D. Lytle Photograph Collection, Mss. 2600, Louisiana and Lower Mississippi Valley Collections, LSU Libraries, Baton Rouge, LA

88 First National Bank
State Library of Louisiana Hp000245

89 Baton Rouge Academy
State Library of Louisiana Hp000260

90 Monument
John B. Heroman, Sr., Photograph Collection, Mss. 4951, Louisiana and Lower Mississippi Valley Collections, LSU Libraries, Baton Rouge, LA

91 First Four Blocks of Main Street
John B. Heroman, Sr., Photograph Collection, Mss. 4951, Louisiana and Lower Mississippi Valley Collections, LSU Libraries, Baton Rouge, LA

92 The Audubon Sugar School
LSU Photograph Collection, RG#A5000, LSU Archives, LSU Libraries, Baton Rouge, LA

93 Trestle Bridge
Andrew D. Lytle Photograph Collection, Mss. 2600, Louisiana and Lower Mississippi Valley Collections, LSU Libraries, Baton Rouge, LA

94 Delegation from Massachusetts
Baton Rouge National Cemetery Photograph: Massachusetts Monument, Mss. 176210, Louisiana and Lower Mississippi Valley Collections, LSU Libraries, Baton Rouge, LA

95 1909 Louisiana State University Basketball Team
LSU Photograph Collection, RG#A5000, LSU Archives, LSU Libraries, Baton Rouge, LA

96 Warship
Andrew D. Lytle Photograph Collection, Mss. 2600, LSU Libraries, Baton Rouge, LA

97 Before the Levee Was Built
Alvin E. Rabenhorst Photograph Collection, Mss. 4110, Louisiana and Lower Mississippi Valley Collections, LSU Libraries, Baton Rouge, LA

98 Cast-iron Turrets
Alvin E. Rabenhorst Photograph Collection, Mss. 4110, Louisiana and Lower Mississippi Valley Collections, LSU Libraries, Baton Rouge, LA

99 Flood Control
Alvin E. Rabenhorst Photograph Collection, Mss. 4110, Louisiana and Lower Mississippi Valley Collections, LSU Libraries, Baton Rouge, LA
Floods

100 State Penitentiary Inmates Working
Alvin E. Rabenhorst Photograph Collection, Mss. 4110, Louisiana and Lower Mississippi Valley Collections, LSU Libraries, Baton Rouge, LA

102 Cracks in the Levee
State Library of Louisiana Hp001856

103 Louisiana State University Men's Glee Club
State Library of Louisiana Hp002321

104 Schoolchildren
State Library of Louisiana Hp000261

105 Mississippi River Flood, May 1912
John B. Heroman, Sr., Photograph Collection, Mss. 4951, Louisiana and Lower Mississippi Valley Collections, LSU Libraries, Baton Rouge, LA

106 LSU Faculty
State Library of Louisiana Hp002320

107 Army Ammunition Trucks
State Library of Louisiana Hp002369

108 Baton Rouge Electric Company Crew
State Library of Louisiana Hp001420

110 Capitol
John B. Heroman, Sr., Photograph Collection Mss. 4951, Louisiana and Lower Mississippi Valley Collections, LSU Libraries, Baton Rouge, LA

111 Boy Scouts
State Library of Louisiana Hp002568

112 Plantation
State Library of Louisiana Hp005333

113 Third Street
State Library of Louisiana Hp000233

114 New LSU Campus Under Construction
State Library of Louisiana
Hp002269

115 Campus Dedication Ceremony
State Library of Louisiana
Hp002308

116 Aerial
John B. Heroman, Sr., Photograph Collection, Mss. 4951, Louisiana and Lower Mississippi Valley Collections, LSU Libraries, Baton Rouge, LA

117 Paving
State Library of Louisiana
Hp001090

118 Rotary and Kiwanis Clubs
John B. Heroman, Sr., Photograph Collection, Mss. 4951, Louisiana and Lower Mississippi Valley Collections, LSU Libraries, Baton Rouge, LA

119 Heidelberg Hotel
State Library of Louisiana
Hp005940

120 Mississippi River Flood Camp, 1927
State Library of Louisiana
Hp000977

121 Distributing Tobacco at Camp
State Library of Louisiana
Hp000855

122 Camp Cooking Facility
State Library of Louisiana
Hp000989

123 Huey P. Long Inauguration
Huey P. Long Photograph Album, Mss. 4495, Louisiana and Lower Mississippi Valley Collections, LSU Libraries, Baton Rouge, LA

124 1929 Aerial Photograph
John B. Heroman, Sr., Photograph Collection, Mss. 4951, Louisiana and Lower Mississippi Valley Collections, LSU Libraries, Baton Rouge, LA

125 Governor's Residence
State Library of Louisiana
Hp003040

126 Plantation Lands Used for Campus
John B. Heroman, Sr., Photograph Collection, Mss. 4951, Louisiana and Lower Mississippi Valley Collections, LSU Libraries, Baton Rouge, LA

128 Louisiana State Police
State Library of Louisiana
Hp005940

130 Huey P. Long with Referees
Huey P. Long Photograph Album, Mss. 4495, Louisiana and Lower Mississippi Valley Collections, LSU Libraries, Baton Rouge, LA
449500008

131 John B. Heroman, Sr.
John B. Heroman, Sr., Photograph Collection, Mss. 4951, Louisiana and Lower Mississippi Valley Collections, LSU Libraries, Baton Rouge, LA
BR012

132 Morning Advocate
John B. Heroman, Sr., Photograph Collection, Mss. 4951, LSU Libraries, Baton Rouge, LA

133 New Capitol
Louisiana State Capitol Construction Photographs, Mss. 3355, , Louisiana and Lower Mississippi Valley Collections, LSU Libraries, Baton Rouge, LA

134 Aerial of New Capitol
State Library of Louisiana
Hp005498

135 Church Street
State Library of Louisiana
Hp000234

136 Huey P. Long's Public Funeral
State Library of Louisiana
Hp000921

137 New State Capitol's Barber Shop
State Library of Louisiana
Hp000420

138 Tommy Gun
State Library of Louisiana
Hp005467

139 Library Commission Bookmobile
State Library of Louisiana
Hp003627

140 Mississippi River Bridge Construction
LSU Libraries, Baton Rouge, LA

141 Downtown Baton Rouge
Jasper Ewing and Sons Photograph Files, Mss 3141, LSU Libraries, Baton Rouge, LA

142 Capitol Christmas
State Library of Louisiana
Hp004131

143 Tennis
State Library of Louisiana
Hp002839

144 Art Deco Detail of Capitol
State Library of Louisiana
Hp004814

146 Tiger Band
State Library of Louisiana
Hp005277

147 Canoeing
State Library of Louisiana
wp002576

148 Land Clearing for Airport
State Library of Louisiana
Hp002579

150 Aquacade
State Library of Louisiana
Hp005142

151 Floating Throne
State Library of Louisiana
Hp005143

152 Huey P. Long Statue
State Library of Louisiana
Hp000946

153 Tessier Building
State Library of Louisiana
Hp004395

154 Louisiana Department of Commerce and Industry
State Library of Louisiana
Hp003780

155 State Library
State Library of Louisiana
Hp008919

156 Works in Braille
State Library of Louisiana
Hp008924

158 Motor Vehicle Bureau
State Library of Louisiana
Hp004075

159 Army Air Corps
State Library of Louisiana
Hp001039

160 Claire Lee Chennault
State Library of Louisiana
Hp001730

161 Library Display
State Library of Louisiana
Hp008069

162 Mike the Tiger
State Library of Louisiana
Hp002826

164 Humble Oil & Refining Company's Refinery Hospital
State Library of Louisiana
Hp001129

166 Library Film
State Library of Louisiana
Hp004966

167 Mardi Gras Parade
State Library of Louisiana
Hp003922

168 Book Dealer
State Library of Louisiana
Hp000069

170 Magnolia Mound Plantation
State Library of Louisiana
Hp000255

171 State Library Branch at Southern University
State Library of Louisiana
Hp008073

172 Negro Librarians Conference
State Library of Louisiana
Hp008089

174 State Police
State Library of Louisiana
Hp005944

175 Bird's-eye View
State Library of Louisiana
Hp000263

176 New Bridge
State Library of Louisiana
Hp000289

178 Christmas Tree
State Library of Louisiana
Hp008711

179 Aerial
State Library of Louisiana
Hp002437

180 David F. Boyd Hall
State Library of Louisiana
Hp002265

181 The Campanile and Memorial Tower
State Library of Louisiana
Hp006905

182 Santa Maria Plantation House
State Library of Louisiana
Hp004167

183 Cabin
State Library of Louisiana
Hp004152

184 Interior of the Santa Maria Plantation
State Library of Louisiana
Hp004155

185 Old Arsenal Powder Magazine
State Library of Louisiana
Hp005128

186 House Chamber of the Louisiana State Capitol
State Library of Louisiana
Hp001191

187 Ku Klux Klan on Capitol Steps
State Library of Louisiana
Hp005943

188 University Terrace Elementary School
State Library of Louisiana
Hp007289

190 Louisiana Oil and Gas Building
State Library of Louisiana
Hp002506

191 Jimmie Davis
State Library of Louisiana
Hp003959

192 Antiwar Protesters
State Library of Louisiana
Hp005933

194 Louisiana State Capitol at Night
State Library of Louisiana
Hp005495

195 Mound
State Library of Louisiana
Hp003942

196 Student Protest
LSU Photograph Collection, RG#A5000, LSU Archives, LSU Libraries, Baton Rouge, LA

198 Downtown
State Library of Louisiana
Hp002482

199 Riverfront
State Library of Louisiana
Hp004772

200 Port of Baton Rouge
State Library of Louisiana
Hp002489

HISTORIC PHOTOS OF BATON ROUGE

With a history tied to the Mississippi River, Baton Rouge has grown from its colonial past as a military outpost favored by the French, English, and Spanish, in turn, into an American city of modern industry and rich diversity. Through the years, the people of Baton Rouge have weathered travails while developing a unique culture and city. Baton Rouge has seen occupation during the Civil War, the destruction by fire and reconstruction of the State Capitol, catastrophic flooding, and political and civil conflict—but also the economic impact of a growing port, the historic arrivals of Louisiana State University and Southern University, and the joyful rituals of Saturday football and the Washington's Birthday Firemen's Parade.

Telling the city's story through words and vivid black-and-white images, *Historic Photos of Baton Rouge* documents 100-plus years in the life of the "Red Stick" as only the camera can capture it.

www.turnerpublishing.com

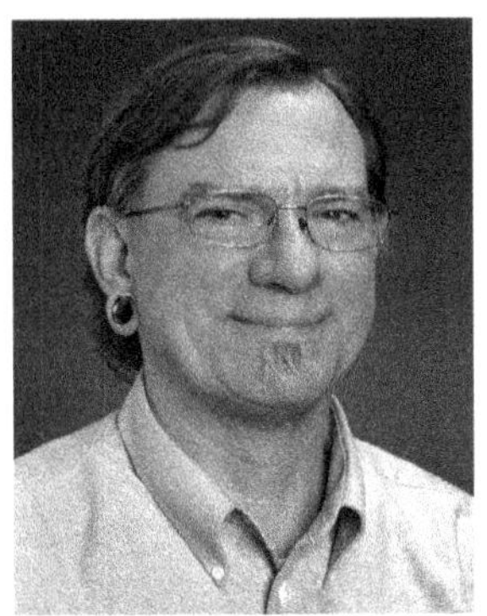

Mark E. Martin graduated magna cum laude from Western Carolina University with a bachelor's degree in history. He then took a master's degree with a concentration in archival enterprise, specializing in photographic archives, from the University of Texas at Austin's Graduate School of Library and Information Science.

For the past 18 years, he has worked as an archivist and has been actively involved with the archival profession at the local, state, regional, and national levels, including serving as chair of the Society of American Archivists' Visual Materials Section. He is the editor of *Andrew D. Lytle's Baton Rouge: Photographs, 1863–1910,* published 2008.